Architecture, Poetry, and Number
in the Royal Palace at Caserta

The MIT Press
Cambridge, Massachusetts
London, England

Architecture, Poetry, and Number in the Royal Palace at Caserta

George L. Hersey

© 1983 by
The Massachusetts Institute of Technology

All rights reserved. No part of this book may be reproduced in any form or by any means, electronic or mechanical, including photocopying, recording, or by any information storage and retrieval system, without permission in writing from the publisher.

This book was set in Mergenthaler Linotron-202 Bembo by Graphic Composition, Inc. and printed and bound by Halliday Lithograph in the United States of America.

Publication of this book has been aided by a grant from The Millard Meiss Publication Fund of the College Art Association of America.

MM

Library of Congress Cataloging in Publication Data

Hersey, George L.
   Architecture, poetry, and number in the royal palace at Caserta.

   Bibliography: p.
   Includes index.
   1. Reggia di Caserta. 2. Caserta (Italy)—Palaces. 3. Architecture, Baroque—Italy—Caserta. 4. Symbolism in architecture—Italy—Caserta.
   I. Title.
NA7756.C3H47 1983   728.8′2′0945725
82-20815
ISBN 0-262-08121-0

Acknowledgments

Many people have been helpful in the writing of this book. Among them are Fronia Wissman, Susan Ryan, and Aaron Betsky. I have greatly benefited from discussions of the material and approach contained herein with my colleagues Judith Colton, Walter Cahn, George Kubler, and Robert Frew. In Italy my thanks go to the immensely cooperative Professors Raffaello Causa, Nicola Spinosa, and Wanda Frizzi, as well as to Giuseppe Portanova and Tommaso Biscardi of the Ente Provinciale del Turismo di Caserta. I am particularly grateful to Dr. Giuseppe De Nitto of the Biblioteca Nazionale, Naples, and to the various institutions these people represent, for information and photographs, and also to Mimmo Jodice, who is not only a superb photographer but a splendid guide. I thank Professor Iris Cheney for last-minute help on the matter of the Alessandro Farnese statue.

My research was funded in part by generous grants from the American Council of Learned Societies and the Vogelstein Foundation. Finally, The MIT Press has been most encouraging and helpful in all phases of writing and publishing the book.

Chapter 5 appeared, in different form, in *The Journal of Garden History*, 1981. All translations and photographs, unless otherwise attributed, are my own.

Contents

Acknowledgments v

1
Introduction: From Caserta to the Pentagon 2

2
The Poetic Myths of Naples 12
Underground Rivers 12
Buried Cities 24
The Sirens 29

3
Architectural Order 32
The Geometric Plan 32
The Absolute Palace 45
Absolutism in Naples 51

4
Royal Architects 64
Carlo di Borbone 64
The Mythic Builder 72
Mario Gioffredo 82
Luigi Vanvitelli 87

5
The River-Road 98
The Site 98
Diana and Actaeon 113
Venus and Adonis 122
Ceres 127
Juno and Aeolus 133

6
Palace Geometry 142
Gioffredo's Project 142
Vanvitelli's "Ideal Royal Palace" 154
The Definitive Design 156

7
Public Poetry 174
The Royal Soul 174
The Pantheon of Hercules 181
The Royal Heart 187
Apollo's Kingdom 196
Marble Guardians 202

8
The Family Romance 208
The Chapel 208
The Halls of Representation 211
The Old Apartments 222
The Library 229
The New Apartments 238

9
Epilogue: Neptune's Victory 248

Notes 257
Bibliography 289
List of Illustrations 303
Index 311

1
Caserta, garden facade. Photo Ente Provinciale per il Turismo

2
Caserta, Fountain of
Diana. Foto Jacelli,
Caserta

3
Caserta, Fountain of Diana, Actaeon and his dogs. Foto Jacelli, Caserta

4
Francesco Celebrano. *Ferdinando IV and His Court at a Boar Hunt*, 1770s. Naples, Museo San Martino. Photo Mimmo Jodice

5
Caserta, stair hall.
Photo Mimmo Jodice

6
Girolamo Starace.
Apollo's Kingdom.
Caserta, stair hall.
Photo Mimmo Jodice

7
Caserta, upper vestibule. Photo Mimmo Jodice

8
Domenico Mondo.
Bourbon Arms Sustained by Virtues.
Caserta, Hall of the Ambassadors. Photo Mimmo Jodice

9
Mariano Rossi. *The Marriage of Alexander and Roxana*. Caserta, Hall of Alexander. Photo Mimmo Jodice

10
Detail of pl. 9. Photo Mimmo Jodice

11
Caserta, Autumn Chamber. Photo Ente Provinciale per il Turismo

12
Caserta, Maria Carolina's bath. Photo Mimmo Jodice

13
Gennaro Fiore. Putti, Maria Carolina's bath (presently damaged). Photo Mimmo Jodice

14
Friedrich Heinrich Füger. *The Age of Gold.* Caserta, Old Apartments, library. Photo Mimmo Jodice

15
Füger. *The School of Athens*. Caserta, Old Apartments, library. Photo Mimmo Jodice

16
Füger. *The Rebirth of the Arts*. Caserta, Old Apartments, library. Photo Mimmo Jodice

17
Antonio Calliano.
*The Death of Hector
and the Triumph of
Achilles.* Caserta,
Hall of Mars. Photo
Mimmo Jodice

18
Caserta, Hall of
Astraea. Photo Ente
Provinciale per il
Turismo

19
Caserta, throne room. Photo Ente Provinciale per il Turismo

20
Gennaro Maldarelli. *Laying the Cornerstone of the Reggia*. Caserta, throne room. Photo Mimmo Jodice

To WYLBUR, WYLMA, and YEDIT

Architecture, Poetry, and Number
in the Royal Palace at Caserta

1 Introduction: From Caserta to the Pentagon

This book has several aims. First, it deals with what is called the poetry of architecture, a phrase that has meant different things to different people. I would like to define it in Vichian terms as architecture's mythic content, a content made poetic by the rhythms, repetitions, gestures, metaphors, and above all the multiple meanings of a building and its pictorial and sculptural decoration.

Giambattista Vico dominated serious thought about myth in Naples in the eighteenth century. He saw the classic tales of religion and history as poems—poems that, rightly interpreted, could read the real world and the world of art as moral histories. Vico's grand philosophy is an attempt to perceive the physical realities that lie behind ancient words like *Ceres*, or *lex*, or *Venus*. He believed that the events in Ceres' life were real even though she herself was never more than a word or composite of words and that these words and composites of words are in fact poems and myths. This was not the allegory of Renaissance tradition but rather a new, harder, philological genealogy of gods and kings called by Vico "the New Science." Vico was no doubt well read in Renaissance emblem books and in treatises on the iconography of the gods. He mentions the *Mythologiae* of Natalis Comes, Cebes' Tablet, Boccaccio's *De Genealogia deorum*, and Gerard Voss's *De Theologia gentili*. He probably also used handbooks such as Ripa's and Cartari's. But his real interest was in turning the literary gloss on symbols and gods, as practiced by Comes, into intuitions about the cruel, illiterate eras of our origins when human institutions were formed, eras that were literally "unspeakable" and therefore were mythicized. Vico's principles of myth-reading are a key to the mythic painting, sculpture, and architecture that the Bourbon monarchy erected around itself like a heuristic carapace. The Neapolitan philosopher and his followers, particularly the poet and librettist Pietro Metastasio, set the tone for Luigi Vanvitelli's conception of Caserta: for its poetic geometry, for its population of sculptured and painted gods, and for its expression of the ideals of heroic absolutism through which the king saw himself as the descendant of such figures as Hercules and Aeneas.

Vico's approach is accordingly the one I use in this book. Some readers will no doubt find what I have done too different from the source-hunting, style-distinguishing, and influence-tracing that dominate the practice of art history nowadays. They will also find that I eschew the pure description, uninflected by interpretation, that characterizes much scholarship, not least that written by Fichera, Schiavo, and others about Caserta itself. (If, on the other hand, there is a book about Caserta that *has* inspired me, it is Marcello Fagiolo Dell'Arco's *Simboli funzioni valori della reggia di Caserta*, 1963.) But if these readers at first miss certain expected discussions I hope they will be happy, instead, to have had a glimpse into one of the great mythopoeic minds of the eighteenth century and an interpretation, in that mind's terms, of the most imposing absolutist palace of the time.

Yet I cannot forbear sketching out one or two aspects of Caserta's influence in order to prepare for this very revelation. Rudolf Wittkower, in *Art and Architecture in Italy: 1600–1750*, makes a comment about Caserta that has often been quoted: "In a sense Caserta is the overwhelmingly impressive swansong of the Italian Baroque." Wittkower then connects the building with Guillaume Cammas's facade for the Capitole at Toulouse (1750–1753), Sir William Chambers's Somerset House, London (1776–1786), and A. F. Kokorinov's Academy of Art at Leningrad (1765–1772). Caserta's stair hall is meanwhile linked to the stairs by Baldassare Longhena at San Giorgio Maggiore, Venice (1641–1647). Vanvitelli may well have known Longhena's stairs; he probably did not know the Capitole, begun a year or so before Caserta was designed. But the real answers to questions about Caserta's sources lie in other Bourbon buildings and projects.

As to the influence of Vanvitelli's masterpiece, Chambers probably *did* know the *Dichiarazione*, Vanvitelli's 1756 book about his palace, and conceivably drew on it for Somerset House. Yet Caserta's elevations (figs. 6.18, 6.19) also have resemblances to English early Georgian elevations, as published in Colen Campbell's *Vitruvius Britannicus* (1715–1721), and even to Baroque structures (also published in Campbell's book) such as Vanbrugh's Castle Howard. The diagnostic elements seem to be the use of a dome on a tall drum in a domestic building, utter symmetry, and an arched rusticated ground-level entrance beneath a main-floor colonnade or pilastrade in lieu of the usual monumental stair. In any event a large number of people came to visit Caserta while it was being built, as Aniello Gentile's excellent *Caserta nei ricordi dei viaggiatori stranieri* (1980) makes clear. Even more people studied the well-illustrated *Dichiarazione*. At the same time one must emphasize that it was Carlo di Borbone who was the moving architectural spirit behind the great enterprise and that when in 1759 he became Charles III of Spain he continued his activities by remodeling his palaces there: the Pardo, Aranjuez, San Ildefonso, and the Escorial.

Another avenue of influence involves Vanvitelli's pupils. One of the closest approximations to the main facades at Caserta that I have found was executed by Giuseppe Piermarini, who assisted Vanvitelli in the great palace. The facade of the Palazzo Belgioioso, Milan (1777), is a miniature of Caserta's (fig. 1.1). Later, working under the influence of another Vanvitelli pupil, Antonio Rinaldi, Luigi Rusca designed a barracks for the Belosersky Regiment in St. Petersburg (1805–1806?). This facade abstracts Caserta's into a pure exercise in Neoclassicism (fig. 1.2). The arrangement of rusticated basement with end and central pavilions remains the same, as does the distribution of arched entrances—one under the central portico and one in the center of each wing. Even Vanvitelli's window of appearances and his temple front flanked by pilaster pairs are repeated. (A few years after Rusca's building was erected Stendhal was to write, "Caserta is only a barracks." Perhaps Rusca had seen the same qualities in the Neapolitan palace and acted accordingly.) Anyway, these examples show how easily this "swansong of the Italian Baroque" translated into Neoclassicism.

But the most unlooked for repetition of Vanvitelli's facade came about as a result of the old campaign to provide Britain with a principal royal residence worthy of her importance in the world. The whole story should be told some day as an epic architectural comedy. Inigo Jones's schemes for Whitehall Palace and those of his assistants are well-known instances, and neither Protestantism nor constitutionalism prevailed against the desire in some quarters for an English Versailles, Schönbrunn, or Caserta. In 1766 John Gwynn published *London and Westminster Improved, Illustrated by Plans to which is Prefixed a Discourse on Public Magnificence, etc.*, with a map showing a colossal palace 1000 feet square in a rebuilt Hyde Park. It is obviously supposed to rival Caserta (1111 by 819 feet): six great courts, and a central corridor going all the way through the building from exterior to exterior. Unfortunately Gwynn includes no elevations. It is not unlikely that he envisioned something Vanvitellesque, however.

But, as everyone knows, there is still no great royal palace in Great Britain. The tiniest princedoms often have more impressive royal residences. Buckingham Palace, which ought to be Britain's Versailles, began life in 1705 as a country villa for the Duke of Buckingham. In 1762 George III's queen, Charlotte, moved in. When her architect for the remodeling, John Nash, had finished, the building was still only a country house. And it was that still when Edward Blore finished remodeling the interiors in 1837, the year Victoria ascended the throne.

Introduction

1.2
Luigi Rusca. Barracks for Belosersky Regiment, St. Petersburg. From Rusca, *Receuil des dessins de différents bâtiments*

1.1
Giuseppe Piermarini. Facade of Palazzo Belgioioso, Milan, 1777. Photo Alinari

Introduction

Then, in 1912, at the height of the Empire, *The Architectural Review* published a new design for the east front by Sir Aston Webb. This was erected in 1913 and it is the Buckingham Palace we know today, though it is obscured by the thick iron railing and gates that stand in front of it. If we can get a look at the facade itself (fig. 1.3) we see instantly that it comes right out of Caserta: the same general parti, the same arched rustic openings in the centers of the wings, the same configuration under the main portico of low, square-headed doorways flanking a high arched one, the same four-column temple front above, the same order (Composite), the same two-story pilastrade, the same Farnese-type windows, the same basement-enclosed mezzanine. The only differences are the greater mass of Webb's portico base and the parapets he built over his three temple fronts and, of course, the fact that Buckingham Palace is tiny compared to the original. Even set beside Blenheim or Castle Howard and despite its hitherto unnoticed Vanvitellization, it is still a middle-sized country house.

All this illustrates the gradual shrinking of a grand idea. But Caserta's true historic place is not as one in a series of facades. Caserta is important for itself, for its uniqueness, and not for what it passed on to or took from other buildings. It belongs to the history of the architectural Sublime. It has the self-reference, the isolation, of the monuments of that grand aesthetic. And Caserta's Sublime in turn leads on to that of the nineteenth century with its love of even vaster palaces for assembly and control. Looking at Caserta one thinks of Boullée, who is one of Joseph Rykwert's "first moderns" and a hero of Emil Kaufmann's *Von Ledoux bis Le Corbusier*. Boullée's "Design for a Vaulted Hall" in the Royal Institute of British Architects, London (fig. 1.4), seems a Neoclassic revision of Caserta's lower vestibule (fig. 7.21); but that comparison is still too Baroque, too multileveled. The lower entrance vault (fig. 1.5), with its simpler columns and its flat, powerful horizontal base makes a better prototype—though one does see a Vanvitellian touch in Boullée's swirled polygonal coffering in the central vault (cf. fig. 7.21). The main difference is Boullée's elimination of the baroque diagonals Vanvitelli used. In Boullée everything is squared into parallels and the walls have been buttressed by rows of ancillary, freestanding columns that form hypostyle guardians for the inner wall-columns, or antae. Yet the projected plans for Caserta (figs. 6.3, 6.17) are hypostyles or regular grids of columns just as much as any plan by Boullée or by his even more geometric and Neoclassical pupil, J.N.L. Durand (fig. 1.6).

The most impressive evidence of Caserta's impact, at least in royal circles (and again involving Boullée) comes in the course of the eighteenth-century debate about the lack of order and symmetry at Versailles. These episodes culminated in the Comte d'Angiviller's competition in the 1780s for a new envelope for the entire palace, an envelope that would wrap it in a colossal set of facades far exceeding in scope and scale anything dreamed of in Naples. Although everyone agreed that Versailles was extraordinary, French critics for years had denigrated its illogical plan and incoherent elevations. Even Saint-Simon called it "a

Introduction

1.3
Sir Aston Webb.
New facade, Buckingham Palace. From
The Architectural Review, 1912

1.5
Luigi Vanvitelli. Caserta, lower floor vestibule. Photo Alinari

1.4
Etienne-Louis Boullée. Design for a vaulted hall. London, RIBA

vast choked-together ensemble" (fig. 3.15). This fact was now all the more humiliating to the French Bourbons because their Spanish cousins at Naples were erecting a more nobly logical, more correct, possibly larger structure.

The balance was to be redressed not by building an enlarged imitation of Caserta but by building an enlarged imitation of Versailles. Boullée's entry (fig. 1.7) does *not* resemble Vanvitelli's building—and that is the point. The competition was in logic, extent, and magnificence, not in motifs. That is the kind of influence at work here; that is how Caserta functioned as a source; that is how its style asserted itself. The positive qualities of the Italian building, and everything that contributed to its identity, were purposely avoided.

If Caserta is read centripetally, as a Vichian poem of myth and number, the huge unfinished palace becomes the proposed Kremlin of Bourbon absolutism. In its very size and universality it is one of the earliest modern megapalaces, the forerunner not only of Boullée's plans for a new Versailles and his other grand projects but also of the buildings of the later British Empire, of Fascism and Nazism, and of America's enormous classical temples in Washington, D.C. If Carlo di Borbone could return from the grave and rule the United States, he would move the seat of executive power from the White House to the Pentagon. (It was with great appropriateness that General George S. Patton made Caserta his headquarters after the Allied invasion of Italy in World War II.)

Megapalatial architecture is therefore still very much with us. The Pentagon was built in 1943 (the architects, Bergstrom and Witmer). The history of modern architecture, from the Crystal Palace in London of 1851, and through its many colossal progeny, into the modern era of vast factories and vaster office buildings, is a history that partly stems from Caserta: for Caserta was intended among other things as an office building, a self-sufficient plant that would house and maintain thousands of servant-bureaucrats who governed the Kingdom of Naples. It is an early monument to central control, to the manipulation of the masses. Carlo di Borbone's motive for moving his court, his army, and his government from Naples to a new town centered on and occupying a massive symbol of his own power was not essentially different from that of the builders of factories and their towns in Germany and America in the nineteenth and early twentieth centuries, and in Japan today. Nor was the Neapolitan king's desire to erect a new capital with an imposing dome and a long grassy mall and with radiating avenues filled with uniform government buildings (fig. 5.5) unconnected with the ideas of the builders of Washington, D.C., for that too, like Caserta, was based on rivalry with Louis XIV's Versailles and on the notion that the safest and most powerful place for a capital is out in the country, far from any existing metropolis. Indeed many buildings of the modern era, from the Capitol in Washington to the phalansteries of the utopianist François-Charles-Marie Fourier, and on to the Pentagon, can be thought of as absolutist palaces with the royal apartments removed or transformed into Halls of the People.

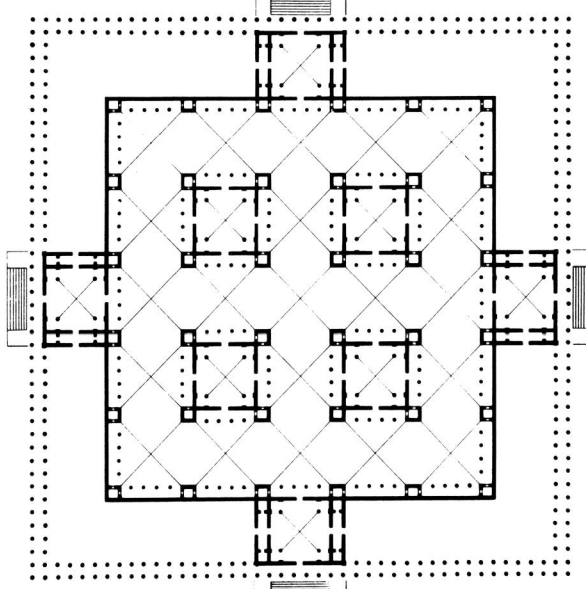
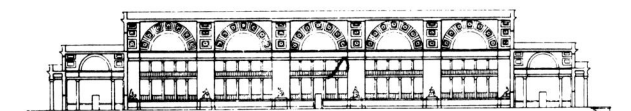

1.6
J. N. L. Durand.
Plan and elevations
of a large hall. From
Durand, *Précis de
Leçons d'Architecture*,
1801–1805

1.7
Boullée. Project for
new envelope for
Versailles, c. 1785.
Paris, Bibliothèque
Nationale

Introduction

In organization this book begins with certain local myths of Naples interpreted under Vico's guidance. It proceeds to the inheritance Vanvitelli and Carlo di Borbone received from the tradition of the geometric plan, to the artistic situation in Naples at the time, and to the personalities and works of the principal performers at Caserta. The book next becomes a visit to the palace itself, beginning with the garden as a historic prologue. On approaching the building there is a discussion of the geometric principles involved in the plans and elevations that Vanvitelli elaborated, showing their debts to an earlier project for Caserta by Mario Gioffredo. We then ascend the royal stairs and move through series of anterooms into the king's and queen's apartments—into the heart of the monarch's house, as that monarch is shown in painting and sculpture to be the descendant of heroes and gods. The book ends with a look at a celebratory performance at Caserta of Metastasio's *Didone abbandonata*, which took place not long before Vanvitelli's death and which is the supreme metaphor for my interpretation.

As we investigate this population of gods, virtues, angels, giants, and commanders, as we witness their life of gesture and relation in the great geometrical vessels constructed for them, we note that the personages counterbalance each other, war with each other, marry, give birth, in ways that as Vico would say (and did say) mimic the human mind itself. Thus in the last chapter some of Carlo's surrogate fathers—Alessandro Farnese, Alexander the Great, Hector—are seen as figures in a Freudian family romance carried out at sublime scale. The whole of the palace interior is seen as the painted and sculptured map of a royal mind or soul. Vanvitelli in fact makes the simile. This interpretation does not anachronistically read Freud into Vico or Vanvitelli. It does something more unusual and more truthful. Freud's theory of the family romance becomes a reinterpretation of Baroque allegory—and we recall that Freud loved myth as much as Vico did.

2 The Poetic Myths of Naples

Underground Rivers

The myths of Naples belong to the landscape of western Campania.[1] It is a marine landscape, subtropical in climate and volcanic. Its sharp, irregular skyline is composed of hollowed seaside hills that form a powerful barricade of red-black cliffs, caves, and promontories suddenly alternating with beaches sunk to sea level. The islands off the coast—Ischia, Procida, Capri—ride at anchor like ancient ships, overgrown with vegetation, abandoned by some foreign conqueror (fig. 2.1). These islands are the relics of offshore craters whose onshore fragments form mythopoeic lakes such as Avernus[2]—the entrance to Virgil's underworld[3]—and lagoons such as Lucrino and Fusaro. Palms, pines, oaks, and willows grow in the lush soil (fig. 2.2).

In Roman times Campania Felix, as the region was called, was celebrated for abundant crops and easeful living.[4] The coast was dotted with villas and baths. But by the eighteenth century, despite the rich soil, the penury that we see today was already in existence.[5] The divinities who peopled this beautiful but fallen land—Hercules, Apollo, and Diana—inhabited a landscape of ruin.

In the eighteenth century, as now, there was a chronic lack of water, and water myths abounded.[6] But Campanian water imagery had a deeply infernal character. Just west of the city, inland from the shoreline cliffs of Procida, Miseno, Baia, and Torregaveta, lie the Phlegraean (Burning) Fields (fig. 2.3). Here volcanic springs bubble from the lake-filled earth, fed by an underground labyrinth of waters that Virgil and his countless

2.1
Pietro Fabris. Ventotene, Capo dell'Arco. From Hamilton, *Campi Phlegraei* (1779)

2.2
Pietro Fabris. The island of Ventotene. From Saint-Non, *Voyage pittoresque* (1781)

The Poetic Myths of Naples

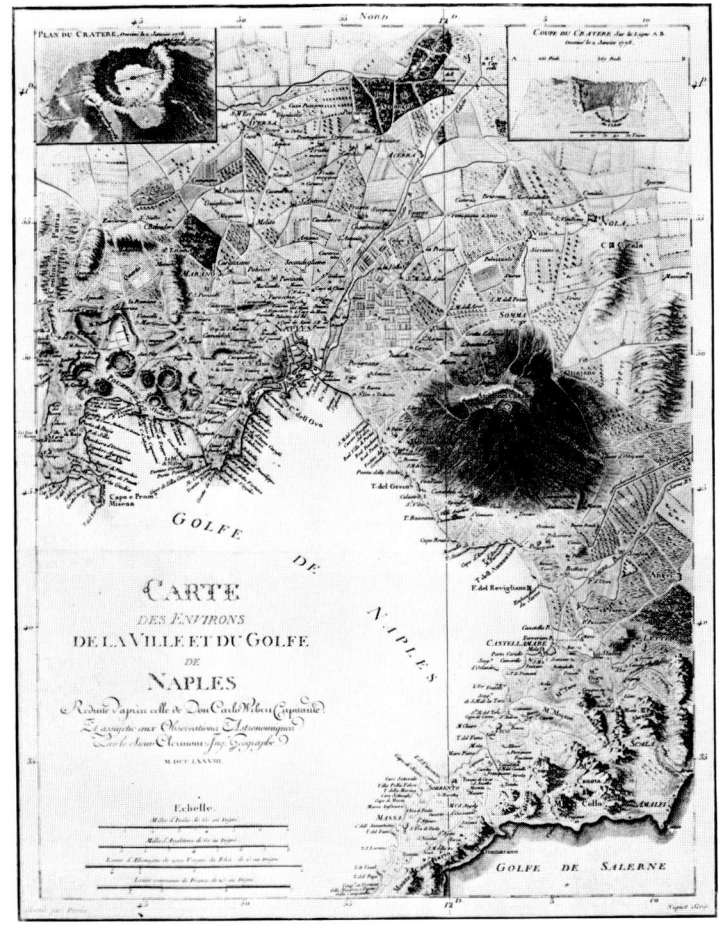

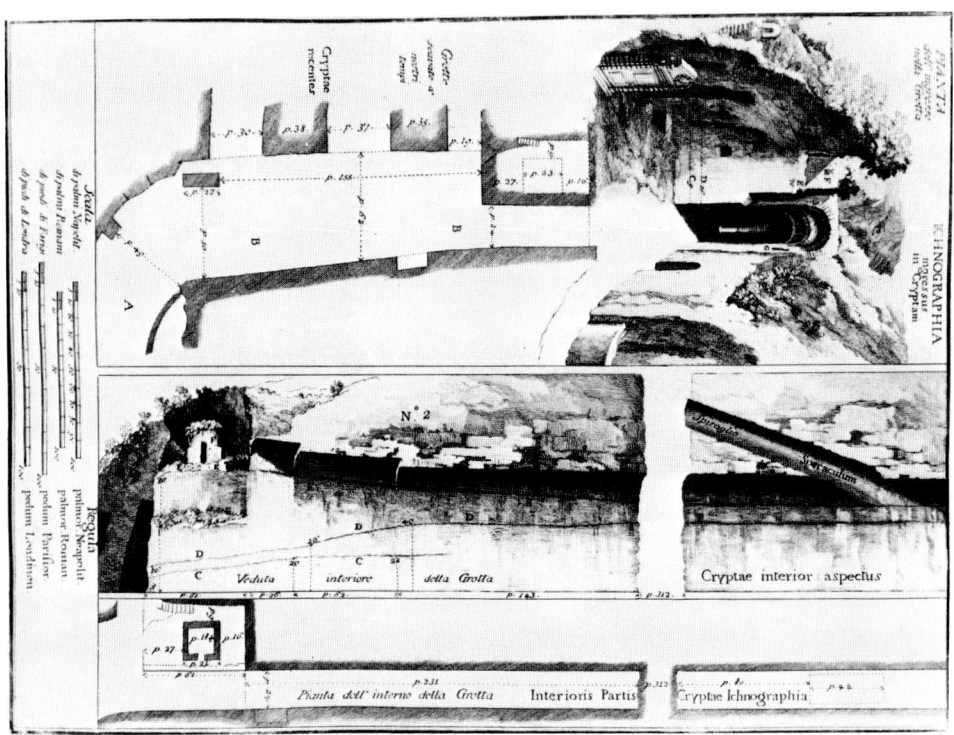

2.3
Map of the environs of Naples. From Saint-Non

2.4
The grotto of Pozzuoli: plan, section, view. From P.A. Paoli, *Antichità di Pozzuoli* (1768)

imitators identified with the underworld city of Dis.[7] It is a quaking, smoking land. Dis is as full of the stink of mounded decay as modern Naples or New York.

The caves and tufa galleries of the region (fig. 2.4) were seen as yet other ruined subterranean cities by a string of visitors from Conrad of Querfurt in the eleventh century to Dryden and Goethe in the eighteenth.[8] The nymphaea, a scattering of small temples that were erected by the Romans beside the region's mineral springs and vapor baths, were the suburbs of these cities, built on the underworld's roof. In these temples, it was claimed, a host of diseases from baldness to bronchitis could be cured. Over the portal of each nymphaeum the affliction treated within was symbolized by a sculptured relief.[9] The whole effect of the rich landscape in Roman times—hills, lakes, and temples—must have been like that of an eighteenth-century landscape garden but one that boiled with the waters of hell (fig. 2.2). It was a paradise for ruin-painters from all over Europe.[10]

Naples itself imbibes this atmosphere. It flowed, and flows still, with waters, though sweeter than those of the Phlegraean Fields. Pontano's eclogue *Lepidina*, the greatest Renaissance poem about the city, celebrates the marriage of the river Sebeto to Naples' mythical queen and symbol, Parthenope. The bride is cleansed and made beautiful by her bridegroom. He symbolizes the new water system, with public fountains, that Alfonso of Calabria installed in the late fifteenth century.[11] Again, in Sannazaro's piscatory eclogues Virgil's landscape poems are rewritten as Campanian seascapes.[12] Fountains much like the small temples of the Phlegraean Fields were erected in the piazzas of Naples to feed and bathe its citizens. Though eternally inadequate as to the volume of water they produced, like the Phlegraean baths these structures were carved with myths pointing out the virtues of their waters.[13] The latter might induce love or snuff it out, beautify the body, sweeten bad tempers, or foster social and economic benefits. Like the nymphaea of the Phlegraean Fields they offered up the waters of an underworld, but this time the waters were cool and mild and their effects psychological and social rather than purely medical.

One such fountain, a typical one, is the Fontana Santa Lucia (figs. 2.5–2.9). By means of the poetry of sculpture—that is, by means of sculpture's power to express trope, allegory, rhythm, and incantatory transformation—the fountain illustrates the Neapolitan myth of underground rivers. I will make it a prologue to the technique I use in this book.

The Fontana Santa Lucia was dedicated in 1606 and is the work of Michelangelo Naccherino and Tommaso Montani.[14] It now stands, in modified form, in the public gardens or Villa Comunale. The water wells up in a great vase, originally offered by sirens but now by nineteenth-century dolphins who squirm into the form of a symmetrical tripod beneath an arch of triumph. Hence the triumphator is he who plunges his face, or his cup, into the fresh pool. The arch's classical members have turned into an orderly swarm of nereids, nereuses, tritons, dolphins, sea horses, crabs, and mussels. The pilaster shafts

2.5
Michelangelo Naccherino and Tommaso Montani. Fontana Santa Lucia, Naples, 1606. Photo Alinari

2.6
Fontana Santa Lucia, relief of Hercules, Amphitrite, and Neptune.

2.7
Fontana Santa Lucia, relief of Neptune, Triton, and Amphitrite

2.8
Fontana Santa Lucia, siren console

2.9
Fontana Santa Lucia,
arms of Alfonso
Pimentel

reinforcing the main uprights are hung with trophies composed of these animals as well as dogfish, sharks, and lobsters. The marble catch may squirm and gasp but inexorably does its duty of decoration and display. The outer support of the arch on each side is a Corinthian column that has turned into a nereus. With both his hands, each of these two divinities steadies the great crown of his capital on his head, though uncertainly, as if still adjusting to the transformed state. Each stands astride a gliding dolphin who smiles wickedly while flourishing a sinuous body around the nereus' legs and slapping a tailfin, a cross between fig leaf and hand, onto the god's genitals.

Rectangular reliefs of Amphitrite, Hercules, Neptune, and a triton separate the seafood-hung pilasters from the nereus columns. On the left (fig. 2.6) Hercules raises his club to fend off the attacking Neptune, who grasps his queen by the leg as she rides off on a wave with her abductor. On the right (fig. 2.7) Neptune and Amphitrite are seated on a wave-throne while a triton, on their right, blows a blast of triumph into his trumpet-shell. Presumably Hercules, perhaps interrupting his swim in the Sicilian Sea as he searches for one of the oxen of Geryon, has seduced Neptune's wife; and the sea god, on the right, has recaptured her and restored the oceans to their proper order. *Amphitrite*, whose name means double triton, is doubly the mate of ocean creatures, the partner at different times of Hercules and of Neptune, and daughter of the triton. These reliefs, curiously much more worn and damaged than the rest of the fountain, are set over niches thickly hung with fruit swags and winged masks. Hence the message is of the pursuit of sea creatures, of reproduction, of new generations of delectable gifts from the sea, and of resolved strife between the garden god and the god of the sea.

These thin, flat niches have bowls at their bases where ancillary streams once ran. Over them are inscriptions, dated 1845, lamenting the dilapidations of time and recording Ferdinando II's renewal of the fountain 250 years after its construction. The dilapidations unfortunately have continued on Ferdinando's own tablets. But Ferdinando II, the great-grandson of Carlo di Borbone, calls the fountain a nymphaeum and hence follows the tradition of his ancestors. For him it is still a temple of nymphs, of water spirits, an underground river of cleanliness, health, and delight. It is the descendant of the Roman bathhouses in the Phlegraean Fields. Ferdinando has, he says, moved the fountain from the narrow square where it had become squalid and ruinous to this new, clean, open place by the shore; so the temple of cleanliness is itself cleansed.

Flanking the attic of the arch proper, the nude torsoes of two daughters of Nereus, as protean as their brothers below, flow lushly out of coiled volutes (fig. 2.8). The attic they buttress is a temple enshrining the original inscription commemorating the gift of Alfonso Pimentel, Count of Benevente and Viceroy of Naples under Spanish rule.[15] He dedicated it for the traditional reason, "that public delight not be absent." In the inscription he defines the original site not in modern language, as the *quartiere*

Santa Lucia, but classically: *ad oram lucullianam*, which refers to Lucullus's nearby Neapolitan villa.[16] The phrase, like the figure sculpture that goes with it, evokes not so much public benefit as public gratification: a Lucullan banquet. Above it all, breaking into the blue sky like foam, the count's arms are set in a divided tympanum bestridden by two putti who with mirror symmetry have pulled a veil from the stately shield. Not: The count unveils the sculpture, but: The sculpture unveils the count—preserving forever, as only sculpture can, beyond the vandalism of time and the pastimes of vandals, this gift from one of Naples' long succession of foreign rulers (fig. 2.9).

Such a conceit, such a reversal of role between donor and gift, carries forward the similar transformation down below, where in essence a marine triumphal arch, dolphin-borne, is beached like a square-rigged fishing boat as its columns and buttresses turn into sea divinities. Natalis Comes says Nereus symbolizes skillful navigation. Meanwhile the nereids and nereuses will themselves be transformed—into water, for the root of their name, νερό, was thought to be 'new water.' As noted, fish and seafood hang in trophylike garlands. The quarry of the fishermen's hunt, like the divinities and like the arch itself they celebrate the conquest of the sea, the cycles of generation and gathering that constitute control of it, and the harvesting of its riches. The marble triumphal bath was originally surrounded by fishermen's stalls similarly hung with lobsters, mussels, and fish and manned by the nereids and nereuses of the quarter, who purified their glistening harvest in the Viceroy's nymphaeum.[17]

It was in Naples, filled with monuments and inscriptions of this type, that Giambattista Vico grew up.[18] Vico was the great poetic mythologist of his age and city. As I have tried to do with the Fontana Santa Lucia, so too Vico interpreted nymphs and nereids, gods and sea creatures, Neptune and Amphitrite, into social and commercial meanings. Water and the landscape of Campania have an especially high place in Vico's mythology. The first towns in history, he says, were built beside sacred waters.[19] And the first great civilized city was Cumae, Naples' seaside neighbor west of the Phlegraean Fields.[20] Nymphs, to Vico, are in essence the 'flung drops' (*nymphae*) of early man's first, fearful religious rituals. And the birth of religion is man's original move toward civilization. Religion arises from man's fear of water and its magical properties and from the desire to subdue it, to control it, to bring it into the service of human needs. The first religion was in fact "a religion of fountains."[21] Control of water in turn meant not only religion but agriculture. And agriculture's consequence was land tenure, which brought settlement and the construction of cities.[22] The powers of water, for good and for bad, are embodied in two key myths, of Diana and of Neptune, which are really accounts of the foundings of religions and of food-gathering institutions.[23] Meanwhile the word *religion* comes from *relegendo* 'accurately reading.' We must accurately read words to understand the myths they carry and accurately read the myths to get back to the unknown ancestors whose personalities and acts lie hidden in them.[24]

The great river that taught human beings the fear of the gods flowed on, and the flung drops were formed into myths, which became beliefs, institutions, ministries, bureaucracies. Modern political systems are no more than the slowly accreted enrichments of early mythical events.[25] To Vico, a code or constitution, a decree, a ministry of agriculture, commerce, or war, an absolute monarch, a parliament (or a president) is as much the creation of myth as are Orpheus, Ceres, Neptune, Apollo, Aeneas, or the Argonauts. The Fontana Santa Lucia, which makes statements about the control of the sea, about the transformation of water, about the marketing of fish, and about the ruling agencies and social benefits of these institutions, does not so much mythicize commerce as accurately read or else reread (*relegere*) their original content. And because the mythic version of that trade, with its nereuses and Neptunes, is original, primordial, "underground" in the sense that its true meaning is overlaid by age and the corruption of language, it is necessary to exhume the myth and use it as a navigational *point d'appui*, marking out civilization's journey down the river of time.

To cite another example, to Vico, Neptune is the "power of the sea which polluted [literally 'flooded'] the first people," while the god's trident symbolizes the sea's ravaging of the land. Hercules, builder of the Gardens of the Hesperides, cleanser of stables, tamer of animals, is preeminently the god of land clearance. He banishes the wild beasts who infest the forests and turns those forests to fields.[26] By sealing an image of Neptune between hanging trophies of fish and a nereus-atlante in an arch built to honor those who have conquered the sea, the designers of the Fontana Santa Lucia make the two reliefs in figs. 2.6 and 2.7 into further trophies, and Amphitrite herself becomes a trophy, or the spoils, of land and sea. Furthermore, before Hercules ravished Amphitrite from Neptune, Neptune himself had ravished his queen. All this was a preliminary to the ravishment of Neptune by these fishermen, early hunters of the sea who would counter the god's power to pollute ('to flood'), to ravage with water, by ravaging *him* of his fish.

Carlo di Borbone was Vico's protector during the latter's last years. The king honored the philosopher, though not spectacularly. Vico, who was professor of law at the University of Naples, became royal historiographer in 1735. He thereupon embarked on a history of the House of Bourbon, of which today we unfortunately only have a fragment.[27] He also gave official orations on the occasion of Carlo's marriage in 1738 and on that of his reorganization of the University in 1742.[28] But Vico's main mythographic ideas are found in his *Diritto Universale* (1720) and *Scienza Nuova Seconda* (1744). Though Vico's thought was indebted to all sorts of earlier thinkers from Pufendorf to Locke and Leibniz, his views stood in opposition to those of the local Enlightenment writers, most of them younger than he and most of them economists, such as Antonio Genovese (though Genovese was Vico's pupil), Ferdinando Galiani and the historian Pietro Giannone.[29] These men saw little or no importance in myth, so the truly remarkable aspects of Vico's thought escaped them.³⁰ At the same time they found the older man's ultramonarchist views repugnant. The Bourbon court on the other hand embraced Vico's ideas, seeing them as a defense against the constitutionalism and republicanism that it feared at home and abroad.

Vico, though he considered himself undervalued and was indeed poor in his declining years, occupied an important professorship and had a number of powerful friends and pupils. Antonio Genovese, as noted, was an antithetical follower,³¹ and the poet Pietro Metastasio a friend.³² Celestino Galiani, the chief court chaplain and titular bishop of Thessalonica, was one of Vico's most powerful supporters, while Vico's pupil Giovanni Battista Filomarino, Prince of Roccaspida, played Alexander to Vico's Aristotle.³³ Filomarino owned a great Baroque palace filled with works of art. Social life there was an important center for Vico's influence. Filomarino also occupied the most important of Carlo di Borbone's ambassadorships, that to Madrid. Both the prince and the poet were well known, in turn, to Luigi Vanvitelli, the chief planner of the town, palace, and gardens at Caserta.³⁴ Still other Vichians were the scholars involved in Carlo's cultural projects, for example Alessio Mazzocchi and Ottavio Baiardi. They applied Vico's philological methods, his doctrine of *relegendo*, to inscriptions and to archaeological research, especially to the ancient local cult of Hercules.³⁵

Although no doubt Vico's mythological approach influenced Caserta's imagery, perhaps it would be better to put it the other way around. In the case of the Fontana Santa Lucia, Vico need not be postulated as its iconographer, but his thought can be used to interpret the fountain as it stands. The same is true of Caserta. Vico need not be considered the iconographer of the palace and garden program, but that program can be usefully interpreted in terms of the Vichian atmosphere that prevailed in the court.

Water, we have seen, was central to Neapolitan myth, and to Vico's theories. Vanvitelli had his own obsession with that element, which became a primary constituent of Caserta. In 1751, shortly after moving to Naples, he visited some of the classical sites—the Piscina Mirabilis, an underground Roman reservoir at Pozzuoli; some of the baths in the Phlegraean Fields; and what he called the "Grotta," by which he probably meant the Grotto of Pozzuoli, a tunnel leading through Monte Posillipo from Naples to the Phlegraean Fields (fig. 2.4).³⁶ Each of these sites can be said to reflect aspects of Vanvitelli's later achievement. The Grotto of Pozzuoli, it was said, had been magically constructed by Virgil in a single night; or, alternatively, by Lucullus, or by Cocceius, using 100,000 men, in a mere ten days.³⁷ Vanvitelli's greatest achievement, after the palace itself, was his demythologized repetition of this event: the immense aqueduct that brought water to Caserta. This too was a prodigious feat and a rapidly executed one involving a huge force of workmen. And it too consisted of a tunnel, some of it going through mountains like the Grotto of Pozzuoli. The feat was even re-Virgilized by the inscription Mazzocchi created for Vanvitelli's structure:³⁸

THOSE BLACK TUNNELS DUG THROUGH ROCKY CHASMS THAT, CONQUERING A MOUNTAIN'S MASSIVE WEIGHT, SUDDENLY SPOUT FORTH A RIVER

The Piscina Mirabilis is a similar great hall excavated from living rock. It belongs to a water system whose very forms, immense tall vaults and piers, are echoed in Vanvitelli's Ponte della Maddaloni. Meanwhile the nymphaea scattered across the Phlegraean Fields suggest the many sources of the Caserta system. These were the objects of hunting expeditions by Vanvitelli all through the 1750s. Often the king and queen joined in. She once remarked that the water system meant more to her than the palace itself—it was more the stuff of the ancient emperors.[39] Eventually the system drew on twenty-eight of these sources, dotted along twenty-odd miles of the aqueduct's course extending northward of the gardens.

The aqueduct was Vanvitelli's pride and joy. Over the years he composed a treatise on it, with illustrations, designs for fountains, Latin verses, and mythological information supplied by his learned Roman friend Porzio Leonardi.[40] In 1762, when water flowed through the pipes for the first time, Vanvitelli brought the flow to the midst of the Ponte della Valle, high over a dramatic cleft in the hills, and staged a "mostra d'acque," a cascade, for the delighted child's gaze of Carlo di Borbone's son and successor Ferdinando IV. The architect described the scene with relish: "Here, at the bridge, a magnificent sight forms itself, wild and natural. For suddenly [water] pours downward for 80 palmi [67.5 feet]. It seems like the Tivoli cascade. It rebounds on rocks, taking various shapes and then, foaming, descends to the lowest part of the road near the central arch, whence it disappears into a culvert." To Vanvitelli, indeed, his achievement was positively Mosaic: "When the water arrived at Caserta it truly brought forth the people's joy because they saw it in a place where it had never been, and because they had believed such a triumph impossible."[41]

The other underground river that fascinated Vanvitelli, as it did so many other visitors and residents, was the river of fire with which Vesuvius, the arch-volcano of Europe, so frequently erupted. Vanvitelli dwelt frequently on this prodigious and fearful fact of Neapolitan life. In 1751, conversing with Carlo di Borbone and Maria Amalia, he described a current eruption as "an image of hell." When the queen then compared Vesuvius's river to Lethe, the river of Dis, Vanvitelli replied, "Majesty, it is worse, I think, because in the river Lethe Charon, though he has only his leaky bark and the help of a broken oar, does cross [his passengers] over. But here, I believe, the damned in their tortures just jump into the infernal liquids."[42] He uttered words more prophetic than he knew. For Vanvitelli was soon to become convinced that he himself had poured his life's energies into the infernal streams of the, to him, infernal land of Naples.

When the queen and her architect spoke about Lethe, of course, they spoke as near neighbors of the physical place, just west of the city under Lake Avernus. And if a second river, a river of real fire, could flow to the east from Vesuvius, then the third, equally real yet equally myth-filled river constructed in the gardens of Caserta will also figure in the comparison. That river was in its main sense Vico's river of time and civilization. But because it was a river of time it had hellish aspects and a sojourn in the underworld: like Lethe, Caserta's river is partly underground. Its construction, moreover, had entailed truly infernal torments, for workmen had died constructing its tunnels,[43] and its waters still gush through the throats of sculptured hell beasts (figs. 5.38, 5.39). It was planned to bring this river beneath the palace and on to Naples, there to furnish the city's fountains. Even this idea, to Vanvitelli, was infernal; for the Neapolitan water system, to him, was thoroughly Stygian, was a swamp like the swamp of Acheron, a squalid morass of open conduits, "a filthy river, muddy, full of soaked hemp and every other kind of garbage, run-offs from fields and roads, as if Rome's sewer were to proceed to Naples to supply its fountains and conduits."[44]

Buried Cities

The underground rivers of Naples flowed not only with myths of water and fire but with urban myths as well. When Aeneas landed at Cumae he descended, bearing the golden bough that would act as his safe-conduct, through a grotto on the shore of Lake Avernus into the underworld city of Dis. After traversing that gray and sunless town he received from his father Anchises the divine commission to go north and become the foreign ruler of another city, Rome, and there to found the imperium of Augustus.[45]

Vico interprets this story in terms of the local landscape. Aeneas's advent is a Roman example of the moment in the cycle of human history that calls for absolute monarchies to replace the republicanism and oligarchic governments that were built up in earlier stages in civilization. When Aeneas lands at Cumae he first makes obeisance to Apollo in the temple that stands above Cumae, which in turn stands above Dis: the fear of the gods is the first step in the founding of religion and of cities. Aeneas's religious activities also included burying his companion Misenus and dedicating a cenotaph to another departed companion, Palinurus. These acts, says Vico, "instituted by nobles, mark the beginnings of the religion of the shades of the gods—the start, properly speaking, of humanity."[46] Once again fear gives birth to religion. Burial of the dead, which Vico frequently connects with garden and agriculture myths, is a second precondition of civilization.[47] Today Miseno and Palinuro, the tombs of Aeneas' two dead companions, are hollow capes on the Campanian shore, one near Cumae and the other near Paestum (fig. 2.3). Miseno is a dramatic rock arch; Palinuro a dome. Both are thrust into the sea, from which they rise like primordial buildings overlaid with centuries of ruin, earth, growth, and decay. Seen thus the underground habitations of Aeneas's dead are like the ruinous nymphaea of the Phlegraean Fields: further suburbs of Dis.

They are also, to return to Vico, part of that greater whole, the Mediterranean basin, which was originally inhabited by fierce uncivilized "Italic" indigenes. These had been mythicized by their more civil descendants into the wild animals of the place—bear, deer, goats, and others. It was overseas strangers such as Aeneas and Hercules who had made true and civil humans of their descendants.[48] Hercules' triumphs in his labors to combat wild beasts, clear land, clean out the Augean Stables, and so on, are similar civilization myths of hunting and farming. They are variants of the stories of the monuments to Palinurus and Misenus.[49]

The city of hell into which Aeneas descends is a place of enervation and eternal darkness. Vico's underworld takes its nature from Virgil's. We have noted that Vanvitelli also endowed the region with a hellish and subterranean character. But Vanvitelli's Neapolitan hell was a Christian one—a black and stinking labyrinth full of devils, disease, and unbearable pain, a place "where nothing pleases, nothing good can be hoped for but only evil feared, and where every effort is thrown into the sewer."[50] In all his 1500 published letters, written over a period of twenty years, there is no mention of Naples' beauty. His enmity for the Neapolitan people, their culture, and the local artistic and architectural style, was religious in its intensity.[51] He saw his professional rivals, notably Ferdinando Fuga and Mario Gioffredo, as downright satanic.[52] So were such ministerial adversaries as Bernardo Tanucci and the Prince of Sannicandro.[53] Vanvitelli's letters make clear that his new palace at Caserta was to be a refuge from this hellish capital for his beloved monarchs, for their court, and not least for himself.[54]

These feelings came to a head in 1764. Vanvitelli's hero and Maecenas, Carlo, had left to become king of Spain. The architect felt forlorn and neglected. Paranoia tinges his letters. In this same year famine struck and the city became a pandemonium of terror. Hordes of semibarbarian *lazzaroni*, the subproletariat, sacked the food shops. There were fearful processions of women who had crowned themselves with thorns and bore great wooden crosses on their backs. Images of saints were demolished when, despite desperate and threatening prayers, they brought no bread. The streets were rivers of death. The terrified court fled to the country, where it lodged in the half-built palace of Caserta, its roofless vestibules towering against the sky. Yet the countryside was worse than the city. Starvation reigned. It had driven armies of peasants into the capital.[55] Vanvitelli wanted to lock them up in Fuga's vast poorhouse (fig. 4.4), designed to hold 8000. He feared a plague: "because what with the misery, the rotten food of the poor peasants, and the ordinary general filth of this place, they stink for miles around like carrion."[56] It was as if an Antichrist had harrowed Hell and sent its denizens into the city by the sea in a mocking evocation of Sannazaro:

> Then came varied creatures,
> The half-wild race of centaurs, blackened gorgons,
> Scyllas, sphinxes, chimeras with blazing faces,
> And hydras, dogs, terrifying harpies.
> (*De Partu virginis*, I 390 ff)

Vanvitelli's Naples was a hell on, not under, earth. But the elements that made it so were nevertheless underground ones: the sewer-aqueduct beneath its streets, the Phlegraean Fields and Vesuvius—that is to say the hells that embraced it—and the underclasses of barbarians or near animals that infested it.

Three other cities that played roles in this mythic complex were more truly buried: the Roman centers at Herculaneum, Stabiae, and Pompeii.[57] All three were excavated by Carlo di Borbone, but the underground city closest to the king's heart was Herculaneum. The dedication of Baiardi's *Prodromo della antichità di Ercolano* (1752) makes the point: "Sire, while the Most Christian King [of France] continues to conquer new cities with the force of arms, and extends the boundaries of his great monarchy, Your Majesty extends his own conquests under the earth."[58]

Herculaneum, the king was assured by other writers, had been built by his euhemeristic ancestor Hercules, who had earlier built the Gardens of the Hesperides in a western country usually identified with Spain (though in the *Aeneid* it is Italy).[59] So, like Hercules, Carlo came out of Hesperia to found a capital and gardens in Campania, another Hesperia. Carlo had an important villa right at Herculaneum, at Portici. Here he housed the hundreds of objects found at the site, and here he convoked the Real Accademia Erculanense, founded in 1755 at Tanucci's urging to study the town and its treasure.[60] Using as his inspiration one of the most famous of all classical statues, the Farnese Hercules (which had become Carlo's property in 1734), Vanvitelli constructed a main part of the iconographic program at Caserta around this figure, who rests after his labors, holding the trophy of the Nemaean lion and the golden apples of the Hesperides, thus appearing as both hunter and garden-builder (fig. 7.11).[61]

At the time much was written and published about the eighteenth-century discovery of Herculaneum, more than about Stabiae or Pompeii or Carlo's great Greek find, the temples to the south at Paestum. Herculaneum must indeed have seemed infernal during its first thirty years of new life. Maiuri writes of it:

Herculaneum was excavated in tunnels by means of subterranean excavations about twenty meters deep, with immense difficulties that were overcome only by the ability of the Neapolitan laborers. They worked by lantern light, with the danger of collapse and the threat of lethal gases from the volcanic subsoil, anxiously having to provide in that darkness for the location and recovery of works of art that had been thrown down, broken, and dismembered by the eruption's muddy inundation; for dislodging and packing up paintings and mosaics, for protecting bronze and marble sculptures, and for bringing them out with slings between the narrow walls of the galleries and light wells.[62]

The early books, especially those by Baiardi and Mazzocchi, dwell on Hercules myths and apply Vico's principles to the newly uncovered city. The myths were seen as verbal encasements for buried truths about the beliefs and ruling institutions of early man in Campania. Baiardi, who published five volumes of his *Prodromo* between 1752 and 1756, never actually got beyond the myths to the antiquities. A disdainful colleague said, "Baiardi has buried Herculaneum under a shroud far thicker than lava."[63] Yet a pan-European interest was by no means all anti-Vichian. Charles-Nicolas Cochin, the Comte de Caylus, and the great Winckelmann, the latter being in many ways the founder of field archaeology, came to study, draw, and criticize. Among the Neapolitans Baiardi, Niccolò Ignarra, Jacopo Orazio Martorelli, Mazzocchi, and above all Francesco Daniele over the years gave Vichian interpretations to the discoveries.[64] Baiardi's *Prodromo* is full of fountain myths, city-foundings and myth-figures that are subjected to the process of *relegendo* and are analyzed into historical actualities. Willamowitz, in the *History of Philology*, castigates the Neapolitans for their fantasy and ignorance but makes an exception of Vico (who was the most fantastic of all), whom he praises for introducing "new and enlivening concepts" into philosophical science.[65]

Myth conditions the scene in one further way. Naples, according to tradition, had originally been a colony of settlers from Euboia, Greece's largest island. Being particularly enterprising and free and being surrounded by small hostile cities of similar folk, some of these Greeks emigrated to Italy; others, we are told, went as far as America. Though made into heroes by later myth, the heads of these colonies in actual fact were "nothing but bold adventurers and assassins." At the time, Greeks knew nothing of the principles of the law of peoples, or of economics, and their only philosophical guide was Pythagoras.

The Greeks had rebelled against their local legal systems and were determined to create one of their own. They first established themselves in Procida, the island just off Cape Miseno. But, significantly, because of lack of water they moved on to Cumae. Then, encountering further problems with water and sickness, they moved nearer to the present city of Naples.[66] First they settled at Baiae (some versions say Chiaia), then at Montevergine in what is now central Naples. This series of legendary capitals, each abandoned in disease and filth for a *nea polis*, is matched by the better attested fact that Naples' rulers had moved through a series of citadels beginning at Monterone, then moving to the the Castel dell'Ovo and on to Montevergine, the Castel Nuovo, to the Viceroy's Palace, and ending up next door to that building with the present Palazzo Reale.[67] When a new castle or palace was built the old one was allowed to fall into ruin. The royal residences were as disposable as the cities they guarded. It was according to this tradition, then, that when Carlo di Borbone arrived at the Palazzo Reale in 1734 it was barely habitable.[68]

These tales of the transported capital were current in the eighteenth century. They form the subject of one of Metastasio's short poetic dramas or "theater acts" that was frequently performed in Naples. The argument of the play, *Partenope*, is given by the poet as follows:

Poets preserve the ancient tradition that the siren Parthenope, daughter of Calliope the muse, chose to dwell on that most pleasant bay of the Tyrrhenian Sea into which the Sebeto empties; that not only was she venerated and paid divine honors by the inhabitants of the region, but that they, inspired by the Cumaean people, who were the first authors of great thought, founded, in the name of their tutelary goddess, the city of Parthenope on that very spot where at present Naples so distinguishes itself among the most celebrated cities of earth; and it is equally credible, by means of historical conjecture and through various unforgotten ancient local names, that many illustrious descendants of heroic stranger-families populated these happy lands in the remotest times, driven from their native soil for domestic reasons, or attracted to their new home by the abundant amenity of the place. On this basis men have built the likelihood that a promise was obtained from the Fates to erect the city of Parthenope. That is the principal action of the present dramatic composition.[69]

The construction of the city is marked in the play by two royal marriages, that of Elpinice to Cleanto, prince of Cumae and descendant of Hercules, and that of Ismene, princess of Posidonia (Paestum) to Filandro, prince of Miseno and the offspring of Aeolus. So the foundation of Parthenope meant the unifying of Herculean Cumae, to the west, with the southern lands associated with Aeneas's voyage from Sicily. The marriages occur at Parthenope's temple, which dominates the opening scene, and whose priest performs the ceremonies. He is in fact Alcmeno, Elpinice's father. In the poetry as in the argument much is made of the Vichian ideas that Cumae was the source of serious thought, and that "heroic stranger-families" had superfertile powers, were the nuclei of kingdoms, and that historic truths are wrapped in ancient names and legends.

When the two foreign fleets, Cleanto's and Filandro's, arrive in the Bay of Naples at the same moment, they converge across it like two great swans. Elpinice exclaims to her father:

The swift Cumaean oarsmen heading south
Whiten our bay, while at Sebeto's mouth
Opposite, as if in rivalry,
Posidonia's sails befoam the sea.[70]

The two brides have been waiting in melodious anticipation on the shore; that shore then begins to be ornamented with balustrades, statues, vaults, pilasters, and architraves. Metastasio's words suggest the gradual assembly of a painting by Claude Lorrain. The ships of Cumae and Posidonia lie next to the harbor works. Calm sea and a wild landscape fill the horizon. Cleanto the Cumaean has been the architect of all this and has signed his masterwork with the symbol of his sacred plough: as we will see, another Vichian touch. The Cumaean prince then becomes the city's founder, priest, and king.

Of all these earlier mythic sites of Naples, Cumae held the greatest importance for Vico. Cumae to him is the first city mentioned in "profane literature" (outside the Bible).[71] And it is with Cumae that he introduces his discussion of agricultural myth. He defines the origins of all cities in garden terms, from the words for plough and for the plough's curve; and from the abundance-producing waters' conjunction with land-clearing fire.[72] The antiquity of Cumae in turn leads him to an important theme in eighteenth-century culture: the claim that Etruscan, or Italic, civilization is actually older than Greek or that its excellence is at any rate older than Greek excellence. Vico claims that Italic civilization flourished when Sparta and Athens were small towns and that Italy possessed a finer art, architecture, religion, military skill, and imperial splendor than those Greek towns did.[73] Italy's superiorities in turn show its greater antiquity. Therefore Cumae, as the oldest of the Etruscan cities, has a privileged eminence. It is, indeed, of Egyptian foundation,[74] with all the further primacy that that implies. And the magnificence of the Cumae that Aeneas admired was precisely this stern, primitive "Egyptian" magnificence. Such primary architecture is stronger, simpler, and cruder than Greek, though in time Etruscan builders ornamented and polished their buildings.[75] This is Vico's version of the question addressed a few years later in works like Piranesi's *Delle Magnificenze ed architetture de' Romani* (1761).[76]

The question affected Vanvitelli too. He worshiped Carlo as an Italic Hercules and believed in an ancient, austere, classical, polished architecture—the antithesis of the Neapolitan rococo that was still (as he might have put it) raging around him. Above all Vanvitelli was obsessed with the preeminence of Rome and things Roman. The hatred felt by Caserta's architect toward the hell of Naples was counterbalanced, in his life and in his work, by this Vichian belief in a proud, stern *romanità*, in the precedence of things Italic and pure, in the capacity of art to be strong.[77]

The Sirens

Presiding over this dark labyrinth of Neapolitan underworlds, of cities buried in lava, disease, or obloquy, shines the marble statue of a beautiful queen. As noted in Metastasio's poem, one of Naples' predecessor cities, located between Cumae and present-day Naples, was called Parthenope. Parthenope herself played several different mythic roles. She was one of the three sirens who lured Ulysses and his sailors as they navigated the Bay of Naples. She was also a Sicilian princess who founded one of the "new cities" that comprise the legendary ancestry of the present capital. And she was the first queen of the city of Parthenope and a goddess who came to be identified with it.[78]

In a kindred way the *Cronaca di Partenope*, the standard medieval account of these matters, says that when the Euboians arrived at Cumae from Procida they were greeted by the sight of a nude, pregnant woman lying on the beach. They named their new city after her: κῦμα, Cuma, 'foetus.'[79] This is an obvious variant of the Parthenope story, though it is told as a separate episode in the *Cronaca*. Virgil, meanwhile, pictured Parthenope as a recumbent nude, he being her nursling, and Ovid saw her as a woman "born for soft pleasure,"[80] while in the *Cronaca* Parthenope lies on a seaside tomb, the victim of strife between factions in her city. Her death leads to yet another refounding, another *nea polis*. The queen dies and her people live, just the reverse of Homer's Parthenope story wherein men die and Parthenope and her companions live on. But we can imagine Homer's Parthenope languidly reclined on a rock much like Queen Parthenope on her tomb, if she rests on one elbow, Etruscan fashion, or like the mother who welcomes the former settlers from Procida to her beach. The *Cronaca* also tells of another recumbent Parthenope-like figure, a marble statue of "a beautiful woman who nourished or fed five little infants, her children," in the Piazza di Nilo or Nido (Nile, or else nest). She nursed the alumni (literally nurslings) of the nearby university.[81]

In all these stories Parthenope is a symbol of the city's magnetism. The city of the dead, the capital of squalor, is starred with irresistible fascination. In the *Cronaca* the fascination is not a summons to death but to life. What really attracts is the city's abundance, beauty, and ease. "Hence," the anonymous author continues with a characteristic double entendre, "it is no marvel that the ancients said that in this sea the sirens lived, and with their sweet song attracted foreigners to live here, since her great amenity and beauty easily drew anyone who saw her, and made him linger to enjoy her completely."[82] Vico follows the *Cronaca* in emphasizing positive aspects of the siren land. He praises the attractiveness of cities in general as a condition of civilization. "How greatly in Homer's time did the fame of their cities and places travel across the sea!" he exclaims, "What were the delights of the Italic peoples! It is the very subject matter of modern civilization, as the sirens drew sailors to their death and Circe turned strong men into swine."[83]

Vico's successors saw the fascination of great cities in the opposite way, though. To them Parthenope is once again Homerically malignant. The economist G. M. Galanti called modern Naples "a fatal siren" and said that its builders had made it beautiful precisely as a form of manipulation, to draw the barons from their estates throughout the countryside and to locate them in the capital as part of a court society subservient to the viceroy or king.[84] With them the barons brought armies of retainers, and Naples became a modern capital in that it was the overwhelming, all-consuming cultural, economic, legal, and military center of the country.[85]

In the eighteenth century the baneful effects of this magnetism became all too evident.[86] Ultimately about one-tenth of the population of the mainland kingdom lived in the capital. This tenth comprised the kingdom's political, ecclesiastical, cultural, and commercial elite. Here the mythic image of a Parthenope reclining beside the waters, calling men, completes itself. And beside her, behind her, was the valley of her former lovers' bones. "All the princes, all the grandees, all the soldiers, all the priests, all the abbés, all the monks, the valets, the merchants, the agents, the artists, the lackeys, have their residence at Naples," complained a French visitor, Ange Goudar, in 1769. "It's the congress of the different orders of the state, the general assembly of the nation." He added that Paris, which was already far too large, contained one-twentieth of France's population, but that Naples contained as much as one-seventh of the population of its kingdoms.[87] As a "congress," Naples drained its constituencies.

All this gave Carlo di Borbone a further reason for erecting a new capital and new royal residences. He could thereby decentralize his rule and soften Parthenope's fatal charm. Caserta was his greatest act in this cause, but the new roads he built to surrounding towns, the harbors he improved elsewhere in the kingdom, and even his new, extra-urban villas, the *siti reali*, contributed to the policy. Carlo also relaxed the law providing that all landholders had to have residences in the capital and thus alleviated some of the in-migration.[88]

Carlo's plans for Caserta were in some respects an antidote to and in others a revision of mythical Naples. At Caserta, as in Naples, are upper and lower labyrinths of waters—waters freighted with mythic images of abundance, rivers of time whose myths must be reread to guard against their Lethe-like burden of oblivion. Naples is also a city set into a penumbra of other cities or ghostly images of cities. These are its legendary predecessors that were abandoned in drought, filth, and disease, its subterranean matrixes, the symbols of the region's antiquity engulfed by Vesuvius's infernal streams; and they are Aeneas's cities built during his passage to his own new capital, Rome, which becomes the fountainhead of the strong architecture Vanvitelli was to revive. The *nea polis* of Caserta is the poetic rediscovery of these buried cities, and the beauty of Vanvitelli's masterpiece, the fascination of its summons, is his contribution to Parthenope's legacy.

3 Architectural Order

The Geometric Plan

Vico was a philosopher of myth. His beliefs about royalty and absolutism were constructed out of the names of gods, heroes, and institutions—names that he had subjected to a process of what Vico called "poetic philology." Yet there is a strong mathematical side to the Vichian philosophy. Pythagorean, mystic, and poetic, this side has more to do with numerology and geometrics than with arithmetic and geometry. It has links with esoterism, with the number theories of such predecessors to Vico as Jean Bodin, and with some of the ideas of Vico's contemporary Leibniz. Vico's efforts are devoted to elaborating his notions of justice, notions that reach architectural expression in the symmetries, distributions, and dimensions of the palatial centers from which absolutism radiated. In short, if Caserta was planned as another *nea polis* and as a more beautiful rival to the fascinating but fatal Parthenope, it also embodies these mathematical ideas. But before we look at these ideas in their eighteenth-century aspect we must examine them in certain earlier forms: namely, in Italian geometric planning and in the French absolute palace.

The subject of Italian geometric planning can best be introduced by glancing at the project made by the Neapolitan architect Mario Gioffredo for Caserta and then comparing it with the plan of Versailles (figs. 3.15, 6.2, 6.3). The measurable uniformity and regularity of the one is as clear as the warrenlike unpredictability of the other. How did such differences come about?

Geometric planning has five basic characteristics:[1]

1. The solids and voids are chiefly located in accordance with a regular or uniform two- or three-dimensional grid.

2. Either walls or sight lines, or both together, may mark out the coordinates (or as mathematicians say, vertices and edges) of the grid.

3. Repeated groupings create various kinds of symmetry and also involve close packing, nesting, and vectors.

4. "Canonical" rectangles and parallelepipeds, such as squares and cubes and derivations of them based on simple fractions such as squares-and-one-third or cubes-and-one-fourth, appear in the principal spaces. (These rectangles were generally known by their Latin names, like *superbipartiens tertias*, 'a square divided into thirds and then extended by two more such thirds.' In other words the shapes were described in terms of their derivation from the square.)

5. Comparable symmetries appear in the arithmetical and geometrical and other series that are found in the numbers generated by proportions, dimensions, and distributions.

This geometric tradition begins, tentatively, in the fifteenth century. Brunelleschi seems to come first. In churches he designed, modular grids dictated the nature of the orders used; he also used grids in experiments with perspective. But perhaps the most imaginative figure was Filarete. Filarete's treatise on architecture, written in the 1460s, anticipates Vanvitelli at Caserta by displaying a capital city filled with large palaces, a city erected on a cubic grid system by a huge work force of more than 100,000. Some of Filarete's palace and fort designs meanwhile anticipate Gioffredo, having large square moats in the form of labyrinths.[2] One is a perfect square 10 stadii (c. 600 feet) wide. At the center is a square palace made up of 9 canonical rooms (fig. 3.1). On a more modest scale Filarete designed a hypostyle reservoir 100 Florentine braccia (191 feet) square, palatial in aspect if not in function, and equally rigorous in its geometric ground plan of 10 bays per side (fig. 3.2). The simple arithmetical series 14, 16, 18, 20 can be used to account for all the dimensions, though the bay system of the upper floors is not consonant with that of the lower (the ratio is 12:7). A symmetrical grid (but not a uniform one, which would call for equally spaced coordinates) produces a clear, isomorphic, instantly visualizable structure.

Later in the fifteenth century Francesco di Giorgio Martini invented similar geometric schemes, using squares, double squares, and the like for government buildings in which the type of government is reflected in the plan and room size and distribution.[3] For Francesco, princes' palaces had to be different from republican ones, the latter having many small rooms for committees and much circulation space. There is also one large assembly room with central access from a series of vestibules, stairs, and courts (fig. 3.3). Princes' palaces, on the other hand, have a narrow *androne*, or entrance vault, guarded by rooms for doorkeepers (fig. 3.4). The rooms are more nearly the same

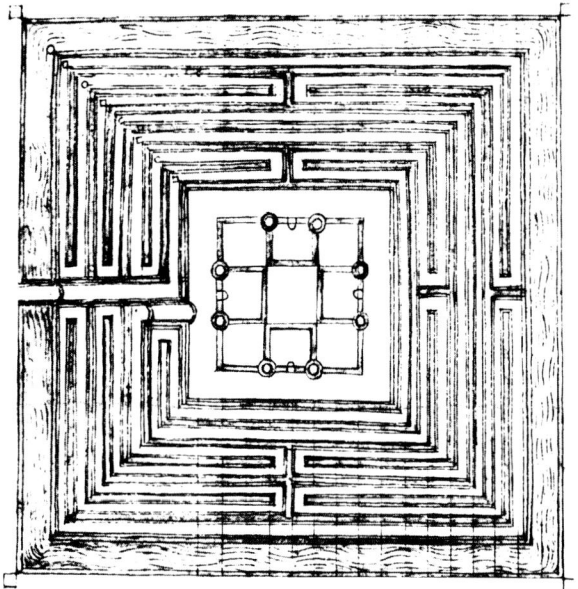

3.1
Filarete. Labyrinth. From Filarete, *Trattato* (1460s)

3.2
Filarete. Reservoir

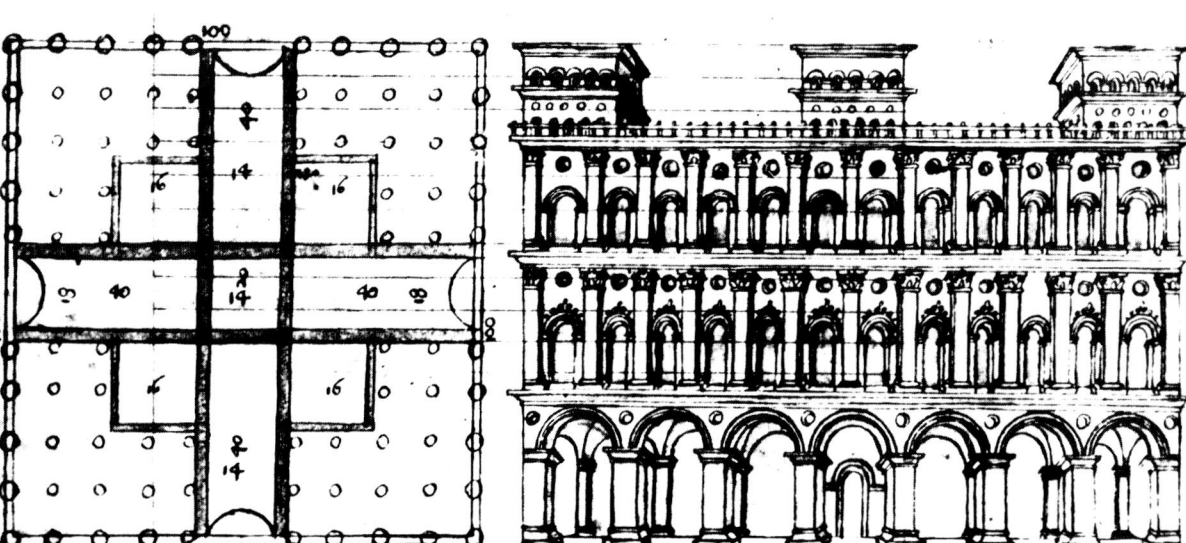

A

B

The Geometric Plan

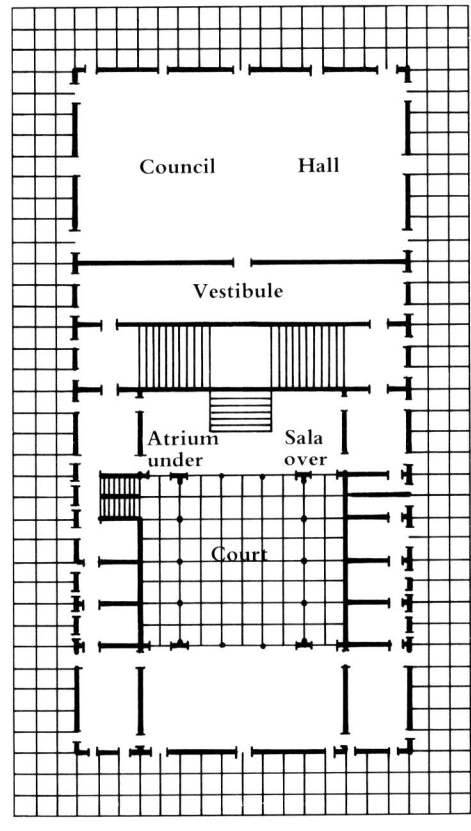

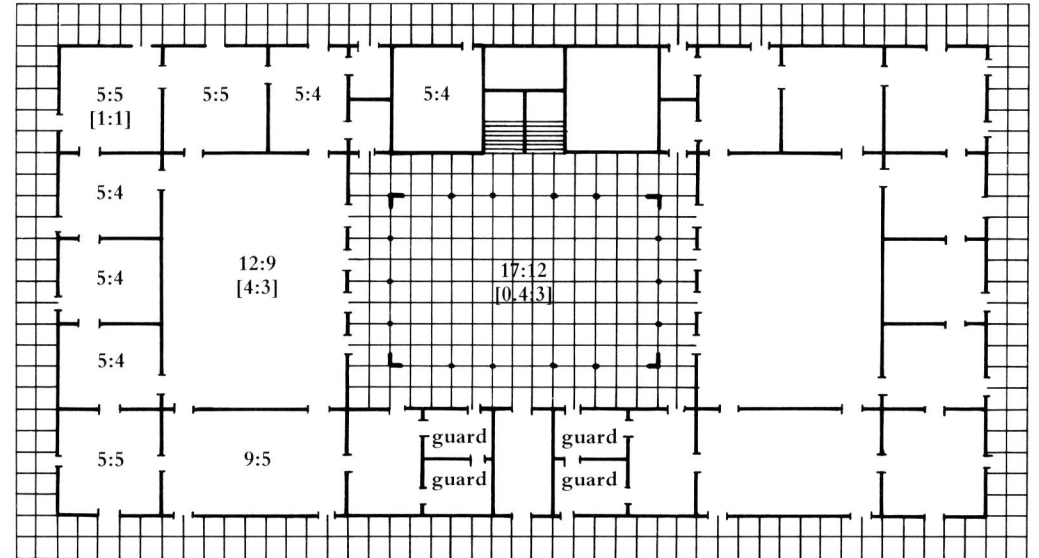

3.3
After Francesco di Giorgio. Republican palace. From the *Trattati* (1480s)

3.4
After Francesco di Giorgio. Prince's palace

size. Princely palaces in general are also larger than the republican ones and contain apartments for courtiers and guests. The republican palace stresses the housing of a governmental machine; the royal palace is a magnificent, hospitable, secure family residence. But in both cases when Francesco's schemes are mapped onto a grid, the various rooms turn out to be proportioned in accordance with the aforementioned canonical shapes.

Francesco's "palatio maggiore in Roma," a fantastic restoration of some Roman ruins, has a massive rectangular plan about 660 by 700 feet, worked out on a strong grid, and with a layout similar to that found in Francesco's princely palaces but with further symmetrical doubling of courtyards and with long lineups of small identical chambers. A similar attempt to restore what is apparently one of the Campidoglio palaces is almost a square (no scale is given) and has four large courtyards in the center arranged in a Greek cross, the corners then being filled in with large rectangular rooms (fig. 3.5). This central area is completely surrounded by strips or banks of chambers, these being 3:2 in plan on the ends and 6:5 along the sides. The banks are punctuated on their central axes by narrow stair corridors. The four corners of the rectangle are expressed slightly outward by means of exterior pilastering that does not match the interior grid. All but two of the eight exterior corner rooms are cylindrical. The central axis of each facade is fortified with a projecting bank of small chambers, making, with the stair corridors, groups of five on the long sides and seven on the short. The geometrical order also involves two twin pairs of facades—an important feature of later geometrical planning. Parts of the plan are marked "separate quarters for conservatori," "separate arch of Marcus Aurelius," "Temple of Jupiter," very different features of the building but completely integrated with the overall grid.

A more important moment in the story (fig. 3.6) came in 1488 when Giuliano da Sangallo conceived a massive cubic grid palace for one of Carlo di Borbone's Renaissance predecessors, Ferdinando I of Naples.[4] It was to house the main officers of the kingdom, setting them and their staffs all within one stately royal building rather than leaving them to their own private palaces where for generations the kingdom's legal, fiscal, and tax business had been conducted by hereditary officers possessing a feudal independence of the crown. Ferdinando's impulse to put his government all under one royal roof foreshadows Gennaro Maria Galanti's theory, also concocted in Naples, that royal palace construction could be a form of political and social manipulation.[5]

Sangallo's palace was to be inscribed within a nearly perfect square measuring about 330 Florentine braccia on each side (just short of 630 feet). The scheme thus called for a building much larger than any seriously intended earlier palace of the period. Visitors were to enter through a central five-arched portico. A swath of circulation space flows through it and then shrinks into three colonnaded corridors forming a triple androne. It widens out into a huge laterally set courtyard

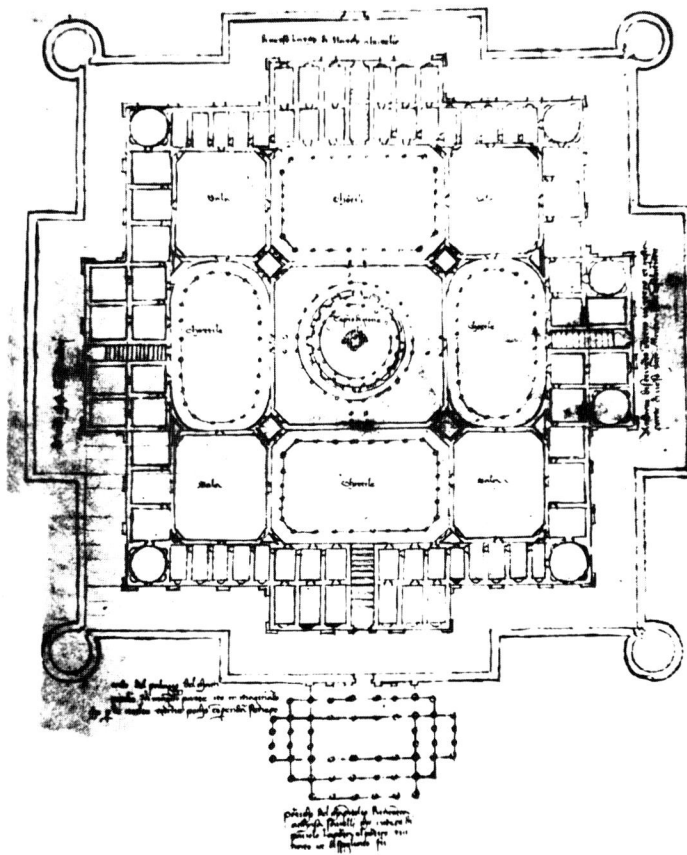

3.5
Francesco di Giorgio. Palace on the Campidoglio, Rome. From the *Trattati*

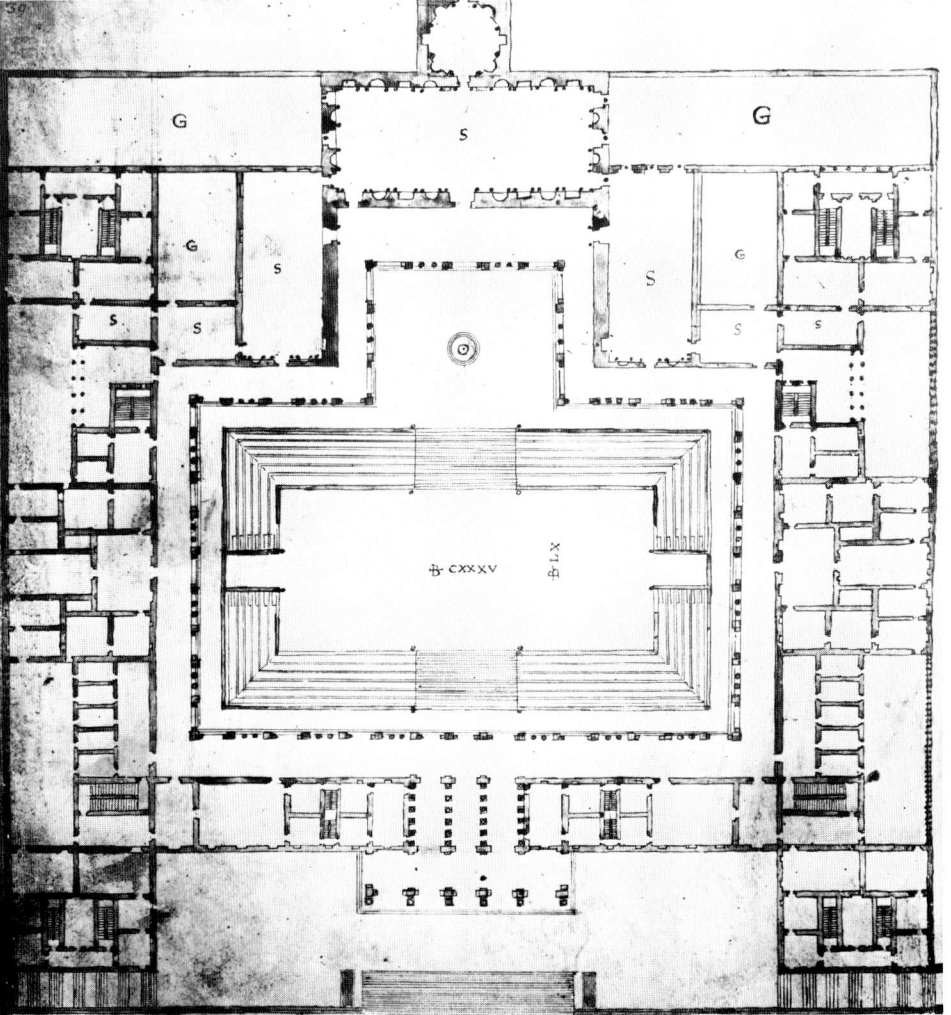

3.6
Giuliano da Sangallo. Projected Tribunali Palace for Naples, c. 1488. Florence, Uffizi

Architectural Order

measuring about 185 by 120 braccia (535 by 229 feet). Beyond a square fountain recess are a rectangular niched salon and a small, square, vaulted room, probably a chapel. The recess is flanked by rooms marked *S* and *G* on the plan, audience rooms, no doubt, and perhaps gardens. All this occurs within the central presentational part of the palace. The remainder consists of two strips, one down each side of the plan, each of them one-eighth the width of the whole. Each strip, in turn, is divided along its length into three large, squarish blocks containing apartments or suites, the end apartments having pairs of stairs and the central ones being without stairs. The arrangement is identical on each side of the palace, and, again on each side, the end apartments are identical. Between these apartment blocks are setbacks fronting narrower suites of yet smaller rooms. So Sangallo's arrangement is basically the same as in both of Francesco's plans, featuring central circulation space that widens and then narrows abruptly, symmetrical banks of small framing chambers, and a large central courtyard with stairs on axis on the far side. But Bramante's scheme is larger in scale and has more subdivisions.

Interestingly enough, construction on Sangallo's building was actually begun. Again, the project reflects the client's desire for control. Finally the fact that the Tribunali Palace, as it was called, should have provided for an amphitheater (for entertainment for the public) as well as for government offices, is still another way, aside from its organization, in which it prefigures Caserta.

In 1506–1508 or so Donato Bramante designed a rather similar building (figs. 3.7, 3.8), also called the Palazzo dei Tribunali, on the via Sistina in Rome.[6] Commissioned by Julius II, its massive foundations still record the desire of a second absolute ruler of the Renaissance to house several bureaucracies under one roof. The structure would have been familiar enough to Vanvitelli, who was a papal architect for most of his life, even after he had moved to Naples.[7] The heart of Bramante's structure is the square courtyard filled with an arcade on piers with attached columns having five openings per side. The central openings of this arcade match the building's main cross axes. The outer parts of the palace are split, also by the cross axes, into four more or less identical *L*-shaped room clusters. These consist of various-sized *sale* and *camere*, 'rooms' and 'chambers,' and each cluster has a double stair at its inner corner. The distribution of the different-sized rooms is as follows: four *sale* (of two different sizes, those on the front over the shops being 10 Roman palmi, about 4.6 feet, shorter than the rear ones), four main stairs, four small courtyards, and five tower rooms (at the corners and at the center of the main front). There are then 16 chambers and various even smaller rooms for guards and the like. The sizes and shapes within each category are about the same. The main court, larger *sale*, the stairs, and tower rooms are all squares or double squares. The dimensions are not a true series but are reducible to a group of five numbers: 18, 20, 25, 30, 46, and their multiples.

The Geometric Plan

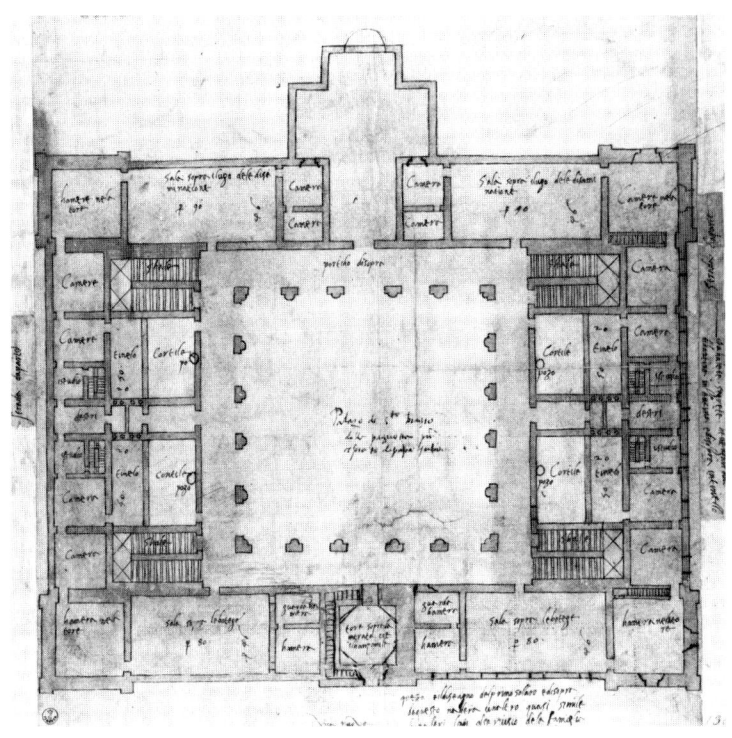

3.7
Bramante. Projected
Tribunali Palace for
Rome, c. 1506.
Florence, Uffizi

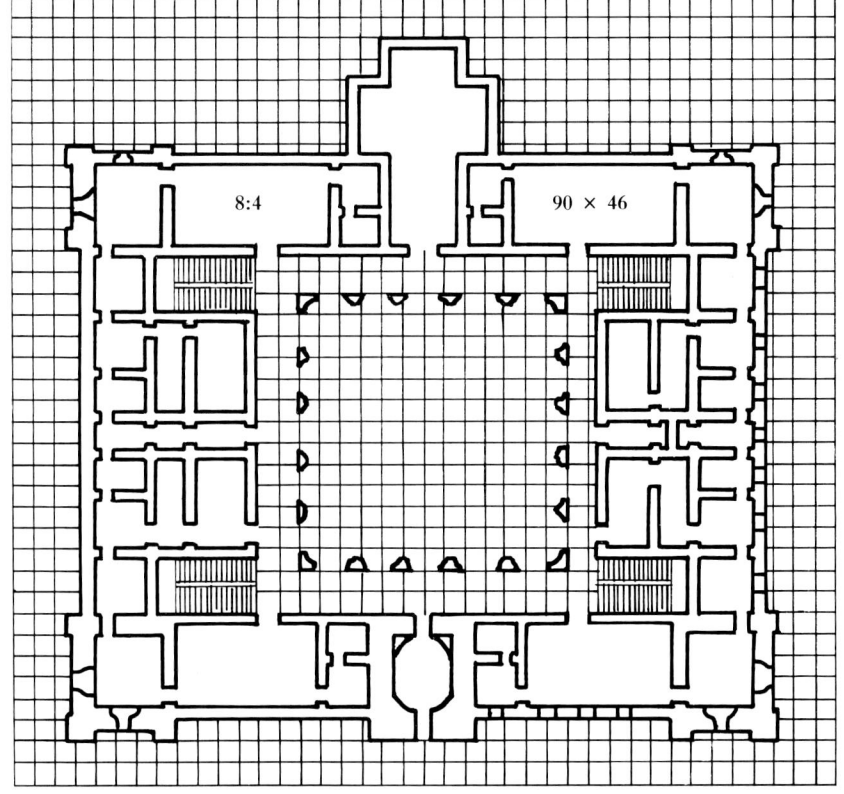

3.8
After Bramante.
Tribunali Palace for
Rome, mapped onto
a regular grid of
11.5-palmo squares

Architectural Order

Bramante's plan can be mapped onto a grid of 11.5 Roman palmi squares (fig. 3.8). Thus mapped, it measures 34 modules, 391 palmi, or 203 feet, by (respectively) 27, 310.5, or 161, not counting the church's projection. Most of the subdivisions of the plan accord with the edges of the graph. The towers are 5 modules square, the court is 17, the arcade 13.5, and all the rooms are measurable in 1 or 0.5-module magnitudes. Slight deformations were necessary to accommodate Bramante's scheme to this grid. Thus the towers are no longer square on the interior but have turned into 4:3 rectangles. The salons flanking the church actually measure 90 by 46 palmi in figure 3.7, whereas in their mapped form they have the proportion of 8:4 modules; that is, they suffer a 5 percent deformation into double squares. But these are fairly insignificant variations.

In certain ways Bramante's conception anticipates the Escorial (fig. 3.9), where Carlo di Borbone spent much of his childhood. Although the builders of four of these early geometric palaces, Ferdinando I of Naples, Julius II, Francis I (who planned such a building at Romorantin in the Loire Valley),[8] and Philip II of Spain, were absolutists who ruled unusually large territories, the Escorial was mainly a residence, not a palace for tribunals, nor was the town of El Escorial a capital. The palace memorializes a Spanish victory that occurred on the feast day of St. Lawrence, famed for his martyrdom on a grille, hence—so goes the lore at any rate—the grid plan.[9] The building was erected in 1568–1584 by Juan Bautista de Toledo and his successor Juan de Herrera.

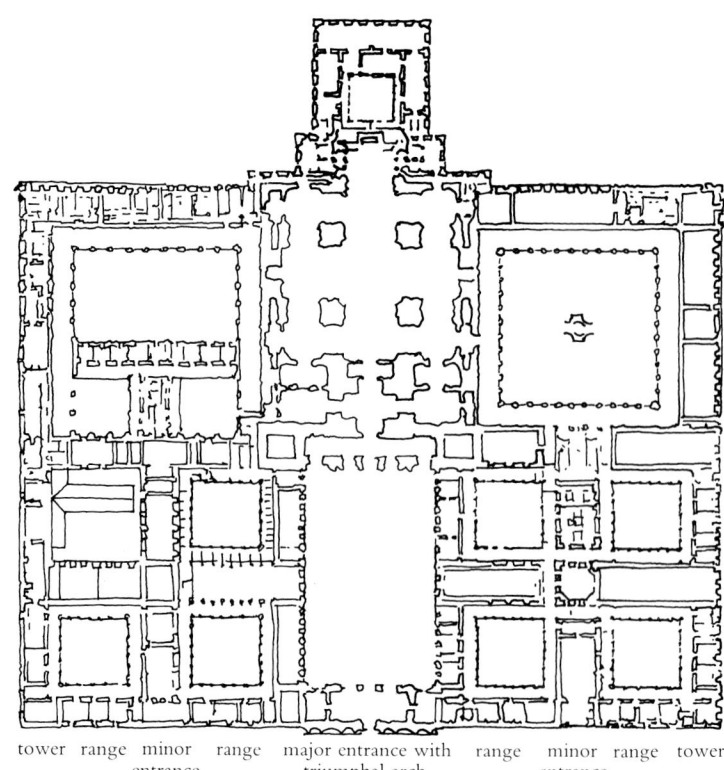

tower   range   minor   range   major entrance with   range   minor   range   tower
                entrance   triumphal arch   entrance

3.9
Sketch plan of the Escorial. After Kubler, *Building the Escorial*

Unlike any earlier building discussed, the Escorial is inscribed (minus the projecting palace) on a rectangle roughly derived from an arithmetical progression based on 180. That is, it is 540 by 720 Castilian feet (c. 641 by 769 U.S. feet), if the Castilian foot is equal to 14.25 U.S. inches), and 540 plus 180 equals 720. The forecourts occupy an area measuring about 360 Castilian feet square, and 360 is another number in that series.

These equivalences are rough; on study the plan is less geometrical than it seems at first sight. Yet with the large Greek cross church on the main axis of the central courtyard and with the similar crosses that form the courtyard complexes flanking the atrium, the Spanish palace is a cousin of Bramante's Tribunali, though of course in actual size it is closer to Sangallo's Neapolitan project. More important, as a single structure containing a royal palace, a cathedral or priory church, a college, and a monastery, the Escorial anticipates Gioffredo's original plan for Caserta (fig. 6.2).

Of the geometrical palaces considered, only the Escorial was erected and put to use. This suggests the tenacity and resources that were necessary to complete these structures. It was a long time before anything really comparable was erected elsewhere in Europe. Meanwhile geometric plans were often used in smaller buildings. The books of Palladio, Scamozzi, Du Cerceau, and many others are there to prove it. Every plan of Serlio, for example, is geometrical, and he brings every building type from peasant's house to church and palace under the sway of grid-based geometry.[10]

In the more elaborate and large-scale projects of the seventeenth century, however, grid-based rectilinear schemes had to compete with the more difficult, more dramatic, more mathematical play of curves that characterizes the plans of Borromini, Bernini, Guarini, Vittone, and, to name a more minor figure, Juan Caramuel Lobkowitz, the Bishop of Vigevano, near Milan, an indefatigable treatise writer. *Architectura obliqua* (his phrase) takes its place beside *architectura recta*[11]—and not only *architectura obliqua* but what I will call *architectura oblata*, *ovata*, and *spiralis*. Nonetheless the exploitation of uniform and symmetrical rectangular grids continued side by side with all this throughout the seventeenth and eighteenth centuries.

In analyzing the plan of the Escorial I extrapolated an arithmetical series from it. Is there any evidence, aside from what is implicit, that architects could design with such ideas in mind? The answer is yes. Caramuel will be our guide. In the eighth *tratado* of his book he describes the plans of famous ancient buildings in terms of their distributions and dimensions, and also in terms of the mathematical means or factors thus generated. For example the Temple of Diana at Ephesus, he says, was 8 columns wide and 16 deep (fig. 3.10). There were thus 128 columns in all (revised from the elder Pliny, *Historia naturalis* 36, 14, which gives 127). According to my reading of Caramuel's text the geometric series 8:15:28, etc. (that is, $15 \div 8 = 1.87$; $28 \div 15 = 1.86$) rises out of the temple's 8-column facade. The third number in the series, 28, is then multiplied by the first, 8, to equal 224, which is the width of the temple. Then 28 is multiplied by the second number in the series, 15, to give

Architectural Order

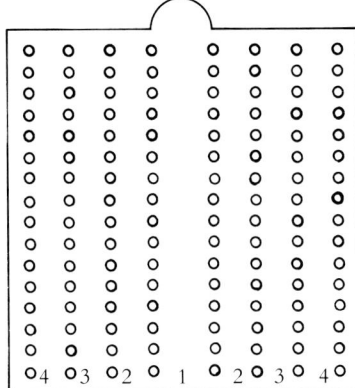

3.10
Juan Caramuel Lobkowitz. Plan of the Temple of Diana at Ephesus. From his *Architectura Civil* (1678)

3.11
Leibniz's system of binary arithmetic. After Leibniz, *Opera* (1768)

								0	0
								1	1
						1	0	2
						1	1	3
					1	0	0	4
					1	0	1	5
					1	1	0	6
					1	1	1	7
				1	0	0	0	8

420, the temple's length (in feet of an unspecified species). Caramuel's system thus links the grid plan, the distribution of columns, and the dimensions through a common factor within a mathematical series.[12] Note also that the facade of this temple, as Caramuel himself points out, is really divided into three parts, since the central intercolumniation, in accordance with classical practice, is wider than the others.

These two types of intercolumniations and their arrangement can be numbered in a way that expresses the reflected or mirror symmetry of the facade (fig. 3.10). The sides of the temple are generated by Vitruvius's well-known formulas, whereby the number of intercolumniations along the sides of a temple must equal the number of columns along the front, minus one. In other words,

$$2(x-1) = y,$$

where x = the side intercolumniations and y = the number of columns across the front. This is a Diophantine equation, familiar in Vitruvius's time. Meanwhile the temple front can be expressed:

```
*  *  *  *     *  *  *  *

4  3  2  1     2  3  4

   3        1        3
```

The asterisks in the upper row represent the columns; the numbers in the second row enumerate the intercolumniations, numbered symmetrically. In the third row are the sets of intercolumniations, distinguished in accordance with size (three equal intervals, one wider one, then three more equal ones). Each bay, thus represented, expresses both its position and its "handedness" or "sense" vis-à-vis the adjacent bays, as well as its position beneath the sloping pediment of the temple. It is thus part of a vector, for it has position, handedness, and direction. *Three* intercolumniations reduce to *two* groups that flank the *one* center intercolumniation, which, being not only central but wider, is the more important. The central bay is in fact a Pythagorean One.

This method of reducing symmetrically or serially arranged sets of numbers to either 1 or 0 is part of a long-standing tradition which, like so much of Pythagorean mathematics, had mystical overtones. The number 1 was thought of as the source of the other numbers, and here it actually seems to be so. Zero is less of an entity in Pythagoreanism; but it was coequal with 1 in a system of binary arithmetic invented by Leibniz in 1697. This reduced all numbers, via a grid somewhat resembling a magic square, to combinations of 1 and 0. Leibniz's system of binary arithmetic can be illustrated by an abacuslike structure (fig. 3.11) in which zeros alternate or pair with ones on the left side of an axis, while their normal-number equivalents are placed on the right. Each new magnitude adds either a new 1 or a new 0 on the left, in accordance with a principle that dislodges the earlier digit one space to the left and simultaneously transforms it from 1 to 0 or vice versa. By following Caramuel's implications the series 420, 224, 128, 28, 15, 8, . . . , which accounted for a whole temple, can be reduced to the sequence 3 1 3, which in turn can be binarized to 1 0 1.

Leibniz praised his system for its simplicity, for the fact that complicated memorization was unneeded, and above all because it expressed the concept of God's creation of Something, 1, from Nothing, 0. Leibniz even wanted his table inscribed on an honorific medallion with the motto THE IMAGE OF CREATION: TO CREATE EVERYTHING OUT OF NOTHING, 1 IS SUFFICIENT, and with a portrayal of God separating the light from the darkness. Galanti, the Neapolitan writer on Magna Graecia mentioned in the last chapter, refers to this system and suggests that it is related to Pythagoras's ideas.[13]

Further into the eighteenth century Jean-François Félibien (in a book owned by Vanvitelli) extrapolates a geometric plan from the younger Pliny's description of his Villa Laurentina near Ostia. Pliny's description of this building is so exact, says Félibien, that "the dimensions of each main part . . . are more or less determined by a comparison of each part with the others, and by the necessity of conserving all the views, projections, and provisions Pliny says are there."[14] Félibien is only repeating Vincenzo Scamozzi, who a century earlier had published similar geometric plan reconstructions of Roman villas. In fact Félibien republishes one of Scamozzi's plans along with Scamozzi's description of it. The Italian writer had claimed, however, that Pliny's text was not systematic enough to produce a graphic figure, and he improves on Pliny's information by positing a hypostyle matrix with "equal spaces as if there were columns dividing it up," assigning to each intercolumniation a dimension

Architectural Order

of 12 feet 18 inches.[15] In other words he creates a uniform rectangular grid on a module just like Caramuel's and extrapolates a number series from it (fig. 3.12, upper left-hand corner). But this time he does it for a complex walled and partitioned building, a building with many articulated functions, rather than for a temple.

Let us apply Caramuel's principle to Scamozzi's villa. The latter is a rectangle of 14 by 32 columns, making a total of 448. The dimensions would be 179 feet 8 inches (Venetian) wide, by 410 feet 8 inches deep (c. 200 by 455 U.S. feet). These dimensions relate to the distribution through a common factor, 12.86, rather than in a series (that is, 14 columns deep by 12.86 = 180, and 32 columns deep by 12.86 = 413.52, close enough to 179 feet 8 inches and 410 feet 8 inches).

Despite the fact that the plan is for a house rather than a temple, the same thing can be done to Scamozzi's plan as to Caramuel's. In this case windows are the intercolumniations and the spaces between windows the columns. The spacing is more varied, yet equally symmetrical if not more so. The lower row of numbers in figure 3.12 begins with the end bay, consisting of one 2-foot column and one 2-foot window. Then comes a 4-foot column, then 10 alternations of 2-foot windows and 3-foot columns, then an axial 3-foot door, and so on across the rest of the facade in exact mirroring. The upper row of numbers shows the number of elements in each subdivision of the facade, as determined by a change in dimensions.

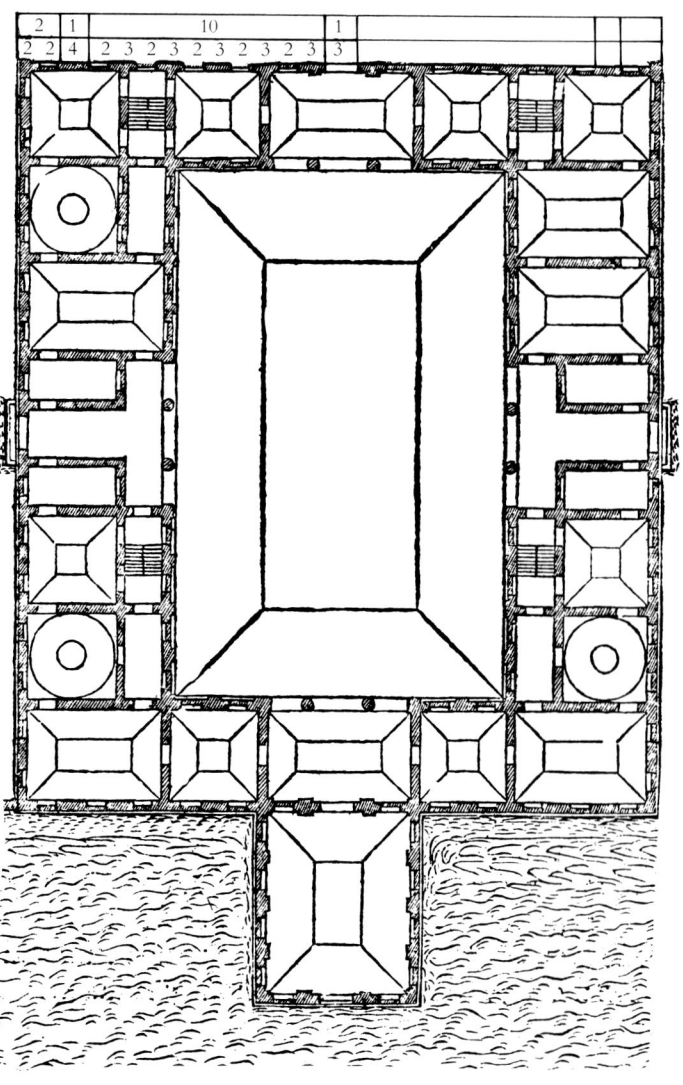

3.12
After Vincenzo Scamozzi. A reconstruction of Pliny's villa at Laurentum, plan. From his *Idea dell'-Architettura* (1619)

In other words there are four types of subgroup or bay: (1) two columns followed by a 2-foot window; (2) 4-foot columns; (3) ten 2-foot windows alternating with 3-foot columns; and (4) a 3-foot door. The advantage to looking at the facade this way is that, instead of assigning arbitrary numbers (1,2,3) to the intervals of the facade, as with Caramuel (fig. 3.10), this method employs the actual dimensions—dimensions that can also be used to state the proportions. The same thing was done in figure 3.8, when Bramante's Tribunali Palace was mapped onto a grid of 11.5-palmo squares. Module, dimension, and proportion coalesce into the same sets of numbers. In figure 3.8, however, the grid was extrapolated and the original design slightly deformed. Scamozzi's own words declare the grid was the matrix of the plan; and the correspondence between grid and plan is exact.

The Absolute Palace

In the eighteenth century the possibilities of such *architectura recta* for very large palaces were reexplored. It was the heyday of absolutism, when the scale of the royal palaces matched that of the new nations and empires ruled from them, and the palaces' size and complexity matched the completeness and depth with which rulers sought to control their subjects' lives. Indeed, as we shall see, the developed absolute palace can be understood as a three-dimensional table of organization, a kind of taxonomic or iconographic working model of the monarchy it housed.

In this sense Caserta is directly, if not consciously, descended from Sangallo's scheme for Ferdinando I of Naples; but it is equally descended from the first modern absolute palace, a building much larger than anything so far discussed. This came into existence in 1566 when Philibert de l'Orme began to extend the Louvre so it would join his newly begun Palais des Tuileries.[16] Together the two structures formed one vast irregular building extending a good 400 *toises* (2400 feet) along the Seine. Here, under Catherine de Médicis and then Charles IX, France housed many of the chief, most representative elements of her financial, legal, military, and cultural structures as well as the royal family and the court. France, which was then by far the largest and most complex unified country in Europe, was governed mostly from this building until Louis XIV moved the court and a great part of the government to Versailles in the 1660s.

The Louvre and the Tuileries were the result of at least twenty building campaigns lasting from the Middle Ages through the nineteenth century.[17] Although the buildings are (or were: the Tuileries was destroyed in 1871) carried out mainly in a Renaissance style they represent the thinking of a dozen or more architects and many different patrons. There is great irregularity. Even the one reasonably regular section, the Cour Carrée, is the work of four different architects (Lescot, 1546–1559; 1566–1600; Lemercier, 1624–1654; Le Vau, 1650–1664; and Perrault, 1667–1674), and betrays several shifts of program. Confusingly, the facades sometimes reflect the interiors and sometimes do not. The module varies. The orders are used as a mere cladding and are not, in the stricter Italian manner, reflected in the proportions of the bays or the compartments they ornament. Lescot, in 1546 and then again in 1598, drew up schemes for realigning the long galleries leading from the Cour Carrée to the one range of the Tuileries that was actually built. These tried for greater regularity, but the vast sizes of the courts and the spindly linearity of the wings would have defeated any geometric effect had the plan been carried out (fig. 3.13).

The layout of Louis XIII's Versailles (1624), on the other hand, is perfectly geometric (fig. 3.14). A firm central axis[18] is flanked by palace and outbuildings with bilateral mirror symmetry. The palace is based on a square and its rooms, including the four projecting corner towers, are either squares or canonical rectangles. The court is a square-and-one-quarter, or sesquiquartal. The plan is at one with those in sixteenth-century treatises.

Yet, of course, the great name to be connected with Versailles is not that of Louis XIII but that of his successor. It was the Sun King who transformed this modest geometric lodge into the greatest palace ever (fig. 3.15). By 1674 Versailles contained quarters for guards, extensive royal apartments, and all sorts of other practical and pleasureful *aménagements*. Living quarters represented different social classes and dozens of occupations; on the right-hand side facing what was to become the Cour d'Honneur was a government office wing. Symmetrically disposed in the form of small, square, separated buildings were further pavilions for government ministries. All these things were expanded, enriched, and interlocked during the seventeenth and eighteenth centuries. Far more than the Louvre, and more than the Escorial or the unbuilt Italian palaces discussed, Versailles aimed to gather separate, semi-independent local offices, nationalize them, and put them under one roof in logical groupings.

Versailles' siting and context were as important to its proclamation of absolutism as was the château proper. On the east the palace was isolated and focused upon by its attendant town, an urban mass split into geometric wedges by three great avenues forming a trident as they move forth from the palace. On the west are the responding geometries of park and gardens. As far as the eye can see, the works of man and nature celebrate this one vast building known at the time not as a domicile, however royal, but simply as the "Château de la France."[19]

At Versailles, in a way that is much more elaborated and complex than at the Louvre, the royal family, ministers, officials, guards, servants, ambassadors, and even the public all had their places—their rooms, their corridors, their stairways grand or small—their spheres. These highly specific spaces and the decoration that adorned and explained them made up a taxonomic grid for rituals that Louis himself constantly enriched. He

3.13
Pierre Lescot. Plan for remodeling the Louvre and the Tuileries, 1598. Paris, Bibliothèque Nationale

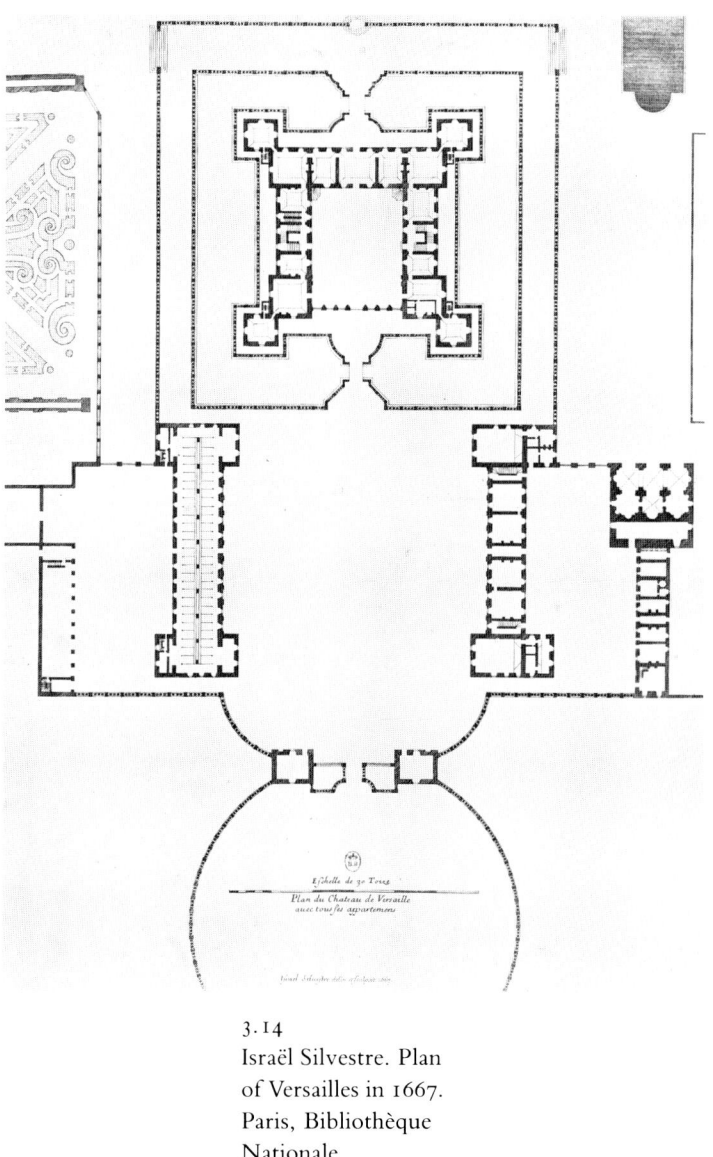

3.14
Israël Silvestre. Plan of Versailles in 1667. Paris, Bibliothèque Nationale

moved through it like a sun through its latitudes and longitudes, from *lever* to *conseil* to Mass to *grand-couvert* to *coucher*. As Pierre Verlet writes:

Louis XIV impressed on his royal métier a luxury and ostentation whose mechanisms no king of France, not even Francis I or Henry III, had pushed so far. The progression of his apartments, the hierarchy of his entrées, the rituals that had to surround his person—rituals in accordance with which one person had to be in this room and another in that—were fixed with a minuteness that could appear ridiculous to us today, but which filled up the existence of most members of his court.[20]

With absolute control went absolute routine. A glance at the plan of Versailles as it was elaborated to house all this, however, reveals it to be very different from the modest geometric palace that is now barely discernible as it demarcates the Cour d'Honneur (fig. 3.15). Around this center has been established a large rectangular envelope of state rooms. But the whole of it, as noted, has been fractured into an irregular web of chambers, galleries, anterooms, and so on. From the original vertical government and stable wings now project two massive horizontal irregular wings, each almost 800 feet long, mainly by Jules Hardouin-Mansart. These contain the theater, the chapel, and dozens of other governmental, residential, and office or ceremonial functions.

The result is ungeometrical both in toto and in detail. Scrutiny of the room alignments, door placements, circulation facilities, and lighting shows this clearly. Look at the king's "interior" apartment, built for informal purposes yet still a place of ceremony, filled with works of art. When the apartment layout is aligned along the rear wall of the transverse range of the Cour d'Honneur (fig. 3.16, *A*), the whole suite is cocked at an angle some 5 degrees from the vertical. The angles marked *B* in fig. 3.16 are therefore all less or more than 90 degrees. This part of the palace was erected beginning in 1677, and is located on the right of the Cour de Marbre. Three major rooms, the bedroom (*a*), the Salon de la Pendule (*b*), and the study (*c*), line this wall of the court. The rooms are all the same width but of different lengths. Only the bedroom (minus its alcove) has canonical proportions in plan (it is about 5:3, a superbipartiens tertias). The central section, comprising the bed alcove (*d*), the *antichambre des chiens* (*e*), the staircase (*f*), the *cabinet de chaise* (*g*) and the *arrière cabinet* (*h*), is random in distribution, proportion, alignment, and circulation. The stair (*f*) has no window at level, nor does the *cabinet de chaise*. Shapes and wall thicknesses are irregular and illogical. The same goes for the other chambers and for the Cour des Cerfs (*C*). The little corridor (*D*) that clings to the outer right-hand margin of the apartment is equally improvisational. There is no logical grid, no module, no meaning or mathematical economy to the sequences of dimensions. The apartments of the dauphin and dauphine are even more chaotic (fig. 3.17). Such planning is fundamentally opposed to geometrical principles. In 1668 a scheme was elaborated to regeometrize the the whole complex, but it was not carried out (fig. 3.18).[21]

The Absolute Palace

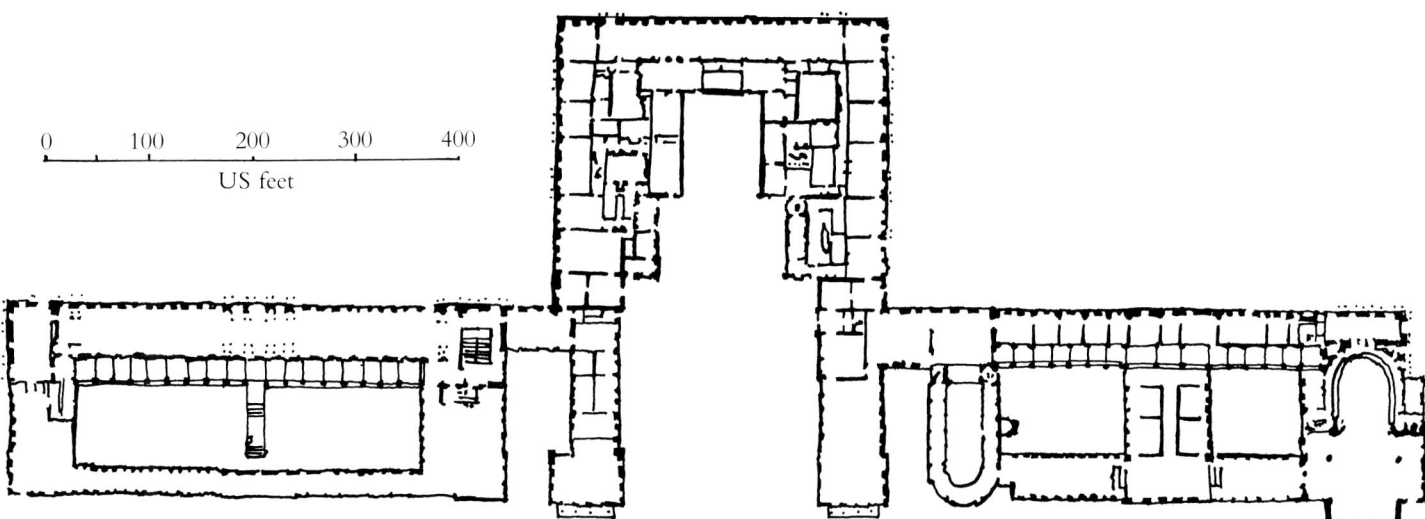

3.15
Versailles. Sketch plan of present building. Courtesy Yale Slide and Photograph Collection

Architectural Order

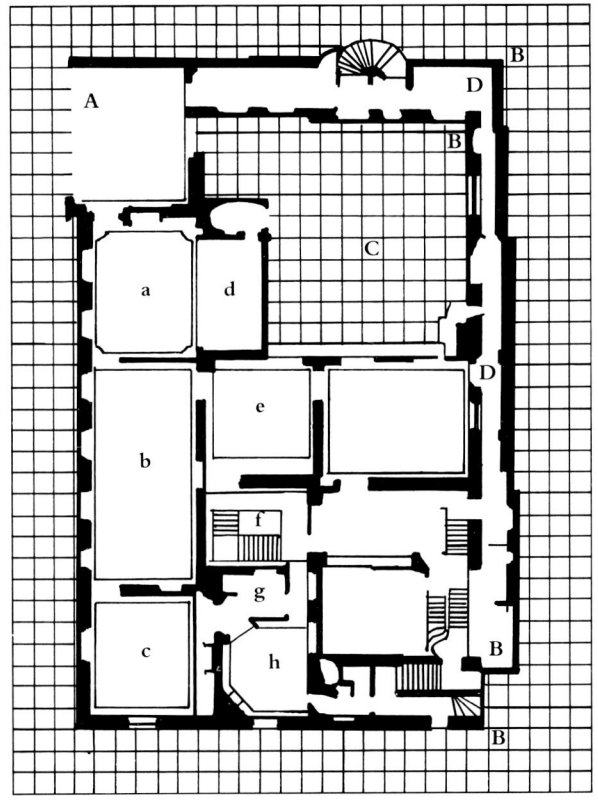

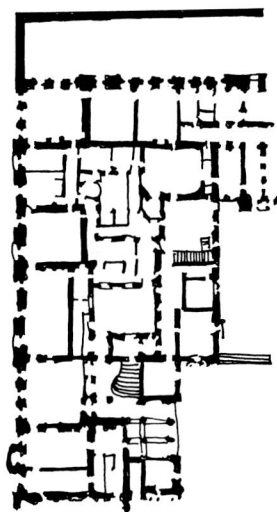

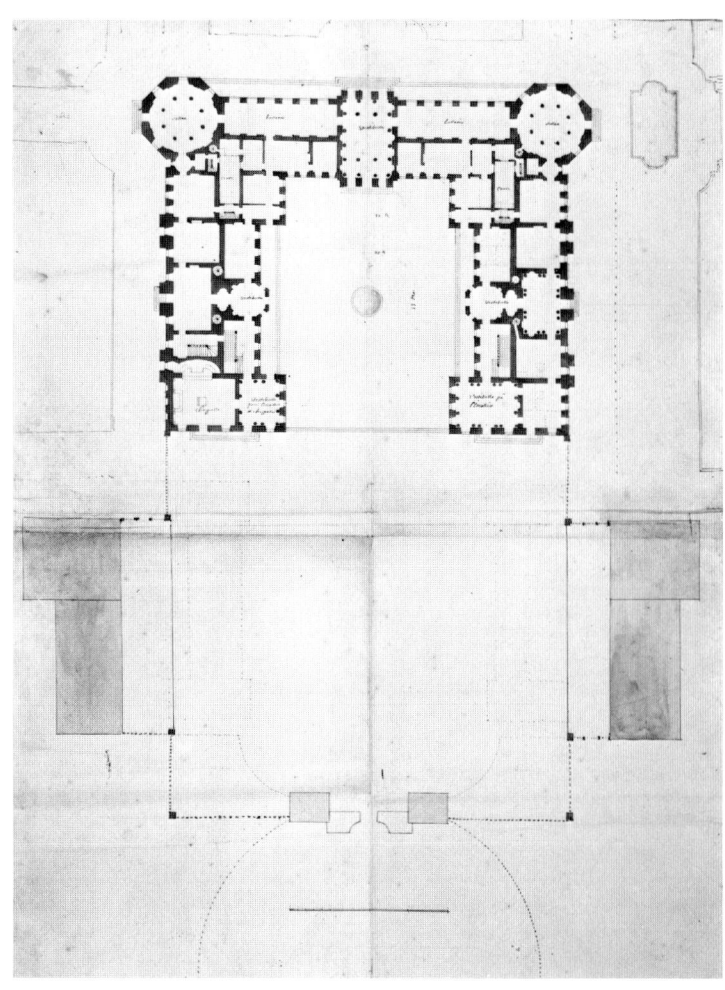

3.16
Versailles. King's private apartments, begun in 1677. After Pierre Verlet, *Versailles*

3.17
Versailles, dauphin's apartments. After Verlet

3.18
Louis Le Vau. Project for a geometrical envelope for Versailles, 1668. Stockholm, National-museum

In short, we are presented with two distinct phenomena: on the one hand the elaboration, mainly in Italian treatises and notebooks, of a geometric *architectura recta*; on the other the absolute palace, developed via the Louvre, the Tuileries, and Versailles, as a matrix for absolutist rituals. Caserta is the most important attempt to combine the two.

Absolutism in Naples

Just as Naples played its role in the development of the geometric plan, equally it played its role in the development of absolute monarchy. The theorists who perfected the eighteenth-century conception of an enlightened despotism deriving from dynastic myth were, among others, Bodin, Hobbes, Leibniz, Pufendorf, and Vico.[22] As by now might be expected, the most important of these for us is Vico—and not only because of his influence in Naples but because his monarchic theory was mythic in tone and lent itself to enhancement by the visual arts. Vico's theories being partly founded on Pythagorean geometry, a Vichian palace is destined to be geometric and mythic as well as absolute.

To Vico, monarchy ('rule by the one') is founded *upon* the One—one single principle, one goal, one source, one "central man." That central man is like the number 1, and his realms, subjects, and laws are like the numbers that rise out of 1 and that are grouped in accordance with the laws of mathematical relation. In other words both equality and hierarchy in society are achieved mathematically.[23] The One produces the other numbers that in their proper groupings reign over human affairs. One, or the monarch, guides society as an architect rules mathematically through lesser virtues, assistants, or skills: this is what is called "architectonic justice."[24] The laws of public order provide that those subjects in a kingdom *count* who are wise and worthy.[25] The scheme is Pythagorean—and Vico in fact pays homage to Pythagoras as *the* Italic philosopher and as the greatest "increment" among philosophers, as the one who founded architectonic justice. "Hence Pythagoras located human reasoning power in number," he explains, "that it might attain to [or perfect] the universe, like a most pure and brilliant light; so that whichever way you turn your mind's eye, Reason directs the eye's rays, and all that is called knowable, and all its parts, you see together as it all responds, accords, and consists as beautifully as is possible in one point of thought." This is the essential oneness of all knowledge through which social damage and benefit can be calculated numerically.[26]

Architectonic justice, anchored in number, is indeed the cause of all things. It surrounds, controls, pervades the laws of private property, of the merit of subjects in a kingdom, and of their dignity in a phenomenon called *lex rectrix*. The *lex rectrix* consists of the laws that correct inequities in acquisition, disposition, or possession. The just measures of the latter things are in turn called the *lex aequatrix*. Both the "restituting" and the "equalizing" law are dependent on architectonic justice because they work through number, and number in turn "plants" propriety in the soul of the legislator, the monarch.[27]

Because for Vico law is basically a variant of mathematics and specifically of geometry, the measures of law are arithmetical and geometrical series. When persons are equal before the law arithmetical justice is invoked. Its magnitudes are equal as in an arithmetical series. Where persons are unequal before the law, as children before parents, tenants before landlords, or mortals before God, a double, or geometric, mode of justice pertains. Contracts, punishments, taxes, rights, property, privileges—all of law and government—are in these cases reducible to geometric principles. The principles are truly geometric, rather than numerical, first because geometry makes concrete the abstractions of mathematics yet does not betray them and second because geometric series, like society itself, are built up from unequal magnitudes.[28]

The power of the ruler, the One, must therefore be absolute. As 1 rules through its subsidiary numbers; as, again, architects rule through subsidiary virtues and assistants, so monarchs rule through courtiers, ministers, departments, armies, which have given up their own power to the mon-arch, the 'one-ruler.' Keys to the natural order, monarchs are driven from office only by their vices, never by the true will of the multitude. They command auspices, consorts, families, tribes, nobility, fields, imperii, rites, and laws of tribute; they are consecrated to the highest religion, sealed to the highest nobility, protected by the highest sovereignty, with power of life and death over their subjects. The laws of war and peace are invoked by monarchs on the authority of auspices and chance. The *respublica* (the common wealth of property and institutions) is composed of pure monarchy. It has one purpose: its own preservation and glory, its dynastic extension back into time, forward into the future, and outward in space. It has one life, which pervades the whole territory of the realm and the soul of every subject within it. As, in Pythagorean mathematics, 1 pervades all other numbers, and as all other numbers proceed from 1 and return to it, so the monarch pervades his people; and so, too, humanity in history proceeds from early, tribal, family-based monarchy to oligarchy, to republics, to democracies, only to return to monarchy—but this time to a massive and civilized one, the "absolute" monarchy in which tribes and families are transposed into nations and empires.[29]

Because of the unique power of the throne the monarch is pure. Forced to give no law except at the bidding of the One God, the monarch is not only free but is freedom itself. The free judgment exercised conforms to the monarchic system that reigns in Nature. The all-pervasiveness of the monarch is that of Nature and of Nature's God. Nor can the ruler's subjects envy this power, for they possess it, being contained within its oneness. The authority of our ancestors, who are the objects of our inevitable mythopoeic powers (like Hercules and Apollo), flows universally to the One Ruler, the embodiment of all deities. And, as with Jove, whatever pleases the ruler or places itself in the ruler's mind as law to be enacted, has the force of law. The freedom of the throne includes and must include the freedom to be utterly arbitrary, and even to seem to be immoral, as a god might be.[30]

As a Bourbon, Carlo di Borbone was ready to fulfill this ideal. For his family dreamed Vichian dreams—or perhaps Vico poeticized Bourbon dreams. In their "family pact" the Bourbons conjoined intimate relationships like those described in Vico's primitive monarchy to the grandeur of an empire that girdled the earth: Vico's modern vast "humane" civil monarchy. As J. L. R. Desormeaux remarked in his *Histoire de la maison de Bourbon* (1772–1788):

A new luster has spread over this house, cherished as it is by Heaven and Earth. Spain, South America, the Two Sicilies, Parma, Piacenza, and Corsica have become Bourbon patrimony. The masters and fathers of so many nations, more united by bonds of mutual esteem than by blood, have laid the foundations of the public happiness by a family pact whose object is to maintain peace and concord in Christian Europe.[31]

Nonetheless, when Carlo arrived in Naples in 1734 there was no royal palace that even began to live up to these implications. The new king found instead the moldering series of earlier residences: a ruinous and haunted Castel dell'Ovo rising from its promontory in the harbor; the Castel "Nuovo," the Aragonese fortress of the 1450s, also on the harbor, with its cramped apartments and quaint classical triumphal arch; the Castel Capuano, a royal residence and partly a courthouse; the Viceroy's Palace, a nondescript building, now destroyed, between the Castel Nuovo and the present Church of San Ferdinando; and various sunk and splintered villas.[32]

There was also the Palazzo Reale (figs. 3.19–3.21). This stood all across one side of a vast semicircular piazza now occupied by the Church of San Francesco di Paola and its flanking colonnades. The Palazzo Reale was a long, low, three-story building 550 palmi (464 feet) wide. It was of brick, *rosso napoletano*, with gray limestone trim, constructed as a continuous open arcade surmounted by two long, low, windowed stories in 10 bays on either side of a projecting Doric-columned arch, with a balconied window of appearances and, on top, a symmetrical set of three baroque clocks (now reduced to a single central clock in a three-tiered aedicule). Domenico Fontana, who also designed the so-called Bacino Angioino, the now much altered Neptune Fountain (1601) in the Piazza Bovio, and the Church of Gesù e Maria (1593–1603), was the architect of the Palazzo Reale.[33] Its length, 550 palmi, its lowness, its plainness and humble brick and limestone; the regular geometry of the facade, where all interest in sculptural event is suppressed, and where number repetition (1, 3, 10), axes, and mathematical distribution reign; these things make of it an understated predecessor of Capodimonte and Caserta. Milizia in 1768 claimed that the original plan had called for three symmetrical entrances with three courtyards behind them—in other words just one-third of Gioffredo's design (figs. 6.2, 6.3). The palace's dilapidation (built on soft ground, it was sinking in the mid-eighteenth century)[34] and its squalid chambers, even though they looked out on magnificent courtyards (fig. 3.20), made it in those years more of a counterpart to the Castel Nuovo than to anything that Carlo would have desired.

Architectural Order

3.19
Domenico Fontana
(with later niches by
Vanvitelli). Palazzo
Reale, Naples, 1600–
1602. Photo Alinari

Absolutism in Naples

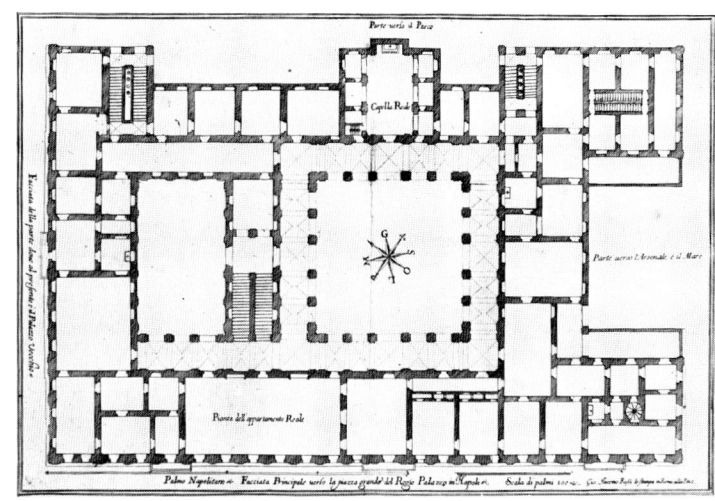

3.21
Engraved plan of the Palazzo Reale, Naples, before 1837. Naples, Biblioteca Nazionale

3.20
Palazzo Reale, Courtyard

Although Vanvitelli's greatest achievement lay in the geometries of Caserta, he did something to add to the geometrical interest of the Palazzo Reale as well. He filled in some of the outer arches in the main facade, supplying the niches for the present colossal nineteenth-century statues of the kings of Naples, including a fine Carlo di Borbone by Raffaelle Belliazzi. He also rebuilt the foundations under the royal apartments (second floor, right-hand side).[35]

In filling in these arches Vanvitelli created a new and interesting rhythm of bays. There are five types of arch: (1) closed, with window; (2) closed, with niche; (3) open, with iron gate and Doric flanking columns; (4) open, with gate and pilasters; (5) central, open, and flanked by pairs of supports and panels or bays narrower than normal. The arrangement, left to right, is

(1 2 3)(2 4 2 4 2 4)(5)(4 2 4 2 4 2)(3 2 1)

(3)   (6)   (1)   (6)   (3).

The second row of figures represents the number of elements in each of the five sets. Unlike the facade sequence in Scamozzi, this one reduces to

3 + (3 + 3), 1, (3 + 3) + 3.

Thus the five bay types are generated out of 1s and 3s, which become the sources of the other numbers or distributions in the design. Something like the principle Leibniz used for his binary arithmetic is brought to bear. But the numbers just listed do not reflect either proportions or dimensions, only types. As can be seen from the plan (fig. 3.21), the bays are irregular in width, and their irregularities do not correspond to the variations in type. Nonetheless there are two kinds of symmetry: the mirroring of the whole facade on either side of the 1 and translational symmetries in two of the sets, namely those constructed of (2, 4, 2, 4, 2, 4) and (4, 2, 4, 2, 4, 2).

Fontana's plan, though in some respects comparable to Bramante's Tribunali Palace in its large main courtyard with five entrances per side and, on axis, a royal chapel, is neither geometrical in arrangement nor absolutist in scale and function. The perimeter is irregular, the grid is ad hoc, and the spacing of repeated elements such as the windows of the main facade is not uniform, though this fact is minimized. Carlo's Spanish soul probably objected to the staircases, which are narrow and ill assorted. All in all the Palazzo Reale was a poor thing after the Escorial, Buen Retiro, and the other palaces the king had known as a boy. Nonetheless, with its vast piazza at the center of the city, the building remained the focus of Carlo's urban ceremonials and was the object of an important program of fresco painting.[36]

The first real step on the road to Caserta was Capodimonte, begun in 1738, only a few months after Carlo became king (figs. 3.22–3.26).[37] Capodimonte stands on a majestic hill, formerly called Miradois, north of the city. In Carlo's time the place was completely cut off from the town. The peculiar topography of the site also meant that it could have no monumental entrance boulevard and no axial relation with its garden

3.22
Antonio Canevari and Giovanni Antonio Medrano. Palazzo di Capodimonte, Naples, 1738–1838. Photo Alinari

3.23
Capodimonte from the side. Photo Alinari

3.24
Capodimonte, courtyard. Photo Mimmo Jodice

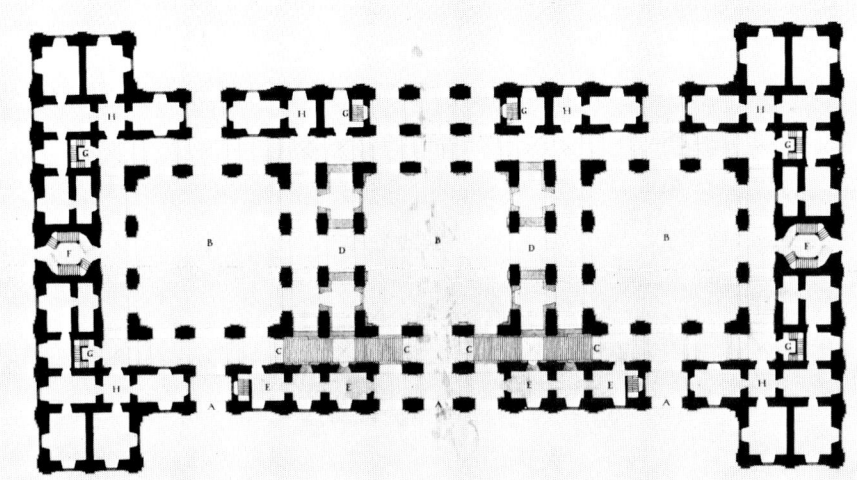

3.25
Capodimonte, plan of ground floor. Caserta, Reggia

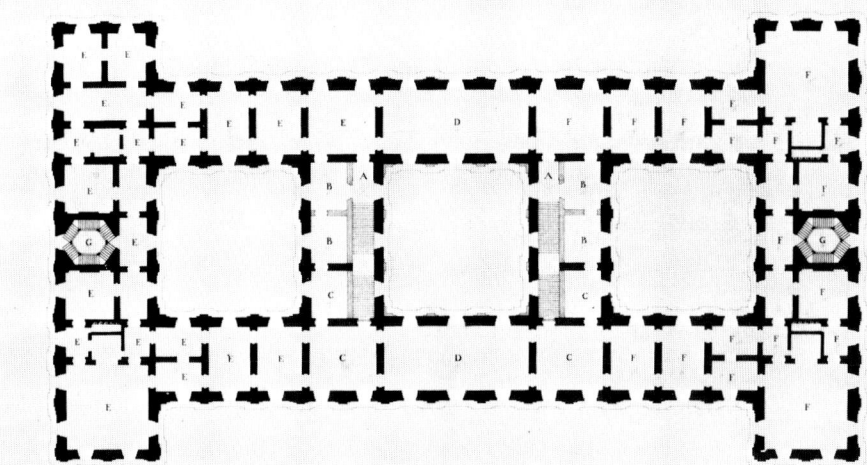

3.26
Capodimonte, plan of main floor. Caserta, Reggia

or with the parts of the city it abutted. But these were not important considerations for a simple hunting lodge perhaps, and at first Capodimonte was only that.

Yet the new palace was potentially much more than a hunting lodge. It was a larger building than the Palazzo Reale itself. The original architect had been Giovanni Antonio Medrano, a military engineer who, according to some, appropriated designs made by his former coadjutor in building the Villa Reale at Portici, Antonio Canevari. Another architect involved with Capodimonte was Angelo Carasale. Carasale had been in charge of erecting the foundations, and their cost greatly exceeded expectations. Confronted by this typical Neapolitan mess Carlo abandoned active prosecution of the building when only about two-thirds of the walling was in place (the south and central courtyards) and only the main floor habitable. The palace remained for years, then, an unfinished ruin (somewhat like Cosimo Fanzago's Palazzo Donn'Anna of 1642 on the via Posillipo). Nonetheless it was eventually completed in accordance with Medrano's plans, though one completely new idea is the present great staircase of 1835–1838 by Tommaso Giordano in a glorious Paestum Doric.

This staircase is not shown in the drawings reproduced in figures 3.25 and 3.26, which seem to have been made in Vanvitelli's office (since their inscriptions make it clear that they are not the work of the original architects, nor of Ferdinando Fuga, who had made a project for finishing the building). Fuga's suggestions, however, are marked out in gray. The drawings probably date from the 1750s. The disposition and assignment of rooms are very much a foretaste of Vanvitelli's own scheme for Caserta. Thus the ground floor consists entirely of circulation and storage space while the main floor is divided into two suites of 26 rooms each, one the mirror image of the other: that on the left is for the king and the other for the queen. Within each of these identical apartments are sequences of guardrooms and waiting rooms (*B, C*); reception halls, or Halls for Greeting (*D*); and living quarters (*E, F*)—exactly as would be the case at Caserta.

Despite its long abandonment and scandal-ridden origins, Capodimonte is undeniably an impressive building. Like the Palazzo Reale it exploits deep colors: a brick of *rosso napoletano* and stone pilasters and entablature, though in this case dark pray piperno is used rather than limestone. Compared to the Palazzo Reale the building is vast, even sublime. Unlike Fontana's structure it is composed of clear, uniform modules consisting of double cubes set vertically within colossal Tuscan pilaster-group bays. It is in fact fully a geometric palace and of the finest type. The two long main fronts are 13 bays in length at the piano nobile and mezzanine levels. The whole is set over a rusticated Doric basement. In this basement are three central arched entrances and, on each side, a single, similar arched entrance. There is thus only one type of bay above and only two below, either arched or windowed. The terminal wings project forward one bay and are two bays wide and nine deep.

The whole outer shell of the building is composed of one-, two-, and three-bay groupings of the module. The two main facades, formed of wings, main block, central axis/door, main block, and wing, make up the reflected distribution:

2 6 1 6 2,

an elegant, self-generating set. It springs, left and right, out of the 1 and moves to a double three (2 × 3), then to 2 (2 × 1). So the facades arise from 1, 2, and 3, and then move back the same way to 1. The flanks are arranged into simpler palindromes of 4, 1 (entrance) 4, the 4 rising out of the main-facade sequence of 1, 2, 3, and leading round the building to the adjacent long facade, hence back to 1. In a word, mirror symmetry prevails, unmixed with the translational symmetry that Vanvitelli used in the Palazzo Reale.

There is a low parapet above the entablature, which appears only in the form of engaged impost blocks over the tops of the main-floor pilasters. Within, the palace consists of three great square courtyards of similar size, symmetrically set, each three bays square, the module here being the same as for the exterior (fig. 3.24). Hence the overall plan comprises a uniform grid or hypostyle of columns that measures 18 across by 10 deep, 180 in all. It can be seen as a geometric abstract of an ancient temple of the larger sort.

The original plan of Capodimonte was greatly altered when the building became a museum after World War II. However, the plans in figures 3.25 and 3.26 reveal much about the original Medrano–Canevari scheme. It possessed a level of geometric precision and interest well beyond that of any of the plans so far discussed. The whole is perfectly mappable onto a regular grid (fig. 3.27). The seventeen bays of the main facade, and the nine of the sides, can be read as modules divided into what may be called micromodules. The latter establish all of the interior and exterior walls of the building, and within this grid the plan of every room is limited to one of the following nine proportions (measured in micromodules):

1:1   3:2   4:2   4:3

5:3   5:4   10:5

10:10,

which can in turn be reduced to

1:1   2:1   3:2   4:3   5:3   6:5.

These are, respectively, the square (1:1), the double square (2:1), the sesquialter (3:2), the sesquitertial (4:3), the superbipartiens tertias (5:3), and the superpartiens quintas (7:5).

Finally, a glance back at the mirrorings generated by the facade piers shows that the rooms along the main (but not lateral) facades are susceptible to a breakdown similar to that given for the micromodular structure—similar in principle, that is, but with different constituents:

(2 1 2) (3 3) (5) (3 3) (2 1 2),

Architectural Order

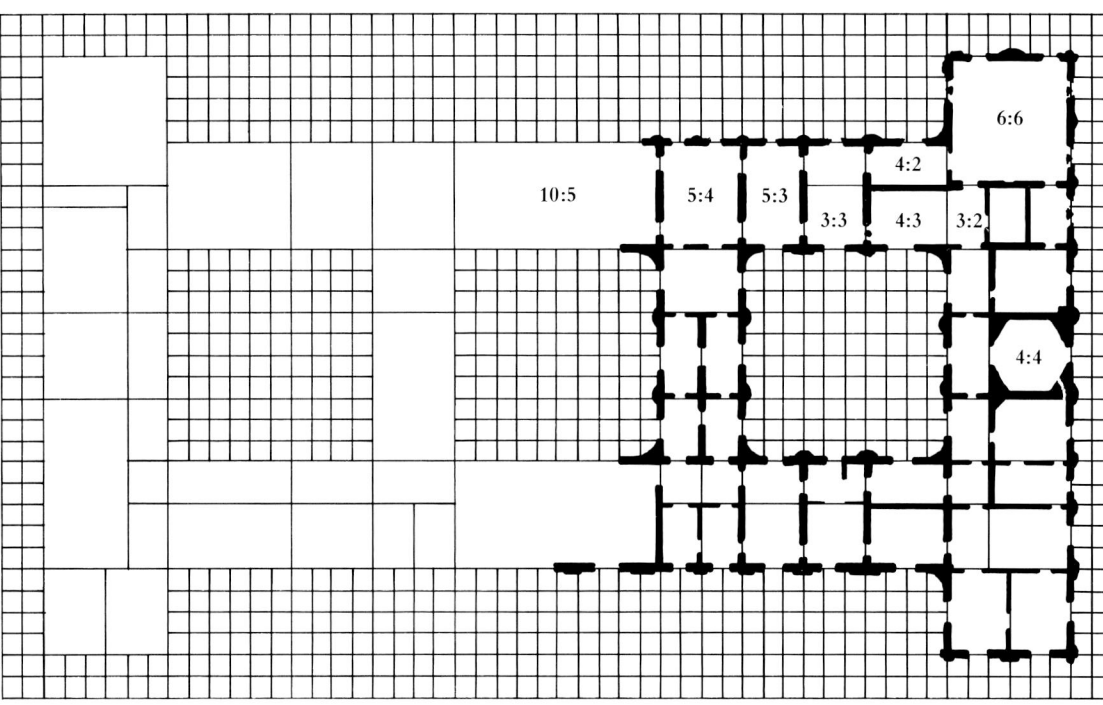

3.27
Capodimonte, main-floor plan mapped onto a grid

which reduces to the following arrangement of three-, two-, and one-member sets:

3   2   1   2   3.

In this sequence, as in the pilaster sequence, there are the reduction to differences of 1 and a palindrome symmetry centered on that number. All these qualities and more are to be found in Gioffredo's and Vanvitelli's designs for Caserta. Such designs constitute a mathematical poetry of architecture that matches Vico's number poetry and his notions of the arithmetic and geometric rule of law.

Not only did these ideas appear in actual Neapolitan buildings; they were given a later, theoretical expression in Niccolo Carletti's Newtonian treatise published in Naples in 1772. This treatise makes architecture into a subdivision of geometry and celestial mechanics.[38] Thus in Book I, Observation I, Carletti states that the best, solidest, most permanent supports are prisms and cylinders arranged in straight lines and groups at right angles, with bases parallel to the horizon, and set vertically or else in accordance with the "lines of direction" of cones and pyramids (Book I, Corollary V). Carletti prints a set of stylized grid plans based on this principle. In placing the supports, the proportions of the human body are used, namely:

1:1, 2:1, 4:1, 10:1, 3:2, 6:5.

These ratios may vary with race, according to Carletti, the Ionians, Corinthians, and Dorians, who invented the three basic orders of architecture, having used slight variants on the formulas. The formulas in turn impinge on the load-bearing possibilities of buildings in the three different styles or in styles such as the Composite that are derived from them. Arithmetical and other series are derived from these ratios to construct plans and elevations. Carletti particularly advocates number sequences whose intervals can produce still other such sequences. And the laws of the mathematical constructs lead, he says, to the "unwritten laws" of the peoples, apparently to something like Vico's primitive *ius naturalis*.

4 Royal Architects

Carlo di Borbone

The title of this chapter is to be taken in two ways. It refers as might be expected to two architects who served the king, Mario Gioffredo and Luigi Vanvitelli. But it also refers to the king himself. For Carlo di Borbone was a royal architect in that he practiced architectural drawing and design, in that he brought to his role as patron a forceful sensibility that contributed specific ideas to Gioffredo's and Vanvitelli's projects, and in that, in the civic festivals held in his honor, he appeared as a mythic builder of cities and palaces, as the architect of a new urban civilization.

To Vanvitelli Carlo di Borbone was truly a "civil, humane monarch," the greatest and best of men and kings. Amid all the paranoia, jealousy, and hatred directed at his fellow human beings in the *Letters*, this golden thread shines, and it shines long after the moment when Vanvitelli finally realized that the king would never call him to Spain to continue the patronage begun at Caserta. Nonetheless, to Vanvitelli Carlo was always an Apollo, an Aeneas, a Hercules, arrived to build capital and kingdom anew, whose abandonment of his protégé was not betrayal but tragedy: "In sum, His Catholic Majesty has been in all ways the Maecenas of his family; the misfortune of his departure, leaving [us] in the hands of two mean-thinking, mean-acting men [the Prince of Sannicandro and Tanucci, in 1766 respectively head of the Regency Council and Prime Minister] has done immense harm."[1]

Carlo, that man of palaces, was born in the Royal Palace at Madrid on January 20, 1716, and lived successively at Colorno (Parma), the Pitti Palace, the Palazzo Reale in Naples, at Portici, and in his various Neapolitan palaces and villas in the countryside; and then in Spain in the Royal Palace at Madrid, at Buen Retiro, and at Aranjuez. He died on December 14, 1788, at the Escorial. He never actually spent a night under Caserta's roof.[2]

He was the son of Philip V of Spain, Louis XIV's grandson, and of Philip's second wife Elisabetta Farnese, Duchess of Parma. Through his mother and through a rather uncertain inheritance derived from her, Carlo was the heir of two nearly extinct houses, that of the Farnese and that of the Medici. His magnificent Renaissance dwellings in Spain and his connection with two of the greatest families of the Italian Renaissance were auguries. Philip's two older sons by his first marriage, Luigi and Ferdinando, at the time prevented any expectation of Carlo's succeeding to the Spanish throne. Everything favored an Italian career, one aimed at the reconstruction of Italian greatness.[3]

It was a period when France and the Italian states feared the power of the Hapsburg imperial hegemony. To forestall this threat a matrimonial tie was established with the Austrians when Carlo and his younger brother Filippo, still children, were engaged respectively to Maria Teresa and Maria Anna, Hapsburg archduchesses. But in the end Carlo married a Polish-Saxon princess, Maria Amalia, daughter of Augustus III of Poland. She was a cultivated woman who, at least in artistic matters, ruled equally with her husband.

In the years immediately before Carlo's accession in Naples the Austrian emperor held Southern Italy as one of his appanages. So the idea of an independent Bourbon-ruled Italian kingdom was welcome to most of that part of Europe that stood against the Hapsburgs. Carlo's accession would be a fourth leg in a family empire—the family pact—with Louis XV on the French throne, Carlo's father Philip ruling "the Spains and the New World," Carlo ruling the new Kingdom of the Two Sicilies, and young Filippo Parma and Piacenza.[4]

The infant Carlo's education had been the business of an *aya*, or nursemaid, of the most conservative Spanish type. When he was seven she was replaced by a male counterpart, the count of Santestebán del Puerto, José Manuel de Benavides y Aragón. The regime inculcated the fear of God, absolute chastity, and fanatical emphasis on the prince's importance, along with the ceremonial recognition of that fact.[5] Carlo also learned the classical languages, history, warfare, drawing, and geometry.

In 1731, at fifteen, he was put at the head of an army representing Europe's anti-Austrian interests. With this army and aided by a number of diplomatic pacts, he made an easy if rather slow progress through Hapsburg-occupied Italy, with long sojourns in friendly cities such as Florence. When he arrived at Naples a large Spanish fleet lay in the harbor to quell any disturbances by the pro-Austrian faction. Carlo entered the city on May 10, 1734. On July 3 of the following year, in Palermo, he was crowned. The Kingdom of the Two Sicilies (which got that

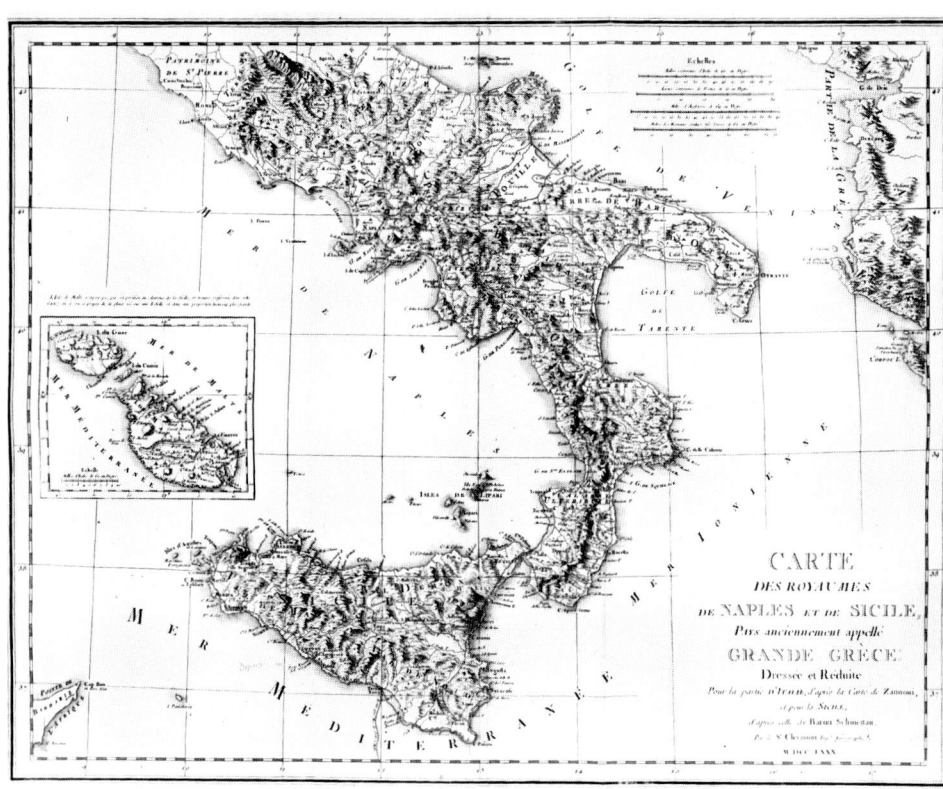

4.1
The Kingdom of the
Two Sicilies. From
Saint-Non

name slightly later) comprised a large territory: all of Southern Italy including Sicily (fig. 4.1). In other words it reconstituted Mazzocchi's Magna Graecia or Pythagorean Commonwealth. Carlo di Borbone, with Carlo Emanuele of Savoy and the Pope, was in fact one of the three most important rulers on the peninsula. And Naples, whose population rose from 270,000 in 1734 to 347,000 in 1766, was one of the largest cities in Europe, if also one of the poorest.[6]

In appearance Carlo was a thin, unprepossessing man. A curvilinear face, two round and popping eyes, and a V-shaped mouth, surrounded by fluttering velvets and armor, appears in the portraits (fig. 4.2). The king's hands and face are said to have been unusually red, the rest of his body unusually white. Sir Harold Acton writes that he resembled "a very distinguished ram."[7] The total effect, however, was of a wry, clever person. Both he and the queen were rawboned and unheroic—though perhaps one ought not to call Maria Amalia unheroic for, astride her cautiously rearing horse and dressed in breeches, frock coat, boots, powdered wig, and tricorne as painted by Francesco Liani, she is a dead ringer for George Washington (fig. 4.3).

Carlo di Borbone was an activist king but suffered from his family failing: depression, or melancholia as it was then known. The reason he had to abandon Naples for Madrid in 1759 was that his elder brother Ferdinando succumbed to this same condition.[8] Curiously enough Mazzocchi's inscription for Carlo's statue in the Foro Carolino makes unambiguous reference to this:

4.2
Francesco Solimena.
Carlo di Borbone at the Battle of Gaeta. Caserta, Reggia

4.3
Francesco Liani.
Portrait of Queen Maria Amalia, c. 1755. Naples, Capodimonte

HE STRETCHED HIS SINEWS AGAINST THE MELANCHOLY OF YOUTH; THAT WHICH DRIVES THE LAZY DRONE FROM HIVE TO HONEYCOMB TURNED HIM IN TIME OF LEISURE TO THE ARTS.[9]

Carlo had absolute power, but (*pace* Lord Acton) he was far from being absolutely corrupt. His policy was ameliorative and reformatory though decisively against Enlightenment principles with their emphasis on the citizen's individual freedom and conscience. Like everyone else in Naples the king was obsessed with the ruinous economy of what is called today the Mezzogiorno.[10] Economic benefits were supposed to derive from the building of Caserta; Carlo's whole program, in fact, involved creating jobs through works of *magnificentia*, or public construction. Building the country villas and palaces, of which there were seven, included the creation of gardens, of forest, field, marsh, and water preserves, and of access roads, aqueducts, and the like, all of which improved the economy and ecology of the region.[11]

Aside from conferring these benefits, Carlo rebuilt his capital as had not been done before. He laid out new streets, erected the Teatro San Carlo (begun in 1737 by Medrano), the Albergo dei Poveri (1751 on, Ferdinando Fuga; fig. 4.4),[12] backed the rebuilding of the great churches of Vanvitelli and Gioffredo, inspired noblemen to build palaces, and created other immense structures of a more workaday nature such as barracks, warehouses, and aqueducts. The Foro Carolino (fig. 4.5), complete with Mazzocchi's inscription, was at first conceived as a rich exedral setting for an equestrian statue of Carlo with colossal rooftop saints and fountains populating a chain of triumphal arches. In this form and in the much simpler form in which it was built, the Foro Carolino was the city's expression of thanks to its urbanist monarch. Carlo seems also to have been involved in the early phases of the much larger Largo del Palazzo (now Piazza Plebescito) in front of the Palazzo Reale,[13] while his porcelain works at Capodimonte produced some of the most charmingly ebullient china (fig. 4.6) made in the eighteenth century.[14] The new palaces and churches were almost invariably decorated with intricate fresco and sculpture programs.[15] The careers of important painters such as Domenico Mondo, Sebastiano Conca, Fedele Fischetti, Francesco Celebrano, to mention only a few, and of sculptors like Francesco Queirolo, Paolo Persico, and Gaetano Salomone were bound up with these projects. It was Carlo, too, who brought to Naples the incomparable Farnese collection of classical and Renaissance art, with its Titians, its Raphaels, its Annibale Carraccis, and its splendid corpus of Roman and Hellenistic sculpture.[16]

But not all was glory and growth. The Farnese collection and its early fate is a case in point. On arrival the objects were stored in the hallways and stairwells of the Palazzo Reale, leaning against the crumbling walls that Vanvitelli's workmen were shoring up and that Carlo's artists were then to fresco with the glories of Hercules, Aeneas, and the House of Bourbon. Visitors complained that in the midst of the mess urchins pissed on Correggios and Titians. In 1755 it was decided that Capodimonte ought to house the collection. But here the squalid scenario simply continued and the masterpieces were displayed,

4.4
Ferdinando Fuga.
Albergo dei Poveri,
Naples. From Sasso,
Monumenti

4.5
Vanvitelli. Alternative project for the
Foro Carolino. From
Sasso

4.6
G. B. Natali. Porcelain cabinet from the royal villa at Portici, 1757–1759. Naples, Capodimonte.

with proleptic surrealism, in unfinished rooms, some of them windowless or even roofless.[17] Contemporaneous descriptions of Capodimonte and the Palazzo Reale, their masterpieces in scattered dissarray, their vaults open to the sky, remind us of Hubert Robert's famous vision of the Grande Galerie of the Louvre in ruins.

It was not until 1782, under Ferdinando IV, that the court painter Jakob Philipp Hackert was charged with setting the pictures in order and restoring some of the damage. Between 1806 and 1808 Giuseppe Buonaparte decreed that the Farnese collection was to go to the Palazzo degli Studi (now the Museo Nazionale). Only in 1834–1836 was Capodimonte completed. And only in 1947 did it become the exemplary museum it is today and the home of the Renaissance and Baroque objects in the Farnese collection, as well as of a large group of works dating from the reigns of the Bourbons themselves.

Carlo not only had studied drawing but was in fact an architectural draftsman as well as a patron of architecture. He is even said to have made a print depicting the Virgin and Child and to have maintained a studio in his private apartments.[18] He was never happier than when at his drawing board, he said, and when Vanvitelli told him that he intended to make architects of his sons the king replied, "You will do well to make them follow that most excellent art, which is the noblest one there is. When I have compass and ruler in hand I cannot help but design something."[19] The king was credited with important specific elements in the design of Caserta. He also designed a new portal for the palace at Portici. Without telling Vanvitelli who had made it Carlo showed it to him, in the form of a model, and asked for Vanvitelli's opinion. The architect cagily replied that the basic idea was excellent but that the iron gate should be wider. The king said, "know then that the idea is mine, but I have not been well served [by the model-maker]," showing Vanvitelli his original sketch to prove the point.[20]

Carlo also wrote about architecture. As soon as he arrived in Italy his interest appeared in his letters to his mother. He was struck, he said, by the superiority of Italian to Spanish buildings. He saw Florence, living there in the Pitti Palace, and was also enthusiastic about Colorno, the Farnese residence at Parma, which had become a Bourbon possession. This palace, Carlo found, was superior to the one at San Ildefonso. Colorno is in fact a standard Serlian form, a rectangle with four projecting corner towers. It is small and skewed but otherwise geometrically the same as Louis XIII's Versailles and as Mario Gioffredo's mighty scheme for Caserta. Colorno also possesses a long chain of similar rooms in perfect alignment, with doors on axis, so that one can look down an endless perspective called a *fuga di stanze*, 'flight of chambers,' as if by aligning enough of these ornate parallelepipeds they would seem to rise into the air like a file of birds. This device reappears in Carlo's own buildings, especially at Caserta.

Carlo was particularly enticed by the mathematics of architecture, so much so that when the *eletti*, or syndics, of Naples in 1758 addressed the king on the subject of the proposed Foro

Carolino, they hoped their design, under Carlo's scientific gaze, would be corrected by his extraordinary mathematical knowledge.[21]

Carlo di Borbone was a royal architect, then, in at least three senses. He was himself a designer; he employed architects whose work he closely supervised with the eye of a designer; and he built on a munificent scale. After more than two centuries of torpor under viceregal rule the city was royal again, and this new royalty was Carlo's greatest monument. Naples became a true capital, not only of and through its architecture, but of music, economics, philosophy, painting, sculpture, and the decorative arts. Its gaiety, beauty, and theatrical *bizzarria* were only sharpened by its sloth and disease. As the king's panegyrist D'Onofri put it: "In the course of a few years, thanks to Carlo's building activities, an astounded Naples scarcely knew herself."[22] It was not only Vanvitelli who wept at Carlo's departure. Tanucci, the architect's persecutor, lamented, "Oh how changed, and daily changing, are country and court, and what sorrow those of us feel who, bred in an age of gold, must live in this age, which turns from iron to lead!"[23]

The Mythic Builder

If Carlo di Borbone rebuilt Naples as a stage set, it was one designed for himself and his family. The major events of the king's life in Naples were marked by civic festivals glorifying Carlo's several mythical selves. These festivals belonged to the people, and they were planned by local architects in the popular *barocchetto* style perfected by Ferdinando Sanfelice, Domenico Antonio Vaccaro, Vincenzo Rè, and the notorious, irrepressible Tagliacozzi Canale.[24] They consisted of large temporary structures—towers, temples, obelisks, arches of triumph, and the like—erected in front of the Castel Nuovo and the Palazzo Reale. Similar, lesser structures were usually built by local organizations such as confraternities and parishes throughout the city.

One type of "machine," as these erections were called, was the *cuccagna*. This was a piece of temporary architecture covered with bread, meat, cheeses, fruit, and vegetables, and equipped with fountains of wine. At a certain moment in the ceremonies, the signal being given by the king, the *lazzaroni* would swarm over the structure and make off with its contents.[25] (One recalls, as an inversion of this custom, the sacking of the food shops by these same street people during the famine of 1764; and also the play of food imageries on the Fontana Santa Lucia, fig. 2.5, which like other Neapolitan fountains can be seen as a marble *cuccagna*.)

What mythical guises did the king adopt on these occasions? Most often he appeared as a city founder like Cleanto in Metastasio's *Partenope*. In 1735 when Carlo returned from his military expedition to Sicily he was greeted as an Aeneas. The title page of the souvenir book issued to mark the occasion shows (fig. 4.7), in an oval frame, Parthenope the siren on the right welcoming the Virgilian savior enthroned on his galley. On the left the Sebeto hails its new lord. The Virgilian note is reinforced by a quotation from *Aeneid* V 150 on a banderole: "the hills respond with thunderous clamor." The phrase occurs in Virgil's description of the nautical games between the Trojan visitors and the Italic natives. It is a prelude to victory for Aeneas and his forces—their first successful foray onto the Italian mainland. And the use of this quotation in Carlo's festival entails what the phrase entails in its original setting: it is a prelude to the hero's rebuilding of a city, for Virgil has Aeneas rebuild Puteolum before he visits the underworld; and ultimately, of course, he will rebuild and rename Rome. Carlo is a second Aeneas and Naples a second Rome, the quotation implies, welcoming its foreign ruler.[26]

The festival proper was in itself a new city. Temporary triumphal arches and a processional way were built leading from the royal barge's dock near the Castel Nuovo up a flight of stairs to the Palazzo Reale. There a large room was decorated with an oval cartouche bearing the words "Beloved of God, Present Guardian of Italy and Worthy King, your Reign Restores to our Lands the Fruits of Our Fields." These lines paraphrase Horace's Ode to Augustus (*Odes*, IV 14). They complete the earlier evocation of Aeneas as the original founder of the imperium that Augustus was to inherit and climax with this second prayer to Augustus himself as yet another rebuilder.

Above the cartouche with Horace's words was an obelisk, symbol of a race well run, and San Gennaro, patron of Naples, blessing the king. Here the souvenir book introduces a mythic tribe of royal ancestors and welcomers for the conquering hero:

"From Astipalea and Neptune was born Anceus; from his wife Samia, daughter of the river Meander, he had Perilaos, Eundos, Samos, Alitersus and Parthenope. From her and Apollo was born Licomedes." In this further variant on Parthenope's multiple ancestries Neptune becomes Parthenope's progenitor, and her marriage to Apollo is perhaps a tribute to, or cause of, her sweet voice. In any event Apollo is another key figure in Carlo's family of mythic cousins and will figure prominently at Caserta. So too will Hercules, who is also present to greet Carlo. On this occasion Hercules stands on a fountain, a triumphator, club on shoulder and the slain Lernian Hydra at his feet. He signifies Carlo's conquest of Sicily—for, explains the text, it was Hercules who had killed Sicily's king Eryx. As Vico would say, Hercules thus cleared the Sicilian wilderness of its barbarian infester and triumphantly harnessed its waters so that agriculture, commerce, and cities could be built.

Vico was only a background figure to the festival of 1735. But he was much to the fore when, three years later, Carlo and Maria Amalia celebrated their marriage with a more poetic festival staged by the university faculty. This consisted of several days' worth of eclogues, orations, and other works including opera. The leading orator was the future royal historiographer. His speech develops many of the mythic themes alluded to here. Hercules-like, the arriving king comes with his ships from Hesperia and debarks at Parthenope's shrine. The queen is hailed as a Saxon princess whose native tongue leads back to the founder of all esoteric knowledge and to the Egyptian fountainhead of all Italic greatness, Hermes Trismegistus. Vico then portrays Carlo in the two mighty aspects of his future reign:

For, when he rides on his horse in amiable ferocity, he is seen to be the emperor worthy of his arms; presiding from the royal saddle he hears the desires of his subjects and is seen as the king entering into possession of his kingdom not by virtue of his birth but by virtue of conquest. When, standing in his royal palace, he admits his princes to the adoration of his hand, he is venerated as the simulacrum of God on earth.[27]

Both portrayals refer to frequently performed rituals: the king on horseback, during processions or even out hunting, and his solemn entries around the countryside, moving from palace to palace or entering a town. The other portrayal shows him at the *baciamano* ceremony.

The latter is described by Vanvitelli.[28] On these occasions an invited circle of ministers, ambassadors, and guests—men and women of the aristocracy of merit as well as hereditary vassals—fill a large salon and one by one approach the sovereign, kneel, and kiss his hand. Conversations ensue. It was on these occasions that Vanvitelli's relationship with Carlo and Maria blossomed, and that the architect showed off his plans and models and received royal criticism and praise. The two planned Halls of the *Baciamano* were to be the principal state rooms at Caserta. The ceremony itself, a form of homage, was a psychological, political, and ceremonial necessity. It was a continual oath-giving by those whose new liege lord was this latest in the succession of conquering kings—in Vico's language, *reges ad regnum ne dum nati, facti videntur*, "kings seen to have been made so, not born to it."

The hand-kissing ceremony, occurring as it did in a royal palace, expressed the double structure of Carlo's kingdom. One wing of this structure consisted of an appointive bureaucracy, which was on the rise and which was composed of what the philosopher called the "optimates." This wing drew its power from the other wing, that of the "patricians" (those who inherited power from their *patres*). The latter wing was symmetrically placed within the political configuration of the realm, but during Carlo's reign it suffered a net loss in power. The two wings were thus truly symmetrical: they were mirror images of each other, one positive and growing, the other negative, shrinking in power, hence illusory.[29] The construction of Caserta, we shall see, is an instance of the seizure of patricians' land by the king and his optimates. The new palace's architecture and that of the gardens and town proclaimed this victory.

This same theme, namely the welcoming of Carlo and Maria Amalia as foreigners who ruled by conquest rather than by birth, is struck by the next participant in the ceremony, Biagio Troisi, who reads some Sannazaran hexameters:

And then, startled by the clamor from
Her cave, which gaped on Capri's eastern cliff,
Beautiful Parthenope did hear
The king arrive and, swifter than the wind,
She crossed the sea with all her nereids.
Round his chariot on the flowery shore

They paused, and knelt across the glassy waves.
Then, crowned head raised to Heaven, she
Gave thanks, and offered with abundant hand
Sea gifts to her lord: a mirror set
With coral and with marvelous blue gems,
Where Persian purple shone like glistening fruit:
"Hail, hope of this disintegrating age
In Italy, sent by noble Heaven."

The scene recalls that in figure 4.7. There follows a long speech in Carlo's praise. The poem goes on to describe Naples' newfound architectural glory, dressed as the city is in the decorations her people have constructed. The whole town seems one great palace ablaze with torches and works of art. But the greatest part of the procession that moves through it all, says Parthenope, is devoted to herself. There are other scenes of Diana and Neptune, and a *cuccagna* is described. Then, after honoring Sannazaro's tomb at Mergellina, the siren and her nymphs slide back into the sea.

Troisi's beautiful poem is conceived as a wave of welcome flooding the city with nymphs and leaving upon it a sediment of abundance as the siren goddess and her cohorts disappear into their blue depths. It is an appropriate reversal of Vico's conception of Neptune who, until the god is controlled, floods the city with devastation. Other poems of welcome struck similar themes. Isidoro Sanchez de Lana's verses end with a picture of Maria Amalia pregnant, another alma mater like the Parthenope who nursed Ovid; and like Parthenope Maria will give birth to poets.

4.7
Carlo di Borbone as Aeneas welcomed by Parthenope and the river Sebeto. From *Descrizione delle Feste* (1735)

In two sonnets (of a group of four) also written to commemorate this event, Vico emphasized the new spirit of pan-European importance that, with Carlo's arrival, filled the capital.[30] Sirri has called it "the reconquest of Europe." Vico duly celebrated a restoration and expansion of the Roman Empire:

Stretching from the kingdoms of the East
West to the sunset lands, and rolling south
To Araby, our empire only ceased
Northward at the icy Istro's mouth.

But then in Italy a prideful king
Whose brethren rule the Frankish lands, arose;
Iberians to his sire their tributes bring,
And his remoter blood is Scipio's.

Still other allies light his holy bride
Her way from that cold land whose western face
Frowns upon Asia's dark and polar blast.

Son of Aeneas! Rebuild Aeneas' pride!
Return the stolen prizes to their place,
And make Italian empire whole at last.

The second sonnet is to the architect of the scenographic machine erected in honor of the marriage, Ferdinando Sanfelice:

With vastness, of all termination free,
Of palace, temple, obelisk and tower,
With kingly thrust of high immensity:
So Memphis stupefied earth's early hour.

But now, Fernando, to the singing world
Your well-praised genius, in time's shortest space,
Has vaster marvels to our age unfurled,
And given it new glory and new grace.

That you might swiftly build this noble scene,
Serving human duty and desire,
Art and Nature lend their richest dress.

So full and lucid is the rare machine
Its sovereign honor lifts it ever higher,
Far above time's deep forgetfulness.

In the first sonnet Carlo appears again as a member of a Vichian noble family whose destiny is to restore and rule what Aeneas had begun. As usual the poet sacrifices fact to fancy, making the empire of old Rome end at Istria. But this shortfall is to be made up by the addition of Poland and Saxony. The summons, at the end of the first sonnet, for Carlo to conquer what, literally translated, Vico calls "the great unjust spoils" taken from Aeneas probably refers to Carlo's imminent military expedition to Sicily. In the second sonnet Parthenope replies to Carlo much as she does in Biagio Troisi's hexameters. Sanfelice's achievement glorifies the arriving god but also Naples herself.

Precisely these ideas—that the King of the Two Sicilies could become the central radiating point of the New Sphere, so to call it, of a worldwide Italy and that this completion of Carlo's role would have occurred in part through architectural works in his capital—are presented by Vanvitelli's vignette from the *Dichiarazione* (fig. 4.8). A winged Amor armed with Cupid's bow and arrows and driving Venus's doves before him makes a triumphal car of an Earth that is set with the Two Sicilies as an orb is set with gems and whose sea is named "Tuscan." It is the Two Sicilies but also the "Etruscan" kingdom of Magna Graecia.

Another festival was staged for the appearance of Carlo's first male child, Filippo, who at birth assumed the title of Prince of the Two Sicilies. This was in 1747.[31] To mark the event an elaborate set of festival machines was designed by Vincenzo Rè, who also composed the sumptuous souvenir book and supplied it with splendid engraved plates. The three main focuses were the Castel Nuovo, which was turned into an enchanted castle of light, its battlements outlined with lanterns and punctuated with airy obelisks (fig. 4.9); the Palazzo Reale; and the new Teatro San Carlo. In the Largo del Castello there was also a fireworks pavilion, a sparkling essay in rococo monumentality built up on a stepped octagon like a great finial (fig. 4.10). In the Largo del Palazzo Reale was a vast *cuccagna* in an arcadian landscape dominated by a rustic fountain of wine and decorated not only with meat, cheese, bread, and other victuals, but with live game and domestic animals wandering in its wooded surroundings: the usual allegorical *salumeria*, in short, but with the added meaning of the royal huntsman who gives provender to his people (fig. 4.11).

The frontispiece of Rè's book, meanwhile, is a temple formed not of food nor marble but of gods and goddesses (fig. 4.12). In the background the landscape of Naples, its bay and Vesuvius, appear. In the foreground is a weedy marsh. The sky is filled

4.8
Vanvitelli. Vignette from the *Dichiarazione*.

4.9
Vincenzo Rè. Castel Nuovo decorations. From Rè, *Narrazione* (1749)

4.10
Rè. Guglia for fireworks in the Largo del Castello. From the *Narrazione*

4.11
Rè. Cuccagna in the Largo del Palazzo. From the *Narrazione*

4.12
Rè. Frontispiece
from the *Narrazione*

with a towering group of figures centered on a tableau in which the swaddled young prince is presented by a winged Victory to Queen Parthenope. She, a massive, draped figure not unlike the Nido river goddess, is enthroned on Misenus's ruined tomb. Beside her is the Abundance figure of Portici, who lifts a tray of produce as an offering to the newborn babe. This perhaps is *his* cuccagna. These fruits of Portici's earth are also the spoils of Herculaneum. On a lower level the Sebeto grasps the spade that had turned him from a wild river into an aqueduct and that symbolizes so much of the subterranean and excavatory nature of Carlo's enterprises. Sebeto rises from his recumbent posture, hailing his new lord. He echoes the gestures of Portici and Parthenope in doing this. Behind him we glimpse the three sirens (and hence Parthenope again, in her other main role), lifting their voices to the sky. A sea horse prances on one side and on the other we see the marshy shore that had given the name of *aquari* to the denizens of Naples.[32] There, a nereid peeks timidly out at the spectacle. On the far right a siren and two putti present a cartouche carrying the words spoken by the queen to the infant prince:

With you, new son, new hope, Parthenope
 Will all her wealth and blessings share.
You are two kingdoms' peace: forever be
 Worthy of your parents' care.

In short, a lower, terrestrial and subterrestrial population, the divinities of the place, equipped with spade and with the earth's produce, welcome the arriving vortex of universal divinities.

Filippo is central to this conquering foreign cohort. At the very top of the flight of gods, floating in the circle formed by the *ourabouros*, the circled snake of Infinity, is Faith. Serenely she opens her bosom to the child, her alumnus, while revealing her sacred volume and the *lituus*, or staff of command. She teaches, she regulates. Seated above the prince and just below Faith, on the allegory's central axis, is Pallas, armored and shielded. She sets a crown on Filippo's head in an action that forms the geometrical center of the composition as a whole, as it is also the central action of this cloud of gods. The Graces meanwhile prepare to grant the boy their gifts. Astraea, on the far left, instructs him in the arts of peace: justice, charity, abundance. She is a prefiguring of the great Astraeas we shall find at Caserta. Her scales, Vico says, signify the Golden Age of the golden number.[33] On the upper right Mars instructs the prince in war. On the far right center, trumpeting Fame consecrates him to an invisible Immortality.

Parthenope is at once queen, mother, and nurse; and as siren she sings the city's fascination. The arriving gods float inward in their great cone of clouds and bodies to the music of her lips. Her voice inculcates the message of newborn peace through a newborn *rex factus* arriving in the weedy wilderness to restore and rebuild. Filippo's arrival from the heavens, rather than from his mother's womb, makes of him a conqueror, not a patrician. *Rerum spes altera* sings Parthenope, in words that can mean 'new political hope' but also 'foreign ruler.'

In Rè's engraving the local divinities are precisely counterpoised, in gesture and position, to the universal divinities above. These symmetries, like the symmetries of feudal versus royal wings in the government, are negative and positive in value, and specular in their mutual reflections: the Sebeto echoes and refracts the figure of Mars. The two venerable males, one the provider, the other the defender, unite in their gestural opposition. The sirens are matched with the Graces in the same way. Song, fascination, and fatality are reflected in the sirens from the upper imagings of Splendor, Beauty, and Laughter. Herculaneum's treasure from the womb of the past is offered in a gestural response to Victory's offering from that of the future. Air meets earth. There are exchanges and equilibrated transfers—"commutative equalizings" in Vico's phrase. Parthenope herself, seated on the Euboean shore, is the prince's other mother, the *mater altera* for the *spes altera*. Indeed she and the prince fully inhabit, almost to the point of indiscretion, the roles of Virgin and Child. Above, Fame flies on the right as pendant to Astraea. The golden age continues, or returns, in the circling architecture of the bodies forming this temple. But that same Astraea also mirrors the cartouche below, which frames Parthenope's invocation and verbally enshrines the prince's parents. Parthenope's poem is, we now see, vague as to who these parents are, and suitably so—or, rather, not vague but all-encompassing. Filippo—poor Filippo, who turned out to be retarded—is here the child of the pagan heavens as well as of earthly civil monarchs. And so Parthenope echoes and visually responds to Faith and to Minerva's discipline.

Rè's frontispiece says all these things and yet exploits the standard language of rococo allegory. But in using these well-understood locutions it manages to restate all the underlying mythic assumptions examined here: the commutation between upper and lower cities and between hell and heaven; a riverlike flow of myth; the notion of the burial of civilized artifacts; that of the arriving god whose epiphany renews a tribal compact and builds a *nea polis* and the magnetic siren figure on her shore, backed by subordinate denizens, who welcomes arriving ruler-gods. The many parental figures who surround and support Filippo, and their divine nature, are a foretaste of the figures of family romance that will fill Caserta. For no matter how much Caserta asserts its Roman, Vanvitellian nature, it too will belong to Campania, to Cumae, to Parthenope and Magna Graecia, to the Pythagorean commonwealths and to their mythic substructures.

Mario Gioffredo

If indeed Caserta grew out of Carlo di Borbone's dissatisfaction with the Palazzo Reale and Capodimonte, one should consider too the shortcomings of a third palace, that at Portici, begun in 1738 by Medrano and finished after 1741 with interventions by Canevari, Fuga, and Vanvitelli.[34] It is not simply that these structures were perceived to be too mean in scale, or that they had design mistakes—though that was true. D'Onofri explains: "However, the late king Carlo III was not content with these two royal complexes—that is, Portici, for it was too near Vesuvius and subject to tremors and eruptions, and too near the sea for an enemy surprise attack; nor [did he like] Capodimonte, which did not come out in accordance with his ideas. And so he wished to add a third."[35] Hence Carlo's third experiment with a residential center, Caserta, is well inland and out of volcanic range. And hence Capodimonte was temporarily abandoned when it was half-built. (See chapter 6 for the architectural ideas that Medrano's masterpiece failed to fulfill.)

It is at this point, with Carlo's first impulses to construct a third palace, that a difficult but learned local architect comes into the picture. Mario Gioffredo was born in 1718, so he was eighteen years younger than Vanvitelli and two years younger than the king himself, Carlo being about thirty-four, Gioffredo thirty-two, and Vanvitelli fifty when the Caserta project was first mooted. Gioffredo had an unhappy life filled with calumny and despair. His existence was dominated by his grandiose rejected plan to build for Carlo di Borbone the most absolute of palaces.[36] Antonio Niccolò Carlini wrote a short vita of Gioffredo after the architect's death in 1785.[37] He says that Gioffredo studied with the Jesuits and had strong literary tastes, then learned drawing from Francesco Solimena. This was good start enough: it is arguable that, in the 1730s, Solimena was the best painter in Europe. Unhappy with the direction Neapolitan architecture had been taking among the followers of Cosimo Fanzago (d. 1678)—artists like Vaccaro, Astarita, and Sanfelice—Gioffredo (like Vico) became an autodidact. And he returned (again like Vico) to what he conceived of as an austere classicism that had been betrayed. Gioffredo took literally Vitruvius's famous advice that the architect should know literature, drawing, geometry, optics, arithmetic, history, philosophy, music, medicine, law, astrology, and divinity (the list is not exactly Vitruvius's but an updated eighteenth-century version). Gioffredo traveled to Paestum to draw the Greek Doric temples there and to Rome. "Thus," says Carlini, "was he seen to occupy the fortress of art."[38] Gioffredo was apprenticed to Medrano, then presumably at work on Capodimonte and Portici, both of which are austere and classical, "Vitruvian" in Gioffredo's word, rather than being, in Fanzago's manner, filled with sheaves of pilasters, serried entablatures, bulbous convexities and concavities, and deep-twined consoles. And though Gioffredo may have been hurt by Medrano's disgrace he nonetheless kept on with his master's geometrical style.

Gioffredo had one key friend at court: the marchese Giovanni Fogliani d'Aragona, one of Carlo's secretaries of state (and later Vanvitelli's protector as well). Carlini writes:

Hence when Carlo in his auspicious Neapolitan reign decided to build a villa at Caserta in Campania he asked the Duke [sic] of Fogliani, Royal Secretary, for a plan. [Gioffredo] then faithfully took up the idea and made a magnificent layout that is in his heirs' hands. To Carlo and whoever else saw it, it was marvelous. But since the erecting of it seemed too ambitious and sumptuous to the king, Carlo prescribed a smaller scheme that would be easier to afford. But then, unexpectedly, Luigi Vanvitelli, a Roman architect, showed him another plan, which the king accepted.[39]

"Yet Rome itself vindicated Gioffredo's taste, continues Carlini, "by commissioning him to build there the [facade of the] Church of San Giacomo degli Spagnuoli." Gioffredo was also responsible, in Naples, for Santa Caterina at Siena (1760) and many other buildings. Assembled together in one group, remarks his biographer, Gioffredo's oeuvre would create a good-sized town.

It is ironic that Gioffredo's buildings are so like Vanvitelli's. Indeed in several cases, notably the Villa Campolieto, Resina, and the Palazzo Casacalenda, which contain work by both men, it is hard to tell where one leaves off and the other begins.[40] This may be due in part to Vanvitelli's penchant for imitating other architects' styles: he has bragged about his mimicry of Domenico Fontana in the Palazzo Reale. But in Gioffredo's case the mimicry or accommodation went the other way: Vanvitelli was the source. What is yet more ironic is that Vanvitelli and Gioffredo loathed each other. The older architect wrote of his Neapolitan competitor that "it was not possible to find in the world a brasher and more shamelessly slanderous tongue, spitting filth in every direction."[41]

What is the style that so marries these two mortal enemies? Gioffredo's masterpiece is the Spirito Santo, Naples, which he totally remodeled in 1774 (figs. 4.13, 4.14).[42] Behind the mainly 1943 facade stands a vast classic vessel supported by beautifully prominent columns forming a colonnade that moves in a great *U* five bays deep all around the nave and apse. The

4.13
Mario Gioffredo.
Church of the Spirito
Santo, Naples, 1774
on Nave and vault.
Photo Mimmo Jodice

4.14
Church of the Spirito Santo, dome. Photo Mimmo Jodice

one-bay transepts are mere cubic incidents in this colonnade, as is the chancel, which breaks the curve of the U in the center. Above the entablature floats a barrel vault. The shafts and Corinthian capitals are of white marble, the simple pedestals and bases of dark gray. Over each chapel, set between the columns, a thermal window (as in a Roman bath vault) breaks the coffered curve of the vault. These windows rise from flat, firm dwarf pilasters. They consist of segmental openings set in front of semicircular ones: a Vanvitellesque feature. Simple, broad moldings and blank panels predominate. Over the crossing is a dome (fig. 4.14) whose cylindrical drum is lighted by aedicular windows. The thermal windows in the apse area have been squeezed narrow. They seem about to spring back into the normative shape, an effect that emphasizes the impression, already present through the grand colonnade, of a hypostyle temple that has been warped by some mighty hand into a basilican hall. The Spirito Santo is a strong and resourceful revision of the rococo in terms of a solemn, doctrinal Vitruvianism that sets the church beside its exact contemporary, Chalgrin's similar St. Philippe-du-Roule, Paris, as a shrine of Neoclassicism.

   Carlini, however, claims that Gioffredo's greatest work is not this church but his treatise on architecture of 1768.[43] This appeared in the same year as Bernardo Galiani's translation of Vitruvius. Together the two books constitute the first Neapolitan treatises on architecture, and both, along with Vanvitelli's *Dichiarazione* of twelve years earlier, go to make up a new, Vitruvian antirococo theoretical wave culminating with Carlini's own treatise of 1772. Only the first of the three planned parts of Gioffredo's book was published, a theoretical introduction. The second and third parts were to be, respectively, on civil and religious buildings.

Gioffredo's treatise really belongs with the literature of Neoclassicism. It is a plea to return to antique simplicity. Mathematics is its basis as mathematics is the basis of all things. Architecture must be rectilinear, "without recourse to capricious strange ornament . . . twisted columns, barbarically transmogrified capitals, animal pelts, cartouches, fronds, wickerwork frames. . . ."[44] The architectural orders, and the orders alone, are to dominate. A vignette at the head of the first chapter of the treatise says it all: the temples at Paestum, the Temple of Diana at Baiae, the Temple of the Dioscuri in downtown Naples, are reconstructed and brought together in one place.

Gioffredo had read Mazzocchi as well as Vitruvius. And like the Vichians, whose work he may well have known, he supposes that Etruscan cultural primacy is expressed in an austere architecture from Egypt, an idea Winckelmann also discusses. Architecture ought to be austere, in turn, because its primordial function was to defend newly civilized man from the invasions of wild beasts and to fight off the horrors of the night. By this we are to understand the night of barbarism. Ancient Near Eastern civilizations, as at Persepolis and among the Assyrians, Medes, and Persians, produced buildings that equaled the vast empires that bore those names, buildings that seem to vie with time itself in duration and sublimity. Equally sublime are the altars early man erected on mountaintops, for example those of the Hebrews, the Scythians, and the Persians.[45]

One element was missing from all this: the orders. Gioffredo not only gives formulas for Etruscan, Doric, Ionic, and others but provides an interesting theoretical basis to explain their differences. Architectural order is "the union of several things that by commutative proportions create the formation of a whole." Hence the very basis of the orders, like that of architecture itself, is mathematical. It is based not only on proportion but on dimension and the distribution of finite values assigned by commutation (partly interchanging number series). One is reminded here not only of Carletti's later book but of Vico's architectonic justice with its own orders: arithmetic, geometric, commutative, and distributive.

Gioffredo continues that it was the Etruscans who first ordered and harmonized the vastnesses of sublime early architecture by means of the orders. Their columns, bases, friezes, cornices, and capitals imposed principles of combination and classification on the inert grandeur of the earlier architectural patrimony. As a result of this native Italic gift for order the greatest of all architecture became the Roman: Near Eastern power was subdued, and subsumed, by Italic intelligence.[46]

But the apex soon passed. With the decline of the Roman Empire, painters, for example, ceased to portray the grand real monuments of their architect confrères and instead began to fantasticate a spindly, playful, structurally impossible style. Herculaneum teaches that this decadent Roman art, with its reedy columns and walls like embroidered banners, is the real beginning of Gothic. This postimperial manner is taken up by the Goths themselves, who were then occupying Italy. By them it was spread over Europe. An architecture resulted that was truly Gothic: barbarous, extravagant, immoral, counter to all primitive classic greatness. And this architecture survived all attempts at reformation until the old architecture of power, correctness, and magnificence was restored by Carlo di Borbone in Naples in the eighteenth century.[47]

Carlini concludes his vita in the approved manner, with a meditation on Gioffredo's character:

Good fortune, when you wait for it, can be utter splendor. But when you try to force it it can be utter evil. The latter kind of fortune manifests its own falsity. Gioffredo was very skilled in his art and quickly mastered all subsidiary disciplines, easily becoming the best of architects. No one was his superior and his work flowered with honesty and truth. But a hard character and abrasive manners and speech showed themselves more and more freely in him; there was a lack of consideration for fellow-architects that embittered them against him despite all forbearance. Rigid in his ideas, Gioffredo built no building that did not breed dissension. His works shone with their own splendor, but nonetheless he would insist on hounding his client into declaring their perfections over and over again. All this gave opportunities to his detractors and did him great damage, though he continued to condemn his critics and praise his own work to the skies. The family finances suffered and his daughters had miserable dowries. However Gioffredo can be said to have provided them with dowries of virtue and education. He was a diligent, by no means indulgent paterfamilias.[48]

In the last act of his life's drama Gioffredo's fortunes were restored. About a year before his death in 1781 the Royal Architect, Ferdinando Fuga, resigned his post, worth 600 gold ducats a year, and it went to Gioffredo. "But Gioffredo's heavy labors and his heavier attitude to life brought on illness. He began to overwork his eyes, losing the sight first of one then of both. Melancholia then plunged him into desperation. The ever stronger medicines he used to restore his sight unbalanced his mind and broke his spirit. He died on March 7 in the year of salvation 1785."[49]

Luigi Vanvitelli

As a courtier Vanvitelli was more adroit than Gioffredo, though his tongue was quite as spiteful and his life almost as unhappy.[50] Indeed his relationship with Gioffredo and the king formed an interesting three-way symmetry. On one side Vanvitelli was the persecutor who succeeded Gioffredo in Carlo's favor and went on to design Caserta. Yet Vanvitelli imitated Gioffredo's style, borrowed ideas from him, and was then in turn imitated by Gioffredo. Both, meanwhile, were ultimately abandoned by the king who nevertheless remained the idol of each and who was considered by both architects to be the restorer of good architecture in southern Italy.

Unlike Gioffredo, however, Vanvitelli, as we have seen, had close personal relationships with the king and queen. He attended the *baciamano* frequently, conversed with his sovereigns in a familiar manner, and was often invited by them to dinner

4.15
Giacinto Diano (?).
Portrait of Luigi
Vanvitelli. Caserta,
Reggia

with distinguished guests. The king and queen went over Vanvitelli's plans at every stage with the utmost minuteness, visited the sites where he was working and in short made a considerable pastime out of the progress of the great palace. In return Vanvitelli treated Carlo as an exalted fellow architect.[51]

It may well be that when Carlo appeared suddenly to accept Vanvitelli's design and reject Gioffredo's it was because Gioffredo was so unpleasant. In any case Carlo had been seeking out other architects well before Vanvitelli presented his project. At least two of these architects, Niccolo Salvi and Alessandro Galilei, were leading figures in Rome like Vanvitelli himself.[52] But only Vanvitelli was willing or able to set about designing the palace, as he did, in his Roman studio before moving to Naples.[53]

Vanvitelli, though born in Naples and though his father, the landscape painter Gaspar van Wittel, was Dutch, remained all his life a Roman of Romans. In this he unconsciously, or perhaps consciously, aided Vico's campaign to exalt Roman religion, law, and myth. On the other land Vanvitelli's puddingish countenance, his massive paunch, his scientific carefulness, his stolidity, and his love of brick and of canals are perhaps traceable to his Dutch blood (fig. 4.15).

Vanvitelli was born on May 12, 1700. Within a year the family was in Rome, driven from Naples by an insurrection and an epidemic. Vanvitelli's grandson, in his excellent biography of the architect,[54] suggests that Luigi was educated more as a humanist than as a practical builder—another point in common with Gioffredo. Besides architecture he studied literature, philosophy, geometry, and physics, and his Latin was good enough for him to pronounce on Metastasio's.[55] He measured Roman monuments. And he read deeply, we are told, in architectural theory. There is much in the grandson's biography on what Vanvitelli learned from the dead but little on what he learned from living teachers. The most prominently mentioned of these is Filippo Juvarra. Vanvitelli does seem to have worked with that architect, though the two were never in Rome at the same time for very long periods. Certainly Vanvitelli was influenced by Juvarra's work and on one later occasion denied that Caserta was influenced by Juvarra's masterpiece in the palace idiom, Stupinigi, near Turin. (But compare figs. 4.16 and 6.14.) Juvarra's project for remodeling the Palazzo Reale at Messina, 1714, with its long axial garden and geometric palace building; the complete project for the Palazzo Madama in Turin, 1721, with its squat triumphal corner towers and three-arched basement entrance underneath a colossal order; similar features planned for Rivoli, 1724; the octagon plans for the Duomo in Turin, and above all sketches for a great octagon stair and circulation center in the Palazzo Reale, Madrid, 1735, also attest to a similarity of ideas in the older and the younger man.[56] But Vanvitelli, for all his taste for literature, emerged as a fine practical builder and civil engineer in a Roman tradition closer to men like Domenico Fontana, architect of the Palazzo Reale in Naples, than to Juvarra. The tradition of civil engineering, of emphasis on mass and vastness followed by Domenico and his descendant Carlo

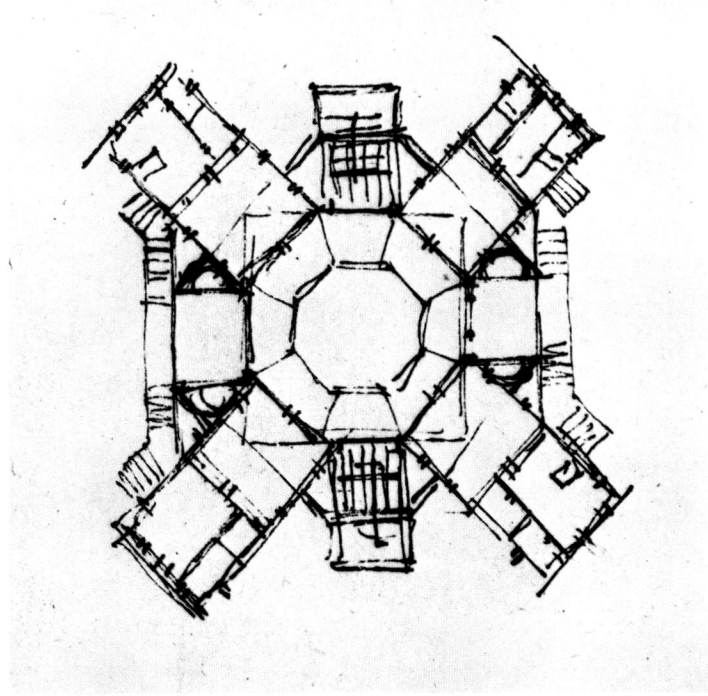

4.16
Filippo Juvarra.
Early scheme for
Stupinigi Palace, c.
1729. Turin, Museo
Civico

Fontana (who was Juvarra's master) came out strongly in Vanvitelli and meshed with the military mode of the Neapolitan antirococo architects Medrano and Gioffredo.[57]

Medrano, Vanvitelli, Gioffredo, and Fuga, in fact, introduced into Naples a new current of Baroque classicism that eschewed the taking of "licentia pro libertate" as Carlini put it, and embraced what he called an architecture "ab aequalibus," of coherence.[58] It was the architecture of Gioffredo's Spirito Santo, an architecture of intricate rectilinear symmetries, powerfully commanded by orders preferably taking the form of colossal monoliths.[59]

Ferdinando Fuga, Vanvitelli's other archenemy aside from Gioffredo, thought along similar proto-Neoclassical lines. The plan for the Cimitero di Santo Spirito, with its 10 by 10 scheme of pierlike tombs, recalls Caramuel's reconstruction of the Temple of Diana at Ephesus (fig. 3.10). In Naples Fuga produced, at about the time Gioffredo was working on his Caserta plans, a scheme for the Albergo dei Poveri that is strikingly similar in its geometry (but with four courts instead of nine) to what Gioffredo was doing (figs. 4.4, 6.1).[60] These things provide all the more reason to sense the mind of Carlo di Borbone behind Caserta. One should also note that these new buildings were far vaster in scale than anything earlier in Naples; their great open courts and forecourts were very different from the small, hidden, exfoliate architecture of the true Neapolitan Baroque.

Vanvitelli's first big chance in architecture had come when he entered the competition for a new facade for St. John Lateran (1732). Though he failed to win, his excellent showing against Alessandro Galilei, whose design was chosen and built (fig. 4.17), and against Salvi (who got the Trevi Fountain job as a consolation prize), made Vanvitelli's name.[61] Galilei's colossal Michelangelesque Composite order clasping a two-story inner elevation, his mixture of pilasters and engaged columns, his temple front, parapet, symblegmata, or gesticulating roofline statues, all reappear at Caserta (fig. 6.19). The same is true of the Trevi (fig. 4.18), except that in this case the Corinthian triumphal arch with its huge niche suggests Caserta's window of appearances.

Vanvitelli's own consolation prize was the commission to build a lazaretto in the harbor at Ancona. This might seem a consolation prize that in itself required consolation, especially in view of the years of agony that Vanvitelli went through trying to collect his fee. But in fact he built a fine, impressive polygon like one of the more elaborate forts or bastions of the period. At Ancona he also erected the Gesù, the Arco Clementino, and the Chapel of San Siriaco.[62] Other work followed, in the Marches, at Perugia, at Macerata, and at Pesaro, as well as the campanile at Loreto already mentioned. Yet Vanvitelli's fame and his accompanying notoriety remained anchored to Rome. There despite his critics he constructed a strong reputation. His main detractor was one of the pope's private chaplains, a Florentine named Giovanni Bottari. The war grew worse

4.17
Alessandro Galilei. Church of San Giovanni in Laterano, facade, 1735. Photo Alinari

4.18
Nicola Salvi. Trevi
Fountain, Rome,
1732–1751; 1762.
Photo Alinari

over Vanvitelli's plans to stabilize Michelangelo's dome, which had developed cracks.[63] Vanvitelli's scheme was adopted and the dome's predicted failure did not come about or at least not at once. In the Vanvitelli archive at Caserta are many drawings of the drum's cracked buttresses, and the *Lettere* allude to continued problems with the dome well into the 1760s. Vanvitelli mentions building a new set of buttresses for the drum: Could he have had in mind something like those he provided for the planned dome at Caserta (fig. 6.17)?[64] If so it is a good thing he did not get to build them; they would have given the famous silhouette a strange character. Anyway, for the immediate present, in 1749–50, Vanvitelli emerged from his critical passage at arms with a strengthened reputation. Other Roman work consisted of wings for the Palazzo Odescalchi (with Salvi), a project for a chapel for the king of Portugal, and the curious, controversial enlargement of Santa Maria degli Angeli, the church Michelangelo had erected out of the ruins of the Baths of Diocletian. More serene in effect and more like Caserta in style is the Convent of Sant' Agostino.[65] Yet even this large, plain, pleasant building, accented with Borrominesque openings but otherwise uneventful, was surrounded by the familiar barrage of public letters, pamphlets, and clerical betrayals. No wonder the *Lettere* show signs of paranoia.

Judging from the books he constantly ordered from Rome, Vanvitelli was well read in mathematics and poetry as well as possessing a fine architectural library. Like the Vichians and like Gioffredo, he believed in the primacy of Italo-Etruscan architecture over Greek and that Greek greatness came with the Greek settlements in Italy.[66] As to France, he owned prints of Versailles, the Louvre, and the Tuileries, to be sure, but only for purposes of pejorative contrast. He acted as Galiani's adviser on the Vitruvius translation, helping to make it a proclamation of his principles.[67]

Vanvitelli's temper and psychic equilibrium were severely tested by Carlo's departure for Spain in 1759.[68] The Regency Council's lack of enthusiasm for his work and for Caserta in general led him into a despondency that was less oppressive but longer lasting than Gioffredo's. Unlike Carlo di Borbone Vanvitelli had to stretch his sinews not against the melancholia of youth but against that more inescapable sort, that of age. In the years between 1759 and 1768, indeed, Ferdinando IV visited the great new palace only once. "The building has a fine effect," lamented Vanvitelli, "but to what purpose? If the Catholic King [Carlo] were here it would be much. Now it is nothing."[69]

Yet despite these complaints and the new ascendancy of Fuga, Vanvitelli built much in Naples after 1759. There are the Foro Carolino of 1757–1765 (fig. 4.5); the cavalry barracks at Ponte Della Maddaloni (1764), the Strada della Marinella and Borgo Loreto on the banks of the Sebeto; the improvements around the port; the facade and stairs of the Palazzo Calabritto[70] and Vanvitelli's ecclesiastical masterpiece, the inspiration for Gioffredo's Spirito Santo, the Annunziata of 1760–1782 (figs. 4.19, 4.20), with its majestic single vessel of a nave supported on forty-four colossal marble Corinthian columns, an apsidal hypostyle like Gioffredo's, with an elegant dome.[71] Comparing

4.19
Vanvitelli. Church of the Annunziata, Naples, 1760–1782. Nave vault. Photo Mimmo Jodice

4.20
Vanvitelli, Church of the Annunziata, dome. Photo Mimmo Iodice

Vanvitelli's work with Gioffredo's (figs. 4.20 and 4.14) one notes the greater geometric power of Vanvitelli's dome, with its strong scalloping of niches in the drum, and the powerful fretwork of octagrams and hexagons in the vault and dome coffering. Though he was clearly under Vanvitelli's influence, Gioffredo was to be more cautious and *retardataire* as an ornamentist. He supplants Vanvitelli's firm thick grid with borders and looping sculptural accents.

The intertwining of the mutual influences in the careers of the two men is seen again at Vanvitelli's Villa Campolieto at Resina, on which Gioffredo also worked. The festival designs for the Palazzo Teora, on the other hand, were entirely Vanvitelli's. They were executed for Count Ernst von Kaunitz, the Austrian ambassador, when in 1768 he celebrated the marriage between Ferdinando IV and Maria Carolina of Austria. Also his was the Palazzo Fondi remodeling, that of the Palazzo Casacalenda (after Gioffredo had been dismissed from the job in 1766, leaving on the building a facade very similar to what he had designed for Caserta); the Oratorio della Scala Santa in the cloister of SS Marcellino e Festo (1772), as well as the facade of that church; the Palazzo Bovio remodeling of 1772; the facade of the Palazzo d'Angri, 1755, and SS Trinità, begun 1769.[72] All these buildings brought to Naples the clear, geometric, column-oriented architecture Vanvitelli was giving Caserta. They were "lessons in proper modern architecture," as he put it, lessons that almost from his arrival in the city Vanvitelli had been anxious to teach.[73] So despite his complaints much of the building activity that filled the Kingdom of the Two Sicilies as a result of Carlo's and Ferdinando's patronage was tied directly to Vanvitelli and his assistants. Here at last in fact was the great resident architect that the Renaissance kings of Naples had so sorely lacked.

In his sanguine moments Vanvitelli was fully aware of this. He knew he was a success and a great architect but seemed to want to believe himself a failure and a victim and therefore wrote and suffered as one. Perhaps this was in part because of the very nature of that Sublime he so relentlessly sought. He often emphasized the Near Eastern magnificence of Carlo's dreams and the fact that their fulfillment was only partial. He writes in his treatise on the Caserta aqueduct:

> But to speak of the advantages that architecture enjoys from princes especially, I note that without these great spirits who ruled in Babylon, Memphis, Palmyra, Rome, and elsewhere, the stupendous piles would not have risen which whole centuries have worked in vain to destroy, and which so firmly teach to a posterity inundated with barbarism, the just proportions and varied forms of solid and ornamental building.[74]

This tells us, in words prefiguring Gioffredo and Carletti, what the creators of the absolute palace felt to be its ancestry. Babylon, Memphis, Palmyra, and Rome were the seats of the prototypical rulers of the Vichian family state. The words were written by Vanvitelli but could have been written by the philosopher himself, or even by Carlo di Borbone.

And yet as the years go by and Caserta slowly rises, as the gardens are planted and filled with their alleys and sculptured fountains, Vanvitelli himself seems ever more estranged from his creation, ever more prey to melancholy. Complaints multiply about slights, the promotion of nonentities, forgotten or broken promises, cabals. The young Ferdinando, with his pale, perfectly oval face and large red mouth, though he appears charming in Mengs's portrait (fig. 4.21), grew up into a rather loutish *lazzarone*, was quite uninterested in architecture and in Caserta, and ignored Vanvitelli.[75] The deepest disappointment of all, arching Vanvitelli's later years like a great black catafalque, was the summons to Spain that never came. The tone of the architect's last decades—the processes of gaining favor, the attempts to get paid, the state of architectural professionalism in an absolutist court—is summed up in a letter to Marco Pini, a friend at Carlo's court in Madrid:

> Naples, 21 July 1767
>
> Most Illustrious and Beloved Worshipful Lord:
>
> I receive your most welcome letter of June 30 from Madrid, which confirms my situation. Since His Catholic Majesty, God keep him, sees fit not even to ask out of curiosity: "why does one not hear that Vanvitelli, who had served me well, has been given some work?" [your letter] takes from me any hope of aid. This is the unfortunate condition to which I am reduced, dear friend, for having, with a zeal that was true and unfeigned—unlike the zeal of many men—served the commands and oracles of the greatest king on earth. In Naples my every merit has become demerit. God has permitted it. . . .

4.21
Anton Raphael Mengs. Portrait of Ferdinando IV at nine, 1759–1760. Madrid, Prado

Everything has vanished like mist in the sun. I have been left to the mercy of those who wanted me discharged from the service years ago—as I have several times indicated in my letters. I go to the ocean and find it dry. Meritorious service has earned me disgrace. Except for a miracle I am without resource. I do not know how long my courage can cope with this sort of outrage without damage to my health.

If a proper moment should arise, I pray you, place me at the Sovereign's royal feet while I, remaining full of infinite obligation, kiss your hand, being your illustrious lordship's most devoted

Luigi Vanvitelli[76]

Although undoubtedly Vanvitelli did need money and undoubtedly was owed money, things were not as desperate as this letter makes out: he had a lot of work. The whining and the fawning are part of the courtier-architect's professional technique. They are extensions of the principles of the *baciamano*. They underline the dependency that is the principle of absolutism. They are, as Vico might say, made necessary by the monarch's need for utter freedom. If Carlo di Borbone breaks his promise he is right to do so; and Vanvitelli cannot bring himself actually to point the finger of blame even in private letters. This, after all, is how gods are.

5 The River-Road

The Site

The Palace of Caserta was planned as the climax of a ride north from Naples along a revived section of the Via Appia.[1] It was a journey that in the eighteenth century took the visitor through a flat prospect of garden and meadow, the horizon dominated by Vesuvius on the south and the Tifatine Mountains to the north (fig. 5.1). But the visitor also approaches the palace, or reapproaches it, through its gardens (fig. 5.2). Aside from two appendixes,[2] these consist mainly of the almost two-mile-long river-road rising in the bosom of the hill known as the Colina de Briano north of the palace and flowing through a series of sculptured fountains to plunge into earth halfway to the palace's garden facade (fig. 5.3).[3]

The gardens,[4] as Vanvitelli makes clear in the *Dichiarazione*, are a commentary on the site.[5] Caserta Nuova, the planned but largely unbuilt new city, was not only to be a new bureaucratic capital for Carlo but a new capital for Campania, replacing Capua and Naples, which had been the region's chief cities in classical and medieval times respectively. Caserta Nuova, Vanvitelli believes, will reevoke Campania's ancient reputation as an earthly paradise: the Campania Felix of the Romans will now, he says, become Campania Felicissima. Paraphrasing Mazzocchi he describes the early Greek colonies in the area and recalls the sumptuous villas, the nymphaea, and the cities of Greek and Roman times that lie in ruins. The contrast with today's air view is striking (compare figs. 5.4 and 5.5 with 5.6).

The Site

5.1
Philipp Hackert. *The Palace of Caserta from the Convent of the Capuchins*, 1782. Naples, San Martino

The River-Road

5.2
Caserta, principal
facade. Photo Ente
Provinciale per il
Turismo

The Site

5.3
Caserta, gardens.
Photo Jacelli

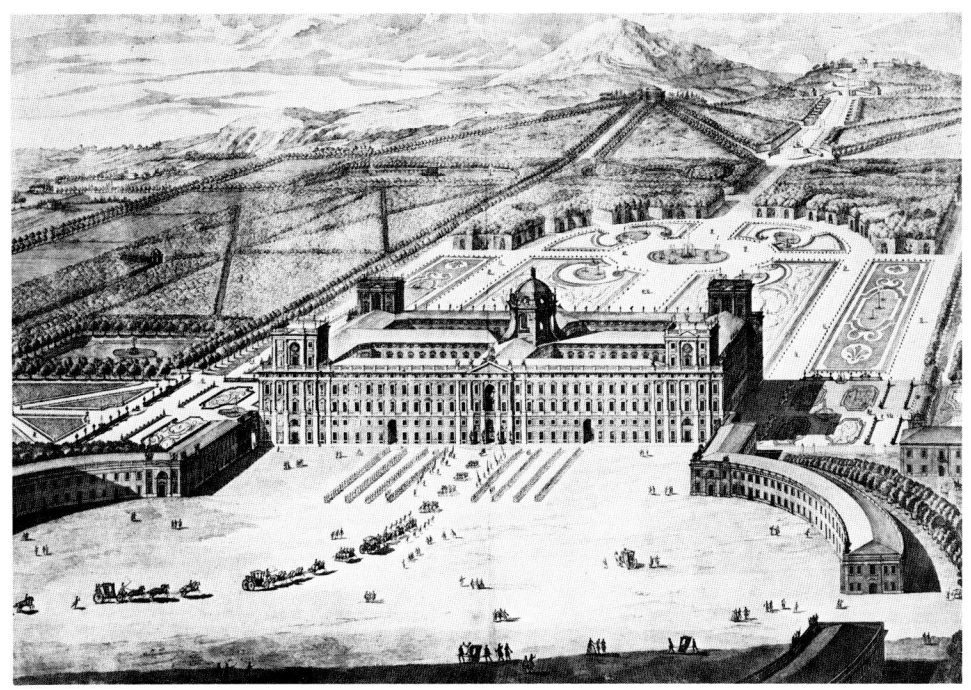

5.4
Caserta, view of the planned gardens of 1756 from the south. From the *Dichiarazione*

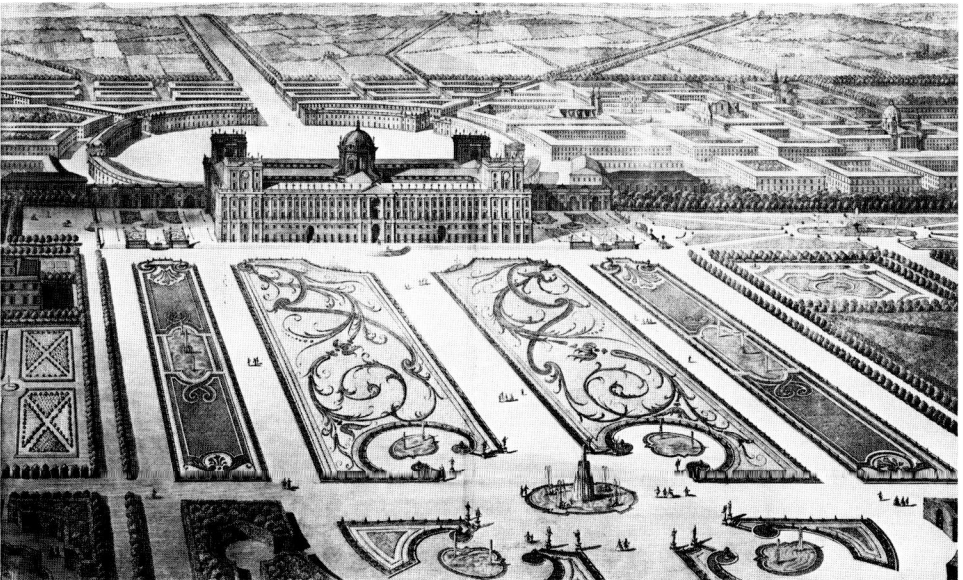

5.5
Caserta, view of the planned gardens of 1756 from the north. From the *Dichiarazione*

5.6
Caserta, air view of the royal palace and gardens. Photo Ente Provinciale per il Turismo

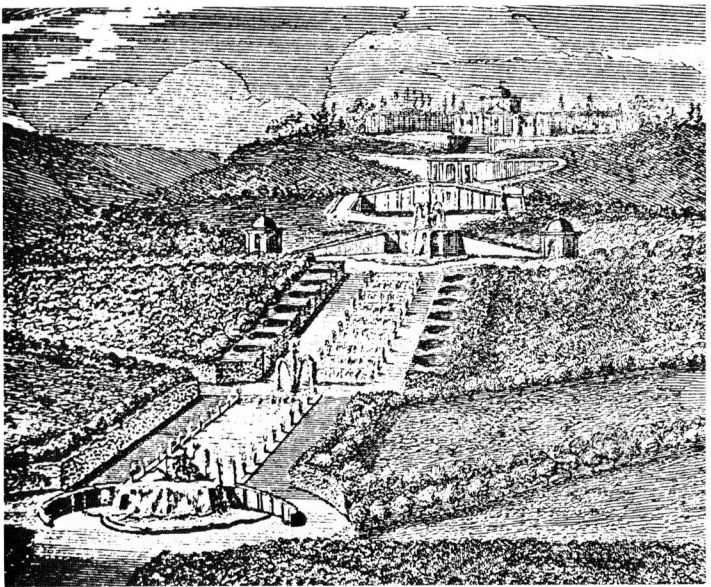

5.7
Detail of fig. 5.4.

In the latter all the rich flourishes have been removed and the flat, regular mathematical forms beloved by Carlo di Borbone dominate.

Vanvitelli goes on: the guardian deity of the place had always been Diana. The site is dominated by Monte Tifata, sacred to her, "which rules an entire countryside not lacking in Campanian magnificences. The western slopes provided an ample situation for the Temple of the Tifatine Diana, long ago transformed into the church of Sant'Angelo in Formis." Vanvitelli lists a nearby circus and wood, both also sacred to the goddess. And it was she who had made Monte Tifata so abundantly favorable to hunting: her temple became rich.[6] A town was built, then the Roman aqueduct that Vanvitelli had thought of reviving and harnessing as a water supply.[7] Meanwhile a temple of Ceres had stood near the grain fields of the region. On the slopes of the Collina di Briano the architect planned a domed coffeehouse, a series of cascades, and a colossal group of Neptune as the source of these waters (fig. 5.7); but Diana and Ceres were not forgotten either.[8]

The first garden scheme of 1756 was clearly influenced by Versailles (frequently alluded to, with a hostility that protests too much, in the *Lettere*), not only in its oval palace forecourt with three boulevards but also in the long axial lagoon and large pool on the left in the garden proper (fig. 5.8).[9] Also mentioned in this context are Vaux, Marly, St-Cloud, Chantilly, Nymphenburg, Cassel, Schoenbrunn, Aranjuez, and Buen Retiro (fig. 5.9; only the last two of course well known to Carlo) as well as the great parks of Holland such as Heemsteede near Utrecht. And although Juvarra's schemes for the gardens of the royal palace at Messina[10] may have been the source for the 1756 design a far more likely source has not been pointed out: the plate in Antoine-Joseph Dézallier d'Argenville's book on gardening labeled "Disposition générale d'un magnifique jardin tout de niveau" (fig. 5.10).[11] I refer in particular to the semicircular exedra, or theater, and the grid of parterres in the central sections of the two plans. In both cases this area is divided by a rectilinear network of pathways dominated by parterres entered quincunx-fashion by diagonal paths. There are then longer, embroidered parterres below them, nearer the palace. These were to be covered with large-scale curvilinear conceits executed in colored gravel or low-blooming flowers or both (fig. 5.8).

The 1756 layout shows that originally the garden at Caserta was to be entered via broad steps behind the palace, with a private raised garden (fig. 5.8, *I*), a single, freestanding statue of Flora and another of Zephyr; a grand parterre (*K*) with more beds and fountains; and (*L*) a focal fountain representing the Sebeto and the Vistula, the latter being the principal river of Maria Amalia's homeland in Saxony and Poland. The royal rivers of Iberia were also to be symbolized. If these central rivers were actual, the four accompanying fountains (2–5) were populated by mythical river characters: Perseus, Atalanta, Bacchus, Hercules, Pallas, and Hippocrene. This notion of the garden as a mixture of real and mythical rivers was to develop considerably in the final scheme.[12]

The Site

5.8
Caserta, planned gardens of 1756. From Vanvitelli, *Dichiarazione*

5.9
Robert de Cotte. Proposed garden at Buen Retiro, 1714–1715. Paris, Bibliothèque Nationale

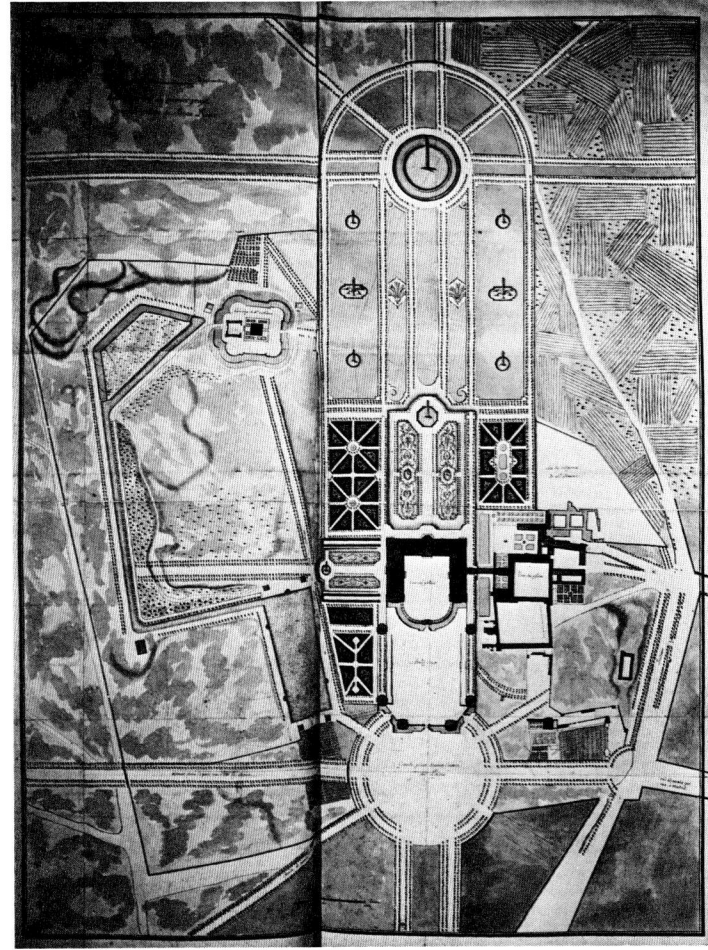

5.10
A. J. Dézallier d'Argenville. "Disposition générale d'un maghifique jardin tout de niveau," from his *La Théorie et la practique du jardinage* (1709)

The *M*s mark an open air theater backdrop made of boxwood hedges. There are also open air "salons" with "cabinets" (*R*) filled with statues or fountains. The whole complex was to be a wide, intricate grid crisscrossed with alleys, "boulevards," and blocks (*N*, *P*, *Q*) and even *piazze*: a veritable labyrinth—literally a garden city—in contrast to the boulevards and piazzas of the real city that Vanvitelli, in some of the *Dichiarazione's* plates, indicates on the southern side of the palace. This early plan for the garden is quite different in its broad labyrinthine geometry from the rigorous directionality of the final scheme. Within the early plan a population of sculptured figures marked out the visitor's routes. The 'main boulevard' (*vialone P*) led to a belvedere, or summerhouse. The main cross axis (*Q*) led all across the park and was almost three miles long. At *S* was to be the Neptune Fountain already mentioned. *T* was another outdoor salon, with an interior portico made of boscage and with fountains of Amor and Psyche. Above it, at *V*, was another salon with fountains of Narcissus and Echo. *X* marked a large pool with a central island, a colonnade, and an outdoor conversation room. Even the vegetable garden had a statue, a fountain representing the birth of Venus. Other, smaller gardens were to take the form of roofed quincunxes (*b*) decorated with separate fountains of Adonis, Endymion, and Diana (*c*). The orchard (*d*) was ornamented with a fountain of Pomona; other vegetable and fruit gardens had fountains of Vertumnus, and so on. The Ω represents the *boschetto antico*, an existing grove that Vanvitelli intended to preserve despite its irregularities.

Although this scheme recalls earlier garden designs, it nonetheless has originality, not so much because of the garden per se as because of its relation to the plan of the palace. It is an extension of the latter's grid of corridors and chambers. The palace's vaults, stairs, domes, and so forth, as diagrammed in figure 5.11, are replaced by alleys, pools, and architectural hedges. The same diagonal axes, the same offsets, the same interpenetrating wall-thicknesses and sight lines; the same cylinders, quincunxes, polygons, and *ronds-points* structure both. And, further, where in the palace the characteristic configuration of every room is its ceiling decoration, in the garden this configuration turns into raised or sunken vegetable, sculptural, or liquid constituents, a "floor decoration." The shape of a parterre is established by a hedge, a flowerbed, a pool, or a statue (figs. 5.4, 8.18). Both indoors and out Vanvitelli interpenetrates solids with planes and quincunxes with octagons, these in turn being transfixed by symmetrical crossed diagonals and orthogonals of circulation space. The central octagon of the palace's main floor is repeated in the salons and cabinets of the garden. The latter's central feature, an octagonal "room" centered on an octagonal pool, with either axial entrance paths or else axial apses on each side, is in turn a pattern repetition of the same basic idea, this time using an oval, that would be seen in the Conversation Room in the apartments of the crown prince and princess (figs. 5.8, 6.14). Both are articulated, within the corners of the rectangular mass encrusting it and by small apses. The same principles, either fully applied as in the orchard (fig. 5.8, *d*) or in truncated form (entrance vestibule, palace forecourt) appear throughout the garden, the palace, and indeed the town. Everything is subordinated to this ever varied yet ever present set of shapes. Figure 5.11 shows the types of dihedral or reflective, and cyclic or clock-based symmetry used in representative parts of the palace and garden. The four corner suites of the main floor, or *piano reale*, which (with exceptions in the case of the stairs) make up a complete 360-degree cycle.

Yet the indoor and outdoor arrangements, while in these ways isomorphic, are far from being the same. They are reversed in some instances, sculpture being set into wall niches in the palace or placed near or on the wall (figs. 8.9, 8.41). The powerful three-dimensional compositions on the ceilings lead the visitor into the center of the room where its sculptured and painted program may be observed. In the 1756 garden the centers of the "rooms" are inaccessible because they occur in pools, flowerbeds, or fountains. In the gardens the visitor is always on the periphery, and statues and plants take the center, whereas in the palace the person is the centerpiece of each room. Even where some large piece of furniture occupies the center, the visitor or user is at least theoretically being invited to use or approach the table or bed in question while mythical or historical personages watch from the walls and ceilings. And whereas in the garden the skies are real, as are the trees and vegetation, flowers and water, the palace is filled with fictive skies, trees, vegetation, flowers, and water. The relations between real and

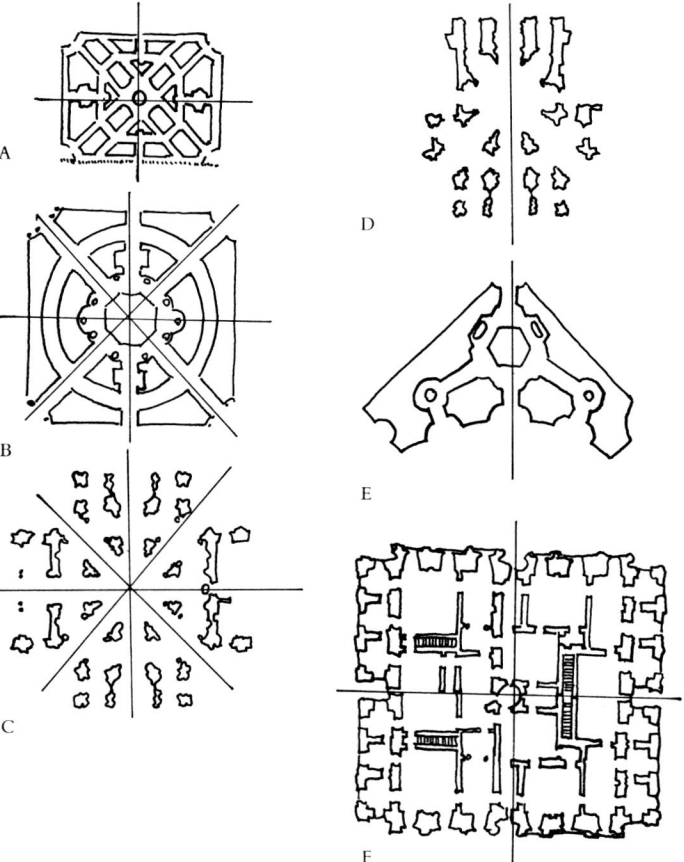

5.11
Caserta, details of the palace plan and of the 1756 garden, analyzed as examples of cyclical and dihedral symmetry. *A*, garden of Pomona; *B*, boscage with outdoor salon; *C*, central crossing of palace at ground-floor level; *D*, southern entrance to palace; *E*, "theatrical prospect with chambers" in the garden; *F*, the four corners of the palace at the level of the *piano reale*, or second floor, showing how room configurations approximate a complete 360-degree clockwise cycle. Examples *A–E* all display dihedral or mirror symmetry. Example *F* shows a four-part cycle symmetry.

mythic, living and representational, moving and still, central and peripheral, are partially reversed, or commutated, when the user moves from garden to palace or vice versa.

The iconography of the 1756 plan is chiefly Ovidian, like gardens all over Europe. But in the *Dichiarazione* the Ovidian imagery is particularly river conscious. The figures come out of chthonic tales of fertility and agriculture and involve transformations of humans into flowers, rocks, animals, and the like. Flora, Perseus, Zephyr, Atalanta, Bacchus, Amor and Psyche, Narcissus and Echo, Adonis and Endymion have to do with pursuit and love, with rocks, streams, grottoes, winds, and flowers. Their presence makes a charming conceit for a garden. Although nothing is unusual in all this, stylistically or historically, it is an interesting foretaste of what was to come, that the sculpture planned for Caserta in 1756 would have frozen and mythicized the transformations and pastimes of the place. The notion that such a garden should have been built at Caserta is particularly happy, Campania being the place where Hercules replanted the Garden of the Hesperides, and of course Campania comprised one of the most imposing of all classical literary garden landscapes, namely the South Italian scenes in Virgil's *Eclogues* and *Georgics*.[13]

But at some point after 1756 Vanvitelli's interest in French formal gardens began to wane. For one thing his hostility to "Versaglia" (Versailles) became stronger. He saw past French Baroque garden design to its Italian Renaissance origins.[14] For another thing he was increasingly employed on the aqueduct and now planned to carry the river right through the garden, under the palace, and then in the form of twin canals flanking the revived Via Appia, south to Naples.[15] The sculpture for this new scheme was apparently all planned, too, though carving was not completed until after Vanvitelli's death in 1773.[16]

Along the way there were other changes, many of them in turn set aside. Thus in December 1763 Vanvitelli informed his brother that he would not, after all, erect an equestrian statue-fountain on Monte Briano, presumably where the cascade now is but, rather, a stepped ramp with many jets and fountains. The planned coffeehouse would stand at the top of this (fig. 5.4). In the same month the idea of erecting a triumphal arch at this point was abandoned as well.[17]

Evidence for another change is a tiny, little-noticed sketch in the Vanvitelli archive that shows an alternative scheme (fig. 5.12); though undated the drawing seems to have been made after Vanvitelli had abandoned the idea of a French platform garden in favor of the present river-road.[18] The sketch also shows the palace and town of Caserta Nuova. Here, as opposed to the partial view in the *Dichiarazione*, the new city is a perfect square centered around a version of Bernini's St. Peter's colonnades. Even more than the printed scheme, the sketch recalls Robert de Cotte's garden project for Buen Retiro of 1714–15 (fig. 5.9). De Cotte's designs were made at a point in time when Carlo di Borbone, of course, would have been in Spain at his father's court.[19] So Vanvitelli's sketch is a likely specimen of Carlo's intervention in the architect's planning of the new palace.

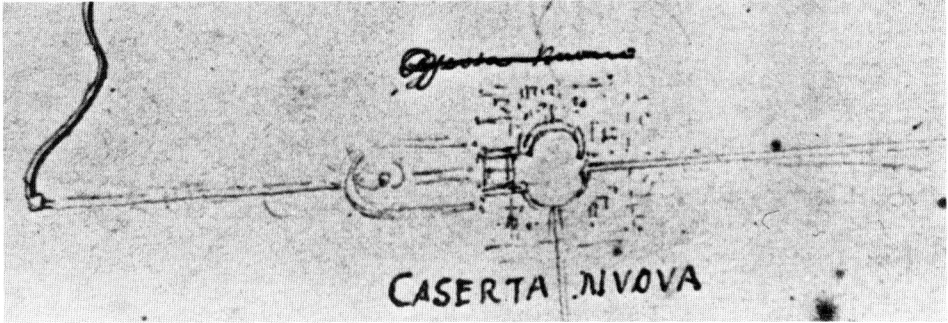

5.12
Vanvitelli. Sketch for proposed garden at Caserta, c. 1760 (?). Caserta, Museo Vanvitelliano

Whatever its source this scheme of Vanvitelli's emphasizes the trident shape of the three canals at the left, or north, and in this is perhaps an outgrowth of the planned Neptune fountain. The sketch also emphasizes the axiality and length of the canals, continuing the aqueduct through the town and on to Naples as Vanvitelli had planned to do. This scheme in turn gave way to what exists today.[20]

The river-road, now beginning in the Collina de Briano,[21] rises out of the hill in the form of a cascade, then turns into a waterfall and pool marked by a large marble group, à la Girardon, of Diana and Actaeon (fig. 5.13). It then dips underground to emerge as a lagoon ending in a fountain of Venus, again goes underground, again emerges, flows beneath a group of Ceres and her court, and finally widens into a second immense waterfall, which introduces the planned climax of the whole: a vast and today incomplete fountain of Juno and Aeolus. The general development, then, is from the great rough rocks above Diana's grotto through measured stages of increasing urbanity and control. The palace of Aeolus forms an arched facade floating above the waters, prefiguring the distant crimson bulk of Carlo's own palace (fig. 5.2). Finally, there was the so-called Dolphin Fountain, the river here having become once again subterranean. The dolphins flank a monstrous sea creature who seems to lurk in Lethe and who spouts forth the river after its passage through hell (fig. 5.44). It is a picture, perhaps, of the things Aeneas had escaped when Neptune saved his fleet from Aeolus's storm. With its dramatic sculpture Vanvitelli's river-road is also a mythic recension of the aqueduct that feeds it, for that too is composed of tunnels, mighty bridges, and causeways and penetrates hunting and agricultural lands.

One probable inspiration for this final conception of Caserta's garden is the Villa d'Este at Tivoli (fig. 5.14). As early as 1751 Carlo himself had examined statues there, and the king's interest in Tivoli is frequently reflected thereafter in Vanvitelli's letters.[22] As for Caserta's debts to Pirro Ligorio's scheme as a whole,[23] the basic conception, at the Villa d'Este, of a great hill punctuated by dramatic fountain groups reappears at Caserta from the first. In particular, the Ceres group at Caserta finds a predecessor in Tivoli's statue of Roma. Piranesi's view of the Este villa (fig. 5.14), dating from about 1761, emphasizes the powerful vertical axis leading down the hill to the foreground, as well as the sequence of rich sculptures and the sense of an intricate river of manipulated waters descending through underground labyrinths, to flow, gush, or cascade into the midst of various marble "allusive poetic fables," to use Vanvitelli's phrase.[24] The Villa d'Este's popularity with Piranesi, Hubert Robert, and Fragonard in the 1760s would have added to its allure for the son of a landscape painter. But Caserta, if it is a revision of the Villa d'Este, revises its prototype by spacing it out along a canal like the one at Versailles or even like a Dutch canal.

Another garden that Vanvitelli looked at or, rather, asked for sketches of was the equally celebrated one at the Villa Lante, Bagnaia.²⁵ Bagnaia is organized like Caserta in that it is arranged on a long vertical axis (fig. 5.15). The visitor walks out along this axis, from the start of the garden, and then returns the same way. As at Caserta the axis rises up a hill, moving from a large sculptural complex featuring a quincunx-shaped pool. In the pool is a fountain of the winds, which can be set down as a distant prophecy of Caserta's Aeolus fountain. Surrounding the pool is a labyrinth of hedges similar to what once existed at Caserta immediately north of the palace. On proceeding through the garden the visitor mounts a symmetrical set of double staircases that surround the arms of Cardinal Montalto sculptured in boxwood. This leads on up to a long table or trough set along the axis of the path and guarded by river gods. The trough has a channel of water down its center and hence can be seen as a miniature river-road. The table was used for summer banquets, the flowing water in its center serving as a convenient way of getting rid of the leavings. More stairs rise over the river gods, Arno and Tiber, who, sweating, saturnine and colossal, flank the head of the table. At this next level the Aeolus Fountain is again foreshadowed, this time by a cluster of dramatic spouts set into a cage like the winds that Aeolus kept on his island. Here there is also a *catena d'acqua*, or water-chain, which again anticipates the river-road. Its margins are scalloped with wavelike curls (fig. 5.15). It leads to a Dolphin Fountain—recall the similarly named one at Caserta—that is black, rough,

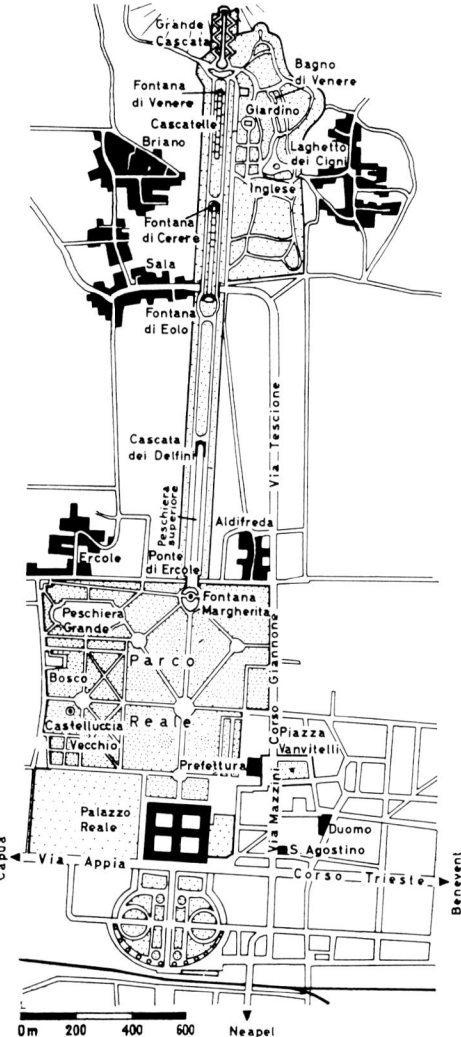

5.13
Caserta, map of the gardens, palace, and palace square. From Thoenes, *Neapel und Umgebung*

The River-Road

5.14
G. B. Piranesi. Waterfall at the Villa D'Este, etching, 1761. From Lamb, *Die Villa D'Este*

5.15
Villa Lante, Bagnaia, upper garden

and hairy with watergrowths. At the summit of the hill two temples flank the axis. Here the visitor returns. And on returning he or she proceeds in chronological order, following the flow of the waters themselves and traveling now from a divine, upper world to a lower, human one (from two temples at one termination to two villas at the other).

In its definitive form, then, Caserta seems to combine the Tivoli notion of a dramatic sequence of sculptural fables with Bagnaia's chronological river-road. A comparison of the 1756 plan with what was built shows that the seventeenth- and eighteenth-century prototypes were deemphasized in favor of a neo-Renaissance garden, a garden derived from cinquecento models but scaled to the sublime ambitions of the age of absolutism.

How is the river-road at Caserta to be read? As at Bagnaia there is only one real path in the central garden. On this path, leaving the palace, the visitor goes back to the beginning of time, a beginning marked by the rocky cascade that issues from the brow of the Colina di Briano. And on returning the visitor must notice that the facade of the palace fronting the garden is actually the main facade of the building—in contrast to normal practice, by which a palace's richer face fronts the town. For only the garden facade has a full complement of pilasters all across (figs. 6.17, 7.1). Each fountain, furthermore, is designed so that the visitor is invited to circle round it to reexamine it on the way back to the palace (figs. 5.26, 5.27).

To follow the sequence in terms of its own chronology, then, beginning at the cascade, recall that a Neptune group had been planned for a site nearer the palace and that at one time there had also been a scheme for a triumphal arch and equestrian statue of the king. Although he had jettisoned the arch and statue, the Neptune idea no doubt remained with Vanvitelli. In any event he took the trouble to draw it on the garden view he published in the *Dichiarazione* (fig. 5.7). Existing at present is only a narrow stair of rustic rocks down which the waters tumble in a foaming ribbon (fig. 5.16). At the foot of the mount the river turns into a series of broad steps, the last of which flings a high cascade into the basin below. This basin is much wider than the cascade and is backed with a cyclopean arc of tumbled boulders. It is sublime, or nearly so—a specimen, with the statues, of the rococo sublime, perhaps.[26]

Diana and Actaeon

Against this backdrop, to the left and right of the cascade and behind the still pool, is the earliest of the garden's mythical episodes (figs. 5.17–5.21). It is a hunt, as Vico would lead us to expect. Diana turns Actaeon into a stag after he has seen her naked. (The group was chiefly executed by Paolo Persico, who carved the two main figures and some of the nymphs. The other nymphs are by Angelo Brunelli, and the dogs by Pietro Solari.[27]) The principles of gestural intercourse exhibited in Vincenzo Rè's allegory of the birth of Prince Filippo are here worked into Vanvitelli's Latin, Italic, and Roman myth. To the

The River-Road

5.16
Caserta, Cascade and Fountain of Diana, mainly executed by Paolo Persico, with Angelo Brunelli and Pietro Solari, 1785–1789. Photo Alinari. (See also pls. 2, 3.)

5.17
Fountain of Diana,
Diana. Photo Jacelli

5.18
Fountain of Diana,
Actaeon. Photo
Alinari

The River-Road

5.19
Fountain of Diana, detail of Diana's group. Photo Mimmo Jodice

5.20
Fountain of Diana, detail of more distant nymphs. Photo Mimmo Jodice

5.21
Fountain of Diana, Actaeon's dogs. Photo Mimmo Jodice

Diana and Actaeon

right the goddess, aided by one of her maidens, gestures at the visual climax of the group while other nymphs, scattered with operatic artfulness over the rocks, indicate supplication, chaste fright, and kindred emotions (figs. 5.19, 5.20). On the left, on the other side of the cascade, retribution: surrounded by a pack of snarling dogs—long, lean, and livid hounds every one (fig. 5.21)—Actaeon, twisting vainly away from one of the bolder brutes, has already grown the head and antlers of a stag. His stag's face echoes perfectly the maidenly fright of the nymphs. Indeed the nymph on the far left of Diana's group is Actaeon's gestural twin; the correspondences between nymphs and dogs are also great. The nymphs are divided into two unequal groups, four on the left and three on the right, with an additional central group of Diana, the one commanding figure, and two companions. The companion on the right readjusts Diana's drapery. The other is seated below, adjusting her robe's hem. The goddess is reasserting her modesty and being dressed even as she reveals to Actaeon (whose mournful, absurd gaze travels across the pool directly to her) that she is indeed a goddess and an angry one. The nymphs on the left meanwhile signal with their lifted arms and eloquent heads, two turned back to Diana, one lingering on Actaeon in powerful regard, aghast at the hunter's fate. The right-hand group, contrastingly, are still bathing, though they are thoroughly startled by what they see. They stare from the water's edge at the miracle disturbing their play and hurry into their garments.

The right-hand group, then, is full of consternation and the still-reigning indecorum of the first discovery. The central group expresses the reassertion of modesty: literally, the goddess's putting on of the garment of authority. And the third group are the *Sprecherinnen*, those who absorb, reflect on, and report the results of the goddess's command.

Actaeon, also disposed as a central figure with attendants, also stands between two groups. But this similarity only plays up the differences between his and Diana's situations. Actaeon is fully clothed in hunter's gear. His pose is a harried and hurried mirroring of Diana's; he urges himself forward, off balance on his right leg while she is solidly and symmetrically erect on her left. Her right hand covers her breast with drapery while his has flown out from his body in alarm as he sees his own dogs turn on him. These similarities and differences all emphasize that *this* central figure, Actaeon, has lost control of his attendants. A terrible reversal has occurred: the hunter has become the quarry. Where Diana's right arm points, commands, quells, Actaeon still absently grasps his useless bow. This reversal is joined by a more basic one, namely that even as Diana is being dressed Actaeon is undressed, his flesh stripped from him by his attendants. They bring him low, slaughter him, while Diana's attendants bear her up and exalt her. Awareness of Actaeon's condition moves outward from the inner dogs who twist around him. There is a central spiral of these fiercer beasts, enveloping him and actually beginning the attack. These are the equivalent of the two nymphs closest to Diana who are dressing her.

Meanwhile, the left-hand group of dogs, preventing Actaeon's escape, equal the still bathing nymphs on the right-hand side of the Diana group. They are the furthest in arrears in the process of the tale's unfolding. Or if one wishes to view the scene with complete synchrony, these have frozen at an earlier moment in the story. In this way the two groups suggest a time-sequence, a step-by-step, articulated revelation. The dogs further to the right are almost heraldic in their cursive immobility (fig. 5.21). The dogs on the immediate right, by contrast, are more aware, fiercer, are in fact assisting in the final action. And so are the nymphs to Diana's left.

The text is Ovid, *Metamorphoses* III 155 ff. The sculptured fable closely follows the poetic one. The tale of Actaeon comes just after that of Cadmus, Actaeon's progenitor, who had built Thebes—a new capital—and married a daughter of Venus and Mars. Ovid begins by attributing Actaeon's misfortunes to bad luck rather than bad behavior, a sentiment he reiterates at the end of the story. He says also that the event occurred before a mountain famed as a hunting spot. Actaeon and his companions have returned from

Gargaphia, a valley crowned with pine
And cypress, holy to the armed Diana.
In its depths there is a forest-hidden cave;
Not art, but Nature imitating art
Built from living pumice and soft tufa
This primal arch. On one side sounding falls
Spread and shimmer to an open pool
Framed beneath a grassy bower. Here,
Weary of the woods and of the hunt,
The goddess-virgin often bathes herself.

In other words Ovid depicts almost exactly what Vanvitelli created, right down to the trees, grassy bower, cave, falls, and even pumice and tufa rocks that look both man-made and Nature-made (figs. 5.16, 5.17).

Ovid treats Diana's bath as a liturgy. The goddess gives her armor and weapons to one nymph-attendant, to another her robe, and two more loosen her sandals. Crocale, still another attendant, knots the goddess's hair. All this undressing, though it occurs before the event depicted, establishes precedents for the sculptured scene in which Diana's attendants so hurriedly put the goddess's clothes back on her. Ovid uses the unveiling also as a foil for another major *narratio*, or closely described consecutive action, in the passage: the dogs' rending or "undressing" of Actaeon. The equivalent device was used in the design of the sculpture.

Actaeon, lost in the woods, comes upon this scene. The nymphs scream and gather round the goddess, trying to hide her, as in the center right-hand side of the sculptured group. But she cannot be hidden. She is a goddess, taller than mortals by a head, as can be seen in Persico's figures. Diana blushes and reaches for her weapons, but they are not to be found, so she flings drops of water on Actaeon. Immediately stag's horns start to spring from his forehead. Actaeon's transformation is described in detail. And when he sees his reflection in a pool, other drops, his own tears, "run down cheeks that are not his own." Hesitating, he is destroyed. His own hounds come upon him: first the attack dogs—Hylaeus, Nape, Poemenis, Harpyia, Sicyonius, Ladon, Dromas, Canache, Sticte, and others:

Then the retrievers, eager for their prize,
Crossing crags, caves, and sudden abysses,
Where here it's steep and there there is no trail,
Pursue the man, right through the places where
He oftentimes before had played pursuer.
Now, alas, his own dogs hunt him down.
He shouts: "I am your master, Actaeon!"
His words die. The air is full of howling.

Melanchactes fastens on him, then Therodamas. The rest of the pack comes behind and Actaeon is rent "till there is no more room for wounds." His moans, not human but also not those of a stag, fill the mountain ridges. His hunting companions come upon the scene and call out "Actaeon!," thinking him far away, and summoning him to look at this splendid kill. How Actaeon wishes he really were far away!

Nor does the anger of the Huntress die
Except in a death that's made of many wounds.

The text like the sculpture breaks the tale in two. There is a Diana-half and an Actaeon-half in both. Ovid plays Diana's nymphs against Actaeon's hounds, as happens in the sculpture. Adding this equation to the poem makes the tale in the sculpture richer in ironies and inversions. Diana's unfindable bow, for which she substitutes drops of water, does not appear in the sculpture. Instead, Actaeon has a useless bow whose inutility is underlined by those lethal drops of water that constitute the great cascade itself, an excellent symbol of the power of a goddess over a mortal. Ovid's naming of the nymphs and of the dogs strengthens the parallel in the poem between the female victims and their canine avengers. But naming also emphasizes the personalities of the nymphs and the dogs by establishing identities for them. This happens, moreover, just as poor Actaeon's own identity is being lost, a loss that would become crucial, of course, when his companions failed to recognize him.

Ovid explicitly deprives his story of a moral. If we reread the tale as Vico does, a moral shows up quickly enough, however. It is the tale of Diana and Actaeon that to Vico classically states the origin of religion in the fear of divine waters. This is

the frightful religion of the rivers, which they invariably called sacred, and which is that of Actaeon who, seeing Diana naked (that is, seeing a living fountain) was sprinkled with water by the goddess (that is, she cast upon him his greatest fear), because a stag (the most timid of animals) was torn apart by dogs (by the remorses [bites] of his own conscience at having violated religion).[28]

It is here that Vico connects the river's "flung drops" with the Greek word *nymphae* and the Latin word *latices* (see chapter 1). Thus nymphs are drops and animations of a river. It is a fine conceit for the group.

The River-Road

Actaeon has broken a taboo: the inviolability of marriage. Water is Diana's shield and protector. It is also the agent of her vengeance and of her punishment. She commutates the elements of her strength into a code of justice that in demoting this man into a beast rightly lessens him in the scheme of things. Diana gets even with Actaeon by making him even with his true equals. The myth holds a legal reality: future law, Vico says, will declare that a man may not look on any naked woman other than his own wife. Actaeon's fear and death are reflections of the fact that the myth of Actaeon appeared in history at the point when primitive hunting communities, which were communities of wanderers, invented marriage. Marriage stabilized them, settled them in permanent places. The institution, he says, therefore stands at the very beginning of civilization. Diana and Actaeon illustrate that aspect of hunting that has to do with clearing land and civilizing, with the maintenance of ownership and the fear of trespass. Indeed Vico makes much of Actaeon as a barbaric hunter with no respect for God. That this nongodfearer should have become the animal that most suffers fear is just.

The balustrade leading from the fable of Diana and Actaeon to the next part of the river-road is decorated with fourteen statues or groups of other hunters in ancient poetry (figs. 5.22–5.25). They have the aspect of guardians as well as hunters. They are as intricately repetitive of the artifacts and poses in the Diana fountain as are Ovid's own strongly patterned tales.

5.22
Fountain of Diana, balustrade figure.
Photo Mimmo Jodice

Diana and Actaeon

5.23–5.25
Fountain of Diana,
balustrade figures.
Photo Mimmo Jodice

The River-Road

They also suggest Vico's further point, namely that dozens of ancient hunting fables are mere revisions of the central story of Diana and Actaeon. And as their brilliant marble bodies shine in the sun above the palace, they usher the visitor back along his path now that he or she has reached and contemplated the first of the garden's "poetic fables."

Venus and Adonis

The next fable, again a mythic hunt, deals with a man and woman who are anything but strangers: Venus and Adonis.[29] It is mainly the work of Gaetano Salomone and dates from the late 1770s and early 1780s (figs. 5.26–5.31). In contrast to the earlier fountain, split in two as it is by the "fearsome" cascade separating the men and animals on one side from the divinities on the other, this has a unified character befitting its theme of amorous union. Indeed, visually, from the axis of the park, it is set directly *between* the two halves of the earlier fountain. Even the rocks that support the figures are more unified, more ledge-like, and less separate than those of the Diana fountain. Venus's and Adonis's rocky support bridges the rushing waters in a single arc. This rock is contained in an architectural frame with gently curving parapets and a low, serene cascade animated by three low jets and several conduits that discharge into a basin taking the form of a long geometric canal. So the effect is less sublimely wild, more controlled and civilized, than that of the earlier fountain.

5.26
Caserta, Fountain of Venus and Adonis from rear. Photo Mimmo Jodice

Venus and Adonis

5.27
Fountain of Venus and Adonis, mainly by Gaetano Salomone, late 1770s and early 1780s. Photo Alinari

5.28
Fountain of Venus
and Adonis, detail of
Venus and Adonis.
Photo Mimmo Jodice

5.29
Fountain of Venus
and Adonis, two
putti and dog. Photo
Mimmo Jodice

Venus and Adonis

5.30
Fountain of Venus and Adonis, putto's face. Photo Mimmo Jodice

5.31
Fountain of Venus and Adonis, boar

The crowd of nymphs and putti mingling on these ledges forms a contrast to the earlier scene. Where the nymphs of Diana focus around the goddess in intricate but singleminded solicitude and consternation, in this second fountain pleasure-bent nymphs and putti rest sirenishly on the rocks or engage in hunting play (fig. 5.29). Others stare at the lovers or at the visitor like midget magistrates (fig. 5.30). Expressing no hint of the coming tragedy, they serve only to bedeck the central couple at the composition's apex. Putti perched behind them ride the higher ridges of stone as if borne along on waves (fig. 5.28). All lead and point to the central couple. Like a Watteauesque lover embarking for Cythera, Adonis takes leave of his kneeling consort, who grasps his left arm as she adjures him not to hunt any fierce game such as wild boar. Adonis, like Actaeon dressed for the hunt, is quieting Venus's fears. Sculpturally indeed, in pose and setting and in the intensity with which he is clung to Actaeon prefigures Adonis, and even Actaeon's dogs prefigure Venus herself in their general form though with a reversed meaning. Look at the interplay between Diana and the nymph nearest her in figure 5.19 and between Venus and her lover in figure 5.28. It is not that the two pairs of figures copy each other but that they suggest movement, rotation, and identity-shifting in a single couple. Venus is the nymph in figure 5.19, sunk down on the rock and lifting her gaze and arms toward the standing figure who is now no longer the huntress Diana but

Adonis the hunter: here is metamorphosis indeed. And he, in turn, seems a Diana who has turned toward his companion, raising his arm in a gesture of comic suffering at Venus's pleas as he supports her with his powerful left arm.

The interplay between the three groups: Diana and her nymphs, Actaeon and his dogs, and Venus and Adonis, makes all kinds of points about hunters and their quarry, love and hate, dissolution and preservation. Adonis like Diana has no weapon but not being divine will not be able to commandeer magical drops of water. (Indeed, with unconscious appropriateness some vandal has broken the bow that one of the putti, on a high outcropping, holds above the couple.) The detail reminds us that it was Cupid who, with his bow, wounded Venus and thus caused her infatuation with Adonis. Meanwhile a pair of putti play with one of Adonis's hunting dogs in a reminiscence of the Actaeon group. They play with the instruments of Adonis's doom. Nor do they fear that doom, the boar beneath them, though his spines are erect and his head seems to shake with a bellow (fig. 5.31).

The scene is thus of events before the hunt rather than a hunt in full career. In this sense the second fountain is proleptic of the first. Both hunts are tragic. Yet there is a lighter note in the Venus and Adonis group. In this second scene the attendants are far from being concerned in the proceedings as Diana's nymphs had been. Their debonair obliviousness is a central point of the scene and sets off Venus's pleading eyes.

Although identities, moods, and emotional directions are different, the basic roles are the same in the two fountains. There are a human hunter, a goddess, water nymphs, a pack of putti instead of the pack of Actaeon's dogs. And there is also in each of the two fables the quarry: the boar that by goring Adonis will turn *him* into the victim, as opposed to the stag that with greater economy but unaltered significance Actaeon simply becomes.

Yet if the roles are similar, the plot like the mood and the emotions takes off in a different direction. This time the human lover is killed by his enemy, not by his allies. The goddess loves and grieves rather than despising and rejoicing. The nymphs do not assist in and react to the climactic event but form its prelude. The playfulness of the putti, in particular, is contrasted with the ferocity, the seriousness, of Actaeon's dogs. The lovers are isolated by their surroundings and their companions. They are tenderly united in a sea of flowing ledges, flamelike seas casting up the white bodies of the nymphs, and putti just like *nymphae* of foam flung from the sea of myth.

The story of Venus and Adonis ends Book X of the *Metamorphoses*. Here it is far from being a tale of simple bad luck, like the poet's version of the Actaeon tale. Ovid fills the story of the love goddess's infatuation with moral meaning. It is the finale of the song of Orpheus, sung to the wild creatures of Thrace in order to civilize them. Vico, meanwhile, claims that the wild beasts Orpheus tamed in the myth were in reality the precivilized people who were tamed by the chanted poetic laws that

Orpheus's stories embodied. The tale does have the spice of fortuitousness: it is because Cupid plays with his arrow that Venus falls in love with Adonis. Here is a recapitulation, in play, of the wounding of Adonis by the boar. That boar, in turn, had accidentally been grazed by Adonis' weapon. Ovid's text provides other connections between Diana and Venus. Venus is so smitten and Adonis so keen a hunter, that she transforms herself into a devotee of the sport:

Inseparably his own, she pleasures herself
In being his shadow, cleaving to his form;
Through hills and woods, through thorn-grown rocks she goes,
Her gown cinched up to kneelength like Diana's.
She urges on the dogs, she starts the quarry:
Low-slung hare, high-horned stag, gazelle—

Venus is in short Diana's progressed reincarnation but one who hunts for love, not hate. She displays the affection or even passion that, with increasing civilization, succeeds to the primitive fears of a solitary hunting race. And when Venus comes upon the bleeding body of her lover after he has been killed she again imitates but reverses the meaning of Diana's action. She sprinkles Adonis's blood with nectar and he becomes the first anemone or wind flower. Not the most timid of animals, this time, but the most timid of plants.

For all its implicit gore, the Venus and Adonis fountain is gentler and more civilized than that of Diana. And if the roles and plots echo each other the emotional meaning is in the end different. Man is not being punished but mourned by the goddess. And, after the introduction of water by Diana, the birth of a flower is an appropriate next occurrence for a garden. Venus in effect cultivates the first anemone ('the wind's daughter'). Vico connects the burial of the dead, the next stage of civilization after matrimony and hunting, with the invention of agriculture, saying that early man "sprinkled" the graves of the dead with religion and divine fear, as Venus sprinkled Adonis's blood with nectar, the liquid siftings of the gods.[30] The flinging of the drops means both the burial of the dead and the planting of plants, just as the word *sepolcro* is linked to *ceppo*, 'root.'[31] Venus, ever inconstant like the fires within her, and ever uncontrolled like those fires, is here subdued with water, flung drops. The laws of marriage are in essential conflict with lawless lust. But Venus's lust is cooled by her loss as it merges with Neptune's flow of time.

Ceres

In the next fountain the fortuitous agriculture of Venus's cultivation of the anemone is replaced by the purposeful agriculture of Ceres (figs. 5.32–5.36). This fountain, also called the Zampilliero, is by Gaetano Salomone and dates from 1783.[32] It is set low in a shallow single cascade at the beginning of which is a second series of equal-stepped cascades like those leading down from the Venus fountain. But the canal here is larger and more riverlike. The forefront of the group consists of two pairs of tritons toward the center and a dolphin on each flanking margin. Behind the cascade, on the upper level, are river gods holding

The River-Road

5.32
Caserta, Fountain of Ceres, mainly by Gaetano Salomone, 1783. Photo Ente Provinciale per il Turismo

5.33
Fountain of Ceres,
river god

5.34
Fountain of Ceres,
river god. Photo
Ente Provinciale per
il Turismo

The River-Road

5.35
Boar's head in parapet (Paolo Persico or Pietro Solari, 1782)

5.36
Fountain of Ceres, triton-satyr

the remains of their broken bronze *litui*. They are seated on wide pedestals, one on each side of the central Ceres group. From the tritons' couches, from the opened jaws of the dolphins, and from the amphorae of the two gods, which represent two Sicilian rivers, spurt long rainbows of water.

In the center is a majestic sarcophaguslike altar of stone, a further development of the rituals of the dead. Its sides curve inward from base to top, and its front is decorated with two sculptured cornucopias flanking a scallop shell from which a bearded mask spouts two jets into the river below. On the altar's incurved sides are pairs of nymphs draped revealingly and seated on the mighty consoles that form the altar's base. The two pairs of nymphs half embrace, twisting to and from each other and delicately gesticulating, like the nymphs of the Venus fountain but with more austerity and decorum. On the altar itself the massive hieratic figure of Ceres is seated holding a large medallion displaying the device of Trinacria (the ancient name of Sicily), which consists of three running legs fanning out from a common center. These stand for the island's three corners, Peloro, Pachino, and Lilibeo. The literature on this fountain states that these capes were also to have been sculptured as crags rising in the river below.[33] Ceres, who once also held a bronze sheaf of wheat, is surrounded and assisted by putti. At her feet on the left a sphinx, now shattered, emits a stream of water. This may be Hesiod's sphinx, the daughter of Typhon, the giant buried under Aetna. The goddess, meanwhile, is buoyant and welcoming amid the activity of her companions.

The Ceres fountain marks a new stage in the development of the river-road. It passes from transformation myth, and from the anger and amorousness of goddesses, to personification, and to the gift to the world of bread and law. Typhon, who had rashly challenged the gods (*Metamorphoses* V 341 ff.), was kept pinioned under the earth by the weight of Sicily: Aetna and the three promontories. Meanwhile Tartarus, personification of the underworld, roams across Sicily's lands because he fears Typhon's struggles will break apart the earth's crust and open his lower kingdom to the light of day. Anxious to claim this kingdom as part of her empire, Venus has Cupid wound Tartarus with an arrow of desire. (Thus does the fable repeat the action of Cupid with respect to his own mother, which had brought on her love for Adonis.) As a result, Tartarus falls in love with Ceres' daughter Persephone. His trans-Sicilian hunt becomes a hunt for his beloved.

In a related episode (*Metamorphoses* V 409 ff.) Cyane, most famous of all the nymphs of that island, who is hunting for her own daughter, informs Ceres, mad with grief, that Persephone has been removed to the underworld by Tartarus. In revenge, Ceres causes the world-famed crops of Sicily to fail. Arethusa, a second nymph of Sicily, rises from her pool and pleads with the goddess to spare the island. She has traveled beneath the earth, she says, and seen Persephone ruling as queen of the underworld. Hearing this, Ceres goes to Jupiter and asks him to restore Persephone to her. A Solomonic judgment is the result: Jupiter divides the year into two parts. Persephone will spend six months with her husband in the underworld and six months on earth with her mother.

Then Arethusa, a former huntress who is now a river, tells her own story, a recension of the earlier ones that forms part of the transformational pattern. Arethusa had been chased by Alpheus, a male river. To save her, Diana had flung a mist around her. Arethusa then became a pool and Alpheus turned back into a river so he could mingle with her waters. At this Diana clove open the earth and allowed Arethusa to escape.

Neither the *Scienza nuova* nor the *Diritto Universale* glosses this tale directly. But the *Scienza nuova* does say that Ceres is identical with her daughter and is in fact grain itself.[34] The Ceres–Persephone seed remains underground for six months and spends the other six on earth in the form of wheat fields. The underground is the underworld, and its river is Tartarus or Styx, which is reached through nearby Lake Avernus. In Vanvitelli's fountain Ceres presides over the point in the river-road marking its emergence from subterranean tract, where it had been bridged over by a lawn. The golden rivers of myth, says Vico, were so called because they watered fields of grain.[35] The Golden Age was golden because it was the age when large-scale wheat farming was invented. Because bonitary laws had to be passed for such farming to work, Vico adds (here following Ovid), Ceres is the goddess of law as well as grain.[36] And it was precisely in Sicily that the first human cities were erected, as markets where the grain was sold.[37] The Ceres fountain brings to the fore the buried-city myth that was a constituent of the region's culture, joining that myth to the equally essential tale of the underground river.

The new quality of urbanism and increased organization seen in the Ceres fountain seems to reflect more of this. Not only is this fountain solemn and presentational; compared to the earlier fountains it is architectonic. Rocks and ledges give way to a true altar. Disorganization and wildness give way to stabilization. The waters that flowed freely in cascades are here channeled and differentiated and made to play tricks conforming to the will of those who control them. The mood is of eternal serene power. Animal heads, trophies of the hunting episodes earlier, or the wild dogs that destroyed Actaeon, or the wild boar that was Adonis' nemesis, are now immured in parapets (fig. 5.35), or else these smooth and powerful architectural forms imprison giants' heads, reminding us of Typhon sunk into his earth, his jungle curls like leaves in lava. The consoles express the architectural notion of compressive force and geometrical order as tropes of slavery. They mark a contrast with the liberty of the waters and the high free bodies of the divinities who sport and reign so superbly in them. Beneath their blackened, barnacled skins, meanwhile, the tritons proclaim that they too are tamed wild creatures, with satyrs' legs (fig. 5.36). Ceres is neither angered nor made love to, neither embarrassed nor pleading. She has no counterpart, no destructive lover, no barbarian voyeur. She is alone and perhaps, since she mounts a sarcophagus, immortal. Or better, her death is the annual death of the Fall and her resurrection the annual resurrection of the Spring. Her companions, including two foam-borne nymphs who are probably Cyane and Arethusa, along with other nymphs who aided her during her hunt on Sicily, are the acolytes of her liturgy of abundance. The two river gods, further off, are probably Alpheus and Tartarus, united in their own way with their lovers.[38]

And yet in pose Ceres is not so different from Venus or even Diana. The three goddesses seem to progress in posture as they move down the river-road through three successive elements: the casting of watery fear, the profession of fiery love, and now this earthy resurrection. But this heavy solemn fountain, once it is seen as an aftermath to Ovid's fable, implies sacrifice and the abandonment of the wild loves of Venus. This stage is achieved, however, through Venus's act, just as the earlier stage had been achieved despite her. Sicily's solidity and civilization's power are fragile. Beneath the weighty tomb is the mutinous Typhon. Tartarus's hunt, Ceres' hunt for Persephone, and Alpheus's hunt for Arethusa all lead to this underworld where inconstant, dangerous Venus, desiring to conquer Diana and Neptune, spreads her fire. But Diana, the thruster, the spout (*iaculatrix*, V 375) has power that also reaches all along the river-road, and the mist that rises from the nest of nymphs around the altar belongs to her. Neptune has revived Ceres' grain, which had been parched by Typhon's fires and reestablishes her agricultural cycle.

The real power is that of Ceres. Her shield with its three fleet legs symbolizes the three earthly hunts of Tartarus, Arethusa, and Ceres herself that took place in the cause of agriculture. The hunts are Ceres' boast and protection. The river-road thus once again speaks of the hunt and is dedicated to its locality: the Two Sicilies, Magna Graecia, or 'Greater Greece.' It embodies *justitia architectonica*. Its more decorous pairing and collocation of the subsidiary figures around Ceres show this. For the first time in the garden's chain of myths, the goddess is truly a sculptured One, a lone sublime untroubled figure toward whom the tritons, nereids, and subsidiary beings all tend. She expresses what Vico calls the oneness of property, tenancy, bonitary lordship, and monarchy.

Juno and Aeolus

The next episode (Figs. 5.37–5.39) is also situated in Sicily, or rather in the Mare Siculum, the 'Tuscan Sea,' that Vanvitelli set between the Two Sicilies (fig. 4.8). Now the river-road becomes yet more urban; indeed it becomes palatial. In the Fountain of Juno and Aeolus the river flows broadly down to a high cascade, crossing over a road, the via Tescione, leading to the town of Ercole as it does so (fig. 5.13). The cascade is marked by a wide parapet approached by gentle ramps from the lower level. The wall thus formed is punctuated by an alternating series of arched and square openings with rusticated pilasters. Thus is the river-road at last truly a raised aqueduct. But the aqueduct is fronted by the parapet over which the water pours. This palace of Aeolus justifies, almost more than does the most imposing part of the aqueduct, the Ponte della Valle, Mazzocchi's epigram for the latter structure: *With this great king what man can vie?/He makes rivers that can fly*.[39] The same sense of hydraulic prodigies permeates the Aeolus Fountain. Indeed the visitor can actually enter the palace of Aeolus via yet another road, a subterranean one: a passageway around the hemicycle, behind the arches and doors of the palace, also leads behind the cascade (fig. 5.39).

The pool was to have contained a colossal group of Juno in her chariot commanding Aeolus to make his winds carry Aeneas away from Italy, where Aeneas and his men were bound, and on to Carthage (*Aeneid*, I 50ff.):

Such wishes turned the fire-hearted goddess
Upon the dark and furious Isle of Winds,
Aeolia, whose king in his huge cave
Imperiously kept the howling storms
Jailed and mutinous in their iron cells.
The mountain thundered with their massive rage.
They roared within; but sceptered Aeolus,
Enthroned above, mastered all their anger,
Lest land and sea and deepest heaven split,
Exploding with this vast torrential might.
God has locked them into sightless caves
Beneath a palace topped with lofty cliffs,
And set a king above them who is vowed
At God's command to loose, or reign them in.

The River-Road

5.37
Caserta, Fountain of
Juno and Aeolus,
by Salomone Persico,
Andrea Violani, and
Angelo Brunelli,
1779–1785. Photo
Alinari

Juno and Aeolus

5.38
Fountain of Juno and Aeolus, relief by A. Brunelli of Peleus and Thetis. Photo Soprintendenza per i Beni Culturali

5.39
Fountain of Juno and Aeolus, gallery behind cascade. Photo Ente Provinciale per il Turismo

The kneeling Juno seeks that king and says,
>"Aeolus, the king of men and gods
Has granted you control of winds and waves.
My Trojan foe is sailing the Tyrrhenian,
Carrying his court to Italy:
Unleash your winds, swallow up his ships,
Or scatter all his men upon the ocean."

She offers Aeolus her daughter Deiopea, most beautiful of her fifteen nymphs, in return for the favor. Aeolus agrees:

>With this he opened up the concave wall
Of the hollow hill. The winds in solid ranks
Roared out from their portals round the world.
As one, Eurus and Notus tore the ocean
From its depths; abundant Africus
Bowled his billows on the shore.
They heard Aeneas's shouting crew, the horses' neighing.
The clouds sucked sight and sky from Trojan eyes:
All across the ocean blind night glared.
The poles thundered, the air was thick with fire.
All things urged the the swift onrush of death.

The passage supplies a number of elements that we can imagine were planned for the fountain: the mighty figures of Aeolus and his supporters confronting an equally mighty but supplicant Juno in her chariot; the three cliffs, Deiopea and her fourteen sisters; perhaps too Aeneas and his drowning horses and men. The present cascade is the great mountain the winds make of the sea, tearing Ocean from its deeps, and the mist of its plunge is the sightlessness the poet mentions. In this fountain Aeneas's vision of a watery underworld succeeds to the volcanic one that Ceres had glimpsed and then, as Persephone, had reigned over. In the Aeolus Fountain the figures strewn around the openings in the palace are the unleashed winds (fig. 5.40). The *latices* and *nymphae* of the earlier fountains get a new incarnation, a new meaning, and a new fearful power. The religion of fountains is seldom so fearsome. The impending outbursts, the rages held in check, sensed in the Ceres fountain, here roll forth fully. The rage is loosed by Aeolus, not Typhon. Air temporarily triumphs over Earth. And the barely controlled superhuman power of the aqueduct itself receives its latest, fullest measure of control.

But not for long—at least not in the poem. Neptune, hearing of these things, knows his domination of the Ocean is under challenge. In his famous "Quos ego" speech he quiets the storm. The son of Venus is able to gather his crew and sail on, and though he goes first to Carthage his true destination is Italy: Palinuro, Miseno, Cumae, Avernus, Puteoli, and Latium, where as Vico puts it he becomes "the monarch of the Roman people."[40] His descent into Avernus, moreover, where he greets his father, imitates that of Ceres–Persephone. In that chthonic city of Dis, that nether Herculaneum, Aeneas gathers the gold not only of grain but of heroic riches and of poets.[41] He sees and knows his ancestors. He begins Roman genealogy. Thus armed he goes on to found the royal house of Alba with its fourteen kings and to build Latium's new capital.[42]

Juno and Aeolus

5.40
Fountain of Juno and Aeolus, the Winds. Photo Ente Provinciale per il Turismo

Imagining a fountain of Neptune at the northern end of the garden, the god perhaps with trident raised as in Vanvitelli's 1776 plan (fig. 5.7), gives an inkling of a splendid pendant to the Aeolus scene. In any event the fountain of Juno and Aeolus, to give it a better name, is reported by contemporaries to have been planned as the greatest fountain in Europe, 131 palmi (110 feet) wide and composed of 54 figures. Salomone actually began work on the Juno group. Her chariot was harnessed to peacocks and sustained by clouds and nymphs. The sculptor is also said to have made the figure of Deiopea, who was to occupy one of the Sicilian promontories, with the four cardinal winds at her feet. The Juno group would no doubt have continued the actions and gestures of Diana, Venus, and especially Ceres, just as the winds that were executed—the minor ones who lunge and fly from their palace—are recensions of the earlier nymphs or even, in their fierceness, of Actaeon's dogs. These winds, twenty-nine in number, are by all four sculptors involved: Salomone, Persico, Violani, and Angelo Brunelli.[43]

Four reliefs, all by Brunelli, are set above four of the openings. They represent Jupiter and the goddesses, the marriage of Thetis and Peleus (fig. 5.38), the judgment of Paris, and the marriage of Paris and Helen. The reliefs form a genealogy of divine quarrels and their matrimonial results. In the first scene, that is, Hera, Athena, and Poseidon threaten to bind Zeus in chains in return for his having flung Vulcan from Heaven. Fire has descended to earth. It is welcomed there by Thetis, who also frees Zeus from his chains. In the second relief

Thetis is unwillingly married to Peleus and takes him to live with her at the bottom of the sea. In further strife, between Juno, Athena, and Venus, Paris in the third relief judges their beauty and Venus, who wins, gives Helen to Paris as a reward. The fourth relief, the marriage between the latter two, brings on that Trojan war that ultimately dispatches Aeneas on his voyage, there to encounter Aeolus's mountain of water.

Thus does Venus stand within a horizontal sequence of events that crosses the main axis of the river-road at its climax, as she also stands within a vertical sequence when she falls in love with Adonis and brings about Ceres–Persephone's annual descent and resurrection. Vico discusses the four events depicted in these reliefs in some detail. He makes them, along with a final marriage between Aeneas and Lavinia not depicted by Brunelli, further stages in the transition from prehistory to history.[44]

Above the reliefs, on the balustrade, are freestanding sculptured slaves, many of them shackled in pairs like the slaves who actually erected the palace.[45] Some struggle under the weight of mighty shell-vases (fig. 5.41) and strain as they hoist great volumes of water, their sweated immobility rendering them unconscious of the modern graffiti that scar them. Similar figures line the two ramps leading down to the level of the pool. Twisted pairs of snakes, Hesperidean dragons perhaps, hold aloft other vases. In the center of this parapet, flanking the cascade, are statues of winged nymphs, boys with game, and so on symbolizing various water and field sports. Originally these vases all emptied into Ocean below. Certain of Vanvitelli's sketches (fig. 5.42) seem to be connected with these figures. As portrayals of practical workers, of constructors, they prepare for the immense size of this fountain and of the palace that is now coming nearer and add to the more historistic flavor of the sculpture as the visitor moves south.

The fountain of Juno and Aeolus would clearly have been the climax of the river-road. It would have brought Vanvitelli's fables out of their earlier mythical world, out of the more generalized topographies of the Diana and Venus stories, through the Sicily of Ceres, and on into a historic moment: Aeneas's voyage and arrival. As Ceres stood for Trinacria Aeneas stood for Magna Graecia, for that revived Magna Graecia that was the Kingdom of the Two Sicilies.

The unfinished state of the last of these great figural fountains bears testimony to the fact that by this stage money had begun to run out, and perhaps energy as well. The powerful, simple Dolphin Cascade, the next fountain on the river-road, dates from 1779 (figs. 5.43, 5.44). Here once more a huge volume of water gushes into an oblong pool, and a number of arching cascades issue from a hemicycle filled with rocks on which are two dolphins flanking the hell monster with a dolphin's head and body but great terrestrial arms and claws. The beast is like one of Sannazaro's "chimeras with blazing faces,/And hydras, dogs, terrifying harpies" that live in hell. In the fountain the teeth of the hell beasts are like massive saws. Their mouths vomit yards of lacy water; their eyes are swiveling globes.

5.41
Fountain of Juno and Aeolus, chained slave-pair on the parapet. Photo Ente Provinciale per il Turismo

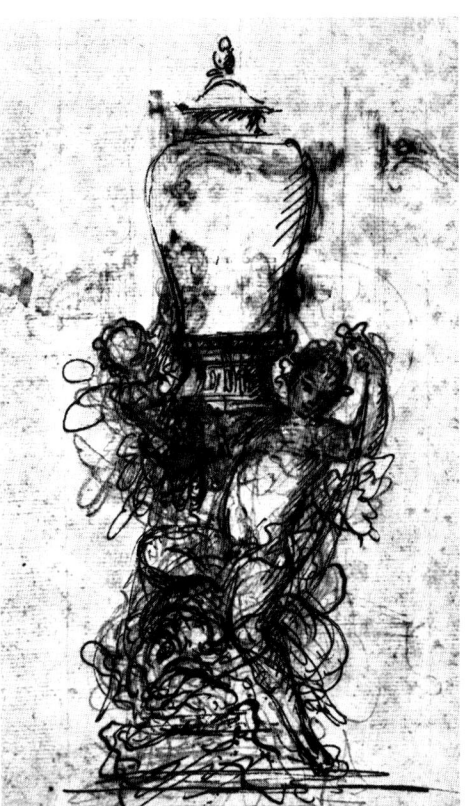

5.42
Vanvitelli. Sketch of balustrade figure. Caserta, Reggia

The River-Road

5.43
Caserta, Dolphin
Fountain. Photo
Alinari

But dolphins, even transformed with claws and tusks, are not simply hell beasts. They were set up in Roman times at the *metae*, or goals, of circuses. They were used to measure the number of turns taken by the runners in a race. Hence a dolphin fountain, here at one end of a long, looplike movement through time and space, represents its turning point. The Dolphin Fountain confirms that the cycle at Caserta, like that at Bagnaia, goes from the heavenly to the earthly to the infernal.

Hell prepares us for heaven or, rather, for the palace that contains both a hell and a heaven. The last of the great fountains was to have been that of Hercules in the lower vestibule, which will be described elsewhere. This was to have stood directly on the river-road's axis.

Caserta was built as a strategic evasion of sea incursions, as a way of countering or controlling Neptune's power to pollute by flooding. The river-road, the mighty aqueduct that makes the waters fly, is Vanvitelli's victory, his enslavement of Neptune's element, as the vast trident of rivers in the second garden scheme would have been a yet greater trophy of that victory. At the same time the enslaved Neptune triumphs in his own way within the garden. He emerges over earth and air and over the fires of hell and of Venus. He shelters Diana, quenches Venus, nourishes Ceres, and short-circuits Aeolus's attack on Aeneas. It is with Neptune, chief god of the Bourbons' maritime kingdom, that we reckon in the end.

5.44
Dolphin Fountain, detail of hell beast. Photo Ente Provinciale per il Turismo

6 Palace Geometry

Gioffredo's Project

Caserta was a geometric temple of government within which the visitor, whether ambassador, petitioner, or official of the kingdom, was to proceed through a geometric labyrinth to the ultimate goal: whichever secretary, officer, or member of the royal family, including the king himself, could be of help.[1] Along the way the visitor would encounter heroes, gods, and allegories. Both the geometric and the mythical aspects of the visit continue the themes of the river-road.

The first architect to design a project for the palace at Caserta was Mario Gioffredo (figs. 6.1–6.5). Gioffredo's designs date from 1750 or 1751.[2] Hence they were drawn up fifteen years or so before he published his treatise on architecture; yet each reveals a lot about the other. Gioffredo's project embodies precisely the notions of Ancient Near Eastern sublimity, of vast palaces configured into geometric logic by the orders, that he was to praise in his book.[3] From the perspective view in fig. 6.1, which contains human figures, the total length of the palace appears to have been about 760 feet (c. 900 Neapolitan palmi). So it was not the supercolossus some have said it was, though certainly its area would have been not quite one-third greater than that of Vanvitelli's present building, which is huge enough: 936 by 696 palmi (1111 by 819 feet). The difference in total area would be about 81,000 palmi as opposed to about 65,000.

Gioffredo's palace was to have been built around nine courts, each square like the perimeter of the whole and composed of uniform ranges flanked by exterior loggias. The central court

Gioffredo's Project

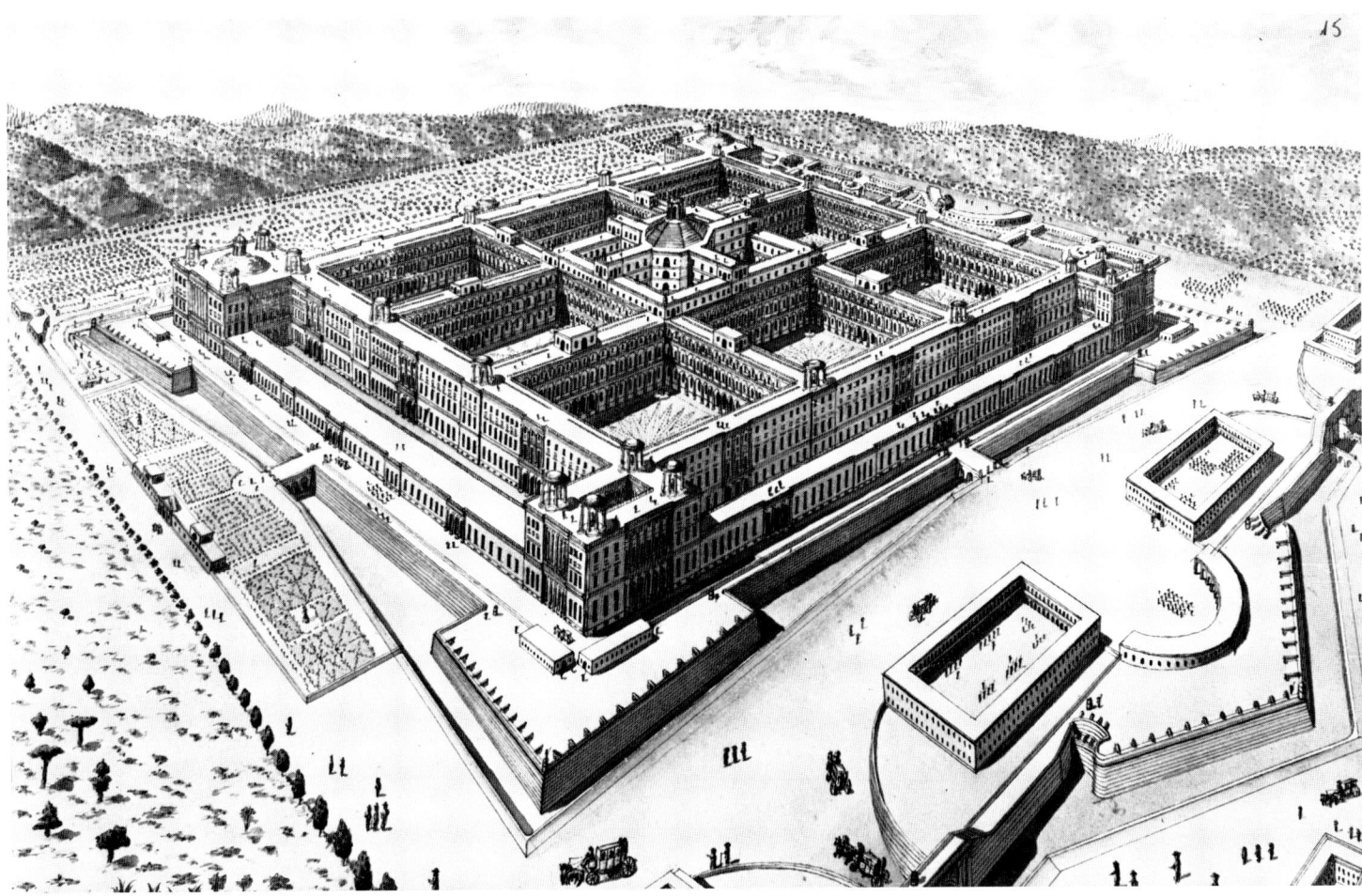

6.1
Mario Gioffredo.
Project for the royal
palace and town of
Caserta, perspective,
c. 1755. Naples,
Biblioteca Nazionale

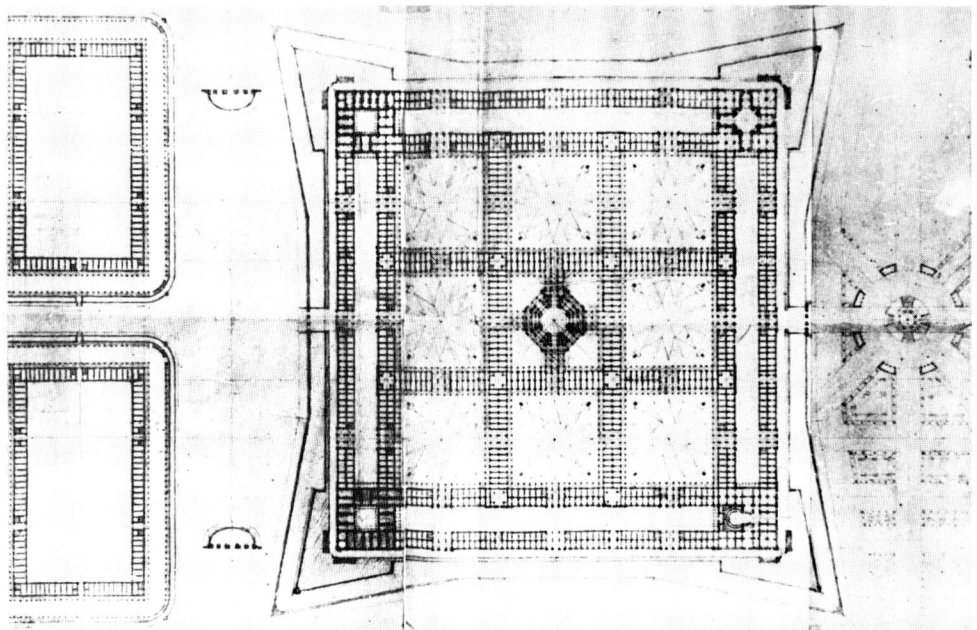

6.2
Gioffredo. Early site plan for Caserta. Naples, Biblioteca Nazionale

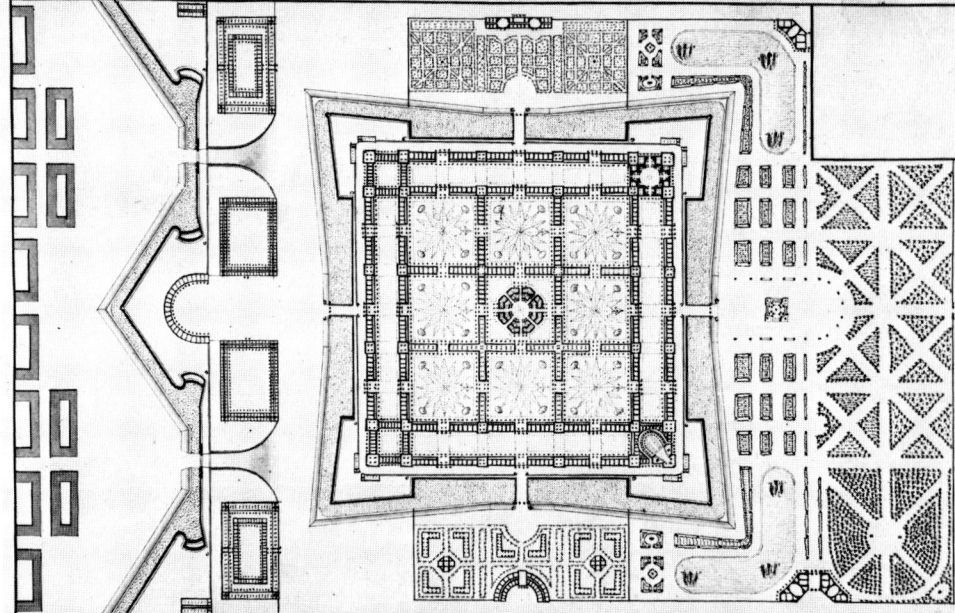

6.3
Gioffredo. Site plan for Caserta. Naples, Biblioteca Nazionale

6.4
Gioffredo. Plan of second and third floors of the palace of Caserta. Naples, Biblioteca Nazionale

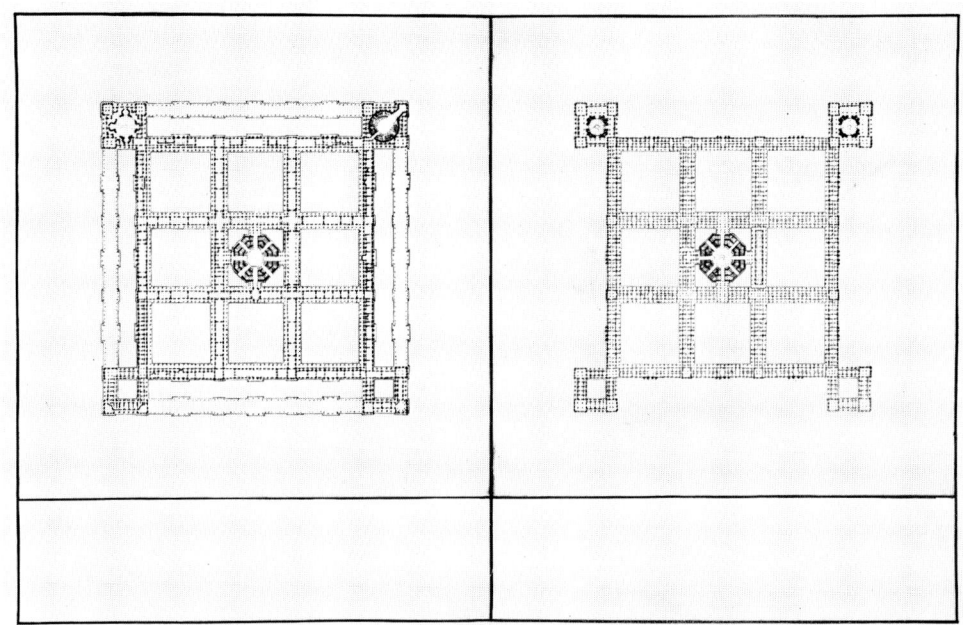

6.5
Gioffredo. Plan of upper floors of the palace of Caserta. Naples, Biblioteca Nazionale

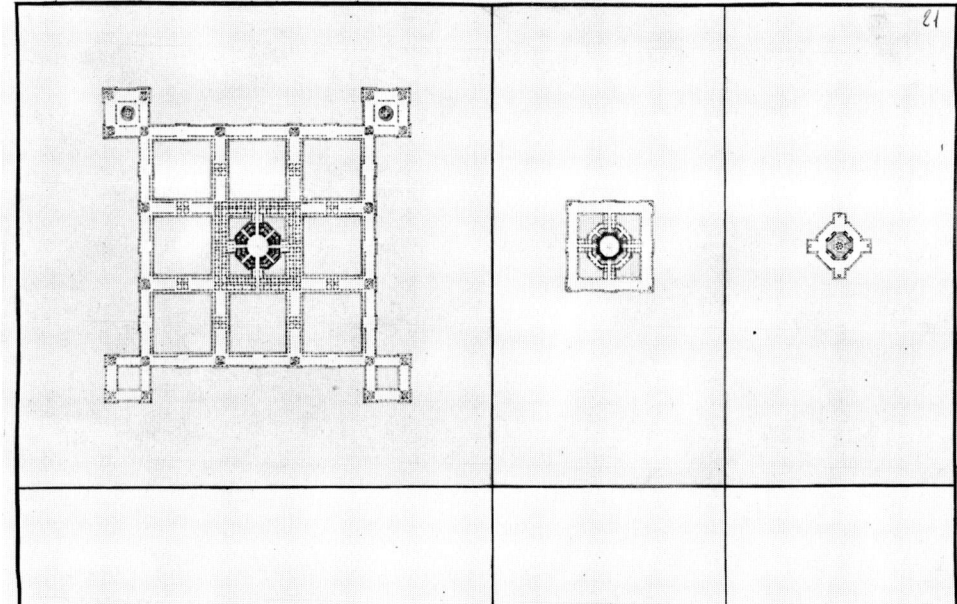

was to have been filled with a cruciform structure one story higher than the others, whose crossing was marked by a large octagonal staircase, possibly a double helix. The outer perimeter was marked by double ranges of buildings separated by immensely long, narrow courts crossing at each corner to form small, square pavilions. Two of the four pavilion towers thus created contained apartments, the other two a theater and a church. The former is set into a frame borrowed from the shape of the Neapolitan Renaissance villa of Poggioreale, with tetrastyle chambers (chambers with four columns in a square at the center) at the corners. The auditorium is a horseshoe of boxes inserted into a domed cylinder. Also to be housed in the palace, according to the program, were the royal family, the court, the upper bureaucracy of the kingdom, and, in the top floors of the octagon, a museum (perhaps including both the Farnese and Portici collections), a Parliament chamber, and a theological seminary (fig. 6.5). This "veritable Kremlin" as Venditti calls it,[4] in its nine-square plan, its scale, and immense corner bastions, evokes not only Gioffredo's Near Eastern prototypes but also specific attempts to reconstruct such buildings, such as Villalpando's essay on the Temple at Jerusalem (fig. 6.6).[5] Note particularly the little penthouses at each juncture of the wings, as well as the arcaded courts. Although Carlo did not erect Gioffredo's palace intended to house whole components of the machinery of state and culture, in keeping with his penchant for building, abandoning, and then building anew,

he did construct separate edifices to house most of the functions. Seven large royal residences were built (two of which, Capodimonte and Portici, contained museums) as well as a library addition to the Palazzo Reale and the Università degli Studi (a long series of remodelings initiated by Carlo, 1738–1818)—all of which echo Gioffredo's program.[6]

The perspective view of Gioffredo's scheme in the Biblioteca Nazionale gives an idea of the whole (fig. 6.1). The view is from the town side. The blocks of smaller buildings, barracks, erected to what is probably the south, provide an orientation and indicate that the architect intended not just a palace but a city as well, as Vanvitelli had. The bastions and moats are fairly low, probably not much higher than the familiar ones that surrounded the Castel Nuovo (fig. 4.9).[7] Not merely ornamental, these bastions are lined with cannon, thirteen to a side. Several of the outbuildings are shown and on the main front a central superbastion whose moat is completed by a wall with two arched entrances flanking it. Beyond there are three gardens at three different scales, and wooded hills (fig. 6.2).

Gioffredo's design proceeds from the concept of the One and spreads eventually into mathematical series. Indeed this plan, like the Canevari–Medrano plan of Capodimonte, is susceptible to full modular analysis. The site layout, for the part of the complex set within the bastioned square that forms the palace's setting, is an axial, regular grid with the octagon at its center (figs. 6.2, 6.3). All the openings in the grid are squares or multiples of squares. This is made clear when the concentric squares are drawn out and crisscrossed by extensions of the vectors formed by the entrances—the latter of a type most familiar in the Louvre *guichets* but also found at Capodimonte (fig. 3.22)— and by the Palladian tetrastyle pavilions located throughout the plan.

The result is what mathematicians call a "plaid graph" (fig. 6.7). Indeed the building is a mosaic of modules and micromodules. The outer circumference is formed by a hollow square made of 32 smaller rectangles, 8 to a side. The corners are squares, and the interior shapes are 6:5 rectangles of the same width as the corner squares. The 9 squares, set 3 by 3, within the frame, all have sides 2 times the length of the surrounding rectangles. The ranges of rooms in the inner courts that make up the ground floor are double squares, and throughout the rest of the building they are 6:5 rectangles. These then are the two different micromodules, marked *a* and *b* in figure 6.8, that measure out all rooms and establish the distribution of the inner and outer colonnades. The omnipresent column grid makes the plan into a plaid-grid hypostyle measuring 6 by 8 (for the ranges) = 48 + 9 × 4 (for the tetrastyles) = 36, or 84 columns per side, 84^2 in total—except that of course those columns are "removed" that would stand within some of the rooms, walls, or courts.

The smaller micromodules or *a*-types comprise several elements, such as the pavilions that are formed of 16 such *a*-micros. The *b*-micros are not integral components of the tetrastyles in the rest of the palace but are determined by the edges established

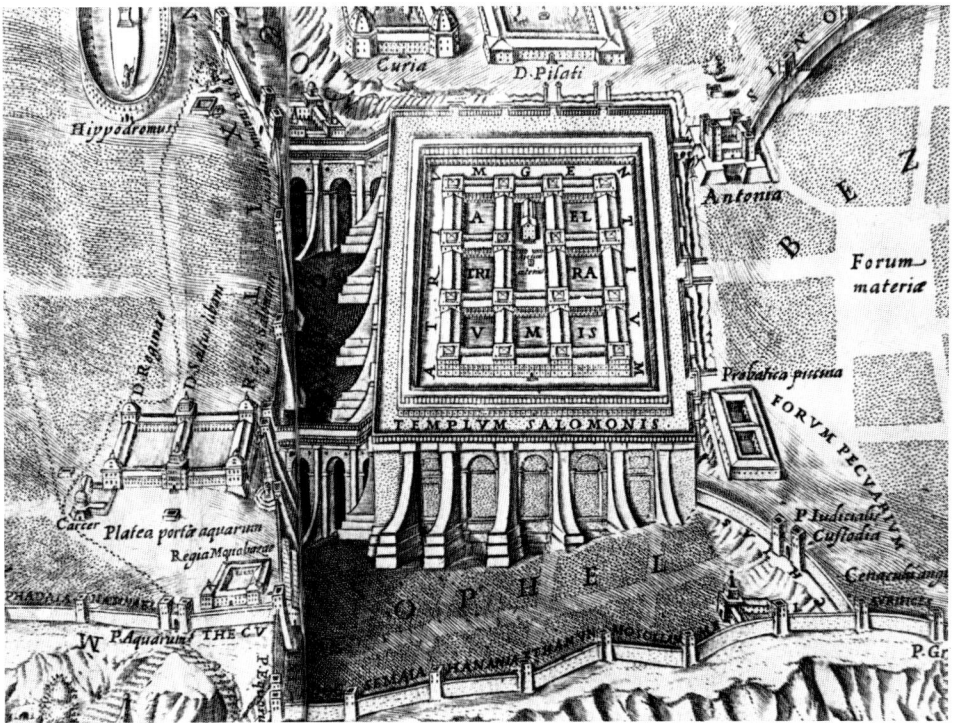

6.6
Juan Bautista Villalpando, reconstruction of Solomon's temple. From Villalpando, *In Ezechielem explanationes* (1596–1604)

6.7
A plaid graph generated by the coordinates or edges of the plan in figure 6.3

by the corner squares. All the gates are 3 intercolumniations wide (3 times the width of 1 *b*-micro). There are two types of tetrastyle. The only geometrical dissonance in the scheme is that the colonnades established by the corner blocks are set closer than those in the rest of the building. This is particularly noticeable in the long bays in the center of each side, whose ends consist of 6-column colonnades with shafts more closely set than those along the long sides. (Incidentally, these immense 52-column colonnades are early instances of a Boullée-like, or Durand-like, Neoclassicism; see figs. 1.6, 6.2) Though Gioffredo's columns are inaccurately marked, his scheme consists of a hypostyle sweep of inner and outer columns, as figure 6.8 makes clear.

The plan is more intricate and thorough than that of Capodimonte (fig. 3.25). But there is no indication in Gioffredo's drawings of the purposes of these rooms. It all remains as mysterious as the layout of a Cretan palace. Nonetheless Vitruvius's well-known principle of the subtractive layout, beginning with a hypostyle grid and then theoretically "removing" columns to form inner spaces, seems to have been followed.

Two of the four corner pavilions—those exceptions with double-square rooms, seven to a range—frame plain open courts. The other two, as noted, have a cruciform church (on the upper left) and a theater (on the upper right) plugged into them, a dense contraction of the tetrastyle principle in the case of the church, whose central rotunda has the same diameter as the rotunda of the staircase. Off the church's central cylinder, which was to have been topped by a dome, are four subcylinders located at 12, 3, 6, and 9 o'clock. These are one-quarter the size of the main cylinder and are articulated by tetrastyles. The corners are filled with tetrastyle cubic sacristies (fig. 6.3). The basic scheme goes back through Juvarra to Leonardo. Less idiomatically the theater's horseshoe has a box tier one row deep, with the stage projecting back to the outer corner of the building. Only these three elements—church, stair, and theater—soften Gioffredo's essay in *architectura recta*.

To telescope somewhat the procedure used in chapter 3, I will reduce Gioffredo's grid thus (since the dimensions are unknown the Scamozzi/Caramuel system cannot be used):

Facade of Gioffredo's Project

5	4	3	2	1	2	3	4	5
T	R	T	R	E	R	T	R	E	R	T	R	E	R	T	R	T
3	7	3	6	3	6	3	6	3	6	3	6	3	6	3	7	3
	1		1		1		1		1		1		1		1	
.5		2		1		2		.5
a-type				b-type				a-type

The upper row of figures enumerates the projecting pavilions in mirror symmetry. In the next row, T = closed tetrastyle, R = range, and E = entrance gate. In the third row come the micromodules, both the a and the b types. In the fourth row are the modules proper, and then in the fifth are the macros. The latter reduce everything to $(.5)(1,1,1,)(.5)$, which equals 4, three central complete macromodules flanked by half-macros. There are totals of 4 macros, 8 modules, and 77 a or b micros on each side of the palace. All four sides are the same. The whole structure hence reduces to 1.

Let us move beyond this level, which is based on Gioffredo's rather small drawings, to the mathematical necessities underlying the arrangement. If we redraw the outer bays of figure 6.8 at larger scale (fig. 6.9), we find that Gioffredo must have wanted to overlay each gate and type 2 tetrastyle with a-micros, such that $4a = 3b$. At the same time the sides of the type 1 tetrastyles are not integrally measurable in a-modules but nonetheless equal $3a$. How can this be? Figure 6.9 shows us: the two systems overlap. In the type 1 tetrastyles the walls obey the rhythm of the a-modules, the columns that of the b-modules. In the type 2 tetrastyles and in the gates, that situation is reversed. Thus Gioffredo defeats or avoids the famous "thickness problem."[8]

The bastions and moat, the garden parterres flanking the sides, and the barrack buildings and bastions to the south are all set along the edges or coordinates established by the palace grid, though in a configuration much less dense than the palace's. The garden pavilions make use of the same geometric constructs and the same scales as does the palace itself, for example in the configuration of central octagon and surrounding ranges vis-à-vis the upper and lower quincunx-parterres on the right-hand side (fig. 6.3). The small square in the center of

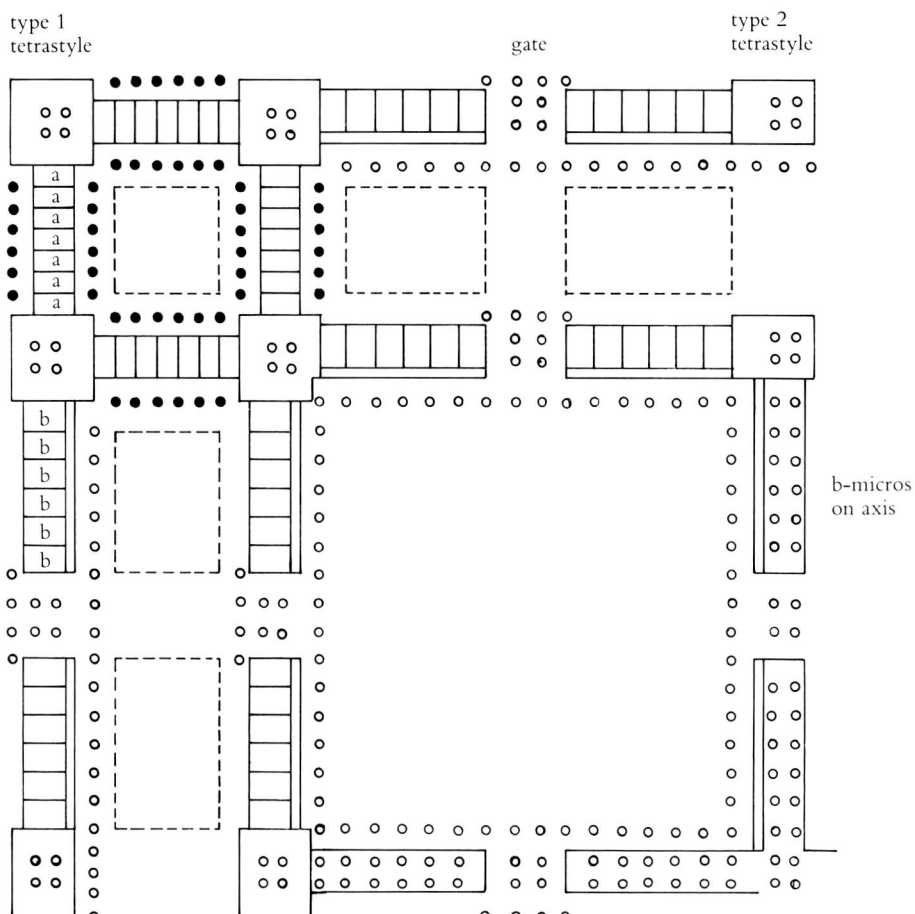

- ● closely spaced, a-micromodule columns
- ○ widely spaced, b-micromodule columns

6.8
The upper left-hand corner of Gioffredo's ground-floor plan

6.9
Redrawn detail from fig. 6.8 showing the outer row of pavilions and ranges and the interpenetrations, within them, of *a*-modules and *b*-modules

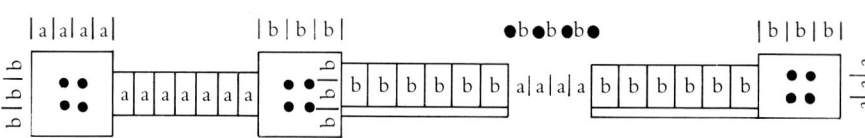

each quincunx has the same width as the central octagonal void of the main stair and as the smaller courts. Each main court is three times this distance; it is also the same as the width of the little temple in the center of the hemicycle in the north garden.

All this relates to the building's geometry. In terms of distribution the plan of Caserta can be analyzed briefly as shown in the table:

Distributions of Gioffredo's Project

Feature	Number	Location	Stories
Octagon	1	Center	6
Central court	1	Center	4
Octagon transepts	4	Center	5
Towers	4	Corners	3
Outer fronts	4	Margins	3
Exterior courts	8	Margins	3
Tetrastyles	12	Inner axes	2
Gates	12	Outer axes	2
Porticoes	16	Corners	2
Cupolas	26	Towers	1

This breakdown shows a relation between the frequency of a given feature and its distance from the center. Thus the closer a feature is to the octagon, the One, the rarer it is, and also the greater its height. These relations can be stated in simple numerical series. The series are not perfect (there are more stories to the transepts than to the surrounding central court, while there are four of these transepts and only one such court). But the trend is unmistakable.

Gioffredo's source, aside from the Villalpando possibility, is easy to trace. The basic layout is a 9-square extension of Capodimonte (figs. 3.25–3.27, 6.10). This can be shown by declaring the areas marked A in figure 6.10 to be equivalent to Gioffredo's corner a-micro courts, while the rooms marked B are tetrastyles and those marked C the entrances. The projecting bays marked D suggest the long narrow courts that frame Gioffredo's plan. Remembering that Gioffredo had been Medrano's apprentice, it is probable that the mathematical principles apparent in both plans are derived from military engineering.[9]

Let us now look at the vertical organization of Gioffredo's palace. A pencil plan of the ground floor in the Biblioteca Nazionale shows each range filled with uniform rooms, the range itself being two rooms deep. The final ink plan of this same floor makes the ranges only one room deep (figs. 6.2, 6.3). Whatever their size, these ground-floor chambers were probably intended for stables, storage, guards, and the like.

In the next two floors terraces appear between the corner towers. The lesser wings cease to rise. Only the inner, greater parts of the palace continue upward (figs. 6.4, 6.5). The church, theater, and two apartments also rise upward in their respective corners. The distribution within the ranges becomes more diverse, with large halls along the arms of the inner Greek cross of the building and smaller suites elsewhere. In the third floor the beehive articulation returns. But the interstices are smaller,

Palace Geometry

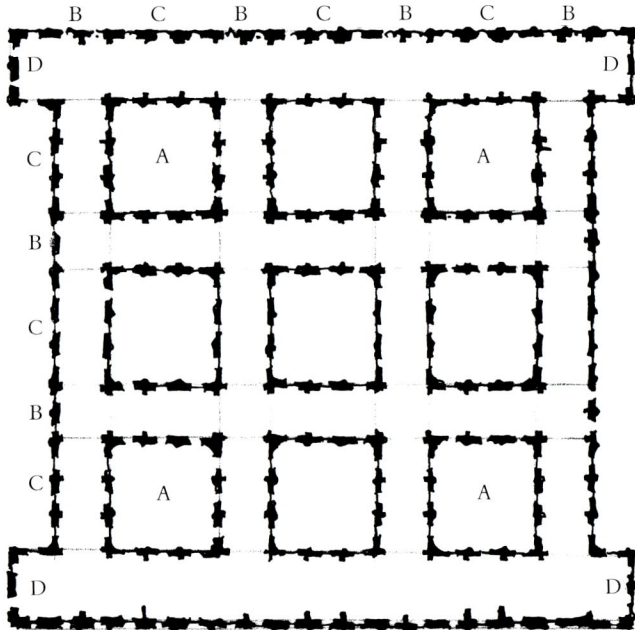

6.10
Plan of Capodimonte redrawn as a nine-court palace

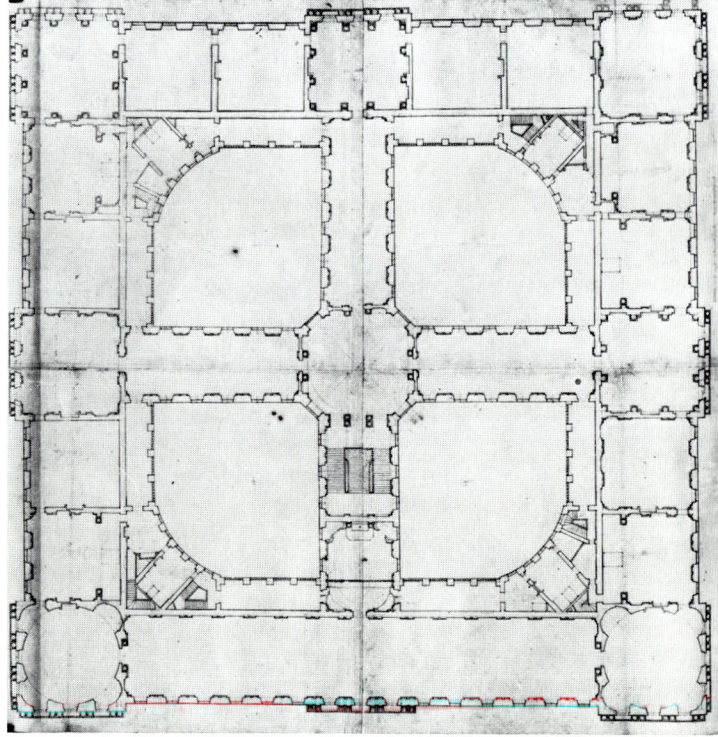

6.11
Buen Retiro at the beginning of the eighteenth century. Paris, Bibliothèque Nationale

three rooms deep. Corridors down the centers of the ranges and external arcades provide circulation. These are probably living quarters for servants and lesser courtiers.

This ascent, like the plan itself, is an essay in subtractive geometry. On the fourth floor only the central elements continue. The roof plan is marked out at the junctures of the coordinates by the round temples mentioned, so that all these outer, lesser components of the palace end in temples. There are twenty-four, each dedicated to one of the patron saints of Naples. Fountains and an astronomical observatory are situated at the top of the dome.[10] In the centers of the ranges leading outward from the middle court are small penthouse stair heads composed of four square units each. The central court meanwhile continues to rise, now divided into many small rooms. The octagon continues too. In the remaining two plans, finally, all surrounding elements are lopped off except the octagon, the One, which rises on alone into a step-pyramid roof.

Not only are the geometrical order of this plan and its two- and three-dimensional hierarchy related to Capodimonte, but so is the architectural style (figs. 3.22, 3.23, 6.1). Both are possessed of the same austere near-Neoclassicism, the same close-set giant pilasters (probably in both cases of gray piperno), the same tall, windowed rustic basement and parapet. There is also the same Louvre-like grouping of arch entrances in threes, which Vanvitelli would studiously avoid and talk about avoiding at Caserta.[11] And there are the same square mezzanine panels, the same slight jogs to mark conjunctions, and the same flat protrusions for axial entrances. On the other hand the square overall shape, the surrounding margin of ranges punctuated at the corners by projecting square pavilions, and the Greek cross of ranges forming the central element with a massive stair-and-octagon complex, all seem to have come from Buen Retiro (fig. 6.11). This shows the palace before de Cotte began to propose remodelings. De Cotte's projects for the Spanish crown were studied in Naples; indeed Vanvitelli's early plan for Caserta palace, like his plan for the garden, seems directly derived from the French architect's Spanish work (fig. 6.12). Carlo di Borbone would have known of this plan, for he was living in Spain when his father commissioned it.[12]

Gioffredo, then, has succeeded in creating a fully absolutist palace scheme that is also fully geometric. He has reinscribed Capodimonte at the scale of Versailles or the Louvre. His project caps the climax of the tradition we examined in chapter 3. As a study of masses his palace is almost comparable to Khorsabad, Persepolis, even Jerusalem, as these complexes lived in the eighteenth century's dream of the Sublime. Yet, to paraphrase Gioffredo himself, the palace is also Greco-Roman: "ordered" and rationalized. It might even be said that it is explained, harmonized, and surveyed by the orders, by its hypostyle armature. The porticoes do not merely provide entrances, they establish the building's rhythms and dictate its mode of composition. They code the geometry into its components, which in turn resolve into the binary number system that leads down to 1.

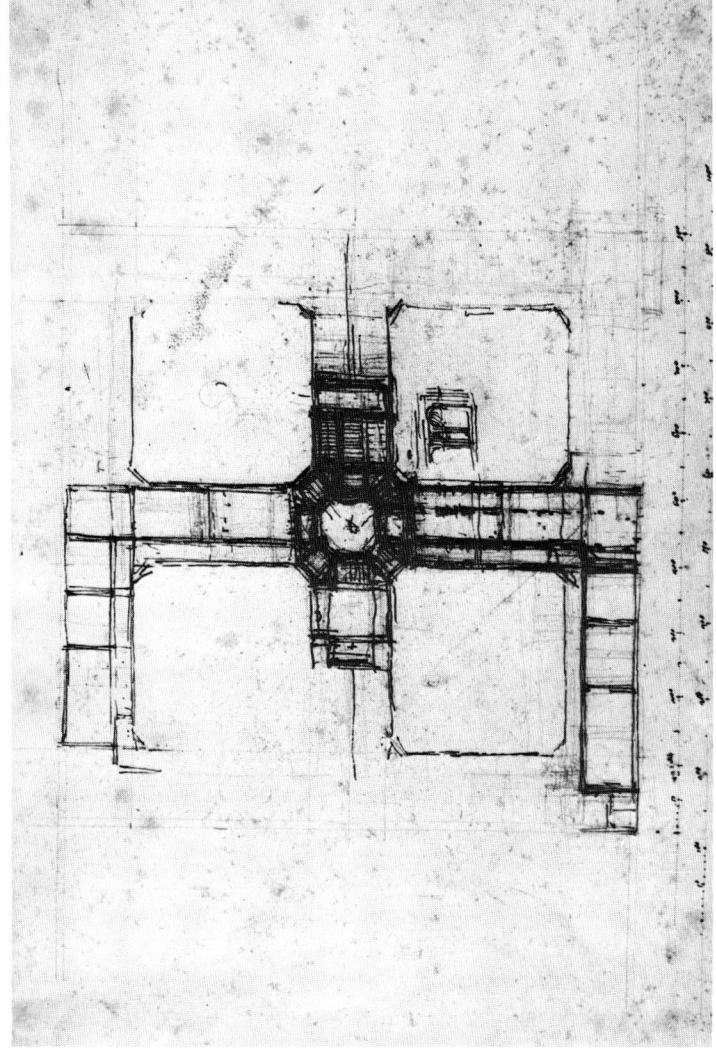

6.12
Vanvitelli. Early plan for the royal palace at Caserta. Caserta, Règgia

Vanvitelli's "Ideal Royal Palace"

In 1750, while he was still in Rome, Vanvitelli wrote out an unillustrated program entitled "Idea of the Plan of a Royal Residence for Monarchs."[13] It may have been composed when he was still unaware of Gioffredo's scheme. And yet it can be read as a comment on that scheme and as an axial splitting-up, with triumphal spaces, of Gioffredo's relentless grid.

Vanvitelli writes: "Firstly, the entrance system (*entrata*) of the royal palace must be magnificent, the stairs ample, grandiose, well lighted, and unimpeded by any inconvenience." This says that Gioffredo's scheme lacks a dramatic entrance. Another departure from Gioffredo occurs when Vanvitelli describes the entrance complex of his ideal palace as if it were a classical temple, which it is, of course, in his finished building. He thus reinforces the separation of circulation space from the palace proper. The entrance temple is to be Ionic, higher than the rest of the palace, and with 5-diameter intercolumniations. There are two minor entrances, one on either side of the main opening. Each entrance leads to a courtyard. The courtyards are correspondingly major or minor, matching their respective entrances in the main front. In short Vanvitelli is calling for a central large court flanked by smaller courts or perhaps by pairs of courts. He thus has in mind a scheme quite unlike Gioffredo's and also unlike Caserta as built, for, in both of these, all courts are exactly equal.[14]

From this central trunk two parterres or raised courtyards are to be erected, one for the king's apartments and the other for the royal heirs. Each is approached by a magnificent stair symmetrically situated in a courtyard. One stair is for the king and queen, the other for the crown prince and princess and for visiting princes. This aspect of the scheme differs sharply from what Gioffredo had planned. Gioffredo's palace had consisted of one single great stair and hives of small geometrical chambers. Vanvitelli's scheme even in this preliminary form divides the building via multiple staircases into zones for the royal family's older and younger generations. In his final version of the plan Vanvitelli would unite his zone divisions with Gioffredo's conception of the great single stair.

A similar sense of a sequential hierarchy fills Vanvitelli's descriptions of the rooms in the Biblioteca Nazionale manuscript. The king's official apartment consists of a series of vestibules and waiting rooms, each accommodating a different type of guardian military personnel: the sergeant of the guard, 100 halberdiers in two "wings," 200 royal guards also in two wings; "two rooms with anterooms, and one [other] for the brigadier of the guard"; so the ideal palace's royal parterre is a sort of architectural dress parade.[15]

The same goes for the "civilian" sequences described in his text. Specific chambers and antechambers are designated for people with titles, people without titles, officials of the kingdom, gentlemen of the king's chamber, ambassadors, and secretaries of the state. In some instances men and women are segregated (for example the women, but not the men, had secret access to the confessionals). Networks of servants' corridors, often like the main corridors restricted by class and sex, bind the whole composition together.[16] There are a grand gallery for the *baciamano* and dressing rooms and bedrooms for ceremonial levées. There is a domestic chapel with its private stair, and so on down to the minutest details. The same arrangements, mutatis mutandis, are provided for the queen, for the crown prince, and for other members of the court. In the center of the whole, as in Gioffredo's scheme, was to be the One, a public chapel with a tribune for the royal family and other tribunes for servants and retainers.

Above all, and unlike Gioffredo's scheme, Vanvitelli's ideal palace and the real, rather different one that was built were buildings for royal ceremonies and audiences. The ladies and gentlemen in waiting literally did wait, in waiting rooms, segregated by status, to be called on for whatever it was they provided, from conversation to chocolate to the *chaise percée*, or to present a petition, a complaint about a pension, or to suggest a candidate for office. And not only the ladies and gentlemen but the rooms themselves wait in line. They comprise flights of anterooms, evaluated by their numerical and topological distance from that royal One, who circulates, resides, and presides in the Throne Room, or in the bedroom, or at the *baciamano*, and who is the fountainhead from whom all change, all recognition, all success, proceed.[17]

The Definitive Design

Now let us turn to Vanvitelli's published plans (figs. 6.13–6.15).[18] These were in essentials carried out as presented in the *Dichiarazione*, except for the central dome and four corner towers. The engravings illustrate the principles of sequence and subdivision used by Vanvitelli to describe the ideal palace, but they do so with a geometry less rigorous than Gioffredo's.

Vanvitelli's plans can nonetheless be reduced to number by the binary process. Indeed he has really only reinscribed Gioffredo's scheme within the narrower bounds Gioffredo's biographer said Carlo wanted. Recall that Gioffredo's palace appears to have been designed on a square approximately 900 palmi in width. Vanvitelli's palace occupies a rectangle 936 by 696 palmi—a reduction of about 25 percent. In other words he has shrunk Gioffredo's square to a 4:3 rectangle by the process outlined in the three sections of figure 6.16. The ranges within that rectangle are 96 palmi wide. The whole can be mapped, without significant distortion, onto a grid as in figure 6.17, where the exact measurements, taken from Vanvitelli's published plan, show that the horizontal ranges equal 306 palmi in length, or about 3.5 times the width of the porticoes, which is 88 palmi. At the same time the 206-palmo vertical ranges equal 2.33 times 88. The inner courts, as noted, are about 200 by 300 palmi. The whole outer 4:3 rectangle is subdivided by uniform ranges into four equal courts. The grid comprises 67 by 52 micros (fig. 6.17), each equaling 14 palmi. Other such mappings are no doubt possible, and we probably will never know which one Vanvitelli actually used. But whatever his actual micro, the principles illustrated here would have prevailed.

Let us turn to the facades. The windows, regularly set in vertical rows, and often between pilasters, extend the vectors established by the pilaster and column systems on the building (figs. 6.18, 6.19).[19] These bays dictate the modular apparatus of the exteriors. They consist, as in Gioffredo's plan, of cubic projecting pavilions marking the junctions of the ranges at the corners, the centers, and the crossings of the palace. However, Vanvitelli has eliminated the crisscross of axial entrances Gioffredo had installed throughout.

Not only is Vanvitelli's Caserta a telescoping of Gioffredo's Capodimonte-derived courts into four related rectangles, it borrows these ideas in consonance with contributions from Buen Retiro. Vanvitelli's facades reflect two of de Cotte's projected elevations for Buen Retiro (figs. 6.20, 6.21), a fact made all the clearer if Vanvitelli's unbuilt towers and drum are removed from the plan as in figure 6.22. In this sense Vanvitelli simply regularized de Cotte's more baroque temple front and set the lateral pavilions one bay in from the ends of the facade. De Cotte's section (fig. 6.23) shows that the handling of the octagon and stair hall in his plan were very similar to what Vanvitelli was to do (fig. 6.24), though the French architect has an open two-story atrium while Vanvitelli's atrium consists of four separated stories. Nor should we forget that behind these more recent schemes there is the same sequence of tower, range, dome, and temple that existed at the Escorial (fig. 3.9). On the

6.13
Vanvitelli. Plan of the ground floor of the palace at Caserta, 1756. From the *Dichiarazione*

6.14
Vanvitelli. Plan of the main floor, or *piano reale*, of the palace at Caserta

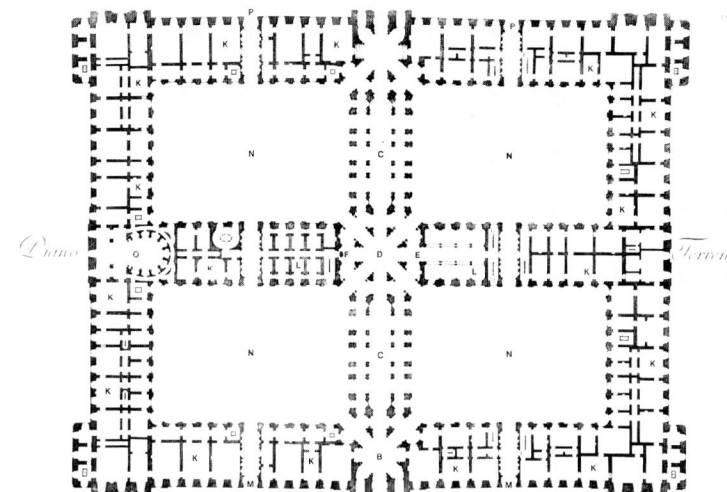

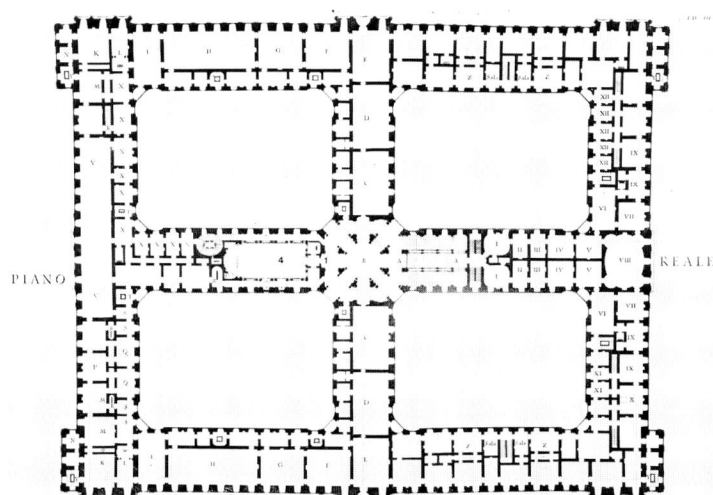

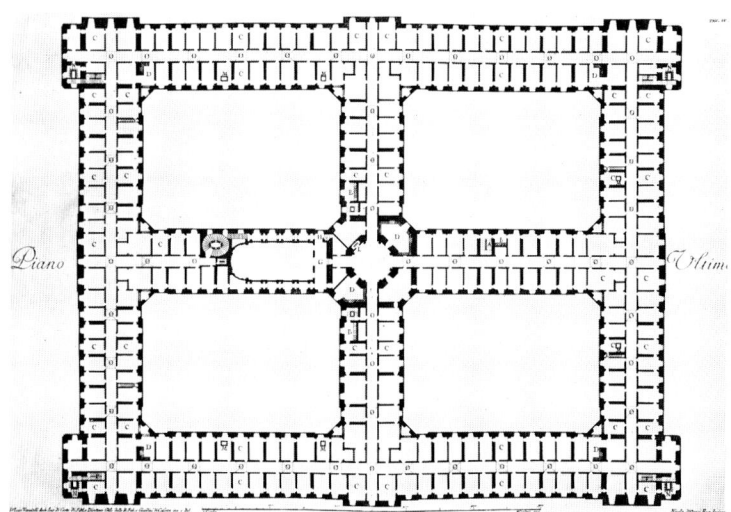

6.15
Vanvitelli. Plan of upper floor of the palace at Caserta

Palace Geometry

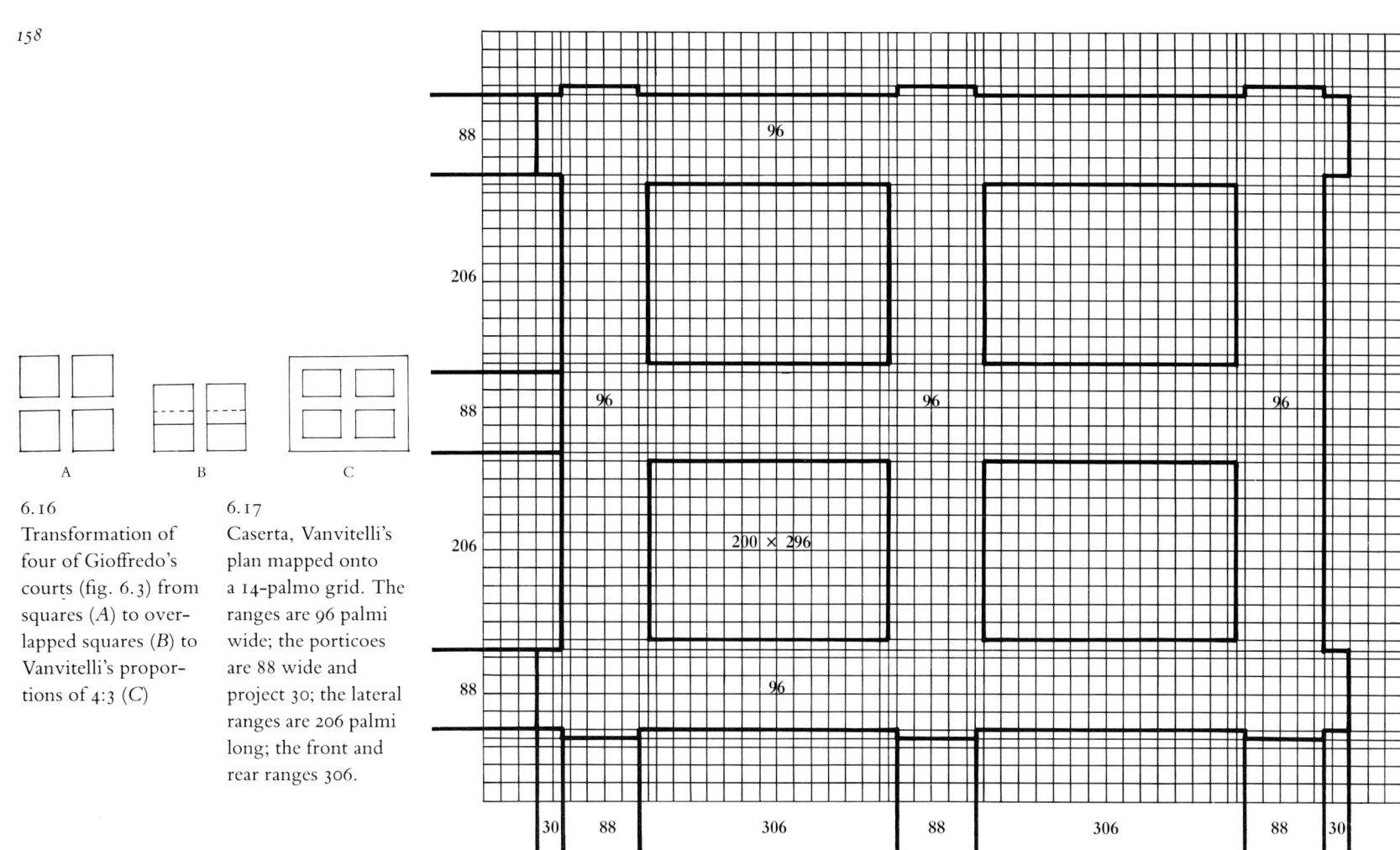

6.16
Transformation of four of Gioffredo's courts (fig. 6.3) from squares (A) to overlapped squares (B) to Vanvitelli's proportions of 4:3 (C)

6.17
Caserta, Vanvitelli's plan mapped onto a 14-palmo grid. The ranges are 96 palmi wide; the porticoes are 88 wide and project 30; the lateral ranges are 206 palmi long; the front and rear ranges 306.

6.18
Vanvitelli. Garden facade of the palace at Caserta, 1756, from the *Dichiarazione*

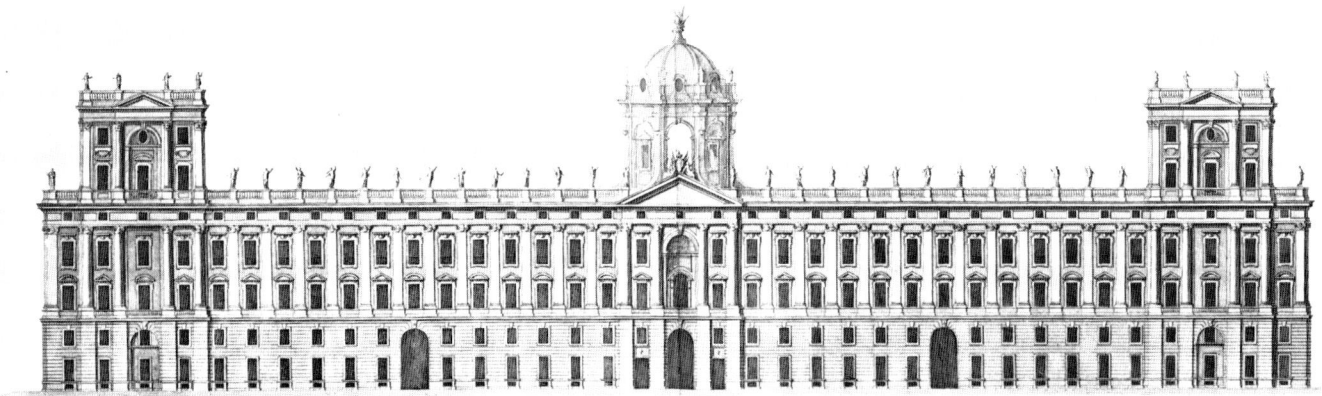

6.19
Vanvitelli. Town facade of the palace at Caserta, 1756. From the *Dichiarazione*

Palace Geometry

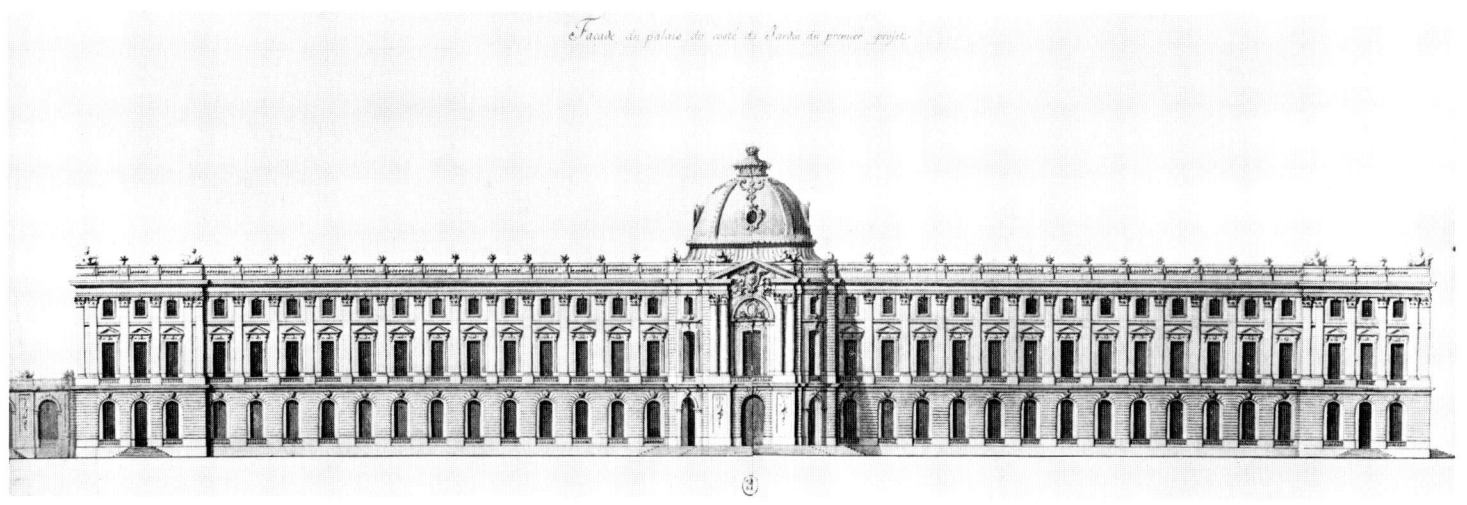

6.20
Robert de Cotte. Garden facade of first project for Buen Retiro, 1712–1714. Paris, Bibliothèque Nationale

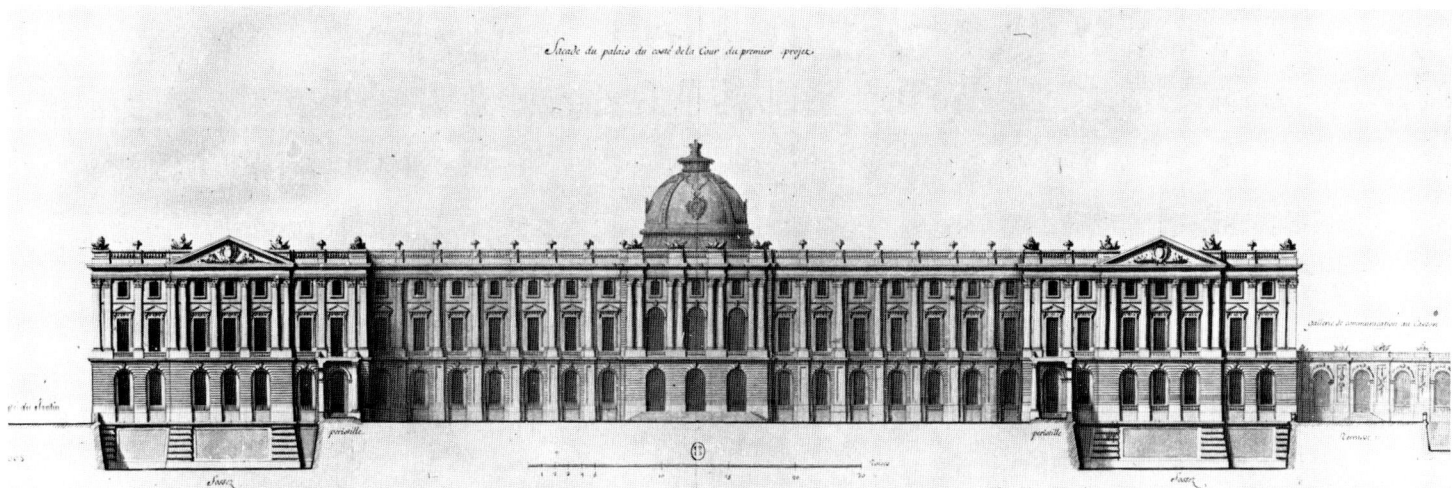

6.21
Robert de Cotte. Buen Retiro, court facade. Paris, Bibliothèque Nationale

The Definitive Design

6.22
Figure 6.19 with drum and towers removed

6.23
Robert de Cotte. Section of an alternative project for Buen Retiro. Paris, Bibliothèque Nationale

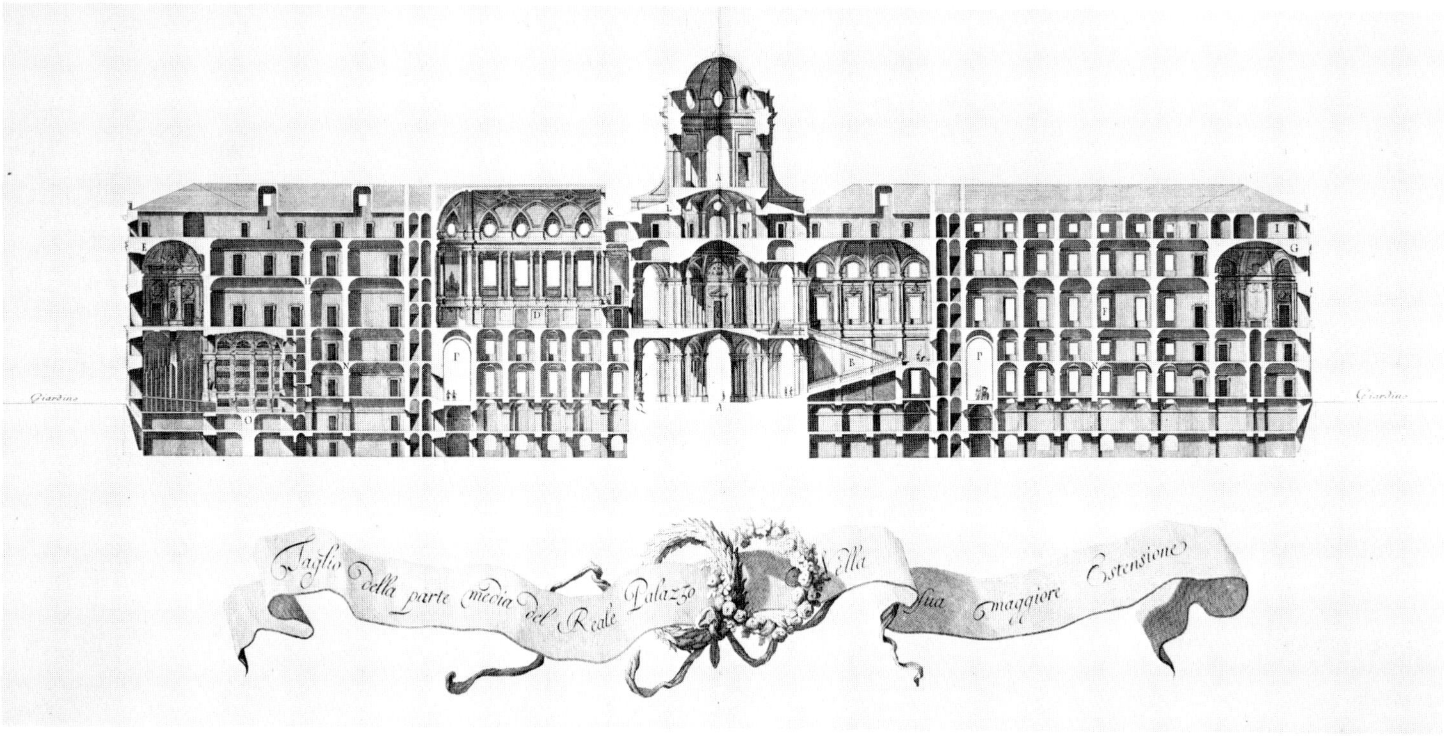

6.24
Vanvitelli. Section through the palace at Caserta, showing the stair hall in horizontal section. From the *Dichiarazione*

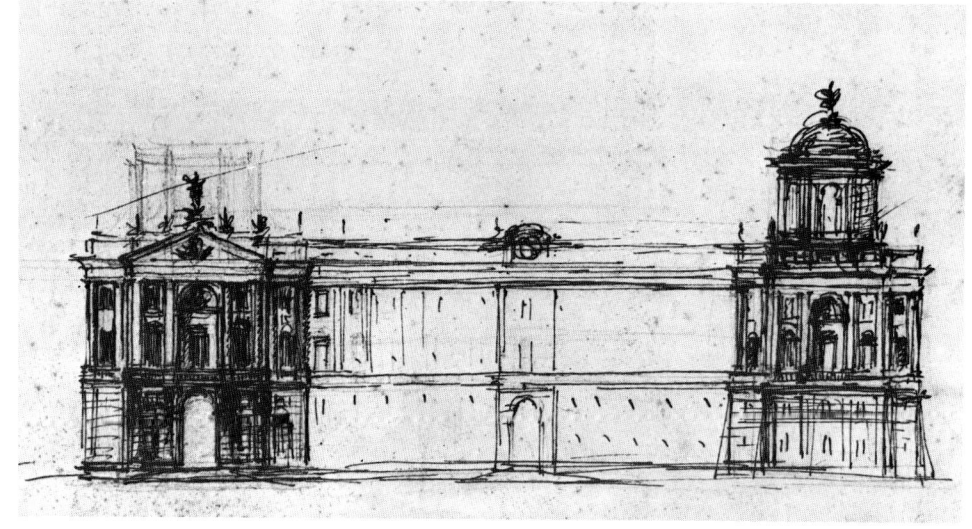

6.25
Vanvitelli. Study for Caserta facade. Caserta, Reggia

other hand the idea of stretching out the octagonal vestibule, stair, and chapel all along the northern interior stem is, in Vanvitelli, transposed to the central part of the east–west stem, which contains the sequence chapel/vestibule/stair. Thus seen, the French component in the design of Caserta is sharpened and increased. But, since the French architect de Cotte was working on Spanish projects, we also see the project's Spanish-Bourbon side more completely.

One more link between Gioffredo and Vanvitelli may be mentioned: Vanvitelli's towers and dome reflect, in a solider, nobler fashion, Gioffredo's little pepperpot cupolas (fig. 6.1). Indeed one of Vanvitelli's preliminary drawings has a particularly Gioffredesque cupola (fig. 6.25). And, just to make the interlinkings even more complicated, Vanvitelli's "Buen Retiro" plan, so to call it (fig. 6.12), has an octagonal complex almost exactly like Gioffredo's. The overlappings in the two architects' styles and careers are particularly intense at Caserta.

Let us reduce Vanvitelli's bay system. First of all, counting the bays uniformly, we get the following subdivisions (see figs. 6.18, 6.19):

Portico Arch Arch-Portico Arch Portico
1   4   5 2 5   4   5 2 5   4   1
    3   3 3   1   3 3   3
    1   2 1   1 2   1

In this array the top row of numbers lists the distribution of pilaster groups separating bays, where the second and third rows give the differences between these groups and the bottom row counts the magnitudes of these "differences" in each subdivision of the bay. Not only does Vanvitelli's series reduce to 1 in the center (at the point of the arch-portico), it is also a numerical palindrome. In this it is like the remodeled facade of the Palazzo Reale and Gioffredo's project for Caserta. But another sort of reduction explains a relative novelty in this facade: there are three porticoes and three arches, but only in the center, only in that "One" situation where a portico stands directly over an arch, do temple and triumphal motif coincide. The scheme is based on reflected symmetry.

Meanwhile the side facades are:

4 8 4 8 4
 4 4 4 4

These facades are without entrances. Note that there is a total of 38 bays across the front and 28 down the sides, and that 38:28 is just about 4:3; so Vanvitelli's bay division echoes the geometry of the plan. Put differently, the 67 by 52 grid in figure 6.17 may be considered as mapping out a potential hypostyle, since it corresponds to the main internal and external subdivisions of the building, with intercolumniations of 14 palmi. The total count of hypostyle "columns" is 68 by 53 = 3604, a figure unrelated to the values for length and depth in palmi. Caramuel Lobkowitz's formula therefore cannot be applied as he used it for the Temple of Diana. But Caramuel was not simply interested in the relationships between column distribution and area.

Palace Geometry

He also evolved a geometric series out of his hypostyle. And Vanvitelli's facade contains just such a series, one that is in fact more elegant than Caramuel's:

$$1[+3] = 4 \times 3[=12][\div 3] = 4[\times 3] = 12[\div 3] = 4[-3] = 1.$$

This is neater and more significant than Caramuel's; neater because it is done by using the number 3 in each of its arithmetical operations and more significant because the series begins and ends with 1.

The side elevations are simpler variants of this idea:

$$4[+4] = 8[-4] = 4[+4] = 8[-4] = 4.$$

The 4s and the 8s can be reduced to 1s and 0s, thus achieving binary access to the One.

Finally, on the question of bay dimensions a number of inconsistent measurements have been published for Caserta, some based on Vanvitelli's preliminary drawings. I have used those printed in the *Dichiarazione*. Looking at Vanvitelli's facade elevations and measuring the chief magnitudes, shows the facade to be divided into six types of bay:

1. Having 14-palmo pilasters
2. Having 7-palmo windows
3. Having 21-palmo pilasters

These correspond to the 14-palmo module extrapolated in figure 6.17. They create all areas except those forming entrance features. And the entrances are composed of the following types of bay:

4. With 10-palmo piers with pilasters or columns
5. With 10-palmo arches
6. With 20-palmo arches.

All this may be arrayed as follows: Let a = a half-micro of the 14-palmo type and b = the 10-palmo type. There are 75 bays made up of these modules. The scheme can be condensed as follows:

Left wing:

$(2a + a)$ (Group A)
$[(2a + a)(3a + a)][2a]$ (Group B)
$[(a + 2a)][a]$ (Group C)
$[(b^2 2b^5 b)]$ (Group D)
(Group C)

Central section (Group E):
$|3|b|2b|3|b|$

Right wing (a mirroring of the left),

where A = the jogs at the exterior corners, B = the temple fronts without entrances, C = the main wings separated by D, the lateral entrances, and E = the central section. The superscripts represent repetitions of the modular clusters in the parentheses. Reduced to a series of bay groups it comes out to

2/7/11/3/11/7/11/3/11/7/2

and to the following dimensions in palmi:

21/91(7 × 13)/112 (7 × 16)/40/112/80/112/40/112/91/112/21.

So within the micro system of 7 and its multiples established for the plan, there is a 10 system as well, one that is used compatibly with it, in Gioffredo's manner, and that exists throughout but appears only in the center of the facade. It is composed of 7 elements but adds up to 80 [10 × 8]. Thus does the number system perform the same tasks performed by the array of temples and triumphal arches mentioned earlier: it is woven separately throughout the whole and then coincides at one central point and one only.

So much for Caserta's geometric structure. As to function, more is known about Vanvitelli's ideas than about Gioffredo's, since Vanvitelli in the *Dichiarazione* explains the purposes of the planned rooms and spaces (figs. 6.13–6.15). After entering on the ground floor at *A*, the *porta reale* (fig. 6.13), the visitor traverses the first vestibule, *B*, with its monolithic marble shafts of *bigia siciliana*, and then chooses between going directly ahead into the triumphal corridor, *C*, or turning left or right, diagonally, into one of the two front courtyards, *N*. At point *D* is the principal vestibule, where a similar choice awaits: directly north into the gardens, northeast into the right-hand rear court; east to the royal stair, southeast back into the right-hand front court; southwest to its mate; or northwest to the left-hand rear court. The visitor cannot go directly west, for that arch is blocked by a statue, *F*. He or she thus stands at the point of maximum possible choice.[20]

The courts themselves are three-and-one-half stories high, with rusticated basements treated with alternating one-story and story-and-a-half arches, a variant of Vanvitelli's treatment of the Palazzo Reale exterior in Naples (fig. 3.19). But these wrap around the offset corners of each court, somewhat as at Buen Retiro. Originally the *piano nobile* was to have been treated with blind arches alternating with open pilastered bays containing temple fronts (fig. 6.26), but this was abandoned for the simpler present scheme (fig. 6.27). As volumes, each court is 3:2 in plan, and 2:2 in elevation on the short side, 3:2 on the long, measuring from ground level to rooftop. The cornices are set at four-fifths of the height of the whole. In other words the values in palmi are 200 (short side, plan), 300 (long side, plan), 160 (cornice height), and 200 (height of roof); see figure 6.28.

Aside from the main staircase other, smaller staircases can take the visitor to other destinations within the geometric temple. In general the central crossed arms of the palace consist of guardrooms, circulation space, and chapel; the southwest L-shaped arms of the king's apartments, both public and private; the northwest L of corresponding apartments for the queen, and the northeast and southeast arms for the royal offspring, including the crown prince and his family. In a more general sense the entire *piano reale* may be said to consist of sets of family living quarters, each divided into male and female halves and also into halves separated by generation. In other words the southwest corner of the palace is devoted to the king, the

6.26
Vanvitelli. Drawing for longer facade of typical court, with temple front for the palace. Caserta, Reggia

6.27
Caserta, narrower court facade of the palace. Photo Ente Provinciale per il Turismo

The Definitive Design

6.28
Caserta, section along main axis of the palace. From the *Dichiarazione*

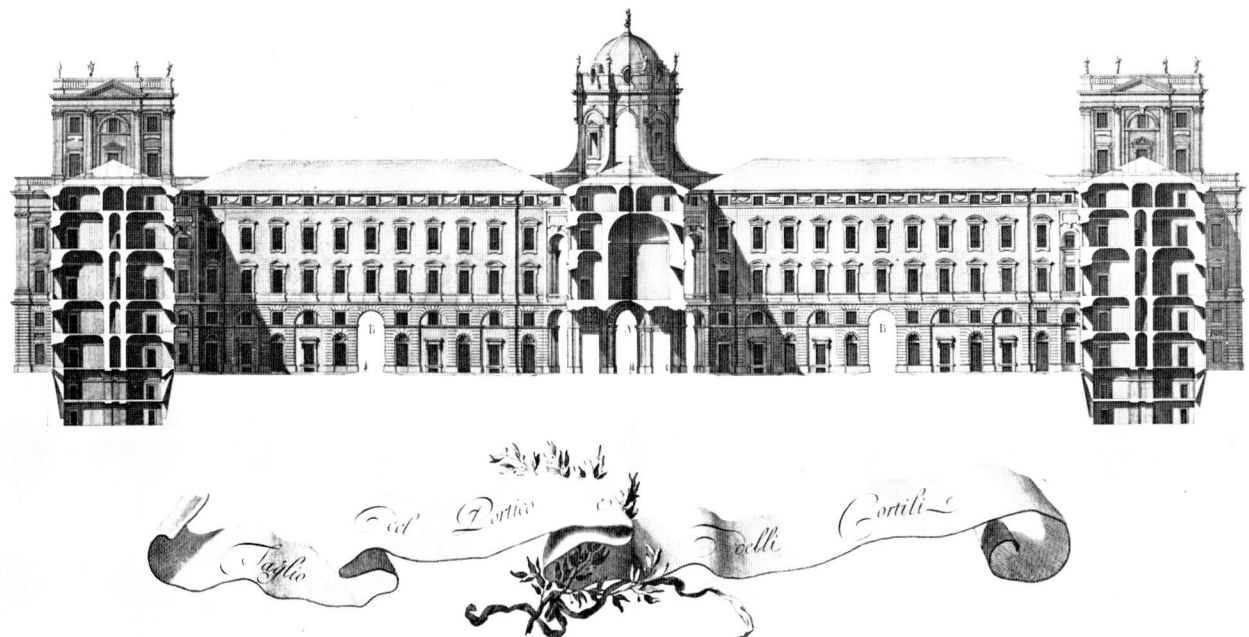

Palace Geometry

northwest to the queen, the northeast to the crown princess, and the southeast to the crown prince. The king's and queen's apartments meet only in their joint bedroom. The apartments of the two younger members of the family are joined together in the procession of guardrooms and anterooms along the horizontal eastern inner range of the palace but split into separate northern and southern apartments when the eastern edge of the building is reached (fig. 6.29). Vanvitelli's *piano reale* therefore realizes Vico's idea that the family unit is the module of a monarchy, dilating that family pattern to the scale of modern "humane and civil monarchy."[21]

Figure 6.13 shows more. The left gate, *M*, takes the visitor to the quarters of the lesser royal children; the right gate, *M*, to those of the crown prince. The main entrance, *A–E*, leads to the king's and queen's apartments. Those of the adult children are located in the areas of the front and rear wings not occupied by major apartments. The fourteen rooms marked *K*, embedded in the family apartments that govern the whole perimeter, are offices for the four secretaries and for certain other government ministers. (The four secretaries are not named. There would probably have been offices also for the secretary of the sacred royal council; there were also the heads of the army and navy and the heads of the central tribunals, Camera di Santa Chiara, Vicaria Criminale, and Vicaria Civile.) Special tribunals, *giunte* and *sopragiunte*, might also have been provided for as there were both a *giunta* and a *sopragiunta* for the palace of Caserta itself.

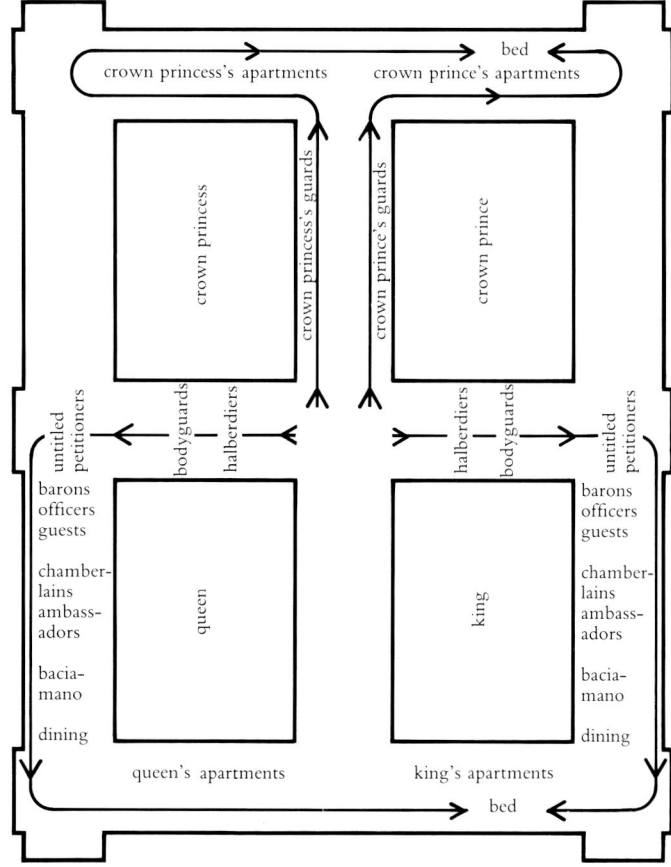

6.29
Caserta, circulation system of the palace. From the *Dichiarazione*

The structure of the Bourbon government did not remain static, and the changes that occurred were probably reflected in Carlo's decision to give up the idea of a new capital city at Caserta with all important functions under one roof. From 1734, to 1737, for example, there was a single secretariat for the royal house. This was then split into the four secretariats of state mentioned. At first these were respectively devoted to grace and justice, commerce, the royal house, and war. Other secretariats or ministries were added, including economic affairs, the navy, ecclesiastical affairs, and foreign affairs. Often a single minister or secretary supervised more than one department.[22] All these officers and their staffs, however, were thought of as the king's personal servants, and at Caserta their business quarters were embedded in suites of other servants' chambers. The *L*s mark the kitchens and wardrobes, respectively, beneath the second-floor chapel and the royal stair; *O* is the theater; and *P*s mark the portals to the gardens.

Having ascended the royal stair visitors find themselves in an upper vestibule (fig. 6.14). Directly to the west are the chapel entrance, 1, and the chapel, 4. The diagonal vaulted passages, imitated from those below that lead up to the four main courtyards, here lead to the *nicchione* in the inner corner of each courtyard, which in each case serves as a window of appearances. *C*s mark the large halls for halberdiers with anterooms for the officers; *D*s, halls for the bodyguards, with similar anterooms. Then at the end come the first true waiting rooms, both marked *E*. For untitled petitioners or guests, these have their own side rooms and give asymmetrically on the windows of appearances, the queen's looking north into the garden and the king's south to the town. With its great half-oval, designed to accommodate crowds of his subjects, the piazza too was a kind of waiting room.

The king's and queen's apartments (fig. 6.14) now move to the left in identical sequences, through rooms marked *F–K* and then toward each other, maintaining mirror symmetry, to meet in the form of a long hall, the queen's corridor, which leads to the bedroom. In this sequence the rooms marked *F* are for titled people, barons of the kingdom, military officers, and foreign guests. Next in line, *G* is for gentlemen of the king's chamber, ambassadors, and secretaries of state; *H* is the great royal salon for public audiences and the *baciamano*. This has several exits and entrances to avoid congestion. All these rooms have access to small anterooms provided with fireplaces and private stairs.

Other families of rooms were focused in other ways on the central family. *I*, at the end of this southern suite, is the public dining room, where privileged guests could watch the king and queen dine or even on occasion join them for a meal. *K* begins the western sequence of private and government rooms. At each corner, *K* is a dressing room, *L* a private chapel, *M*s mark various council rooms, *N* is the king's private study. *O* is the private stairs for secretaries of state, *P* is the king's bedroom, *Q* marks two bathrooms, *R* another private stair, *S* service rooms, *T* still another private stair, this one leading up to the third floor. Xs mark the bedrooms of the royal infants and various minor chambers. *Z*, along the northern wing, marks separate apartments for the older royal children, more guardrooms, and sets of antechambers, chapels, and so on corresponding to similar apartments on the next floor and reached by private stairs. *Y* represents yet other sets of stairs including those that lead to the theater on the ground floor and to the garden.

The central east side of the palace, devoted to the *T*-shaped suite of apartments of the crown prince and princess, is a miniature family sequence within the greater family complex of the whole: I, halberdiers' hall; II, bodyguards'; III, first antechamber; IV, second; V, third; VI, audience hall; VII, dining room; VIII, conversation room leading to the crown princess's apartment; IX, chapel; X, bedroom; XI, dressing rooms; XIII, childrens' room.

The major interior spaces of the palace, like its courts, are shaped by simple mathematical series. The upper vestibule is 50 palmi in diameter and 60 high. Rooms *C–H* are 50 palmi wide by 120 high with cornices at 40. Rooms *F* and *G* are 70 long, *H* is 130 long, *C* and *D* are 90 long, and *E* is 70 long. *I* is 40 × 80 × 120 high. The stair hall is 80 × 100 × 120 high, a 4:5:6 series; the chapel has the same dimensions, and the theater 50 × 50 × 80 high, with the stage area the same. A very select number of dimensions, derived from the series 4, 5, 6, 7, 8, 9, 10, 12, and 13, construct all the major spaces.

The upper floor (fig. 6.15) is devoted to servants' quarters. It includes stairs, dumbwaiters, six kitchens, *D*; access to the loggias at the corners of the palace, *F*; a "tribune" for Mass, *G*; and skylights for the lower-floor corridors, *O*.

All of these arrangements follow the micromodule grid (fig. 6.17). But they do not, as Gioffredo's rooms do, obey the implications of the major exterior geometric divisions. The porticoes do not even give symmetrically on interior spaces, and the spaces they do give on can be small and unimportant. The king's dressing rooms are behind the two lateral temple fronts on the main facades, while the temple fronts on the palace's sides stand before servants' stairs. Only in the cases of the central northern and southern porticoes are there major rooms situated behind major porticoes—and, as is often noted, these rooms are not on axis.[23] If Vanvitelli has borrowed his unsuccessful rival's approach, he has tampered with Gioffredo's rigor.

More important, Gioffredo's idea of a city under one roof is clearly not present in Vanvitelli's final scheme. No mention is made of a library, a seminary, a museum, or an observatory, or of any of the other provisions in Gioffredo's written program. All this was presumably to be included in the new city. The palace Vanvitelli built, like the one described in his Biblioteca Nazionale manuscript, consists of courts or parterres corresponding to the main figures in the royal family. Hence the building is not absolutist in Gioffredo's sense; it does not house a complete national bureaucracy. That quality comes, rather differently, from the embodiment, or embedding, of certain bureaucratic offices within the geometric pattern of a four-part royal family.

Vanvitelli's less than perfectly geometric plan loses its perfection largely because of the small, sometimes irregular armatures of service space that run alongside the regular cubic volumes of the antechambers. The feature is found also in Buen Retiro (fig. 6.11). This off-center pattern is given emphasis and a sudden powerful rhythm when one of the greater spaces opens up vertically, for example the royal stair itself or the upper vestibule (*A* and *B* in fig. 6.13), which would have been a lantern of light crowned by two further central spaces, designed but not executed, and climaxing in the dome uniting the whole (fig. 6.24). I have mentioned de Cotte and could again mention Gioffredo. But Vanvitelli's dome, which is his own, is unforgettable (figs. 6.18, 19). It has the helmeted ferocity of one of Carlo's medieval ancestors patrolling his lands in the Bourbon d'Archambault. The other "great" spaces, rising through two floors like giants, are the chapel, the theater, and the sequence of royal chambers and antechambers on the west (marked *E–I* in fig. 6.14). Thus both the plan grid and that of the elevation are syncopated into climactic emphases by the asymmetrical doubling of volumes. These moments of peak assertion are only the more prominent in the orderly rhythms of the lesser rooms, including the two-level cellars.[24] And they point up the dominance of the overall hive; one now understands Mazzocchi's description of Carlo as a drone seeking sustenance in his honeycomb prison.[25] The heavy basement piers rise slowly and solidly, lightening and lengthening as they go through the horizontal section to flatten into the pedestals of the chapel columns, thereafter to pair off into marble shafts, while the chapel windows become wider and higher than the windows below; the system divaricates into a rib vault to return to its columnar form on the other side (fig. 6.24). The same thing happens, more soberly, in the stair hall and in the royal salon series and more frivolously in the theater, which balances that series, lower down, in the center of the northeast side, *O*. Meanwhile, again in section, the dome separates itself out like a spindle around which all the rest revolves. It is an interruption in the beehive, yet one that is also its motor, or rotor, displaced upward in the scheme like Gioffredo's octagon. This central unity, or One, is not rooted like everything else in a hived underworld but floats over the underground river that was to flow beneath the palace, bearing the traffic of time, fertility, and justice to Naples.

One final element in Vanvitelli's geometrical temple is the octagon, which sets up powerful symmetries of focus. The room shapes of the palace, like those of the 1756 gardens, are based on radial and dihedral symmetries (fig. 5.11) that contrast with the mirror and translational symmetries of the facades. In a way not true of the other plans discussed here, Vanvitelli uses his octagonal elements to plot out crisscrossing paths from vestibule to courts and across the courts to each corner *nicchione*.

Palace Geometry

6.30
Caserta, palace courtyards seen from central octagon. Photo Ente Provinciale per il Turismo

The junctures of the massive vaulted corridors and entrances thus formed, the angled triumphal arches plus the shadows of the interiors against the light-filled courts create effects similar to those in the theatrical scene designs of the Bibiena, or, for that matter, in Vanvitelli's own scene designs (figs. 6.30, 8.45). They throw a beckoning cave of shadow and deep perspective over the whole. They continue, extend, and double into labyrinths the pathways of the garden and river-road. By being purely visual and suggestive, by being optical thrusts across open space rather than remaining tactile and exact like the rectilinear sequences of the interior hive, they affirm the hive and its hierarchies all the more. These Baroque biases were to be fulfilled in the final moment of Caserta's inauguration, the 1773 production of Metastasio's *Didone abbandonata*. Meanwhile these diagonal elements suggest also that the distances of the palace were struck off with a pair of compasses. And indeed we have already heard that this is precisely what happened, and that it was the king himself who did so.[26] He can almost be envisioned as a Blakean god kneeling on the floor of his majesty and ruling his universe.

As the foregoing chapter implies, there was held to be a connection between rule and rulers of the governmental sort and those of the architectural sort. Vico says that geometry and geometrical thinking not only form the basis of justice and monarchy but are the basis of human thought itself. Geometry, he says, is the principal origin of man's virtues and arts. And the arts, in turn, including architecture, must be subject to "irrefragable geometric proofs."[27] Writing, drawing, and design are "geometrical syntheses," modes of establishing magnitude. Works of art must therefore be visible, visualizable, measurable. They must be forms that can be constructed and deconstructed logically.[28] Gioffredo's and Vanvitelli's geometrical constructs, like all ambitious geometrical plans, are such Vichian temples. Their symmetries, uniformities, and repetitions bespeak absolute hierarchy, measure, and harmony. They express a justice that is meted out arithmetically and geometrically; and architectural symmetry is not merely architectural but organizational and taxonomic. It fortifies the judicial. Or, to alter Carlo's meaning only slightly when he commanded Vanvitelli to create four absolutely equal courts rather than one large and several small ones: "the union and the symmetry of things reinforce one another."[29] Here I think he means by "union" a One that is also unity and unison. The construction (or analysis) of such a building is a mode of reducing it to its principle or origin and to the identical principal or origin of the law pronounced or administered in the building. The proofs of geometry, as Vico does not explain but as we can easily supply, are then simply complex and elegant tautologies, achieved by translating form into number and refining, simplifying, reducing, the numbers in accordance with mathematical series. By extension a nongeometric building could not similarly embody justice. Justice might be done in it and governing might be done in it, but they would not be seen to be done.

7 Public Poetry

The Royal Soul

The poetry of the royal palace at Caserta resides in the decorative as opposed to the geometric forms of the building, and in its sculpture and painting. The geometric grid might be said to control the movements of Caserta's users while its mythical poetry woos, admonishes, and informs them. The emphasis is on the relationship between the king's personality and those of his subjects. Modes of access to the central man were numerous—through his family, his counsellors and secretaries, his vassals and servants. But the approaches were also barriers. To visit the king meant getting through a series of baffles and conduits, rather like the water in the river-road. The sculpture, frescoes, and ornament justified the screening process and, it was hoped, polished and purified each petitioner's motives.

The geometry of Caserta was analyzed by geometric means, by number, shape, magnitude, distribution. The mythic aspect of the building can be examined textually and pictorially. In presenting his ideas Vanvitelli did the same. In the text of the *Dichiarazione* he spends little time on the functions of the rooms or on the practical facilities of the palace. Their presence in the book is graphic, not verbal. On the other hand eleven of the nineteen enormous pages of text are devoted to the entrance system's figural poetry. The style is hortatory and dramatic; the *Dichiarazione* is itself a poem, part of the mythic sequence that punctuates the river-road as it flows into the palace. Indeed, Vanvitelli's language, when he addresses the king and queen, is very similar to his poetic and allegorical language in the *Dichiarazione*.

The two matching facades of Caserta, then, have two great entrances, two royal portals that are almost exactly identical, on the north and on the south (figs. 6.19, 6.20). One is for the visitor from the town with its civil institutions, the other for the user who has meditated on the origins of those institutions in the garden (fig. 7.1). These entrances are in fact the two faces of a triumphal arch with a long corridor between. Insofar as they are palace entrances and make use of a two-story elevation with a proposed array of sculptured royal virtues and insofar as they include upper windows of appearances and (unexecuted) roofline statues, they go back to a Neapolitan precedent, namely to the royal gates erected under the Aragonese kings in the fifteenth century. One of these, near the Foro Carolino, was even called the Porta Reale, like Vanvitelli's entrances at Caserta.[1] The inset corner pavilions (fig. 7.2) prepare for the courtyard treatment of linked palace fronts (fig. 6.28). There is the same sense of articulated masses; but on the exterior of the building the arches corresponding to those that fill the courts are widely spaced and blind (fig. 5.2). This further stresses the contrast between the planar flatness of the exteriors and the thick plasticity of the courts and vestibules. The triumphal arch motif is omnipresent although its treatment is varied.

The royal portals each consist of a story-and-one-half rusticated Doric triumphal arch surmounted by a two-story temple front with a second triumphal arch enclosed inside it. The columns are 21.5 palmi high, of gray Sicilian marble veined with metallic yellow. These read brilliantly against the somber pinkish-red brick of the palace wall. The order is Composite. The window of appearances is two stories high and consists of the window proper, which on the south side of the building gives on to the Hall of the Untitled. This window is set into a tall vaulted niche. It was from here, in Vico's phrase, that the king was to appear to his subjects below "as a simulacrum of a god," so its temple form was appropriate.[2] As the king entered the palace below in his carriage, through this rustic arch (fig. 5.4), now he reappeared standing above in the "urban" Composite one. On the garden facade, at the apex of the tympanum, was to have been a clustered trophy with flags and helmets. On the city side was to have been an equestrian statue of the king as victor riding forth, exactly as had been planned for Alfonso I in the Castel Nuovo triumphal arch 300 years earlier.[3] Here, again to quote Vico, the king was to appear "in amiable ferocity" as an eternal triumphator. The vertical ascent of the architecture is itself hieratic: from rusticated pier to marble column to roof statue.

The smaller triumphal arches on the towers (fig. 6.18) repeated these ideas. In a way too the central dome's drum, which remained unbuilt, was to have been a continuous cylindrical triumphal arch wrapped around an octagon. This fact is particularly emphasized in that the central arch of that drum is open to the sky (fig. 6.19). It goes clear through, like the triumphal corridor of the ground floor. This drum-arch serves as the topmost element within a total planned complex of no less than

Public Poetry

7.1
Caserta, detail of northern facade. From the *Dichiarazione*

7.2
Caserta, southern facade, corner pavilion. Photo Ente Provinciale per il Turismo

seventeen such arches, counting four for each tower. And finally it is the arch through which the equestrian king would seem to have just ridden, leaving behind the dome and, by remoter implication, the whole of the river-road. The drum is not Corinthian as one might expect but consists of buttresses swerving up into square piers topped in Michelangelesque fashion with projecting Doric triglyph blocks with little tails formed of guttae. The St. Peter's-type dome is continued by the ribbed cupola with its oval lights framed by squat aedicules.

The roof statues of the garden facade, meanwhile, are more figures in that long train leading, with the equestrian monarch, from the river-road. The sequence, in the garden, of hunters, of slaves, then of released winds (figs. 5.21, 5.36, 5.33), and finally of these rooftop statues silhouetted and gesturing against the sky, makes up the steps in a gradual liberation. The climax of that progress toward freedom is of course the king.

Similarly the windows of the facades become more elaborate, "freer" as they ascend. At ground level they have the simplest surrounds; at upper levels there is more richness. The *piano reale* looks out of windows each of which is a small temple (the literal meaning of *aedicule*). The upper floor windows are suitably less sacral in nature, though nonetheless elaborate, reductively quoting those designed by Michelangelo for the courtyard of the Palazzo Farnese in Rome, and hence a compliment to Carlo di Borbone's Renaissance patrimony (figs. 7.3, 7.4). This window system, also, moves from the inner faces of the central

7.3
Caserta, courtyard,
window in *piano reale*

7.4
Caserta, window in
upper story

portals and spreads horizontally all throughout the building and its courtyards. At the corners of the exterior facades the rusticated gates are blocked by sections of wall containing panels carrying the ground-floor and mezzanine window systems, so at these points the two types of grid fuse (fig. 6.28). The courtyard entrances are all simplified versions of the royal portals, but in them two-story triumphal arch motifs chained together are embedded between the outer elevations of colossal pilasters and the inner ones of aedicules surmounted by attic windows. In the courtyards the entrances to the wings consist of deep semicircular niches with symmetrical radial coffering in the form of shells for vaults but with the door to one side of the central axis (figs. 6.28, 6.32). The whole palace is a concatenation of linked windows and triumphal arches, leading on to lesser and to greater climaxes, around corners, into centers, interiors, or courts, and marching along roofs, all to climax in the central dome—the One.

At Caserta, the royal portal facing south was to have been flanked by four colossi, two on each side (fig. 7.5). These were to have been set on the ground-level pedestals, which still await them there and which act as cube modules for "all the running moldings and all the jogs that adorn the palace exterior," as well as for the vestibules, stairs, and chapel.[4] The arrangement recalls the figures of Rachel and Leah on Michelangelo's Julius Tomb (fig. 7.6) but, much more, the four colossi Perrault planned to set, two on either side of the central arch of the Louvre's east front (fig. 7.7). (Note also the equestrian statue on

7.5
Caserta, southern portal, detail of Colossi. From the *Dichiarazione*

7.6
Michelangelo and assistants. Tomb of Julius II, finished 1547, Rome, San Pietro in Vincoli. Photo Alinari

7.7
Claude Perrault. Design for the east front of the Louvre, detail. Paris, Bibliothèque Nationale

Perrault's tympanum, and the corner towers.[5]) Vanvitelli's colossi are described and illustrated in detail in the *Dichiarazione*. Reading from left to right they are Magnificence, Justice, Clemency, and Peace—a switch from the more common Justice, Temperance, Prudence, and Fortitude, as Vanvitelli himself implies. "They are not," he writes, "the usual symbols used by sculptors, for I have not pretended to represent them abstractly but to particularize them as they reside and are enthroned in His Majesty's great soul."[6]

The territory wherein these virtues sojourn, then, is an architectural and sculptural trope for the monarch's personality. How are we to read it? The "particularities" of Magnificence are that her mantle is wide and noble, that she is crowned, possesses a cornucopia, and, since the palace itself is the king's greatest act of magnificence, that she carries a scroll with the plan of Caserta inscribed on it in her right hand. She wears a battlemented crown, like Tyche or Cybele or some other city goddess. On her pedestal were to have been the words ARTIUM ALTRIX, 'Nurse of the Arts.' Vanvitelli explains: "the arts arrive at the height of their perfection when the peoples, obeying the magnificent genius of the prince, and in order to merit his generosity, employ the full force of their minds, as one knows of Rome in the times of Augustus, Trajan, Hadrian; in Paris in the celebrated reign of Louis XIV; and now in Naples."[7] Magnificence, literally 'making large,' was well portrayed by the image of the palace, by the *Altrix* and her horn of plenty: new jobs through public works. This is part of what, politically, might be called the Declaration of Caserta. The idea will be taken up again in the interior.

Next on the left is Justitia. She turns her eyes to heaven indicating that His Majesty receives his authority from there alone. Her crown indicates his "norms for governing," her queenship of all virtues, and the fact that she is herself the king's principal virtue. In this setting, next to Magnificence, she is a fit embodiment of architectonic justice. As a measure of her equality she wears a toga that is "ample but not magnificent: Justice must refuse all superfluity." She carries consular fasces with axe and military crown, and open compasses and a balance. Justice's usual attribute, aside from the balance, is a sword; but Vanvitelli, like Vico, advocated the idiosyncratic or critical *relegendo* of traditional emblems. The compasses reveal Justice's geometric preoccupations. Vanvitelli in fact tells us that the open compasses and the balance signify commutative and distributive justice.[8] And to Vico the fasces are the symbols of civil empires. Fasces are bundles of *litui* bound together like a compact group of kingdoms. Fasces are the world's first scepters. The fathers, or natural kings of barbarian families, subdued their servants, clients, and attendants, or *famuli*, bringing them from the wilderness to the cities through the power of their *litui*. These marked the agrarian laws passed for the benefit of these lesser breeds, and in turn brought about "Herculean commonwealths," the first commonwealths of armed men in public assembly. The fasces are thus symbols of the universality of

Justice:⁹ *De universi iuris fine uno et principia uno*, to quote the full title of the *Diritto*: "universal justice begins in the One, and ends in it." The fasces and the compasses form a proper prelude to Caserta's measured sequences, its distributive and commutative geometries and to its single monarch's crowning unity.

Justice's pedestal is inscribed FELICITAS MATER, 'Happiness the Mother.' By carrying the means to measure both weight and magnitude Justice reinforces Vico's equivalence between the two measurable forms of well-being.¹⁰

On the right of the arch is Clemency, whose benignity we are told must be evident in her placid face and pose. Dressed in a mantle and crown, she sheathes her sword. She has it, that is, but wishes not to use it. Her face is set upward yet her eyes are lowered in pity for the wretched ones who seek her out. Her pedestal is inscribed MISERORUM CONFUGIUM, 'Asylum of the Miserable.' She too, as the author of the very concept of asylum, is a Vichian virtue.

Finally Peace, whom Vanvitelli calls the Genius of His Majesty, is a tranquil-faced woman in a citizen's toga, since when there is no war, the king is the realm's paterfamilias, cultivating its fields and commerce. Peace wears her traditional olive leaves, carries sheaves of wheat, and holds a tiller to symbolize navigation. The tiller, we are told, refers to Carlo's enlargement of the harbors at Naples, Agrigento, and Barletta; but the wheat and the tiller also parallel the themes of the fountains of Ceres and Aeolus. Peace is labeled OPUM AMPLIFICATRIX, 'She Who Increases Wealth,' which links her also to Vico's conception of Minerva. Peace has many repercussions throughout the rest of the program. She also rounds out the job-creating proclivities of Magnificence and extends Justice's function of measuring out restitution and Clemency's role of affording asylum. By omitting such classic iconographic items as Justice's sword and such entire virtues as Fortitude, Temperance, and Prudence, Vanvitelli's program becomes more ameliorative and enlightened than it would have been otherwise. Virtues that suggest withholding, deprivation, and physical harm are replaced by those suggesting nurturance. The Porta Reale at Caserta is in this sense a recension of the Vincenzo Rè allegory described in chapter 3. Magnificence, Clemency, a Justice that has to do with commerce and contracts, and a Peace that has to do with income production; these are the contents of the king's soul. By "particularizing" the Virtues as he does, by giving them this strong economic and numerical bias, Vanvitelli and his royal advisers have created a legal and economic imagery filled with the spirit of the Neapolitan settecento—of Vico, Genovesi, and Galiani.

The Pantheon of Hercules

On entering Caserta through the southern portal the visitor meets the axis of the river-road as the latter enters through the northern portal (fig. 6.13). The living subject and the king's sculptured forebears join in the lower vestibule at the statue of Hercules that stands at the center of the architectural whole (figs. 7.8, 7.9). This lower vestibule is Hercules' underground city. It is a *pian terreno*, a ground or subground level beneath the *piano reale*. The visitor looks directly out the north portal to the so-called Dolphin Fountain with its underworld creatures and beyond to the upper, ever more distant pasts of Ceres, Venus, and Diana (fig. 6.20). The visitor is thus within the subterranean river of time, ready to be raised, like Proserpine, through the good graces of Hercules to the upper world of life.

In a letter of 1756, the year in which the *Dichiarazione* was published, Vanvitelli records another royal desire, which strengthens this emphasis: "to introduce all the possible symbols of Hercules."[11] We noted in the *Dichiarazione* itself the planned group of Glory crowning Hercules occupying the great niche (fig. 6.13, *F*), where Andrea Violani's single figure of the hero now stands.[12] Without doubt the statue was to recall the most famous of all images of Hercules, the Farnese, which now belonged to Carlo.[13] It also abets the meaning of Vanvitelli's quotation of the windows from the Farnese Palace and has correspondences with the sixteenth-century statue of Alessandro Farnese above in the Hall of Alexander. In the antique statue the hero stands, fatigued with his labors, leaning on his club, which is wrapped in the Nemaean lion's skin. Behind his back, in his right hand, he holds the apples of the Hesperides. He is thus shown after ridding the land of beasts, as he prepares to replant the Gardens of the Hesperides. As noted, Violani's Hercules has an ox's head at the god's feet, in what may be a reference to Hercules' voyage to Sicily to reclaim one of the oxen of Geryon. De Venuti connects these animals with Italic civilization, claiming that in Etruscan 'oxen' were *itali*.[14]

I have already mentioned, fleetingly, Carlo's self-identification with Hercules in a civic festival.[15] At the same time Mazzocchi was seeking to reveal wider connections between Hercules, Pythagoras's school and "commonwealth" in the same region, and Carlo's nation of Magna Graecia. In fact the title page of Mazzocchi's book on two ancient bronze tablets that record a boundary decree illustrates a coin showing Hercules on the obverse struggling with the Nemaean lion (fig. 7.10). The lion's defeat, we are told, mythically records just this type of agreement.[16] Recall too that Caserta is built on the site of a village called Ercole, where a temple to Hercules was thought to have stood.[17] At Caserta, above all, Hercules' clearing the land of infesting beasts[18] would also stand for Carlo's seizure of the estate from his Austrianizing foes the Gaetani. In these ways Caserta becomes a temple to a Farnese Hercules who, in a more than merely Euhemeristic sense, is Carlo himself.[19]

Vico accords a major role to Hercules in the development not just of Campanian but of all civilizations. Every people, he says, has its Hercules.[20] Like Ulysses, Menelaus, Diomedes, and Aeneas—Hercules' successors—Hercules is par excellence "a sea-wandering hero" who settles among unknown lands, peoples, and towns.[21] Thus his trip from Hesperia to Campania to found Herculaneum and receive the religious devotions of his adherents there was a paradigm for Aeneas' journeys from

The Pantheon of Hercules

7.8
Caserta, lower vestibule. Photo Mimmo Jodice. (See also pl. 7.)

7.9
Andrea Violani. Adaptation of the Farnese Hercules, 1770–1773, Caserta, lower vestibule. Photo Ente Provinciale per il Turismo

Public Poetry

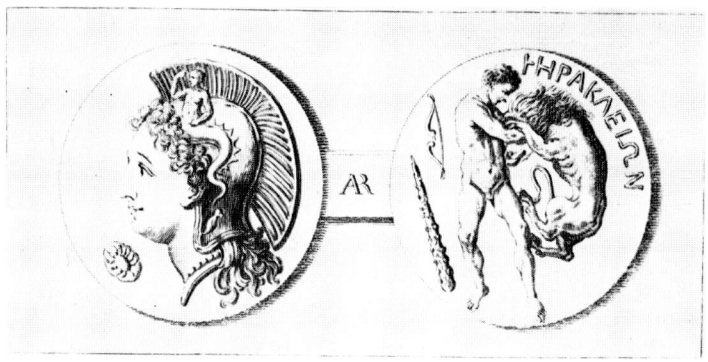

7.10
Hercules and the
Nemean lion, after
an antique original,
from Mazzocchi,
Aeneas Tabulas (1754)

Troy to Rome. Hercules' golden apples are conflated with Aeneas' golden bough. They are the talismans of an underworld voyage. And in extinguishing the Hydra Hercules clears land in another way. He mythically reenacts man's discovery that, by burning over forests, agricultural fields can be created. Hercules was thus a tamer, a civilizer, not only of beasts but of Earth itself.[22] The golden apple of discord, which is one of the apples of the Hesperides, in fact means land tenure among other things and the claims of owners and tenants—in short, agriculture as a social institution.[23] And this, with its concomitants of settled communities, is what leads Hercules to become a city-builder. His act is reflected in the founding of Rome. Romulus dedicated the main altar of his city to Hercules.[24]

Hercules' exploits are reenacted by his many successors. These later Herculeses are the kings of early men. They civilize their peoples under the sign of Hercules' epithet *ferarum extinctor*, 'annihilator of beasts,' converter of barbarians or human beasts into civil men.[25] The lion skin with which Hercules is portrayed signifies his hero's status, his *fortia facta*.[26] He is everywhere. He has the pervasiveness of remote ancestral blood. Seeing his statue in Hell, Ulysses said: "I am in Heaven, for I see Hercules."[27] In the underworld Hercules liberated Ceres' grain so it could rise to earth. It is Hercules' very presence in the center of the ground floor of the palace that makes it an underworld and an atrium to the underground river that was planned to flow beneath it. Hercules' statue reenacts Ulysses' vision. Hercules pities the pitiable and originates asylum.[28] He is the "miserorum confugium" like Vanvitelli's statue of Clemency. And he is, finally, Glory. For Glory is the fame of human merit, a point to be made again by Vanvitelli's stair-hall statues. The very name, Hercules, means 'Glory of Hera.'[29]

Hercules, who slew the Erymanthian boar, the Hydra of Lerna, and much other monstrous game, was one of the great huntsmen of antiquity. His example was followed to the point of obsession by Carlo di Borbone. The estate at Caserta was one of the *siti reali*, or royal hunting preserves. Carlo's panegyrist, D'Onofri, explains the king's obsession in terms that allow for it, indeed demand for it, the kind of mythic rationale that Vico supplies for the hunts of Hercules.[30] To D'Onofri the sport was an exercise in primitive royal continuity. Since man had come into existence in a garden, or in The Garden, among beasts and birds, D'Onofri argues, he must return periodically to their company as to his primal source. Hunting is a return to Eden. In fact the first thing man did on being cast out of Eden was to hunt. Only later came herding, agriculture, mining, and so on; again, the quarry, the spoil of the hunter's search, becomes an allegory of civilization, as was to be the case with the allegorical sculpture in the gardens of Caserta. Hunting, says D'Onofri, is particularly the sport of kings and emperors. It develops their military skills while "ameliorating the motions of the sovereign's soul." It also benefits the sovereign's subjects, for Carlo gave his spoils to the poor. Hunting is a form of magnificence. Royal hunts create jobs for hundreds, even thousands, of keepers and servants. The lower orders, who were not admitted to the king's presence in his palaces, had access to him during his hunts and could even kiss his hand in a rustic *baciamano*. Hence Carlo's hunts, like his palaces, were temples of government, royal ceremonies that softened the royal soul and at which the royal heart might be opened; they were interludes of peace when justice might be measured out.

Looking at such a painting as Francesco Celebrano's *Ferdinando IV and His Court at a Boar Hunt,* painted sometime in the 1770s and now in the Museo di San Martino (fig. 7.11), we witness a Bourbon Hercules engaged in just such exploits or ceremonies.[31] A field, bordered on the right by a windbreak of trees, is seen. Behind, to the right, the low ranges of the volcanic hills beyond the Phlegraean Fields are visible. On the left the picturesquely curved branches of a young oak bow toward the "central man." The foreground is filled with the complex orderly activities of keepers, beaters, guests, observers (with more of the latter behind a curtained enclosure to the right). There is a crowd of carriages, dogs, horses, oxen. It is a genre scene, yet with epic overtones; or, it is a battle scene become a hunt. For the king, central, astride the one white horse in the picture, calmly faces left in full profile, hand and *lituus* extended—a commander, a Marcus Aurelius of the hunt leading his troops and surrounded by his closest advisers, his optimates, and his family. He "shows himself in amiable ferocity" in the midst of a Vichian civilizing siege.

The emphatic pursuit of Herculean iconography at Caserta, recorded in Vanvitelli's 1756 letter, proceeded. Violani's statue had a predecessor. In March 1759 Vanvitelli erected, in the center of the lower corridor, an antique Hercules statue sent

Public Poetry

7.11
Francesco Celebrano.
Ferdinando IV and His Court at a Boar Hunt, 1770s. Naples, Museo San Martino.
(See also pl. 4.)

from Rome in 1756 and attributed to the Athenian sculptor Glycon. Vanvitelli set the work into a temporary fountain. There were various underworld creatures, including four harpies in the form of sphinxes squirting jets of water from their mouths. These sustained a central pedestal for the god himself. A vessel above him also emitted water. The temporary fountain delighted the king, who insisted that another, which he did not further define, be erected there as well.[32]

So, at this point, on the eve of Carlo's departure for Spain, we have further evidence that the river-road was planned to penetrate the palace. Hercules the gardenist and city-builder would join the line of precursors, emerging from the underworld, leaving behind its troops of basilisks, rising above its harpies and sphinxes, in a resurrection within the magnificent chambers of the king's soul.[33]

As noted this 1756 scheme was only an outgrowth of what is described in the *Dichiarazione*, published in that same year but under preparation earlier:

In a place so visible to him who enters the king's staircase as the lower vestibule there ought to be a statue inspiring the viewer to virtuous exploits. Heroic virtue is commonly symbolized by Hercules, who is represented as being muscular and gigantic, to denote strength of body and robustness of spirit. The club in his right hand is the inflexible vigor of reason, which triumphs over every rebellion of the inconstant, ever-returning appetites of man, figured in the Hydra upon which Hercules sets his right foot [which became an ox in the final statue]. The lion skin he wears is a trophy of his hard-won victories. He stands with his head gazing upward, to show that the virtuous man does not so much prize that which he has won in the past—indicated by the cornucopia at the feet of Glory, the winged, trumpet-bearing woman (for her uncertain gifts are largely bestowed by Chance)—so much as to seek the immortal renown symbolized by the laurel with which Glory crowns him and which she signals to the world by the sound of her trumpet.[34]

In her magnificent toga, Vanvitelli goes on, Glory also denotes majesty, as does her generous face. Yet she is uncrowned; crowns are merely signs of the splendor Glory already possesses. On the pedestal are the words GLORIA VIRTUTEM POST FORTIA FACTA CORONAT, 'Glory Crowns Virtue after His Great Deeds.' Andrea Violani's statue (fig. 7.9) has this inscription but no figure of Glory. But the hero-god has completed his work. He turns away from the next mythographic stage: the royal stair.[35] In smaller niches flanking the Hercules are are two more pseudo-antique statues by Violani, a Medici Venus and a Germanicus, and two more by Solari, Apollo and Antinous (figs. 7.12–7.15). The whole forms a miniature Neoclassical museum. The effect is sober and cool, the dry copies being given a drier and more taxonomic air by Vanvitelli's generous niches; they are in the spirit of some contemporaneous antiquary—Gavin or Sir William Hamilton, or Winckelmann.

Seen as a continuation of the fountain sequence on the river-road, the vestibule group adds to it three gods, Hercules, Apollo, and Venus, who play important roles in the iconography of the inner parts of the palace. There are now also two characters who figure prominently in Vico's pantheon: Germanicus, says Vico, was a model builder-emperor who admired and explored the ruins of ancient Thebes, ruins that bore witness to the opulence and power of that civilization. The great piles, the hieroglyphs, armies, the sway over distant lands, tribute: all imprinted themselves forever on his memory. In this way, he says, Germanicus recapitulated the most ancient past and became heir and successor to Ramses. As to Antinous, he of course was the muse of another builder-emperor: Hadrian. However, in Vico Antinous is no Roman catamite but Penelope's son and Ulysses' companion on the sea and in hell, who exemplifies the permanent loyalty of a hero's sworn followers. Because of one disloyal word Ulysses had wanted to behead Antinous. Antinous is a symbol of the ancient *ius heroicum*, the law of loyalty and obedience for followers, a law that was also meant to keep women in perpetual submission to their fathers or husbands. Thus, whether we assume the Hadrianic or the Ulyssian reading of Antinous here, or both, he fortifies the admonitory nature of the architectural vessel that is the king's heart. He signifies family or imperial loyalty. He and Germanicus, like Hercules, Apollo, and Venus, stand for legal and civil institutions, for continuity with the imperial pasts, and for heroic and absolute family laws.[36]

The Royal Heart

Mounting the steps, which are carved with imposing Neoclassical trophies of Medusa shields, flags, helmets, and the like by Nicola Morosini and with other decoration by Gaetano Magri, one sees at the top of the first flight a pair of lions by

7.12
Violani. Adaptation of Medici Venus, 1768–1773. Caserta, lower vestibule.
Photo Mimmo Jodice

7.13
Violani. Copy of Roman Germanicus, 1762–63. Caserta, lower vestibule.
Photo Mimmo Jodice

The Royal Heart

7.14 Tommaso Solari (after Pierre Legros the Younger). Apollo, 1761. Caserta, lower vestibule. Photo Mimmo Jodice

7.15 Solari. Antinous (after Campidoglio type), 1759. Caserta, lower vestibule. Photo Mimmo Jodice

Solari and Persico (figs. 7.16, 7.17). They are heraldic, like Actaeon's dogs (fig. 5.20) and recall Hercules' victory over the disorderly force represented by the lion of Nemaea; here, however, according to Vanvitelli, they stand for the forces of Reason and Arms, which guarantee to the king his realms: another proclamation of territorial entitlement. The lions also guard the upper two flights of stairs, one of which moves visitors past the statues of Royal Majesty and Truth, while the other moves them in the opposite direction past statues of Majesty once again, and Merit. The statues are in lofty niches over the central door. They are full-scale stucco models for unexecuted marbles. *Truth*, by Gaetano Salomone, is on the right (fig. 7.18); *Royal Majesty*, by Solari, is in the center (fig. 7.19), and *Merit*, by Violani is on the left, (fig. 7.20).

Truth and Merit, says Vanvitelli, are the two principal concerns of any petitioner approaching the king.

But, however, among those who come to make complaints there will be calumniators. And among the petitioners there will be brazen hypocrites. So, to keep these persons away from the Prince's ears, at the beginning of the stairs everyone is warned that he cannot succeed by vilifying others, nor can he ascend and make requests if he is without merit; while the majesty of the king, justly discerning truth and merit, will not let itself be seduced by such people's representations. To express all this, statues with the following symbols and mottoes will be made: In the central niche, more majestic and richer than the others, there will be the simulacrum of Royal Majesty, greater in stature than the flanking statues, dressed in a royal mantle and wearing a royal crown, and in the action of command. She will hold in her right hand a scepter whose point consists of an open eye, to denote that she knows what it is that she commands. She will be seated on a lion, which aside from the relation it has with the royal arms of Spain, is the only one among the animals in which Clemency strives with Fortitude—virtues that reside in the king's heart and check not only his lowlier vassals but his great ones . . . The pedestal will bear the following words: AD MAJESTATEM ACCEDENS PERPENDE QUID AFFERS, 'Think well what you bring with you when you approach His Majesty.' [By the way, none of these inscriptions was ever put in place.]

Truth will wear a toga, seemingly transparent, since however much it covers her it always shows the beauties of her nakedness. With the right hand she will raise a sun because, as that illuminates the universe so she spreads light on invisible things. She will hold the fingers of her left hand closed, except for the index finger, with which she points to the sun, since what we call the truth is nothing else but the conformity between the enunciation and the thing enounced. She shows that this sun is unique to her, and unique in its effect, which explains her character. She will rest her left foot on the world, because Truth triumphs over all things. She will have the inscription: VERA FERENS VENIAS LATURUS FALSA RECEDAS, 'Truth-bearers may approach but let the false go away.'

Merit is richly dressed. The laurel garland that binds his brow will be a symbol of his victorious accomplishments. He will be youthful-looking because Merit is too young to be remunerated; to indicate that Merit is formed through service to the king, or in civil or military affairs, he will hold a book in his right hand and rest his left on a sword. This will be sheathed and the book

7.16
Caserta, stair hall from entrance to crown prince's quarters. Photo Mimmo Jodice. (See also pl. 5.)

Public Poetry

7.17
Caserta, lion by
Paolo Persico. Photo
Ente Provinciale
per il Turismo

7.18
Gaetano Salomone.
Truth, 1776. Caserta,
stair hall. Photo
Soprintendenza per i
Beni Culturali

7.19
Solari. *Royal Majesty*,
1776–77. Caserta,
stair hall. Photo
Soprintendenza per i
Beni Culturali

7.20
Violani. *Merit*, 1776.
Caserta, stair hall.
Photo Soprinten-
denza per i Beni
Culturali

closed, because Merit does not make a show of itself without diminishment. With his right foot he will make as if to climb over steep rocks since, to make himself meritorious, he must overcome difficulties. So as to invite to the prize only those aspirants who deserve it there will be written on the base: QUI GRAVIS ES MERITO GRAVIOR MERCEDE REDEBIS, 'You who are heavy with merit will depart heavier still with rewards.'[37]

Vanvitelli thinks of all these statues as embodiments in an almost Freudian sense of the motions, tendencies, checks, and urges within a human personality. The stair hall is a vessel containing competing, reinforcing, paralleling, emphasizing, and selecting passions. The groupings of the statues, the three in the stair hall and for that matter the four at the south portal, are special "teams" or *équipes* not unlike the id, the ego, the superego and Freud's other embodiments of the passions and counterpassions of the heart. In effect the stair is a great ribbed shell (figs. 7.16, 7.20, and 7.21), the scallops of its clustered arches at the top sending forth inward-curving ribs that support the rim of an oval crest or summit that contains more inner ribs repeating these shapes. The whole container is like a great reliquary. The lions of Clemency and Fortitude confront each other, and Hercules the Founder, and Truth, Majesty, and Merit each have their actions. Each in his or her way also shepherds visitors, exhorts them, questions them. The sculpture equalizes and rectifies: *lex aequatrix* and *lex rectrix*. Majesty's lion recapitulates but with new emphasis—with a new burden one might say—the lions below. Majesty is thus sovereign not only over Clemency and Fortitude but over Reason and Arms. The inscriptions explain to the visitor the traffic and the intentions of the beings in this psychic temple. So do the gestures, costumes, and attributes of the statues. For instance Majesty (fig. 7.19) seems about to dismount and is commanding with her seeing-eye scepter that some action take place. Over her head hangs a luminous gray shell like a halo, a half-sun blazoned on the pale red wall. And we remember that Majesty presides over the entrance to the apartment of the king's successor. It is as if Diana-Venus-Ceres had reappeared in actions subsequent to their actions in the gardens, here to set about the king's business.

Merit (fig. 7.20) and Majesty, meanwhile, are subtly paired with each other. Both are dressed in medieval clothing. They are like a medieval king and queen, or a queen and her suitor. Majesty is not only like Ceres; for that matter she has the same spread-kneed, outgoing seated pose we see in Parthenope and Astraea in Vincenzo Rè's vision of the gods and goddesses welcoming Prince Filippo in 1749 (fig. 4.12), though she has less languishing urgency and a more Neoclassical resoluteness. Truth (fig. 7.18), in contrast, is alone. And she seeks companionship. She is a rococo goddess whose toga or gown does indeed show off her charms. Who would not be attracted to Truth? She has a siren's fascination. She shows her sun, pointing to it as if it were a flower she had just picked: the "thing enounced," to use Vanvitelli's phrase, points to the enouncer, and yet is both. She is One. Truth is also lighter and more buoyant than Merit and Majesty. She is a more decorous recen-

7.21
Stair hall, view from above. Photo Mimmo Jodice

sion of Bernini's *Verità* in the Vatican. With her sun above, her earth below, she readies us for that other sun god, Apollo, who stood below in Hercules' subterranean shrine and who reappears in glory in the vault.

Apollo's Kingdom

Most of these lower figures are not truly gods but personifications. They lead, however, to true gods, who are found, appropriately, in Heaven. Rising on the powerful lifted arms of the stair vault is the oval summit of the reliquary (fig. 7.22). The inner recess in which Apollo rules is a gold-framed and frescoed sky thick with clouds and drifting, feathery divinities. The central frame contains a musicians' gallery, almost invisible from below, so that during the concerts accompanying royal entrances and exits, the music seemed to issue from the inhabitants of the fresco. Below the main scene in that fresco, in four oval panels, are the four seasons: on the southeast, Spring, an enthroned young goddess being crowned by a bee-winged genius with a wreath; and thereafter, counterclockwise, a Boucher-like reclining nude in an orange robe, luxuriously symbolizing Summer; a rampantly naked pink Bacchus for Fall, and finally Winter, a freezing old man clutching his shivering body. The constant elements in these four scenes, the similar enframements, poses, and colors, suggest a single continuous action stopped at four points and with a metamorphosed single character appearing at each stopping point.

These paintings are the work of Girolamo Starace Franchis, with the assistance of Giuseppe and Gaetano Magri. They date from 1768–69.[38] The work is not mentioned in the *Dichiarazione*, though the wooden model of the stair hall in the Museo Vanvitelliano provides for it. In any case Vanvitelli speaks frequently of Starace in his letters and made designs for paintings that Starace executed in Rome.[39] It is probable that the same thing happened here. Unfortunately there is no published program for the fresco, so it is necessary to rely on internal evidence with help from the iconographic handbooks; the following identifications of some of the inhabitants of the painting will therefore be tentative. Nonetheless, Vanvitelli was no doubt as willing to depart from the standard repertoire of meanings here as he was in his programs for the sculpture.

The gods form an equator of blue, white, and rose-clothed bodies across the center of the oval (fig. 7.23). On the left Mercury rushes forward carrying a trumpet and gesturing to two goddesses seated below him. The one on the left passes a caduceus to her companion who is embraced in turn by a third woman seated beside her. The first of the three has a small bird on her head. If the bird is a crow the goddess may be identified as Pity, one of whose attributes is this supposedly merciful bird. The central goddess of the three is Astraea, with her close companion Pudicity (fig. 7.24). Astraea wears the crown and rich breast ornament Ripa specifies. She is being handed her fasces by a putto, filled with servile joy, who floats just below the hem of her gown. In the center, remote and royal, is Apollo. Enthroned on a Parnassus of rococo cloud, from which a gilded

7.22 Girolamo Starace. *Apollo's Kingdom*, 1768–69. Caserta, stair hall. Photo Mimmo Jodice. (See also pl. 6.)

7.23
Apollo's Kingdom, central panel. Photo Mimmo Jodice

Apollo's Kingdom

7.24
Apollo's Kingdom, central figures. Photo Mimmo Jodice

7.25
Apollo's Kingdom, lower figures. Photo Mimmo Jodice

7.26
Apollo's Kingdom, right-hand figures. Photo Mimmo Jodice

pedestal projects, rather resembling Majesty's pedestal below, he offers a crown to . . . to whom? Silhouetted against the sun-filled void above, the crown is extended out over the void below. It awaits the arriving king, perhaps, or at least the meritorious and truthful petitioner. It matches Majesty's eye-tipped scepter. Minerva, like Astraea armed in a cuirass equipped with breast cups like Helen of Troy's, stands to Apollo's right, grasping a spear, her helmet plumed and surmounted by an owl, as with slightly curled fingers she designates the sun god.

Minerva's spear, and Astraea's caduceus and fasces, are prominent Vichian tropes, as is Astraea's link with Pudicity. Quintus Fabius, we are told, had sent the Carthaginians a spear and a caduceus as emblems of an alternative: war or peace. But normally the caduceus is sent as an announcement of war, while the spear is war itself.[40] Vico makes Mercury Apollo's protégé in royal heraldry as well as his messenger, or *legatus*, bearer of *leges*, laws, from the gods to their people below.[41] The caduceus, normally associated with Mercury, is in Pity's hands and is being presented to Astraea as goddess of justice. In Pity's hands the caduceus draws souls from Orcus, the underworld forest below a hellish grove that once devoured barbarian humankind because of the inconstancies of Venus.[42] Hence the caduceus is another form of asylum for the miserable. It civilizes and brings peace. It quiets the rebarbarizing tendencies of the goddess of inconstant fire.

From this very complex of divinities and their meanings, says Vico, comes commerce.[43] The word commerce derives from *merx*, or payment, from which *Mercury* also comes: goods, or the exchange of goods. Commerce can occur only in times of peace. Any war is war against that which would disrupt the peace. The spear that Minerva carries is the latent instrument that keeps the plebs in line. Minerva is the goddess of internal order within the state,[44] as Mercury with his caduceus addresses himself to external disorders. So Minerva carries her spear much as Pity carries Mercury's caduceus. Both objects are talismans and protections, like Aeneas' golden bough, or the Hesperidean apples that Hercules has with him in hell. By carrying the caduceus announcing the decrees of the *respublicae* against promiscuity, Pity projects and defends herself, as she is guided and shielded by Justice and Pudicity. The entire fresco restates the reasons for the palace's emphasis on the royal family as a module of the realm. These central gods, ruled by Apollo, are muses of fecundity, family unity, civil order, and peace.

Below this, and contributing to Apollo's eminence, is a chain of twelve female figures proceeding upward in two groups of six. All are dressed in gold or rose (fig. 7.25). They carry dividers, brushes, sculptors' tools, masks, trumpets, books, and other impedimenta of the muses. Meanwhile in the lower right Immortality, armed with her golden circlet, rushes forward with flapping wings and pushes Time, or Death, with his scythe, from the heavens. He may gather his harvest on earth but not here.

Upward on higher clouds are more muses (fig. 7.26). The first reclines with majestic ease on a cornucopia; with her generous smile and gesture she is Liberality, or perhaps the Nurse of the Arts from the royal portal. Beyond her are Clio (with trumpet and book); Thalia with her mask; and Euterpe, or perhaps Pastoral Poetry, for she holds a wooden flute.[45] The lower group of muses all have to do with number, these upper ones with poetry. There are more than the traditional nine. Indeed, in the background on the right other faces and figures crowd forward into the scene: other, undefined arts seek to join the sacred company. But all in their mingling gazes and gestures move psychologically and physically toward the central form of Apollo.

Higher still, above Apollo, four figures accompanied by putti flutter on dusky bees' wings (fig. 7.23). It is likely that they are Spring, Summer, Autumn, and Winter, for they recapitulate the seasons' succession below. Lit by Apollo's splendor, they dance their round dance and crown his glory. Further off, in the golden empyrean, similar seasons perform the next year's round. In the center Apollo's lyre melts into a golden presence whose form loses itself in radiance. He and his lyre emanate those "chords of force" that govern the dance of time, commerce, and rule.[46] This lyre is one of the many that fascinate the unruly into the siren spell that civilizes. The lyre was "discovered by Mercury and taken over by Apollo" to sing the muses into existence, thus founding the arts and skills of humanity and of its early, premonarchic republics.[47]

Vico claims that fascination with song brought the barbarian into a state of social organization. This in turn reflects the myth of Parthenope as well as that other myth, equally local to Naples, that made Apollo Parthenope's mate. Indeed Vico builds on these ideas and makes the Muses' river, the Hippocrene, the stream on whose banks they erect their city of art. Apollo, who rules Parnassus, rules that city. He and his lyre, who make cities out of muses and out of men, are one with Amphion, whose lyre's sweet sounds made stones (that is, plebs) dance into the form of walls, and who thereby erected Thebes. Apollo and his fellow gods, the months or hours, and their music, are a further *corps de garde* for king and visitors. They recapitulate the tale of the river-road. But now that river gushes upward like a fountain to heaven.

Vico uses the phrase *fortia facta*, which also appears on Hercules' pedestal at the foot of the stairs, to describe another aspect of Apollo's lyre. This sings the "fortia facta heroum domi," the heroes' great deeds of taming;[48] in other words actions like Hercules' taming of the Nemaean lion, a taming that turned it into a trophy of cleared agricultural land. These lyre strings, these "chords of force" that bind societies together, are laws. They are the guts of the body politic. They are the "fortia facta belli," the great deeds of war that preserve nations. And these great deeds are also poetry, art. Poetry and art were originally codes of law. The law of Apollo is this: The lyre of kings consists of the sayings of poets. Apollo, like Minerva and Mercury, is a *conditor legum*, a founder of laws, just as Hercules is the founder of agriculture. Apollo is also the "eternalizer of names" who assures immortality to the family, to those who obey the law. The imperium he invents guides his other invention, the *respublicae*, whose skills and disciplines are administered by the muses.[49] Apollo showers the allegorical stair below him with the explanatory gold of myth.

Marble Guardians

If Hercules is the Atlas-like sustainer of Olympus and the stairhall world (fig. 7.8), he has the character of an Atlanteean column, of the human figure as architectural support. This idea is taken up throughout the most public interiors of the palace: the vestibules, stair hall, chapel, and theater. The point is made, for one thing, by the colors and materials in the vestibules (figs. 7.27, 7.28). The walls are paneled in scagliola and marble of pink, gold, gray, and dark red. The statues are of white marble, the vaults of white stucco with yellowish plaster bordering. The architraves and marble cornices are gray, the unadorned friezes of veined red marble. Throughout this pale world trimmed with darker line, armies of columns with dark gray or pink marble shafts stand out like mighty Herculean lifters (fig. 7.29). The paler, white-and-pink pilasters they front upon are not bundled like so many *litui* in the Neapolitan Baroque manner but are formed into mighty piers. The effect is like that of the more complex parts of St. Peter's or of that other Michelangelo church in Rome remodeled by Vanvitelli, Santa Maria degli Angeli. The rooms and halls of Caserta have an atmosphere at once airy and imperial. It is as one imagines Apollo's music to be, or that of the slowly turning seasons.

Within this airy world the guardian deities are these dark, powerful shafts. The lower vestibule has twenty of them, of polychrome marble from Sicily, and there are twenty-four more in the upper vestibule. They come from Monte Sant'Angelo in the mainland province of Apulia.[50] Others had been extracted from Roman ruins such as the "Serapeum" at Puteoli. Saint-Non quotes critics of the palace who say that it represents the simple theft of the precious spoils of antiquity throughout the kingdoms.[51] But the shafts gleam throughout the palace with a power that immediately overshadows both the clustered piers, pedestals, and entablatures that clasp them, and the vaults they lift into whirling crowns (fig. 7.30). On the exterior other monoliths, more weathered and more remote, sustain the royal portals.

The column shafts of Caserta were one of Carlo's obsessions. The king saw them as tribute sent from his kingdom's quarries and archaeological sites and as the produce of his soil.[52] In a way they were a means of political representation, a stately parliament in stone. When each was set in place an engineering spectacle was staged. The court and royal family would come out to Caserta to watch, as at the accreditation of some immense ambassador. The shaft would arrive prone, wrapped in a cage of wood, and would be rolled into position. Once there it was raised to its pedestal and revealed to the applause of the court. The progress of Caserta's erection can be measured in the *Lettere* as Vanvitelli counts the columns that have risen to support the

7.27
Caserta, royal palace, lower vestibule.
Photo Ente Provinciale per il Turismo

7.28
Caserta, upper vestibule. Photo Ente Provinciale per il Turismo

7.29
Caserta, upper vestibule. Photo Ente Provinciale per il Turismo

Marble Guardians

7.30
Caserta, upper vestibule, vault. Photo Mimmo Jodice

vaults of the triumphal corridor, have marched through the lower vestibule, up the stairs, and then into the upper vestibule where to this day they stand ready to support the great unbuilt dome.

These shafts are like the forms of men and women who, according to the myths of Vitruvius and his commentators, are encased or imprisoned metaphorically as forced guardians within all columns and who, as caryatids, termini, atlantes, and other architectural monsters, lift the weights of the vaults and roofs that offer shelter (fig. 7.31). A Corinthian maid from Aeneas's city of Puteoli, a Sicilian scholar, an Apulian matron,[53] and others delimit the visitor's route through the palace's public rooms. The marble shafts are architectural halberdiers and bodyguards whose brigades hold aloft the palace created for similarly colorful brigades of human guards, servants, and courtiers. Continuations of the sculptured guardians without and of the allegorical statues of Majesty, Merit, and Truth, they reinforce the double nature of Caserta's expression—geometric matrix for justice and palace of mythic admonition. They inhabit and transfigure a base material, brick, and a baser one, stucco. Optimates in the social temple, they animate the palace's geometry with more of the sublime music of myth.

This reading is strengthened by the nature of the foundation-stone ceremonies, to which Vanvitelli gives much space in the *Dichiarazione*.[54] In October 1751 the site had been cleared. The cornerstone was laid, well before the foundations were actually begun, on Carlo's thirty-sixth birthday, January 20, 1752. At

7.31
Columns, pilasters, termini, and atlantes. From Guarino Guarini, *Architettura Civile* (1737)

7.32
Pasquale Mattei. *Manovre al Campo di Marte*. Caserta, Reggia

dawn regiments of infantry from the Molise and L'Aquila appeared, plus squadrons of cavalry and dragoons. The soldiers turned into living columns formed up so as to outline the plan of the future palace; the long sides were composed of cavalry, the short sides of infantry. The corners were created by eight cannon and their crews, two at each corner. (One thinks here of the corner bastions, lined with cannon, in Gioffredo's design.) On the spot near the center destined to be occupied by the royal chapel, a rectangular platform was built and covered by a canopy. Here were the royal party, the first and finest pillars of palace and of state. A table in the center formed the upper part of the device that would lower the first stone into the cavity beneath. That stone was given a strange, "bonitary" inscription:

Let Bourbon palace, Bourbon race,
Remain upon this Bourbon place
Until the gods receive this stone
Flown up to Heaven on its own.[55]

To pursue the possibility suggested in these lines, the Bourbons remain below, a standing family, until the very stone on which they stand flies to heaven like the Immacolata in the chapel. One thinks again of Amphion.[56] A century later this ceremony became the central icon of the throne room that was adapted from the original Hall of the *Baciamano*. In the ceiling fresco by Gennaro Maldarelli (fig. 8.42) the long-limbed king and queen, in the center, sway along a crimson carpet leading to the silk-draped pavilion marking the site of the chapel's future high altar, where Bonito's Immacolata will be. Round them in seemly shoals are court and army. A heroic foreign family reigns in the center of its bowing tribe, having seized local land. Maldarelli emphasizes the tent rather than the military formations. But the spirit of Vanvitelli's description of the ceremony also recalls Bourbon military exercises, as recorded for example in Pasquale Mattei's *Manovre al Campo di Marte* (Caserta, Reggia): a flag-flying royal tent, again, but this time well back and framed by a vast geometric arch of troops, and a colorful foreground of *popolo minuto* who explain, admire, and contrast with the rigid masses beyond them (fig. 7.32).

The army that marked out Caserta's shape in colorful uniforms, anticipating the columns inside the palace, was now replaced by another army, one that would cast the palace into permanent form. This was the army of craftsmen and laborers, jointly commanded by Vanvitelli and Lorenzo Maria Neroni, Superintendent of the Fabric of Caserta. The new army also had many ranks—master craftsmen, journeymen, apprentices, day-laborers, convicts, Christian slaves, heathen slaves. Men, women, and children worked.[57] The feeding and keeping of these thousands was a major logistical problem. We have seen that the soldiers in this army are commemorated in the form of chained slave-pairs on the parapet of the Fountain of Juno and Aeolus (fig. 5.36). The army of plebs created the shell of the palace in about twenty years. By 1762 the main-floor rooms were mostly roofed in. By 1768 the chapel columns were being set up. The shell of the whole was virtually complete, and the chapel and theater were decorated by the time of Vanvitelli's death in 1773.

8 The Family Romance

The Chapel

We now enter the precincts of the court and of the inner royal family that that court was designed to surround. We will visit first the chapel, then the rooms through which access to the king is gained, then the family's living quarters, and finally (in chapter 9) the theater. All these rooms were designed in accordance with Luigi Vanvitelli's general wishes, though the style varies from rococo to Neoclassical and Empire, and though the New Apartments were not under way until the 1840s.

The chapel emphasizes the Bourbon court's domestic nature and the themes of conception, infancy, and guardianship. It is one of the splendors of the palace (figs. 8.1–8.4).[1] It is perhaps rather too often compared with Robert de Cotte's chapel at Versailles. Certainly the latter was Vanvitelli's inspiration, though Caserta's chapel has more templelike proportions and is more of a *U*-shaped basilica in the manner of Vanvitelli's and Gioffredo's two great churches in Naples (figs. 4.14, 4.19); and it is warmer, more theatrical, and more colorful than the French prototype. Note its hexagonal coffering in the apse vault and its freestanding back-lit pairs of columns. The Caserta chapel is in many respects a typical Italian eighteenth-century church.[2]

The columns, gray monolithic marble shafts, support gilded capitals, a rich entablature, and a richer vault, a vault in which circular thermal windows nestle into wreaths and garlands set just above the cornice. The columns' immense pedestals meanwhile serve as piers for the main-floor chapels.[3] The piers open into aisles, or aisle compartments, connected with each other

8.1
Caserta, chapel of the royal palace, 1768.
Photo Alinari

8.2
Caserta, chancel of the palace chapel. Photo Ente Provinciale per il Turismo

8.4
Caserta, chapel, winged head in door. Gaetano Salomone, 1777. Photo Ente Provinciale per il Turismo

8.3
Caserta, chapel, entry beneath royal loge. Photo Ente Provinciale per il Turismo

by wide, squarish doorways (fig. 8.2). The balustraded gallery or colossal plinth thus formed runs all the way around the room, not omitting the chancel.

Most of the sculpture is by Violani and Salomone and was completed in 1768. The chapel's great artistic feature was Giuseppe Bonito's *Immaculate Conception* (fig. 8.2) over the altar,[4] which was damaged in World War II when much other harm was done to the chapel. The iconographic impulse, therefore, here as in the palace as a whole, is toward the celebration of the family. Naples' clan of tutelary guardians watches over a chapel focused at one end on a loge in which the king, his wife, and children worshiped and, on the other, on an altar dedicated to an epic enactment of the Virgin's own conceiving. She floats like the risen Parthenope of Rè's frontispiece (fig. 4.12), one who has yet to be delivered of her prince. The king, as father of Naples, framed in the loge of his chapel, faced those holy genealogies that constituted his patrimony as royal priest of Christ and that exalted him in the company of his capital's family of saints.

The family nature of the chapel is enhanced by the many infants' heads, representatives of angelic hierarchies, that punctuate the polychrome marbles and scagliola lining the walls, floor, and vault (figs. 8.2, 8.4). These heads, borrowed directly from Borromini's work in St. John Lateran, Rome, are indicated in the *Dichiarazione* designs, as is an altarpiece much like Bonito's. The angels, done by Salomone in 1777, mostly consist of long, fluttering, limblike feathers and ephebic heads. They flutter at the corners of architraves, guard the summits of the piers, and preside over the altar aedicule. The floor is meanwhile patterned like an immense carpet; indeed, throughout, there is the feel of monumental domesticity. The Bourbon court, in its private and public comings and goings, in the continual confessions and masses, would have underlined this sense of a holy family and set upon it Vico's tribal understanding of that term.

The Halls of Representation

By the time of Vanvitelli's death in 1773 the gardens had been planted and much of their sculpture was in place. The palace's 1200 rooms were structurally complete and the whole shell roofed in. The upper and lower vestibules were decorated, as were the stair hall, chapel, and theater. At this point work slowed down until the early 1780s. In that year the rooms leading south from the upper vestibule and the two apartments along the south front were worked on in campaigns lasting until the fall of the dynasty in 1860. None of the other apartments, not the crown prince's on the east, the queen's on the north, nor those of the royal children on the northeast, were ever decorated. As to the existing decorative work, Vanvitelli had apparently prepared plans for it and his son Carlo supervised the execution of most of it.[5]

In these entrails of the palace the vestibule and stair-hall allegories, whose purpose is to admonish the visitor, give way to statements about the Bourbon family itself and the heroic and mythical forebears of its Neapolitan branch.[6] The rooms along the southern arm of the central cross (C, D, and E in fig. 6.14), which Vanvitelli called the Halls of the Halberdiers, Bodyguards, and the Untitled, are now collectively known as the Halls of Representation. Their decoration dates mainly from the late 1780s, with some elements much later. The basic lineaments of all three rooms are illustrated in the *Dichiarazione* (fig. 8.5, I, L, M). The cornices and frames are of black Mondragone marble and the walls of dappled scagliola in various colors. Vanvitelli's simple massive geometric enframements, flat planes of colored marble, elastic gilded arabesques, oval niches, coved ceilings with thermal windows, widely set pairs of pilasters, and utter symmetry, prevail.

The Hall of the Halberdiers is also known as the Ambassadors' Hall (fig. 8.6). The decoration is spare and rich. It is vast and dim, gray and gold. Colossal baroque candelabras hang from the vault, which is in fact a coved ceiling enriched with ladderlike gilded panels. Over the doors there are eight stucco busts in oval niches by the nineteenth-century sculptor Tommaso Bucciano (fig. 8.7). Antonio Marotta has identified them as portraits of the Bourbon queens of Naples.[7] Their ancestresses are in the garden: Ceres, Venus, Diana. The ceiling painting, *Bourbon Arms Sustained by the Virtues* (1787), is by Domenico Mondo (fig. 8.8). In it we have another of those flying processions of divinities, gesturing and gazing at each other against the background of a thundery empyrean set as if seen through a great skylight.[8] At the bottom Hercules raises his club to slay his monstrous earthly enemies, including the Hydra and the Giants who occupied the earth before the advent of man: it is, again, that Vichian deinfestation of territory that appears so frequently throughout the palace. In the next group, above, and of course later in time, are various virtues including Majesty, who twists on the lion she rides to admire at the fleur-de-lys on the mighty shield in the center; Fortitude with her column and sword; Justice, whose attendant putti play with her sword and scales; and Peace with her goat-horned cornucopia, accepting an olive branch from yet another attendant putto. Other figures represent more sui generis Bourbon virtues; for example, Eminence of Rank floats above the great shield and with her left arm prevents an eagle from flying higher. She herself gazes into the limitless beyond. Next to her, on the right, Loyalty deploys a staff and basilisk-bird (whose gaze kills him who offends). On the left Obedience bears her burning brand and sets her eyes on heaven, while she is given, by her putto on the far left, a bridle and bit. Below these ladies, toward the center, Puissance is recognizable with her key to power, her table of laws, which are other such keys, and her helmet. Most of these ideas are taken from Cesare Ripa's handbook rather than being inventions like the stair-hall and vestibule programs.[9] Yet the array of qualities represented is very personal to the family that was to

8.5
Vanvitelli. Planned Halls of the Ambassadors, of Alessandro Farnese, and of Alexander the Great at the royal palace at Caserta. From the *Dichiarazione*

8.6
Caserta, Reggia, Hall of the Ambassadors, late 1780s. Photo Alinari

The Family Romance

8.7
Tommaso Bucciano.
Bust of Bourbon
queen in the Hall of
the Ambassadors.
Photo Mimmo Jodice

8.8
Domenico Mondo.
Bourbon Arms Sustained by Virtues,
1787, in the Hall of
the Ambassadors.
Photo Soprintendenza per i Beni
Culturali per la Campania. (See also pl.
8.)

live in the palace. To the normal civil virtues were added those of power, rank, obedience, and loyalty, expressed by means of the instruments of fire, compulsion, memory, and death. The violent lustrations of Hercules, below, are carried on, above, more precisely and subtly. The females in this weighty and powerful fresco are very different from Starace's delicate, billowing beauties in the stair hall. They are powerful and large of body, and almost as rough looking as Hercules and his giants below.

The Hall of the Bodyguards (figs. 8.9–8.11) is also called the Hall of Alessandro Farnese. Alessandro (1545–1592) was the greatest of Carlo di Borbone's Farnese ancestors. Though Duke of Parma, he established the family's Spanish connections. He was raised in Spain and served Philip II as governor general of the Netherlands. He was a great military leader and diplomat and a skillful, unscrupulous ruler. The walls of this room are more classically ornate, less abstract, than those of the Hall of the Halberdiers. But the tone is still mainly gray. Widely set pairs of flat, channeled Ionic pilasters sustain a rich stucco entablature whose frieze is a rolling march of rinceaux. Thermal windows, true and false, fill the margins of the coved ceiling. Most of this is in Vanvitelli's plans of 1756 (fig. 8.5, *L*, with relief panels as in *M*), except that Vanvitelli's thermal windows are there shaped like inverted hearts rather than having their present segmentally headed form. Between the pilasters are rectangular stucco reliefs of episodes in the ancient histories of Magna Graecia—battles, marches, meetings, victories—by Bucciano, for example: *The Flight of Hannibal from Capua in 211 B.C.* (fig. 8.10). The artist has made use of large-headed, squat figures, abrupt shifts of linear alignments, and other devices borrowed from Roman sculpture. The reliefs represent a degree of Neoclassicism beyond what Vanvitelli envisioned, and they replace the trophies Vanvitelli had planned (fig. 8.5). Vanvitelli also designed a much plainer vault, rather different from the richly etched and feathery forest of fronds, putti, birds, and the like that exists today (fig. 8.9). Except for the reliefs, the room was completed in 1787.

To the right, on entering, one sees a colossal marble statue of Alessandro Farnese crowned by a Victory (fig. 8.11). This was carved in the sixteenth century by Simone Moschino, in Rome, based on a design by Gaspare Celio, who served the Farnese court in Parma. It was quite possibly made for the *sala grande* in the Palazzo Farnese in Rome. It stood in that building until Carlo di Borbone or his son had it set up at Caserta. It was probably intended to be part of an unexecuted decorative program for the Farnese Palace chronicling the deeds of Alessandro Farnese.[10] The work is traditionally said to have been carved from a shaft taken from the Basilica of Constantine, an appropriate *Entstehung* for such a sculpture and, if true, a possible reason for its severe though typically Mannerist compaction of bodies. At Caserta, as a sort of statue-colonne, it extends the theme of the marble guardians in the vestibules.

The Family Romance

8.9
Luigi and Carlo Vanvitelli. Hall of Alessandro Farnese at Caserta, late 1780s. Photo Ente Provinciale per il Turismo

8.10
Tommaso Bucciano. *The Flight of Hannibal from Capua*, 1787. Caserta, Hall of Alessandro Farnese. Photo Ente Provinciale per il Turismo

8.11
Simone Moschino, after a design by Gaspare Celio. *Alessandro Farnese, Vanquisher of Heresy and Liberator of the Province of Escaut, Crowned by Victory*, late sixteenth century. Caserta, Hall of Alessandro Farnese. Photo Mimmo Jodice

8.12
Camillo Guerra. *Carlo di Borbone at the Battle of Velletri.* Caserta, Hall of Alexander the Great. Photo Mimmo Jodice

Alessandro appears in classical military dress, his musculature Herculean; bearded, curly-headed, grasping his baton, and striding on the prone and massive corpse of Heresy. Alessandro is indeed a colossus, bigger than the goddess who crowns him, who stands behind him, a palm frond in her other hand. A third figure, in a Liberty Cap, symbolizing the Flemish provinces freed by Alessandro, supports the Victory goddess from behind. Vanvitelli probably knew this group, and he may well have been thinking of it when, in the 1750s, he planned the somewhat similar Hercules fountain for the lower vestibule, in which the god is crowned by Glory as he tramples his enemies. It is in any case yet another repetition of the image of the deinfestor, of the giant-killer. In the vault is another Starace fresco, not currently photographable: *The Glory of the Prince with the Twelve Provinces*, dating from 1785. The program's association between provinces—territory—and Alessandro Farnese, whose blood was brought to the Bourbons by Carlo's mother, is thus made clear.

The third of these great family halls is the central one of the palace front, leading out onto the balcony through the window of appearances over the main south gate (figs. 6.14, E; 8.5, M). Vanvitelli designated it as the Hall of the Untitled, but is now the hall of Alexander the Great. In it, single clusters of dark red marble Ionic pilasters with white marble bases and capitals support a Corinthian entablature with modillioned cornice and a geometrical spiral frieze. Huge easel paintings dating from the 1840s fill the walls. On the right is *Carlo di Borbone at the Battle of Velletri* by Camillo Guerra (fig. 8.12): the king on his white horse with leopard-skin blanket prances with his generals into the midst of a group of the wounded, while war still rages below. A battlefield pietà, complete with prayer book, pillow, Byronic victim, aged priest, and even a Magdalen, fills the right-hand corner. A landscape, vaporous with the aftermath of battle, forms the background. It recalls Celebrano's hunting scene celebrating Ferdinando's similar Herculean cleansing of the land. But this time the quarry consists of Austrians, not wild boar (fig. 7.11). Vanvitelli had also called for an equestrian picture (figure 8.5, M). As a pendant to Guerra's canvas, on the wall opposite, is *The Abdication of Carlo di Borbone in Favor of his Son* by Gennaro Maldarelli, 1849 (fig. 8.13). In this painting we see the court as it was in 1759, depicted in the Palazzo Reale, surrounding a throne pavilion and draped table; the king, the young Ferdinando, and before them the kneeling Tanucci. A peaceful family transaction opposes the violent victory on the opposite wall.

Both these pictures were executed long after Carlo's death. They look back on him as on a heroic ancestor. But another ancestor, more ancient and more universally heroic, is evoked in this hall. On the left, over the fireplace, is a porphyry medallion with a portrait of Alexander the Great. And over each door is a relief, in stucco or grisaille, of an episode in Alexander's life by Tito Angelini, dating from the 1840s. We see acts of valor, but there is great emphasis on compassion and regard for inferiors. These range all the way from a scene of Alexander with Bucephalus, his horse, to the hero's pity for the dying Darius, or for Darius's family (fig. 8.14). These works are even more Neoclassical than the reliefs in the Hall of Alessandro Farnese; but again the ideal of the clement, all-powerful ruler is stressed.

The wall decorations of the Hall of Alexander the Great were executed during the second phase of the Bourbon reign and, like much of the other work by Angelini and Bucciano, probably replaced Napoleonic imagery that had been set in place during Murat's reign. But this room had been intended as a hymn to Alexander at least as early as the period of Carlo Vanvitelli's supervisorship, for the ceiling vault is filled with a massive, all-consuming painting by Mariano Rossi dating from 1787: *The Marriage of Alexander and Roxana* (fig. 8.15). The architectural vaults and fictive skylights of the two earlier rooms are here replaced by a scheme that covers the entire ceiling. A great concentric pattern, of an earth, forms the outer rim. This earth is filled with forests, walls, mythic episodes, encampments, flights, greetings—all glimpsed, *da sotto in su*, like the vault fresco of a Baroque church. Rossi does not paint a flying procession across the sky, occupying more or less a single plane, as in the vaults discussed earlier, but creates a centrifugal cone rising upward to the blazing godhead. An inner, upper

8.13
Gennaro Maldarelli.
The Abdication of Carlo di Borbone in Favor of Ferdinando IV, 1849. Photo Soprintendenza per i Beni Culturali

The Family Romance

8.14
Tito Angelini. *The Family of Darius Seeking Mercy from Alexander.* Caserta, Hall of Alexander the Great. Photo Ente Provinciale per il Turismo

8.15
Mariano Rossi. *The Marriage of Alexander and Roxana*, 1787. Caserta, Hall of Alexander the Great. Photo Ente Provinciale per il Turismo. (See also pls. 9, 10.)

ring of divinities is assembled in groups, their garments floating gracefully into a halo of golden clothes concentrating on the central Zeus, remote, resplendent, who becomes a more majestic version of Starace's Apollo in the stair hall. In return the king of the gods blesses all below him, radiant on his throne of rolling air. The marriage couple is meanwhile blessed again by a concatenation of goddesses, plumed and draped like the gorgeous divas in an opera by Metastasio. Deities, beauties, and virtues converge, showing off their gifts and themselves, bringing kingdoms' crowns, the spoil of continents, the exotic flowers and game, and the yet more exotic fashions, of Africa and Asia. On the left, the never-to-be-omitted Hercules reclines after his labors. Magnanimity's lion and Victory's flag are beside him as a group of putti sport with his attributes. Opposite, on the right-hand side of the vault, a queenly bacchante raises a bunch of grapes like a pagan Host as putti and servants scurry with wine vessels. All assemble in a hovering canopy round the bride and groom. Alexander and Roxana rise to the visitor's eye out of a distance as one approaches, splendid in rose and blue, while exactly opposite them, functioning as a sort of repoussoir across the entire chamber, are the blacks and silhouetted browns of a grouping of the emperor's field commanders. The whole conception is like that of a Metastasio epithalamium, for these poems could be of just such epic scale and population.

The three Halls of Representation are romances of the royal family. The sequence begins with the Bourbon queens, the wives and mothers of the kings and princes of the Two Sicilies. They form a pantheon round a painted emblematic hymn to Bourbon virtue. We then move on to another constituent of the family, its Farnese blood, celebrated in a hall dedicated to the greatest of the Farnese condottieri and Spanish "deinfestors." Alessandro Farnese arrives as a god in a panorama of scenes depicting the territorial extent of Magna Graecia. We end with a great Alexander's marriage. And Roxana, princess of an Indian land, like the Bourbon queens represents territory.[11] This third room focuses both on the legendary conqueror and on Carlo di Borbone's own most precious territory, the road that was to lead directly from Caserta to Naples. It includes two pendant scenes that mark the beginning and end of his Neapolitan career, setting these acts into the context of Alexander's family and loyalty.

The introduction of Alexander the Great sets an imperial dimension on the iconography of Caserta. Alexander, we are told by Vico, built the first (Greek) empire and vanquished the last eastern one. The pupil of Aristotle and lover of Homer's poetry, he brought the lares of the west to the Ancient Near Eastern labyrinth of failed sublimity whose names—Persia, Babylonia—are now mere echoes. Their beautiful and impoverished remnant, Roxana, forlorn, anxious to be reconquered, symbolizes the mighty fall of territories waiting to be occupied by a new foreign god. Alexander's magnanimous family-founding was imperial in another sense because of the social abyss between the partners, because of the sublime power gap they represented. That difference marked the hugeness and inclusiveness of Alexander's territory and his heart's magnanimity.

All this comes from Vico: to him Alexander was also important as a person. He united African sharpness with Greek delicacy, expressing this when he founded a Greek city, Alexandria, in Africa. Far more than Tyre, Troy, or Carthage, Alexandria was a great capital and a city of artists and philosophers.[12] The emperor's peregrinations and his magnetism brought back to Greece essential knowledge of foreign lands, of their flora and fauna, as in the fresco. He made Greece the capital of an empire of knowledge. Alexander, indeed, "considered the whole of the earth to be one city—his own."[13] Rossi's heaven of gathering gods, with its Hesperidean gardens and groves, its camels and lions, alarums and excursions, is just such a mating of East and West and of ancient and modern empires, worthy of the Bourbon family pact.

The Old Apartments

From the Hall of Alexander, marked *E* in figure 6.14, sets of apartments lead off in either direction at right angles to the axis of the Halls of Representation. To the right, or west, are the major public anterooms to the king's apartments. These were decorated in the nineteenth century. To the left, or east, *Z* in figure 6.14, are the apartments Vanvitelli intended for the *principini*, decorated mostly in the 1780s and used by Ferdinando IV and Maria Carolina as their own living quarters. There are dozens of rooms in this set, known as the Old Apartments, all quite small, and I shall not attempt to describe each one. But they do serve to represent the most intimately domestic aspect of the palace.

The walls of many of the rooms are covered with silks woven at Ferdinando's nearby model factory and town of San Leucio.[14] The overdoor panels are by Bonito and G. B. Rossi. The style is in accordance with Vanvitelli's predilections. The greatest emphasis, the greatest color, and the greatest fantasy, are in the ceilings, as was the case in the Halls of Representation. These ceilings (figs. 8.16–8.23) swarm with fictive architectures, skies, landscapes, and figures. All is impossibly held together by interlacings of girandoles, garlands, swerving moldings, and guilloches.

The first four rooms are devoted to the seasons, beginning with Spring (fig. 8.16). The iconography here is rustic and Neapolitan, in line with Ferdinando's personality (he was known as the "*lazzarone* king"). Peasants and urchins prevail. Arts and leisure are personified by buoyant, roseate young people who frolic on balconied hanging gardens and among urns and trellises. Putti fly about with garlands curved against the sky in perfect circle-segments (fig. 8.17). Below this skyey paradise is an austerer, late Louis XVI arrangement, with slender noble mirrors and panels, and symmetrical wreaths of gold.

8.16
Antonio Domenici. Spring Chamber of the Old Apartments, late 1770s. Caserta, Reggia. Photo Jacelli

8.17
Spring Chamber, Caserta. Photo Soprintendenza per i Beni Culturali

The Family Romance

8.18
Antonio Dominici.
Autumn Chamber of
the Old Apartments,
late 1770s. Caserta,
Reggia. Photo Ente
Provinciale per il
Turismo. (See also
pl. 11.)

8.19
Studio of Ferdinando IV. Caserta, Reggia. Photo Ente Provinciale per il Turismo

8.20
Antonio Dominici. *Apollo and Minerva*, 1782–83, for Maria Carolina's *salottino*. Caserta, Reggia. Photo Mimmo Jodice

The Family Romance

8.21
Maria Carolina's bath, 1782–83, Caserta, Reggia. Photo Mimmo Jodice. (See also pl. 12.)

8.22
Gennaro Fiore. Putti, Maria Carolina's bath. Caserta, Reggia. Photo Mimmo Jodice. (See also pl. 13.)

8.23
Fedele Fischetti.
Ceiling, Maria Carolina's bath. Caserta, Reggia. Photo Mimmo Jodice

The Family Romance

This first room is mainly by Antonio Dominici;[15] the next, whose sky or vault depicts Summer in very similar ways, is by Fedele Fischetti and features Persephone and Ceres as well as Bacchic peasants. Autumn (fig. 8.18) is by Dominici again. The walls are paneled with gold silk. Still lifes of autumn fruits and flowers hang on the walls; Bacchus, Ariadne, and harvesters of grapes fill the vault. Winter is by Fischetti, presided over by Boreas, Orythia (his daughter) and Vesuvius. In contrast to the open skies of Spring, Autumn and Winter have enclosed vaults consisting of great golden shells with scrolled openings, as in Vanvitelli's schemes for the Hall of Alessandro Farnese. The designer of these four rooms was undoubtedly Vanvitelli himself, for the scheme is almost a direct repetition of his ceilings in the Cappella delle Reliquie, Santa Cecilia, Rome, though the figure style at Caserta is more sedate.

The little studio mentioned in Lampedusa's *The Leopard* (I, "Royal Audiences") is a bijou of a room decorated by Brunelli, Hackert, and Tischbein (fig. 8.19). The style is newly Neoclassical, with a vault by Giuseppe Magri covered with griffins and spirals of a severely symmetrical sort. The studio marks the ascendancy of German taste at the court and is in line with Maria Carolina's German background. In 1789 Johann Wilhelm Tischbein had become head of the Accademia di Disegno.[16] The furniture is of German manufacture as well, in what might be called a Sino-Pompeiian taste.

A *salottino* leading to Maria Carolina's bath was decorated by Dominici with crisp and rubicund gods and goddesses enthroned in clouds. The divinities surround a delightful Vanvitellian construct of arabesques: an octagon of concentric arcs formed from palms, volutes, stalks, ribbons, and tendrils. It is the quintessence of Vanvitelli's informal mode (fig. 8.20). But within these curly enframements the gods of Olympus—Apollo and Minerva; Mars and Astraea; Mercury; Jupiter and Venus—have a hard-shelled Neoclassical weight.

The bathroom also speaks this more rococo language (fig. 8.21), with intertwining twists of gilded shells, flowers, and the like, against deep pale skies. The bathroom decorations are more thinly and loosely woven than those of the *salottino* but with Vanvitelli's omnipresent golden tendrils. It has a marble tub by Salomone resembling a Napoleonic sarcophagus, and wall paintings by Fischetti. The Graces dance above the golden faucets, and over the doors stucco putti by Gennaro Fiore make as if to bring amphorae of waters and oils to the bathing queen (fig. 8.22). Above, gilded swags hang over other female divinities. Venus, just born, steps down a staircase of ripples. She is decorously draped, to the point of unrecognizability. In the ceiling a summer sky arches over clusters of water nymphs, reeds, dolphins, and other aqueous things, all bending down toward the presumed bather (fig. 8.23). The whole room sums up Vanvitelli's informal mode. It is in fact a conceit on the theme of Diana's spied-upon bath at the beginning of the river-road. All this dates from 1782–83, just a few years before Tischbein's advent.[17]

The Library

The rooms we have looked at (even the study) are in a relatively familial, fantastical mode, strikingly less majestic than the Halls of Representation. But in Maria Carolina's library, further along in this same wing, we find a room that definitively returns to the earlier mood.

In Mengs's Prado portrait (fig. 8.24) Maria Carolina of Hapsburg-Lorraine, daughter of the Emperor Franz I and Maria Theresa, and sister of Marie Antoinette, appears as a courtly woman with long whitish face and hair and wary eyes. She was a person of ebullience and strong passions. It was Maria Carolina who halted Carlo's habit of continuing to govern Naples after he had moved to Spain, and she who fired Vanvitelli's old enemy, Tanucci, in 1777—too late to do Vanvitelli any good, of course. In the 1780s Maria Carolina was a reformer; she protected the Freemasons and dabbled in political theory.[18] After the French Revolution, naturally, she turned from any sort of liberalism. But she remained relatively bookish and intellectual if one may judge from the contents of her library, which, besides being an excellent general collection of history, military affairs, and literature, includes works by most of the important local eighteenth-century writers including Metastasio and Vico.

These books are housed in several rooms, the main one being decorated with four large wall paintings, frescoes completed with tempera, by Heinrich Friedrich Füger. The style of the room is Vanvitellian: heavy abstract enframements, hexagonal

8.24
Anton Raphael Mengs. Portrait of Queen Maria Carolina. Madrid, Prado

coffers picked out in brilliant contrasts in the vault, medallions of famous writers over the doors. For the pictorial decorations Fueger was a good choice. He had been educated at Halle as a jurist and carried the imprint of his humanistic training into his art. When he was in Naples in the early 1780s he painted many portraits of the royal family, including miniatures (his specialty). The four pictures in Maria Carolina's library, dated 1782, are *The Age of Gold* (fig. 8.25); a picture now known as *Envy and Wealth* (fig. 8.26); *The School of Athens* (fig. 8.27), and *The Rebirth of the Arts* (fig. 8.28). The first and third of these are the two larger, and are horizontal in format. They are on the room's end walls. The others are square and are on the window wall and the wall opposite.

The Age of Gold represents that period of Hesperidean unity when Aeneas's golden bough and its many fellow talismans were one. We are in the primordial garden of the gods. Accompanied by the Graces and Abundance, Apollo, a tall, fair, plump Nordic youth with abundant curls, dressed in reddish gold, enters a wilderness glade from the right. On the left and on the far right he and other divinities are reverently hailed by a group of barbarian families. One of these men, kneeling in the center, carries a crook, or *lituus*.[19] Another leans on a spade; a third holds a bow; a fourth, a fishing rod and net. Hunting, fishing, and agriculture begin with the arrival of law and land clearing. Continuing in this Vichian sense, the Graces stand for natural contracts and for commerce and trial—the agreements and adjudications necessary among men for marriage.[20]

The next scene, labeled *Envy and Wealth* or *Envy and the Virtues* in modern publications,[21] shows on the left the kneeling Midas, who was Orpheus' pupil—hence his lyre and laurel crown though he is also a pleb, a fool in fact. Midas nearly dies of hunger because everything he touches, including food and water, turns to gold. Here he bends over the banks of the river Pactolus drinking from it. Midas's real story, says Vico, is not that he exemplified greed or envy—though he did do so, and Füger has heavily cloaked Envy stabbing herself with hostile anguish in the background (fig. 8.29)—Midas' real story is that he mythicizes the river-of-gold trope. The true river of gold, the true Pactolus is like the Nile, the Arethusa, or even the Tartarus, a river that irrigates golden wheat fields planted along its shores.[22] Füger's river, a glow of cloud, splits the scene into a left half devoted to the pleb or pseudo-Apollo, and Envy; while on the right the divinities arrive in a repetition of the event in figure 8.25. Like the river-road this Pactolus gilds Ceres' lands and summons her from her underground city.

In the upper left-hand corner, far above Midas and Envy, at the origin of the episode and of the river, there is a mountain on which white Pegasus rears, his hooves breaking the banks of the Hippocrene that now flows down the slopes of Parnassus into human lands. This identity between Vico's Hippocrene and the Pactolus is, again, the mountain cascade of the religion of the waters, of fear, and of *latices*. The Hippocrene had been loosed when Pegasus kicked the parapet of the Muses' well—

8.25
Friedrich Heinrich
Füger. *The Age of
Gold*, 1782. Caserta,
Old Apartments,
library. Photo
Mimmo Jodice. (See
also pl. 14.)

8.26
Füger. *Envy and
Wealth*. Photo
Mimmo Jodice

8.27
Füger. *The School of Athens*. Photo Mimmo Jodice. (See also pl. 15.)

8.28
Füger. *The Rebirth of the Arts*. Photo Mimmo Jodice. (See also pl. 16.)

that is, when man had learned his first art, which was that of taming horses, which in turn allowed him seemingly to "fly."²³ On the other side of the scene, as its agent of fulfillment, is Minerva, the protectress of commerce. Within the realm of riches she is Midas's antithesis. She offers her cup to gold-bedizened Wealth, who treads on Apollo's lyre, for she is subsequent to the poetic laws of Parnassus, and replaces them with the laws of historic society (fig. 8.30).²⁴ Wealth, in gesture and regard, has learned from Envy's self-immolation. She is to Envy as Minerva is to Midas. A winged genius, the genius who comes with the founding of human sciences, crowns Wealth in honor of her learning, her prudence, and her modernity. Wealth has gathered wisdom from every corner, every incident in the scene. And finally two real historical people, the old man and his son or grandson behind Minerva, do the same. They benefit from the process portrayed, and they continue it. The scene fits in well with the Neapolitans' double fascination with economics and mythology at the time.

The School of Athens continues humanity's lessons (fig. 8.27). It came into being when Socrates introduced mankind to more subtle sciences than horsemanship, for example, dialectic, and when he taught Pythagorean mathematics. "By this unifying road in the times of Socrates and Plato, Athens shone with all the arts in which human genius can be admired: with eloquence, history, music, bronze-casting, painting, sculpture, and architecture; with syllogism, sorites [a type of verbal logic], and inductive reasoning."²⁵ These disciplines arise from geometry. In Vico's mind they developed as poetic institutions, that is,

8.29
Detail of fig. 8.26, Envy

8.30
Detail of fig. 8.26, Wealth treading on lyre

abstractly according to inner laws as all other civilizing discoveries have done. But humanity, in its inveterate mythologizing, embodies the poetic laws into personalities, not only into gods but into the famous humans credited with the great discoveries made by unknown predecessors. In the same way, the personages who inscribe geometrical constructs, teach, and demonstrate, are all allegorical. But they stand and sit like the historical figures in Raphael's famous fresco of the same title. Füger's allegories, the abstract histories of real life, literally *replace* Raphael's historical individuals. The crowd of new arrivals with which the two previous scenes were filled are here, on the right, headed by two main "real men," rather resembling Raphael's Plato and Aristotle, who had stood center stage and reigned over the whole scene in the Vatican picture. That they should here be so radically deposed from that centrality; that Raphael's tableau should in face have been rotated ninety degrees, makes Vico's point well. The real men enter upstage, on the far right, followed by various characters, including the artist himself (fig. 8.31). The historicity even of Plato and Aristotle is tinctured with myth. They too were late arrivals, belated, even magical in that they were credited with the miracles of their nameless predecessors.

If Füger has borrowed from Raphael, from the tapestry cartoons as well as from the Vatican stanze, it is with cause. The main event in *his* School of Athens is on the left: a priestess removes the veil from a shrouded statue standing on an altar (fig. 8.32). Altars, says Vico, are the true foci of cities where men congregate to learn. For *ara* 'altar' is *arces* 'strongholds.' From the same word comes *ager*, originally an 'urban district': "In Greece Theseus founded Athens on the famous Altar of the Miserable, assuming correctly that the miserable were the men and women who were impious and outlawed and who, from the quarrels of their unholy societies, returned to the strong lands of strong men . . . alone, weak, and needing all the benefits that pious humanity had produced.[26] The "altar of the miserable" was therefore the first urban civilization.[27] In *The School of Athens* the miserable are probably the students and seekers who come to learn "the benefits that humanity had produced"; but we also think of Hercules again, for he is a similar if less learned asylum, as is Vanvitelli's planned statue of Clemency, the "miserorum confugium." Asylums and altars are indeed the central foci of Vico's city; think of its hundreds of churches, its monasteries, and its Albergo dei Poveri. The altar of Füger's school is inscribed: "What I have been, am, and shall be is never uncovered." The process of learning never ends. The new historic discoverer, or uncoverer, is always mythologized. His predecessors always siip back into namelessness, that is, into allegory. Hence Füger makes of his *School of Athens* a reversed recension of his *Age of Gold*. The mortals, now, are those who arrive on the right, led by the Plato-Aristotle figures. They replace Apollo and Abundance. And it is now the gods or allegories who, most of them, are recumbent on the left and who grasp their symbolic tools.

The object that is being uncovered but that will never be completely known is a statue of Venus. Venus is the principle of all generation, including the intellectual kind. She may also be Cartari's "image of Venus weeping beneath her mantle, which represents the land in winter when it is mostly covered with clouds and appears all sickened because it does not see the sun." Some Cartari editions illustrate a totally shrouded female like Füger's (fig. 8.33).[28] Like Vico's, Cartari's unveiling will occur to be followed by the season of reveiling. Knowledge, like the seasons, like Immortality herself and the arts as in Starace's stair-hall fresco, is cyclical and never more than partial. In any event, in Füger's scene *Astronomy*, stars glowing on her crown, begins to unveil this figure to the assembly of arts and sciences. A priestess in the rear, on the left, clouds the altar with incense. It is not strange that Raphael's *School of Athens*, thus reinterpreted, should surround the altar of a mourning Venus. The mourning veil is being lifted by the queen of sciences. Astronomy, the major achievement of the geometric art and the most celestial embodiment of its laws, is the Springtime who ends the sorrows of the winter Venus, even if she does not reveal what that Venus has been, is, or shall be. Astronomy, the "long turning of the year," in Vico's phrase, serves to fascinate the crowd of arriving human gods. She is the good siren of science. She is the science that is ἀπὸ τό οὐρανοῦ, "by Heaven," the sky's contemplatress, who instituted the first auspices of humanity, mother of Hymen and of marriage, dressed as a "doc-

8.31
Detail of fig. 8.27, self-portrait of Füger as Raphael (on far right)

8.32
Detail of fig. 8.27, the unveiling of Venus

8.33
Mourning Venus. From Vincenzo Cartari, *Imagini degli dei*, 1625

8.34
Detail of fig. 8.28, goddess

8.35
Detail of fig. 8.28, putto

tor."[29] She is thus to be connected with the Immortality of Starace's stair-hall fresco (fig. 7.25), with the crowd of famous figures in Füger's painting, and with those whose names are engraved on the base of the obelisk behind them: Marcus Aurelius, Epaminondas, Socrates, Homer, and Phidias.

Finally, in the fourth picture is an event that caps the Athenian climax (fig. 8.28). A flying genius like the one in *Envy and Wealth* descends upon a commanding, right-of-center goddess figure (fig. 8.34) who is a kind of twin both for Minerva and for Wealth. Replacing the bending, groping Midas on the left, meanwhile, is the recumbent Sebeto, with spade, crown of reeds, and upward gaze. His role and aspect in the picture resemble Midas'.[30] The figure is also linked, like Midas', to the barbarians in figure 8.25. And in front of Sebeto a putto, who mimics Midas not in role and aspect but in pose—and thereby remakes the point about rightful as opposed to wrongful discoveries of treasure—inscribes COSMUS DE MEDICIS on a tablet (fig. 8.35). Here is a visual pun about gold, the Apollonian gold misused by Midas but transmuted into true wealth by Cosimo. In this scene the Bourbons' Medici heritage appears more subtly than does the Farnese patrimony in the Hall of Alessandro Farnese; and Cosimo's stone-carved name is meanwhile added to those on the obelisk in the *School of Athens*. At the same time the place of Greed, or Envy, is taken by two wondering, approaching, discussing ladies who will join this episode just as Envy is abandoning the event in which she had been taking part (fig. 8.26). In another sense, by similar trope-transformation, the man and his son, right-hand-side recipients and explainers in *The Age of Gold*, become left-hand-side and female recipients and explainers. And the Evil that flees the scene, who is the Envy of *True Wealth*, becomes in this scene Blindness with bandaged eyes, ass-eared Ignorance, and another Envy, this one male but making as if to stab himself like the Envy in figure 8.29. All three of them clamber over the foundations of a Greek Doric temple in the ruins of an excavated ancient town. Again there is a clear reference, in the mythic mode of the buried city, to the room's riches as a library.

This fourth picture seems to conflate Herculaneum and Paestum. Below, on the ground, are the broken artifacts of the civilizations recovered in Carlo's and Ferdinando's excavations, now to be revived and re-known. A commanding goddess (fig. 8.34), Tyche or Cybele in civic crown, a goddess of cities, points with her right arm to those who approach and, with her caduceus, indicates the buried past: a bust of Homer, a torso, a Composite capital, a palette, books, a broken lyre like the one in *The Age of Gold* and also like that in the Midas scene, but this one richly wrought. That caduceus is the instrument of civilized struggle that we have seen before. Pity, in Starace's stair-hall fresco, hands it to Astraea. It is one form of the golden bough and of all other produce of the Hesperides, including the spears of wheat that will flank the Hippocrene/Pactolus. The goddess points to the "superseded" yet now also re-known artifacts of the underground city. These dead shall be raised, as

Aeneas with his bough brought up from Dis his father's mandate and as Ceres' gold is yearly raised to the rivers of the surface world. Like Parthenope, Tyche or Cybele builds new cities. Her genius brings the fire of learning to buried metropolises. The goddess will illuminate the Stygian rivers of dead towns and their dead arts. The boy who writes Cosimo's name is Midas' redeemed successor as the wealth-rediscoverer, and he is also a re-visioning, with altered pose but continued gesture, first of the barbarian king in *The Age of Gold* and then of that other astonished, fascinated seeker in *The School of Athens* who recoils from the unveiling of Venus (fig. 8.27).

The New Apartments

In contrast to these small rooms decorated during the reign of Ferdinando IV and mainly under Carlo Vanvitelli's supervision, the "new apartments" occupy what Luigi Vanvitelli had intended as the king's living quarters along the southern front of the palace. The rooms continue the majestic scale of the Halls of Representation. Vanvitelli called them, respectively, the Halls of the Titled, of the Ambassadors, of the *Baciamano*, and the King's Dining Room (fig. 6.14, *F*, *G*, *H*, and *I*). They lead to the rooms Vanvitelli had originally intended as the king's private apartments and where Ferdinando IV's successors did indeed live. But here, stylistically if not conceptually, we take leave of both Vanvitellis and move beyond even the Füger–Tischbein world of the 1780s into something new. The decorations of the New Apartments date from 1807–1845—that is, from the reigns of Murat, Bonaparte, and of Ferdinando IV after his restoration in 1815 as Ferdinando I. Francesco I, who reigned from 1825 to 1830, and Ferdinando II, king from 1830 to 1859 (he was the restorer of the Fontana Santa Lucia mentioned in chapter 2) also contributed.

The first room is the Hall of Mars (fig. 8.36), begun in 1807 under Giuseppe Bonaparte (fig. 6.14, *F*), and with Carlo Vanvitelli's successor Antonio de Simone in charge. The dado and door frames are of black Vesuvian basalt. Paired Ionic pilasters support an Ionic entablature with frieze of addorsed griffins and a coved ceiling filled with stucco reliefs. Thus the architectural enframement is derived from Vanvitelli's Halls of Representation. But the spaces between those immaculate marble pilasters and in the paneled coves of the vaults are here filled with monumental relief figures in self-conscious, often exact symmetry. The larger reliefs are allegories of Fortitude, Prudence, and similar martial qualities. The smaller ones, over the doors, are devoted to episodes from the *Iliad*. Most of them feature the god of war. They replace the original Napoleonic decorative scheme, and are by Domenico Masucci, by another sculptor known only as D'Antonio, and Valerio Villareale.

The vault painting is by Antonio Calliano and depicts *The Death of Hector and the Triumph of Achilles* (fig. 8.37). With its flailing, friezelike composition, plunging white horses, and stylized sunset, Calliano owes equal debts to David, Gros, and perhaps someone like Josef Anton Koch.

8.36
Antonio de Simone and others. Hall of Mars, 1807 on. Caserta. Photo Alinari

The Family Romance

8.37
Antonio Calliano.
The Death of Hector and the Triumph of Achilles, 1815. Caserta, Hall of Mars. Photo Ente Provinciale per il Turismo. (See also pl. 17.)

What does this painting have to do with the functions of the palace? Vico tells us that Achilles and Hector play key roles in the realm of justice. Achilles was the greatest of the Greek heroes, one of the optimates of the harsh early republics; but his refusal to bury Hector meant that he was behaving like a barbarian, an animal. Furthermore he had brought about the ruin of Troy and that of his own country simply to right a private wrong.[31] This sort of interpretation of the *Iliad* is what Vico calls "the discovery of the true Homer," and he devotes a major part of the *Scienza nuova* to it. In one sense it is the search for the first of all the great mythic tellings of a race's civilizings. In another, Homer is simply a *primus inter pares* among epic poets. For all peoples have their Homers, as they have their Aeneases and their Herculeses.

In a more topical sense the selection of this subject for the Hall of the Titled, that is, of the optimates, may tie in with the Treaty of Casalanza, signed May 20, 1815, by which after the Napoleonic interregnum the Bourbons returned to rule, cleansed of their humiliation. We would then see Hector as the heroic victim of a foreign invader, defending his capital with Mars at his side, a feature not in Homer's text but, interestingly, very much the case in Calliano's picture. Furthermore, it is the funeral of Hector that ends the *Iliad* and sends Aeneas forth on his journey to Italy, thereby beginning the next stage, the Latin one, of the story. The presence of Mars in Hector's chariot fits the themes of the hall and takes the curse off Hector's failure. And since they traced their ancestry euhemeristically back to

Aeneas, the Bourbons would have seen Hector as a kinsman too and the reestablishment of their capital on the Bay of Naples as a reestablishment of a Troy perished because of Achilles' fury. That fury, which culminated in the Greek hero's dragging Hector's naked body around the walls of Ilium, is prefigured by the artist in Hector's stiff white nakedness. The similarity of this scene to Gavin Hamilton's dramatic portrayal of that same culmination, *Achilles Dragging Hector's Body around the Walls of Troy*, engraved by Domenico Cunego in 1766 and well-known to Neoclassical painters, would complete Calliano's prolepsis.[32] Meanwhile the original notion of the Halls of Representation, namely that of joining wall episodes in the lives of great commanders and rulers who are then apotheosized in a painted ceiling, is here continued. The Hall of Mars is a direct continuation of the Hall of Alexander. With its matrimonial emphasis the latter moreover serves to introduce Ferdinando IV's domestic apartments, but serves equally well to lead on, as here, in a more public sequence, to Mars and his Homeric actions. Especially in 1815 that vision of the Trojan victim, sustained by a Mars who seems about to kill the invader chief, would well express the Bourbon state of mind.

The room marked G in figure 6.14, Vanvitelli's Hall of the Ambassadors, is now devoted to Astraea (fig. 8.38). The decoration is very similar in style to that of the Hall of Mars but possesses a more restful rhythm and is filled with the symbols and figures of peace. Astraea had appeared in Starace's stair-hall fresco under Mercury's protection, embraced by Pudicity and receiving the fasces from Pity. Vico writes much of Astraea. Indeed her reappearance here bears out and continues her actions in the Starace fresco. Astraea combines aspects of Justitia and Majestas; in this sense she continues the theme of barbarian "justice" (as in Achilles' punishment of Hector) as well as the themes of the royal portal and the stair hall and of Ceres' fountain in the gardens. Astraea is the "bringer to earth of justice in golden summer." She holds the instruments of measurement because it is through the measuring of grain that distributive justice came into being.[33] She is the antithesis of Mars's fury and of Achilles' barbaric justice.

The ceiling of this room is painted with a *Triumph of Justice with Astraea between Verity and Innocence* (fig. 8.39) by Giacomo Berger (1815). Widows and unfortunates advance imploringly toward the goddess, who stands on an Altar of the Miserable. She holds, with self-conscious symmetry and delicacy, the fasces of modern monarchy and the scales of mathematical justice. Around her a bevy of personifications stand, taken mostly from Ripa, or from Ripa as reinterpreted in the Vichian mode.[34] In the sky on the left, reclining in a throne of clouds, are Jupiter and Juno arm in arm, the symbol of a marriage made in heaven. Opposite them, hellish as opposed to heavenly, the dispersed as opposed to the joined, devils and evils are expelled into a gray storm. Below these, on the ground, Hercules, as ever exemplifying heroic virtue and dressed in the skin of the Nemaean lion, slays a prehuman giant. In the *Scienza nuova* Hercules is particularly linked to Astraea, for as the lion's slayer he

8.38 Antonio de Simone and others. Hall of Astraea, c. 1815. Caserta. Photo Jacelli. (See also pl. 18.)

is in the house of Leo, which is attached in the heavens to the House of Astraea.³⁵ Behind this explusion other exiles form the central band of the painting, Democracy with her handful of serpents and *litui* among them. In contrast, next to Astraea's throne a nearly naked Innocence crowns Modesty, seated at Astraea's feet. Modesty, or Gentleness, thus crowned, is a feature of the *Scienza nuova*. On the left, more expulsions: Calumny exits, grasping by the hair the naked boy she has maligned, her torch symbolizing the fact that her viciousness can burn abroad throughout all states. Indolence, resting on Astraea's platform, reacts to everything with slow dislike.³⁶ Throughout the painting Berger has used some of the same elements found in Calliano's *Hector*: the naked hero in the foreground, though active here, not passive; the band of weary refugees on the left; and the significantly raised arms respectively of Mars and Astraea.

The room's walls are of unmolded scagliola panels. The Composite pilasters, in heavy unfluted pairs, are of porphyry and *fior di pesco*. A rich neoclassic entablature supports a coved ceiling articulated into rounded-off panels tightly woven with golden boughs and flowers. Swans sustain festoons. Along the rich granular sheen of the walls, large, graceful, golden relief figures disport themselves freely as in air, nude and without enframements. Winged geniuses hold instruments and attributes of Justice, Fortitude, and Magnanimity. Grasping their tables of the law, their fasces, and their wreaths, they fly, their gods' veils billowing filmily behind. At one end of the room is an

8.39
Giacomo Berger.
The Triumph of Justice with Astraea between Verity and Innocence, 1815. Photo Ente Provinciale per il Turismo

8.40
Gaetano Genovese and others. Throne room at Caserta, 1839–1845. Photo Ente Provinciale per il Turismo. (See also pl. 19.)

8.41
The throne at Caserta. Photo Ente Provinciale per il Turismo

altar-fireplace with three goddesses standing on it in an embrace: *Minerva between Legislation and Reason*, by Villareale, who did much of the room's sculpture along with Masucci. At the other end of the room is a similar altar-fireplace on which Astraea and Hercules appear again, as full-round statues, with representations of the Two Sicilies.

This room is clearly conceived as a pendant to its immediate predecessor. Barbaric justice gives way to civilized. The cruel vengeance of the early heroic republics is replaced by this allegorical restatement of the symmetries and the measures of modern monarchy. This succession permeates the pictorial and decorative content of both halls. In Berger's painting, as in Vanvitelli's inscription intended for the stair hall, the truth bearers approach and the false go away.

Vanvitelli's Hall of the *Baciamano* is now known as the Throne Room (figs. 6.14, *H*; 8.40, 8.41). It continues the basic membrature of the two preceding halls. But now the wall treatment is richer yet more geometrical and the vault more abstract, as if Astraea's justice with its serenity and inevitability had prevailed into this further realm. The room's great barrel vault is penetrated by eight thermal windows along its length, the four along the interior wall being fictive. A project by Pietro Bianchi for decorating this room, undertaken during the Napoleonic interregnum, exists in the form of a model for the throne and its niche, now in the Museo Vanvitelliano. But it was Gaetano Genovese who in 1839 definitively decorated the chamber, and his work is fully in line with the more muted, more architectonic manner of the Halls of Mars and Astraea. Work was completed by the spring of 1845, in time for the Naples meeting of the Seventh International Congress of the Sciences. Nine local sculptors were employed, including Tito Angelini and Tommaso Arnaud.

The Throne Room is a pantheon of Neapolitan decorative art of the period: rich, classical, geometric, yet imaginatively eclectic. The names of the twelve provinces of the kingdoms are inscribed over each pair of pilasters—recalling the sculptured episodes in the South Italian provinces in the Hall of Alessandro Farnese—as the widely set pairs of pilasters do also (fig. 8.5, L). But now the order is Composite and the pilasters zone off powerful geometric panels trimmed with beaded gold. On the interior wall a troop of double doors leads to the *retrocamere* that line the exteriors of all these apartments. The doors stand opposite a symmetrical lineup of windows. Over the openings, tightly framed, are thick, robust rinceaux—more golden boughs—and in the entablature a frieze with forty-four roundels of the kings of Naples (omitting Murat and Bonaparte), a secular pendant to the chapel's tribe of patron saints. As in the Hall of Astraea there is a striking contrast between free, unframed wall figures and the tightly framed beings of the Hall of Mars.

In the ceiling is Maldarelli's 1844 fresco of the cornerstone ceremony, already described, set into a geometric garden of golden fretwork and blossoms—a flowery tale friezed with birds, wreaths, tendrils, and hieratic growths (fig. 8.42). As in the Hall of Alexander the Great, Ferdinando II here remembers, in his Throne Room's major event, and as its major personality, his own most important forebear, not Alessandro Farnese, Cosimo de' Medici, Alexander, or Hector, but Carlo di Borbone. The procession of heroes in the procession of antechambers, therefore, has led inevitably to this recalling of Caserta's own beginnings in its Hesperidean garden whose stones now indeed fly up to heaven to form a heaven for its Bourbon race. In mood and energy the painting in the vault stands midway between the twisting fury of Achilles and Astraea's dispassionate geometry. At the same time it recalls the settecento tradition of court scenes in the manner of Celebrano or Joli. The canvas pavilion, the dimly discerned masses of troops, and the deep landscape culminating in Monte Tifata, all have their earlier echoes in Bourbon court art.

Now, having traversed these sequences of ancestral blood and fame, it is time to justify the title of this chapter. Freud first used the term "family romance" in 1908. It means a child's dream that his true parents are not those he lives with but people of much higher station or even a mythic hero and heroine. When, at a later stage of development, the child learns that the identity of his mother is certain but that in the nature of things his biological father's identity must remain relatively open to question, he concentrates on dreaming up a substitute father. He imagines that his mother has had affairs with great men, heroes, gods. Freud writes:

These works of fiction which seem so full of hostility [to the true father], are none of them really so badly intended, and . . . they still preserve, under a slight disguise, the child's original affection for his parents. . . . These new and aristocratic parents are equipped with attributes that are derived entirely from real recollections of the actual and humble ones; so that in fact the child is not getting rid of his father but exalting him. Indeed the whole effort at replacing the real father by a superior one is only an expression of the child's longing for the happy, vanished days when his father seemed to him the noblest and strongest of men and his mother the dearest and loveliest of women. He is turning away from the father whom he knows to-day to the father in whom he believed in the earliest years of his childhood; and his phantasy is no more than the expression of a regret that those happy days have gone. Thus in these phantasies the over-valuation that characterizes a child's earliest years comes into its own again.[37]

Without knowing it, it seems to me, Freud is here being very Vichian. The child's family romance, in his fantasy about a mythic, supernal father whose lineaments are paradoxically those of his biological father, recreates that aboriginal family in which the father was indeed a great king, a poet and lawgiver, an Apollo-Hercules. It goes directly back to Füger's *Age of Gold* with its mixture of arriving gods and the barbarian families who welcome them. It justifies the roles of all the other "fathers" from Hercules to Alessandro Farnese.

8.42
Gennaro Maldarelli.
Laying the Cornerstone of the Reggia, 1844.
Caserta, throne room. Photo Ente Provinciale per il Turismo. (See also pl. 20.)

9

Epilogue: Neptune's Victory

It is the Chapel of Apollo, so to call it—the theater—that rounds out this study. The theater weaves together the several threads of the reading of Caserta: the family romance, the Vichian poetry, and the absolutist doctrine. The tiny auditorium, with a capacity of about 500 (fig. 9.1) is of horseshoe shape in plan and contains separate entrances for public, court, and royal family. The audience seats itself in a cage of coral-red pilasters capped with amber gilt.[1] There are five tiers of boxes and a central royal box three tiers high. This is nothing less than a second proscenium arch, smaller but denser and more ornate than the proscenium arch itself, and crowned with an imperial crown (fig. 9.2). The system of very broad low openings echoes that of the chapel (fig. 8.1), again serving as a punctured plinth for a giant order. But this time the columns are immured in piers and the spacing is even. The chapels here are orchestra boxes, and the chancel has become the auditorium. The panels between the ribs are filled with scenes of mythic triumph rather than the geometric coffers of the chapel. Bonito's *Immaculate Conception*, meanwhile, is replaced with a certain appropriateness by the royal box. What more exalted family romance is there, indeed, than that of the Immacolata? Members of the court and staff occupied these boxes and loge seats in descending hierarchical order, depending on nearness to the royal box, on the day of the week, and on the number of performances already presented.[2] So the seating arrangements of the theater formed a half-world based on distributive justice. Court and government confronted the stage world with their own unities of time, action, and place.

The theater is decorated with frescoes and with marble and alabaster sculpture. The vault (not presently photographable) is a disc raised by the ceiling ribs, whose interstices are filled with energetic bevies of personifications. It is by Crescenzo La Gamba. In that disc Apollo reappears, here not as a reigning lyre player but in battle with the serpent Python. The god stands like a powerful archer and suppresses the snake. This action, says Vico, marks the severity of Apollo's original law, for Python is in reality Apollo's lyre. He is also, in a typical bouquet of conflations, the Golden Bough, and Apollo's own bow with which Python is slain.[3] And indeed La Gamba's Python, writhing rigidly above the worlds of court and stage, does have his bowlike, and boughlike, aspects, and even the aspect of the scroll of a lyre, a scroll the musician is unaccountably struggling with. Meanwhile the arrow that accomplished Python's death means, like the arrows of Diana, or her flung drops, the sudden death met by transgressors of cruel primordial law.[4]

There is more of this unifying: Python is the Hydra, the snakes that Hercules fought in his cradle, and also the dragon Ladon whom he slew in the Garden of the Hesperides in order to pluck its apples.[5] Throughout the palace this all-purpose talisman is ever the purifying adversary. It is only in degenerate times that Apollo's lyre, and law, were reinterpreted so as to delight rather than admonish, and to sing of wine and flirtation.[6] Vico would therefore see the frolicsomeness of the scenes in the Old Apartments as a screen for *fortia facta* looming behind them.

There are other paintings in the theater, supporting this program, by Domenico Mondo, Mariano Rossi, and Starace. The proscenium is flanked by statues of Vico's other two mythic lyre players, Orpheus and Amphion.[7] Guardian columns of the stage picture, they resonate to Apollo's struggle above them and with the many harmonies, geometric and mythic, that fill all the palace and garden.

To what ancient and austere laws did Apollo, Amphion, and Orpheus echo? The operas of Metastasio and Paisiello sang such myths and with such glosses as Vico makes. The theater was inaugurated in 1769, in the reign of Ferdinando IV, and was used mainly during Carnival.[8] In 1772 there were performances of Metastasio's *Didone Abbandonata* that served to baptize the whole complex, including the gardens. As it happened they took place not long before Vanvitelli's death on March 1, 1773.[9] It is probable that Vanvitelli designed the scenery, for all his life he was active in the theater both as a designer and, in his letters, as a critical operagoer.

The 1772 revival of Metastasio's opera at Caserta marked a return to the iconographic beginnings of Caserta's program. For on this occasion, during the final scene, the back wall of the stage was removed to reveal the garden parterre outside, on the west flank of the palace. In 1756 that section of the garden had been labeled "theatrical prospect" (fig. 5.8, I, M). So the idea of an outdoor stage-setting had been part of the conception from the beginning. *Didone Abbandonata* deals, of course, with city-building, and ends with a storm at sea, a storm that is in

9.1
Theater of the royal palace at Caserta, 1768–1772. Photo Jacelli

9.2
The royal box at Caserta's theater. Photo Ente Provinciale per il Turismo

every sense a twin to the one depicted in the Fountain of Juno and Aeolus.[10] Aeolus's tempest, that is, had driven Aeneas's fleet to Carthage, where the hero fell in love with Queen Dido, who was there erecting her new capital. But Apollo and Aeneas's father Anchises command the hero to continue toward Italy. Aeneas recalls the words of his father in a dream:

"Son"—I marked his words—"ungrateful son,"
Is this the kingdom you were to have won?
This sinful bed, is this the Italy
Ordained for you by Phoebus and by me?
Unhappy Asia waits for you to rear
A second Troy upon new land—the peer
Of Asia's Troy and of Aeneas' power:
This was your promise at my dying hour.

Despite his passion for Dido, and despite the machinations of Venus, Aeneas follows his father's command. Overcome with grief, the queen throws herself into the flames that Vulcan has caused to consume her city, and is herself consumed. Her new palace, not yet completed, sinks into flames. The stage directions continue:

At the same time on the distant horizon the waves begin to rise and slowly move towards the palace, all darkened above with dense clouds and accompanied by a tumult of stormy music. On approaching the fire the waters' violence grows as that of the flames resists it. The furious rhythm of the waves, breaking and foaming around the ruins, the constant roar of thunder, the guttering lamps and the continual howling of the sea storm's accompaniment—all represent the implacable mutual hatred of the elements.

In the end, commanded by Neptune, the waters triumph. The finale of *Didone Abbandonata* is thus in effect a substitution, an example of what I will call commutative mythography. The Neptune fountain that Vanvitelli had planned at the beginning of the river-road was to have shown the god surrounded by his court, enthroned, and raising his trident in command. What other scene could this be, given the rest of Caserta's program, than the moment in the *Aeneid* when the god quells Aeolus's storm with his famous speech beginning "Quos ego"?[11]

Is this the duty that you owe your king?
Without permission throwing sky and sea,
Wind and land, into a rage of mountains?
You, whom I . . . but first I calm these waves.
And then I punish you as never yet before.

We see that Metastasio was paraphrasing Virgil, putting Neptune's rhetoric in Anchises' mouth, while at the same time reconstructing the war of the elements that occurs also in the garden. This way, the beginning of the river-road would not have been Diana's transformation of Actaeon but rather Neptune's planned, earlier, higher assertion of his rule of the oceans (fig. 5.5). Such an assertion would make the fountain of Aeolus a foil for the Neptune statue; it would bracket all the events in the river-road with these mighty Neptunian parentheses. The sea god would speak down the length of the whole garden, marshaling its fables along the whipline of his gesture. The whole complex would be a composition of warring air, earth, fire, and water; of "sky and sea / Wind and land," brought forcefully into a mythic kingdom.

With this in mind let us return to the opera. Its span embraces the construction and ruin of Carthage as a foretaste of the construction (but not the ruin: the immortalizing) of Caserta. And as a sign of that second, greater palace, a second greater palace now appears on stage. The seat of Neptune appears as Dido's palace falls into embers. It is dawn, an hour of glistening morning splendor. The god rises on his shell-throne, trident in hand, supported by festive shoals of monsters and beauties. The sense and direction of the opera turn from interior turmoil outward to the other theater in this room, the theater of the court. Neptune addresses the royal couple who sit opposite his stage within their own proscenium. True majesty, on its corresponding thrones, within its corresponding palace of painted myths and perfectly numbered form, hears the poem of a mythic majesty. The sea god, backed now by a real garden echoing that palace in its boxwood geometries, speaks:

Benignant planets of the Spanish sky,
If on our strife you turn bewildered eye,
Know, we four elements have equal might
And hence in honor's name are doomed to fight.
Thus eager Vulcan's spectacle of flame
But tempts the water god to join the game.
If trusty Vulcan to the battle runs
And booms your royal ire from sonorous guns,
Then, in his turn Neptune crosses seas
Bringing your law to the Antipodes,
And coming back with their devotion. Hence
It's right that I for glory should commence
To make this far-resounding trial of skill
To harness winds and drive them to my will.
But now, obedient storms, my sign debars
   Your further noise; the enemy
     Surrenders this terrain to me.
       I hold the palm.
The nightly saraband of Spanish stars
   Serenely modulates in key
     And all the kingdoms of the sea
       Return to calm.

These words are another, yet more rococo, gloss of Virgil. Neptune's final speech also seals Ocean's triumph over Vulcan. Vulcan's fire had not only been the holocaust that consumed Carthage: its flames had joined the fires of Venus that filled the bodies of Dido and Aeneas, or that had established Adonis's role as the first flower of agriculture and Typhon's as the prisoner beneath Ceres' land. The speech moves out from the local scene, with its underground rivers and buried cities, to the vast realm of an ocean that, wherever it rolls, breaks on Bourbon shores. And in 1772, let us remember, the Bourbon Hesperia stretched from Ceres' Sicily to Fray Junipero Serra's California.

As to the appearance of this stage palace, the Museo Vanvitelliano at Caserta contains many scene designs by Vanvitelli for palace interiors that suit the spirit if not the letter of Metastasio's text (fig. 9.3). And Metastasio's mighty apparition also matches and concludes the architecture of Vanvitelli's theater (fig. 9.1). The combination of the two, the mythic palace of the stage and

Epilogue

9.3
Vanvitelli. Design for an opera setting. Caserta, Reggia. Photo Soprintendenza per i Beni Culturali

the real one of the auditorium, also brings to mind the great amphitheater of the stair hall (fig. 7.16).

As to the emotional content of all these scenes, Dido's love fills the whole of the opera. She is its siren singer, its Parthenope. She is the mother in the family romance in which Aeneas and his line enact their parts. Hers is a love both erotic and maternal; her sons are also her lovers. Thus Metastasio makes Dido the lover of Aeneas, and then Aeneas's mother, then the mistress and mother of Carthage itself. Yet all these love objects, these sons and lovers, are portrayals of Dido. The city, especially, is a recumbent, resplendent portrait of her, whose arches, towers, streets, and temples are her offspring. Metastasio (and his designer) give us this, visually and poetically, in the setting for Dido's entrance. She walks out from the vaulted labyrinths of the citadel and says:

Aeneas, splendor of Asia and sweet care
Of Venus and of Dido, look how fair
The face of Carthage grows as it is born,
Its body rising like a lightening morn.
Arch and palace, dome on temple piled,
Of Dido's labor Carthage is the child;
Aeneas is yet more her offspring—why
Then does Aeneas not meet Dido's eye?

That turning away of Aeneas from Dido is a sign of his inevitable treachery. But it is also the shyness of the son contemplating the fantasy of his mother's lovers. In joining mother love to lover's love the queen is a second Cythera, a second Venus; she mothers and loves Aeneas and in this latter role is like the city of Parthenope. For she, the city-builder, had been a mother to Carlo di Borbone's son, and had greeted Carlo himself as Aeneas. Parthenope like Dido was a princess who had sailed across the seas (Dido had sailed to Africa from Tyre), founded a city, reigned in it, been slain and set upon a seaside tomb and, in consequence, had become the occasion of a *nea polis*, and of a new palace. In this last look at the Bourbon court, as it is addressed by its parental gods in Vanvitelli's theater in Vanvitelli's palace, we are returned to the primal myth, the primal romance, of the beginnings of human settlement in this region.

Undoubtedly both Vanvitelli and Vico knew Metastasio's text, as Metastasio knew Vico's, the two latter being close friends. Indeed, Metastasio read and praised the *Diritto*, whose third volume appeared only two years before the original premiere of *Didone Abbandonata*.[12] Like Metastasio Vico stresses Dido's fate and the idea that ruined Carthage would live again in Aeneas' Neapolis in Latium. This rebirth, he says, is built into the very name of Dido's people. They are Phoenicians, or phoenix persons. Dido flies up reborn from her own ashes. She is a bird, incidentally another likeness to Parthenope. And she had already abandoned an earlier infested city, Tyre, when she sailed to Africa.[13] In building Carthage there, furthermore, she claimed and cleared land. When she met Aeneas, who had abandoned the infested city of Troy, they copulated in a cave;[14] this was a sign of their twin roles as "founders of peoples" and as arriving gods come through the wilderness of the sea to build cities in a wilderness of land.[15]

Dido's and Aeneas' "errant natures" are *errores*, which are wanderings, waverings, from the path of history and *errors*, or sins, as well as discoveries, colonizings, and buildings. Vico links this exploratory and constructive colonial character to the wanderings and foundings of the very explorers who compose the myths of Daedalus and Hercules, Orpheus and Amphion. They, and Dido, and Aeneas, are the predecessors of those who were to go beyond the Mediterranean: namely Columbus, Vespucci, Magellan, and Vasco da Gama.[16] These Italic Herculeses make the whole world their Mediterranean. They claim land and found colonies. They are in search of "lucre," they quest after the ever-shifting Hesperides, after the gold, the women, and the dragon-dueling that are to be found in those magical gardens. Their new worlds of beast-killing, land-clearing, of gardens of gold and poetic law, are not different in kind from, and are the necessary results of, earlier new worlds such as Carthage, Puteoli, Neapolis, Cumae, and Rome.

The "Iberian skies" ruled by the royal planets whom Neptune addresses, namely Ferdinando IV and Maria Carolina and their Spanish Bourbon brethren are, as Neptune says, world-encircling. The sea god brings back devotion (*vota*, 'vows,' and even 'votes') from all parts of that globe, a globe whose two miniature halves confront each other at the moment when Dido's palace turns into Neptune's and the city of the Phoenix queen is replaced by that of her sea-wandering lover. The hemisphere composed of royal family, court, and government stands to the east. Opposite is the other hemisphere, that of the rest of the world, of the gods—Hesperia, the endless western land.[17]

Notes

2 Poetic Myths of Naples

1. For these foundation myths see first of all Giovanni Antonio Summonte, *Historia della città e regno di Napoli . . .* [1601–1643] (Naples, 1748), vol. 1, pp. 1 ff. Summonte was a main source for later historians and guidebook writers, such as Petrini, Sarnelli, and others cited below. An earlier collection of myths, read throughout the eighteenth century because attributed to the famous historian Giovanni Villani, was the anonymous *Cronaca di Partenope*, edited by Antonio Altamura (Naples, 1974), which was compiled in the fourteenth century. For the landscape, see R. Liberatore, *Viaggio pittorico nel regno delle Due Sicilie* (Naples, 1829); G. P. Carratelli, "Il Mondo mediterraneo e le origini di Napoli," in *Storia di Napoli* (Naples, 1975), vol. 1, pp. 99 ff.; and Antonio Scherillo, "Suolo e sottosuolo di Napoli," ibid., pp. 17 ff. The classic work remains Julius Beloch's *Campanien* (Berlin, 1879, new ed. Breslau, 1890).

2. Pompeo Sarnelli, *Guida de' forestieri . . . della regal città di Napoli e del suo amenissimo distretto* (Naples, 1697), s.v.; A. Parrino, *Nuova guida de' forestieri* (Naples, 1725), s.v.; plus the essays in the *Storia di Napoli* cited in note 1; Beloch, *Campanien*, s.v.; Giovanni Carafa, *Lettere di Giovanni Carafa, duca di Noia, continente alcune considerazioni sull'utilità, e gloria, che si trarebbe da una esatta carta topografica della città di Napoli, e dal suo contado* (1750; Naples, 2d ed., 1770), pp. xiii ff.; and Sir William Hamilton, *Campi Phlegraei: Osservazioni sui vulcani delle Due Sicilie* (Naples, 1776) with its excellent plates.

3. *Aeneid* VI 42.

4. Summonte, *Historia*; G. M. Galanti, *Saggio sopra l'antica storia de' primi abitatori dell'Italia*, 2d ed. (Naples, 1783), esp. 160 ff.; B. Capasso, *Napoli Greco-Romana* (Naples, 1905); Jean Bérard, *La colonisation grècque de l'Italie méridionale et de la Sicile* (Paris, 1951); Bérard, *Magna Graecia* (Turin, 1963), which is useful on the historical possibilities of the legends analyzed by the Vichians, for example pp. 13 ff. Bérard disregards the works written by Vico and his school, however. See also Amedeo Maiuri, *Saggi di varia antichità* (Venice, 1954).

5. Pietro Napoli Signorelli, *Vicende della coltura nelle Due Sicilie* (Naples, 1811), vol. 1, pp. 211 ff.; G. M. Galanti, *Nuova descrizione storica e geografica delle Sicilie* (Naples, 1786–90); Domenico Bartolini, *Viaggio da Napoli alle Forche Caudine ed a Benevento . . .* (Naples, 1827); Giovanni Aliberti, "Economia e società da Carlo III ai Napoleonidi (1734–1806)," *Storia di Napoli*, vol. 8, pp. 77 ff.

Notes to Pages 12–20

6. See my "Water-Works and Water-Play in Renaissance Naples," in E. R. MacDougall, ed., *Fons Sapientiae: Renaissance Garden Fountains* (Dumbarton Oaks Colloquium on the History of Landscape Gardening, V; Washington, D.C., 1978), pp. 61 ff., with bibliography on the Renaissance and later periods. Also Leone Gasparini, *Antiche fontane di Napoli* (Naples, 1979), pp. 8 ff. Curiously enough, the Bourbons had a fountain as the source of their name. See Vittorio Gleijes, *Carlo di Borbone, re di Napoli* (Naples, 1976), p. 11; Gleijes speaks of the *aquae borbonis* in the family's ancient lands (chiefly the present Département de l'Allier in France).

7. *Aeneid* VI 397; see also Hamilton, *Campi Phlegraei*; also N. Del Pezzo, "Siti reali: i Campi Flegrei," *Napoli nobilissima*, ser. 1, 5 (1897):119–22; 149–53; 170–73, and A. Maiuri, *I Campi Flegrei* (Rome, 1958).

8. Bartolini, *Viaggio*, passim; Carlo Celano, *Notizie del bello, dell'antico e del curioso della città di Napoli*, edited by G. B. Chiarini (Naples, 1856–60) and variorum edition (Naples, 1970), s.v. "Tomba di Virgilio," "Grotto di Posillipo"; E. Mele, "Viaggiatori stranieri a Napoli, II," *Napoli nobilissima*, ser. 2, 15 (1906):27 ff.; Louis Guimbaud, *Saint-Non et Fragonard* (Paris, 1928).

9. Pompeo Sarnelli, *Nuova guida de' forestieri curiosi di vedere e di riconoscere . . . Pozzuoli, Baja, Cuma, Misena, Gaeta* (Naples, 1782), pp. 106 ff.; Franco Strazzullo, ed., *Le Lettere di Luigi Vanvitelli nella biblioteca palatina a Caserta* (Galatina, 1976), letter 652 (1759) and passim.

10. G. Doria and O. Ferrari, *Vedute napoletane della raccolta Lemmermann* (Naples, 1957); [Raffaello Causa], *Il Paesaggio napoletana nella pittura straniera* (Naples, 1962); Alste Horn-Oncken, *Ausflug in Elysische Gefilde. Das Europäische Campanienbild des 16. und 17. Jahrhunderts und die Aufzeichnungen J. F. A. von Uffenbachs* (Göttingen, 1978); P. Walch, "Foreign Artists at Naples: 1750–1799," *Burlington Magazine*, 121 (1979):247 ff. See also Liberatore, *Viaggio pittorico*.

11. G. L. Hersey, *Alfonso II and the Artistic Renewal of Naples, 1485–1495* (New Haven, Conn., 1969), pp. 18 ff., with earlier bibliography.

12. Wilfred P. Mustard, *The Piscatory Eclogues of Jacopo Sannazaro* (Baltimore, 1914) investigates the Virgilianism of these poems.

13. Felice De Filippis, *Piazze e fontane di Napoli* (Naples, 1957). Gasparini, *Antiche fontane*, pp. 74 ff.

14. See note 13 and G. Ceci, "La Fontana Santa Lucia," *Napoli nobilissima*, ser. 2, 9 (1902):145 ff. It was Ceci who discovered the true authors of the work. The fountain was moved from its original site in the Santa Lucia quarter to a location nearer the harbor edge in 1620, a fact recorded in a now destroyed inscription, and then moved again in 1845 when another inscription was installed—this one still in place—falsely attributing the sculpture to Giovanni da Nola. The fountain was finally set up in the Villa Comunale in 1898.

15. For Pimentel see D. A. Parrino, *Teatro eroico e politico dei governi dei viceré del regno di Napoli*, in Giovanni Gravier, ed., *Raccòlta di tutti i piu rinomati scrittori dell'istoria generale del regno di Napoli* (Naples, 1770), vol. 9, pp. 295 ff. See also Giuseppe Coniglio, *I Viceré spagnuoli di Napoli* (Naples, 1967), pp. 163 ff. The building of the Fontana Santa Lucia can be linked to the famine of 1604–1606. The inscribed and sculptured praise of seafood may relate to the rise in grain prices during that period, as well as to the food scandals that filled Pimentel's reign.

16. Touring Club Italiano, *Napoli e dintorni* (Milan, 1976), p. 317; but for an eighteenth-century belief, see Alessio Simmaco Mazzocchi, *Della Chiesa cattedrale di Napoli* (Naples, 1751), s.v.

17. The fountain was actually paid for not by the viceroy but by the Commune of Naples (Coniglio, *Vicerè*, p. 172), which gives an added twist to the actions of the putti on the upper tympanum. For nereuses and nereids as symbols of navigational skill see "De Nereo et Nereidibus" in Natalis Comes, *Mythographiae* (Geneva, 1641), pp. 833 ff. and 1051. As to the word *nereus* itself, it is now thought that νερὸ means 'new water' only via modern Greek. See Pauly-Wissowa, *Realencyclopädie der classischen Altertümswissenschaft*, s.v. "Nereus." However, for the period I consider such an anachronistic derivation held good. For the fishermen's stalls see Gasparini, *Antiche fontane*, figs. 58, 59.

18. For Vico bibliography in general see Maria Donzelli, *Contributo alla bibliografia vichiana, 1948–1970* (Naples, 1972), which updates Benedetto Croce's and Fausto Nicolini's *Bibliografia vichiana* (Naples, 1947). The latter conveniently cites authors, such as Montesquieu and Boulanger, who borrowed from Vico without acknowledgment. For items of specific interest consult the bibliography of this book.

19. Giambattista Vico, *Il Diritto universale*, edited by Fausto Nicolini (Naples, 1936), p. 11.

20. Ibid., pp. 7, 407, 627.

21. Ibid., II, p. 145. Vico, *Scienza nuova seconda*, edited by Fausto Nicolini (Bari, 1953), paragraphs 528, 714.

22. Vico, *Diritto*, p. 496.

23. Ibid., p. 45.

24. Ibid.; Vico attaches his definition of *relegendo* to two of the dominant myths at Caserta.

25. Vico complains that mythology, which holds the key to the development of human thought, has always been misunderstood: "Why is mythology, which is the first history of politics (*rerum*), so ill thought of (*infelix*)? During the eras of fable, mythology considered it sufficient to be concerned not with the mores and government of those eras, but with the nature of the gods that were hidden inside the myths, so that divine things would remain unknown to the common people. For this reason, after many centuries, mythology now holds itself ready for exploration, [raising the question] as to whether it is as vague, unpredictable and indeed sterile [as has been thought]" (*Diritto*, p. 12). In short, only in the fullness of time does scholarship become ripe enough to study myth in the manner prescribed by the "new science."

26. Ibid., p. 496.

27. This work, had it been completed, would no doubt have led on to further honors. Vico's *L'Origine della giurisprudenza romana* (1744) was dedicated to the prime minister, Bernardo Tanucci, which meant it had his approval. For other details about Vico's relationship with the court see Michelangelo Schipa, *Il Regno di Napoli al tempo di Carlo di Borbone* (Naples, 1923), vol. 2, p. 275 n., though in general this book is excessively anti-Bourbon; G. B. Vico, *Autobiography*, as continued by Carlo Antonio de Rosa, marchese di Villarosa in Vico, *Opere*, vol. 5 (Bari, 1911), p. 224; F. Nicolini, "Vita ed opere di Giambattista Vico," *Diritto*, vol. 1, p. xxxv. For Vico's peculiar (and favorable) redefinition of feudalism, which makes the institution both exceedingly modern and monarchic and also Italic and Roman, see Giovanni Vitolo, "Il Feudalismo di G. Vico," in *Atti dell'accademia di scienze morali e politiche della società nazionale di scienze, lettere, ed arti in Napoli*, 83 (1972):83 ff.

28. Schipa, *Napoli*, pp. 690–91.

29. Raffaele Sirri, "La Cultura a Napoli nel settecento," in *Storia di Napoli*, vol. 8, pp. 165 ff.; Signorelli, *Vicende*, vol. 8; Gioele Solari, "Vico e Pagano. Per la storia della tradizione vichiana a Napoli nel secolo XVIII," *Rivista internazionale di filosofia del diritto*, 5 (1925):320

ff., which shows that there was in Naples "a constant uninterrupted tradition [extrinsic to Vico's real thought], but formed of love and admiration for, and legitimate pride in, Vico, whose work seemingly was wrapped in religious mystery. This attracted for the whole of that [eighteenth] century the attention of scholars, provoked curiosity and wonder, excited the imagination, and fed legends" (p. 321). However, Vico taught his mysterious and poetic ideas to the sons of the most exclusive gentlemen in the city in his private academy, we are told. See also Giuseppe Galasso, "Napoli ai tempi del Vico," pp. 320 ff. in *Giambattista Vico nel Terzo centenario della nascita* (Naples, 1971); Nicola Baddaloni, "La Scienza vichiana e l'illuminismo," ibid., pp. 101 ff.

30. Nor have modern authors spent time on Vico's concept of myth. Of those few who have done so, see Isaiah Berlin, *Vico and Herder: Two Studies in the History of Ideas* (New York, 1977), p. 35 ff.; Giovanni Villa, *La Filosofia del mito secondo G. B. Vico* (Milan, 1949); D. Severgnini, *Il Serioso Poema* (Milan, 1953); Giovanni A. Bianca, *Il Concetto di poesia in Giambattista Vico* (Messina/Firenze, 1967); A. M. Isoldi Jacobelli, "Il Mito nel pensiero di Vico," in *Omaggio a Vico* (Naples, 1968), pp. 39 ff.; and A. R. Caponigri, *Time and Idea: The Theory of History in G. B. Vico* (Notre Dame, Ind., 1968). For Vico's notion that ancient jurisprudence was a "serious poem" see *Scienza nuova*, paragraph 1027; also D. Bidney, "Vico's New Science of Myth," in *G. B. Vico, An International Symposium* (Baltimore, 1969), pp. 259 ff., and Severgnini, *Il Seriosa Poema*.

31. Genovese taught Vico's son (Nicolini, "Vita," *Diritto*, vol. 1, p. xxxvi). Vico's importance among other luminaries is shown less in his own work, which ignored the local scene, than in the local attacks on him such as Damiano Romano, *Difesa istorica delle leggi greche venute in Roma contro alla moderna opinione del Sign. D. Gio. Battista Vico*, a book that attacks Vico's claim that Rome and Rome alone was the fountainhead of the best law of ancient times. But it is interesting that Romano's arguments, like Vico's, are based on the literal truthfulness of epics such as the *Aeneid*. Vico's ideas, for all their poetic darkness, continued to be propagated in court circles by disciples like Ignazio della Croce, an Augustinian monk and professor of theology at the University in the 1770s. See Enrica Viviani della Robbia, *Bernardo Tanucci e il suo più importante carteggio*, 1 (Florence, 1942), p. 237; also Schipa, *Napoli*, passim and Vico, *Diritto*, p. 787.

32. Schipa, *Napoli*, pp. 736 ff.; Vico, *Diritto*, p. 787. In the latter a note by Fausto Nicolini says the poet was not only Vico's good friend but had a romance with one of his daughters, probably the poet Luisa.

33. Part II of the *Diritto* is dedicated to Filomarino (Vico, *Diritto*, p. 792 and note). Filomarino was ambassador to Madrid in 1738–1740.

34. Genovese, in addition to teaching Gennaro Vico, also taught Vanvitelli's son Gaspare (Vanvitelli, *Lettere*, 1072 [1763]). For Filomarino's art collection see Charles-Nicolas Cochin, *Voyage pittoresque de l'Italie*, . . . (Paris, 1756), pp. 146 ff.

35. Ottavio Baiardi, *Prodromo della antichità d'Ercolano* (Naples, 1752). See part I, pp. 170 ff., for a Vichian review of river and fountain myths and their role in the founding of cities. Baiardi's political fall came with that of his protector, Fogliani (Vanvitelli, *Lettere*, 377 [1756]). See Mazzocchi, *Commentariorum in regii herculanensis musei Aeneas tabulas heracleenses* (Naples, 1754); also Mario Guarnacci, *Origini italiche o siano memorie istorico-etrusche sopra l'antichissimo regno d'Italia, e sopra i di lei primi abitatori* (Lucca, 1767), vol. 2, pp. 291 ff. Guarnacci speaks of the rivalry of Greek and Etruscan art, showing that Greek art achieved true excellence only in the time of

Alexander. Guarnacci links the Etruscans, his true heroes, to the ancient Hebrews, whose Temple of Solomon was the greatest building on earth. The laws and institutions of civilization begin with these Hebraic Etruscans, who in fact "constituted the first and universal population of Europe" (vol. 3, pp. 108 ff.). Another Etruscan, Pythagoras, gave philosophy its very name and was the first person to call himself a philosopher. His philosophy, like his race, had originally been universal and brought civilization to then barbarous Greece (vol. 3, p. 270). See also G. M. Galanti, *Saggi sopra l'antica storia de' primi abitatori dell'Italia*, 2d ed. (Naples, 1783).

36. See notes 1 and 2. Vanvitelli hunted ceaselessly for water sources to make the water system at Caserta more impressive than that at any other Bourbon palace: *Lettere*, 92 (1752), 133 (1753), 209 (1754), and 211 (1754).

37. Sarnelli, *Pozzuoli*, pp. 1–2, 66.

38. Vanvitelli, *Lettere*, 183 (1753). A longer version of the inscription is in Mazzocchi, *Opuscula quibus orationes, dedicationes, epistolae, inscriptiones, carmina ac diatribae continentur* (Naples, 1771), vol. 1, p. 211 n. and attributed to Salvatore Spirito.

39. Vanvitelli, *Lettere*, 185 (1753).

40. Ibid., letters 364 (1756), 528 (1758), 796 (1760), and 895 (1761).

41. Ibid., letters 952 (1762), 953 (1762), and 966 (1762). The values of all measurements in this book are taken from Vincenzo Scamozzi, *Idea dell'architettura universale* (Venice, 1619), vol. 1, pp. xxiv and 73. Scamozzi prints the relative lengths of the Roman palmo, the Neapolitan palmo, the Florentine braccio, the Venetian foot, and the Castilian foot. In U.S. measures the Neapolitan palmo equals 10.125 inches, the Castilian foot equals 14.25 inches, and the Florentine braccio equals 22.92 inches.

42. Vanvitelli, *Lettere*, 30 (1751).

43. Ibid., letter 781 (1760).

44. Ibid., letters 85 (1752) and 158 (1753).

45. *Aeneid* VI 76 ff.

46. *Diritto*, pp. 499–500; *Scienza nuova*, paragraph 721.

47. *Diritto*, p. 450.

48. Ibid., p. 379.

49. Ibid., p. 690–691.

50. Vanvitelli, *Lettere*, 812 (1760).

51. Ibid., letters 609 (1759), 243 (1754), 838 (1761), 998 (1762), and 1276 (1766). Though he had a house in Pizzofalcone from 1752 (located at the present via Monte di Dio 70) Vanvitelli kept his Roman house in the Piazza San Silvestro until 1766.

52. Vanvitelli, *Lettere*, 111 (1753), which describes Fuga's design for the Albergo dei Poveri as having "bad symmetry, with many inexplicable features." For other judgments on Fuga's talent and character see letters 7 (1751), 13 (1751), 348 (1756), 368 (1776), 756 (1760), 924 (1762), and 1259 (1766); also Luigi Vanvitelli the Younger, *Vita di Luigi Vanvitelli* (Naples, 1828), and a new edition (Naples, 1975), whose editor, Mario Rotili, quotes from a letter to Vanvitelli from his friend Porzio Leonardi urging Vanvitelli to be more stoical about Fuga. J. Garms, "Die Briefe des Luigi Vanvitelli am seinen Brüder Urbano in Rom: Kunsthistorisches Material," *Römische historische Mitteilungen*, 13 (1971):264 ff., demonstrates Vanvitelli's low opinion of Neapolitan artists. He never even mentions Solimena or Giordano in the *Lettere*. See also letters 80 (1752) and 485 (1757).

53. Vanvitelli, *Lettere*, 366 (1756), 660 (1759), and 839 (1761); but then Tanucci seems to have had few friends anyway. For personal descriptions of Tanucci, Sannicandro, and other court figures see René Bouvier and André Laffargue, *La Vie napolitaine au XVIIIe siècle* (Paris, 1956), pp. 186 ff.

54. Vanvitelli, *Lettere*, 1372 (1767): he wants Ferdinando IV's fiancée, Maria Giuseppina of Austria, to see plenty of Rome before she comes to Naples because only in Rome will she see architecture comparable to the palace at Caserta.

55. "La Carestia del 1764 nel Cilento nella cronaca di un contemporaneo," *Quaderni contemporanei dell'università degli studi*, 4 (1971): 180; Harold Acton, *I Borboni di Napoli* (Milan, 1962), pp. 124–25.

56. Vanvitelli, *Lettere*, 1143 (1764) and 1145 (1764). F. Valsecchi, quotes an unidentified eighteenth-century observer: "The people of the countryside are more like American or African savages than inhabitants of Italy. Whoever travels a few miles away from Naples sees nothing but persons, of either sex, clothed in repulsive rags and presenting every evidence of the worst and most inadequate nourishment." "L'Eredità del passato," in M. Fubini, ed., *La Cultura illuministica in Italia* (Turin, 1957), p. 53.

57. See Mario Praz, "Le Antichità di Ercolano," in *Civiltà del '700 a Napoli, 1734–1799* (Florence, 1980), vol. 1, pp. 35 ff. for recent bibliography. Also Fausto Zevi, "Gli Scavi di Ercolano," ibid., vol. 2, pp. 57 ff.

58. Cited by Sirri, "Cultura," p. 265. See also A. Maiuri, *Saggi di varia antichità* (Venice, 1954).

59. *Aeneid* VI 6.

60. Among the members of the academy were Alessio Mazzocchi, Niccolò Ignarra, and Francesco Daniele, so Vico's influence was present. See Fausto Nicolini, *Della Società nazionale di scienze, lettere ed arti . . . Notizie storiche* (Naples, 1950), pp. 18 ff.; also Costanza Lorenzetti, *L'Accademia di belle arti di Napoli (1752–1952)* (Florence, 1952), pp. 13 ff., for Carlo's arts and crafts reforms.

61. For the transfer of the Farnese collection from Rome to Naples, see A. Gonzalez-Palacios, "Il Trasporto delle statue farnesiane da Roma a Napoli," *Antologia delle belle arti*, 6 (1978):168–74; also *Mostra da Palazzo degli studi a Museo Archeologico* (Naples, 1977); for Herculean sites in the area, see Mazzocchi, *Aeneas tabulas*, pp. 64 ff., and for the museum at Portici N. Del Pezzo, "Reali delizie borboniche," *Napoli nobilissima*, ser. 2, 3 (1922): 146 ff.; also Renato De Fusco, "Architettura," *Storia di Napoli*, vol. 8, pp. 374 ff.

62. Maiuri, *Saggi*, p. 365. For representative contemporary works on Herculaneum see [A. F. Gori], *Notizie del memorabile scoprimento dell'antica città di Ercolana vicina a Napoli . . .* (Florence, 1748); D'Onofri, *Elogio sulla Morte del . . . re Carlo III*, p. xciii ff.; Marcello De Venuti, *Descrizione delle prime scoperte dell'antica città di Ercolano* (Rome, 1748). De Venuti says that he was the first to have to explain to his majesty the early finds at Herculaneum (p. viii). In Vichian fashion he fantasticates on the place names of Magna Graecia to picture an ancient world equally linked to the Book of Genesis and to Greek, Roman, and Egyptian myth. See also Scipione Maffei, *Tre Lettere del Signor marchese Scipione Maffei* (Verona, 1748); J. J. Winckelmann, *Nachrichten von den neuesten Herculanischen Entdeckungen* (Dresden, 1764) and *Geschichte der Kunst des Altertums* (Dresden, 1764–1767). Vanvitelli's reactions to Winckelmann, meanwhile, were on the whole favorable. For one thing they shared a hatred of Naples: *Lettere*, 547 (1758), 536 (1758), and 1381 (1767). For modern accounts of the excavations see M. Ruggiero, *Storia degli scavi di Ercolano* (Naples, 1885) and Egon Corti, *Ercolano e Pompeii* (Turin, 1957), pp. 126 ff.

63. Quoted by Sirri, "Cultura," p. 265.

64. See especially Daniele's *Monete antiche di Capua* (Naples, 1802). For J. J. Winckelmann's reactions to the local savants see his *Werke*, edited by C. L. Fernow (Dresden, 1808), pp. 2, 3 ff.

65. Quoted by Sirri, "Cultura," p. 265. See A. De Franciscis, "L'Esperienza napoletana del Winckelmann," *Cronache pompeiane*, 1 (1975):7

ff. and also *Fonti documentarie per la storia degli scavi di Pompeii, Ercolano, Stabia* [edited by "Archivisti Napoletani"] (Naples, 1979). De Fusco, "Architettura," pp. 376 ff. says that it may have been Maria Amalia who first awakened Carlo's interest in Herculaneum. She had admired antiquities taken from the site in her father's collection at Dresden.

66. *Cronaca di Partenope*, pp. 57 ff.; G. M. Galanti, *Saggi*; and Bartolommeo Capasso, *Sull'antico sito di Napoli e Palepoli* (Naples, 1889).

67. Thoenes, *Neapel und Umgebung*, pp. 20, 330, 346, 354.

68. Vanvitelli, *Lettere*, 175 (1753), 197 (1754), and 210 (1754).

69. Pietro Metastasio, *Tutte le opere di Pietro Metastasio* (Florence, 1832), pp. 699 ff. Another, perhaps even more famous operatic version of the myth was Stampiglia's *Partenope*, most famous in its setting by Handel but also set by Domenico Sarro and others, and performed in 1739 at San Carlo and in 1722 at the Teatro San Bartolomeo, and elsewhere.

70. *Partenope*, p. 1.

71. *Diritto*, pp. 3, 7, 627.

72. Ibid., p. 450.

73. Ibid., pp. 346, 396.

74. Ibid., p. 407.

75. Ibid., p. 397.

76. Like Vico, Vanvitelli had much in common with Piranesi. Vanvitelli admired Piranesi's talent while finding his architecture mad (*Lettere*, 1300 [1766]).

77. See chapter 4.

78. See note 1. Niccolo Carletti, *Topografia universale della città di Napoli in Campagna Felice . . .* (Naples, 1776), pp. 243 ff., describes what he takes to be the remains of a temple of Parthenope in the present Piazza Sant'Aniello. See also Summonte, *Storia di Napoli*, vol. 1, pp. 4 ff.; also the engraving opposite p. 29, which gives the genealogy of Parthenope, running from "Cielo, re dei Greci" through Japhet, Prometheus, Deucalion, Hellen, Eulus, Eumelus, and others.

79. *Cronaca di Partenope*, p. 58. The author actually says the word *cuma* means 'to sleep' in both Greek and Latin but is obviously transferring this false translation from the correct one I give.

80. Virgil, *Georgics*, 4, 564; Ovid, *Metamorphoses*, 15, 711–12.

81. *Cronaca di Partenope*, pp. 68–69. There is now a male river god, probably Roman, in the Piazza Nido.

82. Ibid. Similarly, Vico was to see not simply a city but all of Nature as an immense woman or "vast animate body that feels passions and effects" (*Scienza nuova*, paragraphs 377 and 379).

83. *Diritto*, p. 395.

84. G. M. Galanti, *Nuova descrizione geografica e politica delle Sicilie* (Naples, 1789), vol. 3, p. 274.

85. Arnaldo Venditti, "L'Opera napoletana di Luigi Vanvitelli," in R. Di Stefano, ed., *Luigi Vanvitelli* (Naples, 1979), pp. 99 ff., says the population of the capital rose from 270,000 at the advent of Carlo di Borbone in 1734 to 347,000 in 1764 despite the fact that 30,000 people had died in the plague of 1764. By 1798 the figure was 441,000. Franco Venturi, in "Napoli capitale nel pensiero dei riformatori illuministi," in *Storia di Napoli*, vol. 8, pp. 1 ff., shows that it was Giovanni Battista Carafa who took the lead in advocating enlightened absolutism and the continued growth, with improvements, of the big city capital. See Carafa, *Lettera di Giovanni Carafa*, p. xxiv, who felt that a city's buildings were "the first and often the only principle of salubrity in the air, of long life to the inhabitants, of good discipline, the advancement of manufactures and commerce, and finally of the inclinations and customs of the citizens." See also G. M. Galanti, *Descrizione dello*

stato antico ed attuale del contado di Molise, con un saggio storico sulla costituzione del regno (Naples, 1781), vol. 1, p. 225, who says that the countryside was prey to pirates, and that the other cities of the kingdom were so overtaxed that they slowly became deserted. Only Naples was relatively safe and prosperous: hence there was all the more reason to move there.

86. Aliberti, "Economia," *Storia di Napoli*, vol. 8, p. 78, reports that by 1797 the population of the Mezzogiorno as a whole was 4,959,700 while that of Naples was 435,930. It was not only romantics like Rousseau (*Emile*, 1762) who advocated flight from the cities; Tanucci mentions a plan of Carlo di Borbone's to divide Naples into four subcities or "metropolises," and advised his former sovereign, when he was King of Spain, to stay outside Madrid (*Lettere di Bernardo Tanucci a Carlo III di Borbone*, edited by Rosa Mincuzzi [Rome, 1969], p. 318). See also Luigi Barreca, ed., *Il Tramonto di Bernardo Tanucci nella correspondenza con Carlo III di Spagna, 1776–1783* (Palermo, 1976) and Venturi, "Napoli capitale," p. 26, for other cities about which people felt similarly; Aliberti, "Economia," p. 100, and Fausto Nicolini's introduction to his edition of Francesco Galiani, *Dialogues sur le commerce des bleds* (Milan/Naples, 1959). (For Galiani's ironic self-incrimination with Vichian tendencies see ibid., p. 461; also Fausto Nicolini, "Giambattista Vico e Ferdinando Galiani," ibid., *Saggi vichiani* [Naples, 1956], pp. 155 ff.).

87. Ange Goudar, in a book called *Naples, ce qu'il faut faire pour rendre ce royaume florissant* . . . (1769), p. 238. This is a true piece of Enlightenment literature, invoking Montesquieu, Hume, Pitt, and others in an analysis of Naples' ailments—lack of agricultural and commercial planning, the depopulation of the countryside, overtaxation, and bureaucratic misalignment. Above all Goudar cites as a fault the very principle of absolutism, namely that sovereignty, or authority, is indivisible.

88. But Vanvitelli, *Lettere*, 1244 (1766), remarks that Ferdinando IV had renewed another law, stating that all landholders of the Kingdom of Naples had to live in the capital on pain of sacrificing their country rents.

3 Architectural Order

1. Points 1, 2, 4, and 5 are discussed in my *Pythagorean Palaces* (Ithaca, N.Y., 1976), esp. p. 52. For point 3 see Lionel March and Philip Steadman, *The Geometry of Environment: An Introduction to Spatial Organization and Design* (Cambridge, Mass., 1974), pp. 89 ff. and 215 ff.

2. For Brunelleschi's grid plans see *Pythagorean Palaces*, pp. 64, 81, and 129–30; also Samuel Y. Edgerton, Jr., *The Renaissance Rediscovery of Classical Perspective* (New York, 1964), pp. 1 ff.; Leonardo Benevolo, S. Chieffi, and G. Mazzetti, "Indagine sul Santo Spirito di Brunelleschi," *Quaderni dell'Istituto di Storia dell'Architettura*, ser. 16 (1968):1 ff. For Filarete see Antonio Averlino [Filarete], *Trattato di architettura*, edited by A. M. Finoli and L. Grassi, 2 vols. (Milan, 1972). This text, 23 v, actually gives the figure of 103,200 workmen. See also ibid., 40 v, 21 n., and pp. 56–57 n.

3. Francesco di Giorgio, *Trattati di architettura*, edited by Corrado Maltese (Milan, 1967), 2, 21 r, 21 v. Hersey, *Pythagorean Palaces*, pp. 75ff.

4. See my *Alfonso II and the Artistic Renewal of Naples, 1485–1495* (New Haven, Conn., 1969), pp. 75 ff., and Hartmut Biermann, "Das Palastmodell Giuliano da Sangallos für Ferdinand I König von Neapel," *Wiener Jahrbuch für*

Kunstgeschichte, 23 (1970), esp. p. 157. Biermann falsely imagines, however, that Ferrante had planned this mighty complex solely so that he could possess a full-sized replica of an ancient Roman house!

5. G. M. Galanti, *Descrizione dello stato antico ed attuale del contado di Molise* (Naples, 1781), vol. 1, p. 225.

6. Luigi Salerno and others, *Via Giulia* (Rome, 1973), pp. 314 ff.; Arnaldo Bruschi, *Bramante architetto* (Bari, 1969), pp. 593 ff., 946 ff. The scheme is recorded in several versions. My illustration is based on Uffizi A 136, which shows the second floor. The plan consists of a "canonical" sesquialter, or square-and-one-half, rectangle. Though no overall scale is given, I estimate on the basis of room dimensions, inscribed throughout, that the whole was to be about 400 by 320 Roman palmi minus the protrusion of the church at the back. In other words it was planned to be about one-third the size of the Neapolitan Tribunali.

7. See G. Nicolosi, "Luigi Vanvitelli, architetto della reverenda fabbrica di San Pietro in Vaticano," *Atti del VIII convegno nazionale di storia dell'architettura* (Rome, 1956), pp. 65 ff.

8. See Carlo Pedretti, *Leonardo da Vinci: The Royal Palace at Romorantin* (Cambridge, Mass., 1972), esp. pp. 79 ff.

9. See now George Kubler, *Building the Escorial: An Architectural History of Its Fabrication* (Princeton, N.J., 1982), with earlier bibliography. For the grille see Urscino Alonso Mayo, "Heraldica Escurialense," in *El Monasterio de San Lorenzo el Real de el Escorial en el cuarto centenario de su Fundaciòn, 1563–1963* (El Escorial, 1964), pp. 617 ff.

10. See Myra Nan Rosenfeld and others, *Sebastiano Serlio on Domestic Architecture: The Sixth Book* (Cambridge, Mass., 1979) with full bibliography.

11. Juan Caramuel Lobkowitz, *Architectura civil, recta y obliqua, considerada y dibuxada en el templo de Jerusalem . . .*, 3 vols. (Vigevano, 1678), vol. 2, tract 8, p. 6.

12. Ibid., tract 8, section 4, "De el templo de Diana."

13. Meanwhile for Diophantine equations see H. H. Stark, *An Introduction to Number Theory* (Cambridge, England, 1978), pp. 145 ff. For Leibniz see G. W. Leibniz, *Opera omnia*, edited by L. Dutus (Geneva, 1768), vol. 3, nos. lviii, lix. Interest in Leibniz's monadic/diadic arithmetic was expressed in Naples by Innocenzo Molinari in *Parere istorico intorno alla vera idea contenuta nella lettera apologetica . . . de' Quipù* [n.p., n.d.], p. 6 n., where he speaks of Leibniz's number system as being more than merely arithmetical, but "psychological, characteristic, and hieroglyphic" as well; as indeed "a universal philosophical language."

14. André Félibien, *Entretiens sur les vies et sur les ouvrages des plus excellens peintres anciens et modernes* (Paris, 1725), vol. 6, p. 121.

15. Ibid., pp. 159 ff.; see also pp. 171 ff.

16. Louis Hautecoeur, *Histoire du Louvre: Le Château, le Palais, le Musée* (Paris, 1928), pp. 13–42; Yvan Christ, *Le Louvre et les Tuileries: Histoire architecturale d'un double palais* (Paris, 1949), pp. 15 ff. De l'Orme's full project for the Tuileries, insofar as one can judge (ibid.) was quite geometric. It was not realized in anything like its original form and probably had little impact on the line of development that led to Caserta, though Carlo di Borbone, with his interest in architecture, might have seen plans of it.

17. Louis Hautecoeur, "Le Louvre de Pierre Lescot," *Gazette des Beaux-Arts*, 15 (1927): 199 ff.

18. P. de Nolhac, *Histoire du Château de Versailles. Versailles sous Louis XIV*, 2 vols. (Paris, 1911); C. Mauricheau-Beaupré, *Versailles* (Monaco, 1949); Alfred Marie, *Naissance de Versailles*, 2 vols. (Paris, 1968), vol. 1, pp. 5 ff.; Louis Batiffol, "Le Château de Versailles de Louis XIII et son architecte Philibert le

Roy," *Gazette des Beaux-Arts*, 10 (1913):341 ff.; Guy Walton, "'L'Enveloppe' de Versailles: Réflexions nouvelles et dessins inédits," *Bulletin de la société de l'histoire de l'art français*, 92 (1977):141 ff.; Jean-Claude LeGillou, "Aperçu sur un projet insolite (1668) pour le Château de Versailles," ibid., 95 (1980):49 ff.; Robert Berger, "The Chronology of the *Enveloppe* of Versailles," *Architectura* (1980), 2:105 ff.

19. Pierre Verlet, *Versailles* (Paris, 1961), pp. 85 and 181.

20. Ibid., pp. 261 ff. See also Louis Madelin, "Comment le roi soleil dirigeait ses ministres," *Historia* (March 1953):293 ff.

21. Le Gillou, "Aperçu"; Berger, "*Enveloppe*." Also Gerold Weber, "Die Versailles-Konzepte von André Le Nôtre," *Münchner Jahrbuch der bildenden Kunst*, 20 (1969):207 ff., esp. pp. 212 ff.

22. For Samuel Pufendorf the *Elementa jurisprudentiae universalis* (1661) is particularly relevant; for Bodin, see his *De republica* [1568] (Paris, 1586) where in Book I the author exalts the primacy of the family as Vico was to do, making its habits and rules the nucleus of later general law and human rights. Bodin has a great deal to say on another theme that fascinated Vico as well—Pythagoreanism, and the principles of arithmetical, geometrical, and harmonic justice (pp. 415–16, 748, 751). For Leibniz see *Specimen demonstrationum politicarum pro rege polonorum eligendo* (1669). For a modern assessment: Nannerl Keohane, *Philosophy and the State in France* (Princeton, N.J., 1980), pp. 54 ff., 241 ff.

23. *Diritto*, p. 53. See A. Corsano, "Vico and Mathematics," in *Giambattista Vico: An International Symposium* (Baltimore, 1969), pp. 425 ff. For Vico's opinions on the importance of Pythagoras and his mathematical-social teachings see ibid., pp. 398, 678, 681, and 698. Also see Vico's *De antiquissima italorum sapientia* (Naples, 1710), pp. 23 ff. [Book I on metaphysics], which develops very fully the Pythagorean parallels between human thought and mathematical concepts such as point/line/plane/solid, perspective, and the like. For a modern analysis see S. Mazzarino, "Vico, la storia romana e il 'metodo geometrico,'" *De Homine*, 6 (1968):3 ff.

24. *Diritto*, p. 75.

25. Ibid., pp. 105–106.

26. Ibid., p. 506.

27. Ibid., pp. 105–106.

28. Ibid., pp. 63, 65.

29. Ibid., p. 75; *Scienza nuova*, paragraph 1026. The second, universal monarchy is sublime, and defeats the feudalism that had limited the earlier type of monarchy to a small scale. It was such feudalism that so beset Carlo di Borbone. In this, at least, Vico was at one with the Illuminists (Sirri, "Cultura," passim).

30. *Scienza nuova*, paragraphs 1025, 1091 ff.

31. Desormeaux, *Maison Bourbon*, dedication.

32. Renato De Fusco, "L'Architettura della seconda metà del settecento," *Storia di Napoli*, vol. 8, pp. 367 ff.; Anthony Blunt, *Neapolitan Baroque and Rococo Architecture* (London, 1975), pp. 168 ff. (though this account is riddled with errors); Felice de Filippis, *La Reggia di Napoli* (Naples, 1942), p. 34; Michelangelo Schipa, "Un re di altri tempi," *Napoli nobilissima*, ser. 2, 2 (1921):171 ff.; A. Venditti, "Opera napoletana," pp. 131 ff.; Salvatore di Giacomo, "Le Regge di Napoli, Capodimonte e Caserta," (in *I Palazzi e le ville che non sono più del rè* [Milan, 1921]); G. C. Alisio, *Urbanistica napoletana del settecento* (Bari, 1979), and, for a contemporary view, Vincenzo Ruffo, *Saggio sull'abbellimento di cui è capace la città di Napoli* (Naples, 1789).

33. See Venditti, "Opera," 131 ff.; Schipa, "Un re," De Filippis, *Règgia*.

34. Francesco Milizia, *Le Vite de' più celebri architetti d'ogni nazione e d'ogni tempo . . .* (Rome, 1768), p. 303.

35. Vanvitelli, *Lettere*, 175 (1753), 197 (1754), and 210 (1754). Vanvitelli apparently summoned the French sculptor Jean-Jacques Caffiéri, then a stipendiary at the French Academy in Rome, to Naples with an eye to carving statues for the facade in the 1750s. According to Thieme-Becker, *Allgemeines Künstlerlexikon*, s.v., Caffiéri was in Naples for a short period after completing a statue of the Holy Trinity, no longer in situ, for the Roman church of San Luigi dei Francesi in 1753. There is as yet no evidence for the claim in Wend Graf von Kalnein and Michael Levey, *Art and Architecture of the XVIII Century in France* (Harmondsworth, England, 1972), p. 99, that Caffiéri was being asked to contribute sculpture to Caserta.

36. See notes 33 and 34 and Camillo Minieri-Riccio, review of D. Salazaro's "Poche parole dette sul sepolcro di Luigi Vanvitelli," in *Archivio storico per le provincie napoletane*, 5 (1880):197. Nicola Spinosa, "La Pittura napoletana da Carlo a Ferdinando IV di Borbone," *Storia di Napoli*, vol. 8, pp. 453ff.; Vanvitelli, *Lettere* 151 (1753); Ferdinando Bologna, "Solimena al Palazzo reale di Napoli per le nozze di Carlo di Borbone," *Prospettiva*, 16 (1979): 53ff.

37. See De Filippis, *Antiche residenze*, pp. 123 ff.; Schipa, "Napoli," pp. 301–304; De Fusco, *Residenze*, p. 369; Arnaldo Venditti, "Antonio Canevari" in *Dizionario biografico degli italiani*, s.v.; N. Del Pezzo, "Siti reali: Capodimonte," *Napoli nobilissima*, ser. 2, 6 (1902):65–67, 170–73, 188–92. For a contemporary view of Capodimonte's art collection and of its curators, see J. J. Winckelmann, *Werke*, edited by C. L. Fernow (Dresden, 1808), vol. 2, pp. 293 ff.

38. Carletti was the oft-cited guidebook writer; the title of his architectural treatise was *Istituzioni d'architettura civile* (Naples, 1772).

4 Royal Architects

1. Vanvitelli, *Lettere*, 1276 (1766); see also 605 (1759) and 715 (1760). For Naples before Carlo's arrival see Michelangelo Schipa, *Regno*, pp. 1 ff.

2. For Carlo di Borbone see the bibliography.

3. Ruggero Moscati, *I Borboni d'Italia* (Naples, 1920), quotes Antonio Genovese writing of the year 1734, in which "it pleased God to restore to us our king, peace, and our true liberty and greatness; for no people can call itself truly free that does not have a domestic prince" (p. 24). The *Descrizione delle feste celebrate dalla fedelissima città di Napoli per lo glorioso ritorno della impresa di Sicilia della sacra maestà di Carlo di Borbone . . .* (Naples, 1735) says that the Largo del Palazzo was inscribed with slogans redating time, in Naples, from the advent of Carlo—much as the Fascists redated time from Mussolini's revolution—and exalting Carlo for ending the interregnum in direct royal rule that had prevailed since the last of the Aragonese kings in the early sixteenth century.

4. Schipa, *Regno*, p. 71. By the treaty of Aquisgrana (1748) Filippo, brother of Carlo, was to become King of the Two Sicilies on Carlo's death while the Duchies of Parma, Piacenza, and Guastalla were to be divided between Austria and Sardinia. But all this was

changed after Carlo's heir, Ferdinando, was born. According to Moscati, *Borboni*, p. 26, the Venetian resident in Naples, Cesare Vignola, was writing that the Neapolitans believed Carlo was about to declare himself king of Italy.

5. Ajello, "Carlo di Borbone," *Dizionario biografico degli italiani* (Milan, 1953 on), s.v. See also Acton, *Bourbons of Naples*, pp. 11 ff.

6. Schipa, *Regno*, p. 99 ff.; Venditti, "Opera," p. 99; Aliberti, "Economia," p. 78; Franco Venturi, "Napoli capitale nel pensiero dei riformatori illuministi," *Storia di Napoli*, vol. 8, pp. 3 ff.; Sirri, "Cultura," pp. 226 ff.

7. Acton, *Bourbons*, pp. 11, 15; Schipa, *Regno*, p. 73. For Bourbon portrait iconography see Steffi Rottgen, "Iconografia dei Borbone di Napoli," *Civiltà del '700 a Napoli* (Naples, 1980), vol. 2, pp. 387 ff.

8. See Vanvitelli, *Lettere*, 604 (1758), 663 (1759), 645 (1759), and 646 (1759).

9. Quoted in full by Rotili, *Vanvitelli*, p. 46.

10. See Alisio, *Siti reali*, pp. 19–20, for economic experiments among the Neapolitan illuminati, especially as they regarded farming and the construction of villas.

11. Spinosa, "Pittura," p. 508; D'Onofri, *Elogio*, p. xxv, quoting Carlo himself. Each villa or estate was involved with a different "industry," for example Portici for fishing, Capodimonte for goats and deer. The amount of game taken in these vast enterprises was such that one can speak of harvests. The number of people employed probably had considerable economic impact; for example 150 were used at Persano for a single hunt (Vanvitelli, *Lettere* 520 [1757]).

12. For the Albergo dei Poveri, a massive royal attempt at social amelioration in the spirit (but before the age) of Bentham, see Salvatore di Giacomo, "L'Albergo dei Poveri" in *Napoli d'oggi* (Naples, 1900); [L. Bianchi], *Disegni di Ferdinando Fuga e di altri architetti del settecento* (Rome, 1955); Roberto Pane, *Ferdinando Fuga* (Naples, 1956), and especially Giulio Pane, "Ferdinando Fuga e l'Albergo dei poveri," *Napoli nobilissima*, 3rd ser., 5 (1966):72 ff. To Vanvitelli the Albergo dei Poveri was the great counterscheme to Caserta, erected by his enemy. Though the two buildings were of equal scale, the Albergo cost only 900,000 ducats while Caserta cost more than seven times as much—6,133,808 (Aliberti, "Economia," 88). A parallel structure, in Rome, was Innocent XII Pignatelli's Ospizio Apostolico dei Poveri Invalidi, begun during his reign (1691–1700). See Dorothy Metzger Habel, "Piazza Sant'Ignazio, Rome, in the Seventeenth and Eighteenth Centuries," *Architectura*, 11, no. 1 (1981):31 ff.

13. For Carlo di Borbone's other large urban enterprises see Lorenzo Giustiniani, *Dizionario geografico-ragionato del regno di Napoli* (Naples, 1803), vol. 6, pp. 304–309, and Camillo Napoleone Sasso, *Storia dei monumenti di Napoli* (Naples, 1856–1858), vol. 1, pp. 421 ff., 433 ff. Also Arnaldo Venditti, *Architettura neoclassica a Napoli* (Naples, 1961), pp. 51 ff. For an interesting later Bourbon project for urban renewal, see Vincenzo Ruffo, *Saggio sull'abbellimento* (Naples, 1789) with its dedication to Ferdinando IV, which claims that Naples can be made "the first city of Europe and the capital of the universe." The book is written in the spirit of Laugier and Milizia. These things are discussed in Raffaele Mormone, "Architettura a Napoli, 1650–1734," in *Storia di Napoli*, vol. 8, pp. 1087 ff.; Venditti, "Opera," vol 44, pp. 134 ff.; Giancarlo Alisio, *Urbanistica napoletana del settecento* (Bari, 1979), and "Sviluppo urbano e struttura della città," *Storia di Napoli*, vol. 8, pp. 313 ff.

14. E. Romano, *La Porcellana di Capodimonte* (Naples, 1959), with earlier bibliography, and G. Liverani, "Porcellane di scavo di Capodimonte," *Faenza* (1959):120 ff. Also Vega de Martini and Alvar Gonzalez-Palacios, "Porcellana," ibid., vol. 2, pp. 93 ff.

15. See Oreste Ferrari, Nicola Spinosa, and others, "Pittura," in *Civiltà del '700 Napoli*, vol. 1, pp. 128 ff.; also Schipa, "Per l'Addobbo, l'ingrandimento e le decorazioni della reggia di Napoli alla venuta di Carlo di Borbone," *Napoli nobilissima*, 2d ser., 11 (1902): 109 ff.

16. See the exhibition catalogue, *Da Palazzo degli studi a museo archeologico* (Naples, 1977), and A. Gonzalez-Palacios, "Il Trasporto delle statue farnesiane da Roma a Napoli," *Antologia di belle arti*, 6 (1978):168 ff.

17. "Don Fastidio," "Il Museo sotto i Borboni," *Napoli nobilissima*, 2d ser., 15 (1906):30 ff.; Bruno Molajoli, *Notizie di Capodimonte* (Naples, 1964), pp. 9 ff.

18. D'Onofri, *Elogio*, p. cxlvi.

19. Vanvitelli, *Lettere*, 529 (1758) and 18 (1751).

20. Ibid., letter 570 (1758).

21. Venditti, "Opera," 125; Marcello Fagiolo dell'Arco, *Funzioni simboli valori della reggia di Caserta* (Rome, 1963), 36; Acton, *Bourbons*, p. 16; [Regione Emilia Romagna, Commune di Colorno], *La Reggia di Colorno nel '700* (Colorno, 1979).

22. D'Onofri, *Elogio*, p. xiv. See also Sirri, "Cultura," p. 252.

23. R. Mincuzzi, ed., *Lettere di Bernardo Tanucci a Carlo III di Borbone, 1757–1776* (Rome, 1969), p. 129 (August 10, 1762). This deals with what Tanucci felt to be Vanvitelli's derelictions of duty.

24. Franco Mancini, *Scenografia napoletana dell'età barocca* (Naples, 1964), esp. pp. 167 ff., which deals with Vanvitelli as a scenographer; Mancini, "Feste apparati e spettacoli teatrali," *Storia di Napoli*, vol. 8, pp. 651 ff. In "Feste," p. 651, Mancini explains that Tagliacozzo-Canale received his notoriety during the celebrations of Filippo V's decree ceding the Two Sicilies to his son Carlo in 1734. Tagliacozzo's tableau depicting the Gardens of the Hesperides collapsed, killing several people and injuring hundreds. See also U. Prota Giurleo, "I Bibbiena a Napoli," *Partenope*, 1, no. 3 (1960):175 ff., *Feste ed apparati civili e religiosi in Napoli dal viceregno alla capitale* (Naples, 1968), and "Il 'Trucco' urbano," *Civiltà del '700 a Napoli*, vol. 2, pp. 301 ff.

25. For Vanvitelli's version of these proceedings see *Lettere*, 437 (1757) and 1125 (1764).

26. *Descrizione delle feste* . . . (1735). Tagliacozzi did another "Arrival of Aeneas" for the wedding of the Infante Filippo and Luisa Elisabetta, oldest daughter of Louis XV (Mancini, "Feste," p. 662). For Aeneas as a local city-founder see Pompeo Sarnelli, *Nuova guida de' forestieri . . . della regal città di Napoli* (Naples, 1782), p. 164, which names Gaeta as a town built (or rebuilt) by the hero, who then lived in it for seven years c. 1183 B.C.

27. Vico, meanwhile, *Diritto*, p. 400, had already praised Maria Amalia's native language, German, as the offspring of Scythian. The Scythians, in turn, were the offspring of Hercules and founded "the first republics of the optimates." They were characterized by "rectitude, modesty, simplicity, and justice." The quotation is from *Breve ragguaglio della rinomata fiera che sotto la direzione di D. Ferdinando Sanfelice Cavaliere Napoletano si celebrò nel mese di luglio dell' anno 1738 in occasione del real maritaggio del nostro re D. Carlo di Borbone* . . . (Naples, 1738) [irregular pagination].

28. Vanvitelli, *Lettere*, 38 (1751).

29. Vico, *Diritto*, pp. 648–49;

30. Vico, *Versi d'occasione* (Bari, 1949), pp. 122–124. Also *Breve ragguaglio*, s.v.

31. Vincenzo Rè, *Narrazione delle solenne reali feste fatte celebrare in Napoli da sua maestà il re delle Due Sicilie* . . . (Naples, 1749); also N. F. Faraglia, "Il Largo del Palazzo," *Napoli nobilissima*, 1st ser., 2 (1893):9–10. For Vanvitelli's low opinion of Vincenzo Rè see the *Lettere*, 937 (1762) and 663 (1759). Vanvitelli disliked such Baroque festival machines. The *Avvisi reali* or proclamations of festivals for the

capital, now in the Archivio di Stato, describe innumerable similar structures, pagan for the carnival and for royal celebrations, and Christian for religious holidays.

32. *Cronaca di Partenope*, p. 67.

33. *Diritto*, p. 730.

34. N. Del Pezzo, "Reali delizie borboniche," *Napoli nobilissima*, 2d ser. 3 (1922):146 ff.; Giancarlo Alisio, *Siti reali*, s.v. "Portici."

35. D'Onofri, *Elogio*, p. xiv. He refers to the king by his Spanish title. When Carlo was King of the Two Sicilies he was known as Carlo di Borbone since there was disagreement as to the enumeration of the Angevin, Hapsburg, and Capetian kings who had claimed the thrones of Naples or Sicily.

36. See Pane, *Architettura dell'età barocca in Napoli* (Naples, 1939), pp. 305 ff.; Venditti, "Opera," pp. 102 ff.; Blunt, pp. 165 ff.; B. Rocco, "Elogio del Cavalier Gioffredo disteso da Benedetto Rocco," in *Giornale enciclopedico di Napoli*, 1, no. 3 (1785):37 ff., reprinted as a pamphlet (Naples, 1785). On pp. 38–39 the anonymous author claims Gioffredo acquired his taste for literature and mathematics only later in life and that he studied with Martino Buonocore as well as Medrano. He adds that Gioffredo's real masters, however, were Palladio and Daniele Barbaro's edition of Vitruvius. The article also says that Gioffredo received formal mathematical training at the University from Niccolò di Martino. See also Giuseppe De Nitto, "I Disegni di Mario Gioffredo per la reggia di Caserta presso la Biblioteca Nazionale di Napoli," *Napoli nobilissima*, 3rd ser., 14 (1975):183 ff.; reprinted Naples, 1981.

37. *De vita Mari Gioffredi neapolitani architecti commentariolum* [1785; by Antonio Niccolò Carlini, n.p., n.d.]. See also Sasso, *Monumenti*, vol. 1, pp. 489 ff.

38. Carlini, *Gioffredi*, p. 2.

39. Ibid., p. 3.

40. Ibid., p. 4.

41. Vanvitelli, *Lettere*, 876 (1761) and 878 (1761). The latter records Vanvitelli's particularly strong dislike of Gioffredo's success in winning a commission, apparently unexecuted, to build a church facade (that of San Giacomo degli Spagnuoli, now Nostra Signora del Sacro Cuore) in Rome. Later Vanvitelli refused even to meet Gioffredo (letter 909 [1761]). Ironically enough, when Vanvitelli judged the anonymous entries in the competition for remodeling the Church of the Spirito Santo, he found Gioffredo's to be "the least expensive and of the most beautiful symmetry" of the four (Franco Strazzullo, *Il Restauro settecentesca alla chiesa dello Spirito Santo a Napoli* (Milan, 1953), pp. 17, 19.

42. F. Strazzullo, *Restauro*; Thoenes, *Neapel*, pp. 274 ff.

43. *Dell'Architettura di Mario Gioffredo architetto napoletano. Parte prima nella quale si tratta degli ordini dell'architettura de' Greci, e degli Italiani . . .* (Naples, 1768).

44. Ibid., dedication.

45. Ibid., p. 5.

46. Ibid., pp. 7–8.

47. Ibid., p. 9 ff.

48. Carlini, *Gioffredi*, pp. 6–7.

49. Ibid.

50. For Vanvitelli see the bibliography.

51. Vanvitelli was also jealously conscious of his position vis-à-vis other architects and artists—not only Fuga and Gioffredo, but also Corrado Giaquinto (*Lettere*, 606 [1759] and 634 [1759]), and G. B. Sacchetti (706 [1760]).

52. See Roberto Pane, "L'Attività di Luigi Vanvitelli fuori del regno delle Due Sicilie," in R. de Stefano, ed., *Luigi Vanvitelli*, pp. 43 ff.; Venditti, "Opera," p. 101.

53. See chapter 2, note 51. In fact Vanvitelli apparently maintained two architectural offices, one in Caserta (after about 1757) and the other in Rome under the direction of his brother Urbano (*Lettere*, 100 [1753]).

54. Vanvitelli, Jr., *Vita*, pp. 15 ff.; see also Ferdinando Paturelli, *Caserta e San Leucio*, edited by Gaetano Capasso (Naples, 1972). Paturelli was Vanvitelli's student and assisted Carlo Vanvitelli, the architect's son, at Caserta after the father's death. For Gaspar van Wittel see Raffaello Causa, *Pitloo* (Naples, 1956), pp. 35 ff. Gaspar had experience both as a maker of engineering drawings and as a decorator. See Giorgio Morelli, "Appunti bio-bibliografici su Gaspar e Luigi Vanvitelli," *Archivio della Società romana di storia patria*, 3rd ser., 27 (1969):117, 119.

55. Vanvitelli, *Lettere*, 1212 (1765).

56. For Juvarra see [Università degli studi di Messina. Istituto di Disegno], *Mostra di Filippo Juvarra architetto e scenografo* (1966), nos. 52, 53, 112, 119, 156–57, 175, 221. Vanvitelli seems to have been more interested in La Superga, Turin, than in the palace of Stupinigi. He sent for prints of that church and of Juvarra's San Filippo, also at Turin (*Lettere*, 695 [1759] and 703 [1760] and then wrote (732 [1760]) that Juvarra's buildings were "formless and unthought-through (*senza riflessione*), without correctness in composition, but with nice things scattered here and there—though not in a connected way, and mixed with awful things which take away the merit of the good ones. In short, I thank Almighty God and my guardian saints who have given me the light and strength to be an architect as well; but one who is more ordered and regular [in his designs]." See also letters 733 (1760) and 849 (1761).

57. In 1751 Vanvitelli sent to Urbano for a copy of Carlo Fontana's treatise on aqueducts (letter 34). His other books included Guarino's supermathematical *Architettura civile* (1737) treatise (letter 55 [1752]), Vitruvius in the Caravita and Perrault editions, a Vignola, Montano's *Libro d'architettura* of 1608, Borromini, Blondel, and treatises on hydraulics (Jörg Garms, "Die Briefe des Luigi Vanvitelli an seinen Brüder Urbano in Rom: Kunsthistorisches Material," *Römisches historisches Mitteilungen*, 13 [1971]:277).

58. Carlini, *Gioffredo*, p. 2.

59. De Fusco, "Architettura," *Storia di Napoli*, vol. 8, pp. 434–35, describes Vanvitelli's architecture as a form of classicism with Baroque accents, and with its origins in Italian cinquecento architecture—namely in the work of some of the architects such as those discussed above in chapter 3. See also Mario Rotili, "Il Progetto vanvitelliano per la Fontana di Trevi," *Samnium*, 27 (1954):54 ff.

60. For Fuga see Roberto Pane, *Ferdinando Fuga* (Naples, 1956), and Giulio Pane, "Ferdinando Fuga e l'Albergo dei Poveri," *Napoli nobilissima*, 3rd ser., 5 (1966):72 ff. Vanvitelli seems to have been a member of a Roman academy, the Accademia degli arcadi, founded in 1690 around Christina of Sweden partly to oppose the more opulent forms of Baroque taste.

61. R. De Fusco, "Vanvitelli e la critica del settecento," *Napoli nobilissima*, ser. 2, 3 (1967), reprinted in R. di Stefano, ed., *Luigi Vanvitelli* (Naples, 1973); also Pane, "l'Attività," ibid., pp. 43 ff., 59 ff., 71 ff.; Rotili, "Progetto." Rotili discusses what he calls the "great Roman neo-cinquecento movement in architecture" of the eighteenth century, in which Vanvitelli plays a leading part—a point that underscores my linking of sixteenth-century with eighteenth-century palace planning in chapter 3.

62. Pietro Carreras, *Studi su Luigi Vanvitelli* (Florence, 1977); [Comune di Ancona], *Il Lazzaretto di Luigi Vanvitelli* (Ancona, 1980).

63. Giovanni Gaetano Bottari, *Dialoghi sopra le tre arti del disegno*, [1754] (Florence, 1770), one of many such books. See especially in this edition pp. 64–65, where Vanvitelli is not named but is clearly referred to when the author castigates those who have said Michelangelo's dome threatened to collapse, claiming that these architects are setting themselves up against the great man.

64. Vanvitelli, *Lettere*, 1093 (1763). Here Vanvitelli says something rather curious: Bottari, who has attacked his plans for stabilizing St. Peter's dome, is characterized as "one of those damned unbridled Florentine buffoons who adore Michelangelo's shit and want to prove, despite the truth of the matter, that the great man could never have made a fool of himself as in fact he did in the great dome of Saint Peter's."

65. See Pane, "Attività," pp. 59 ff., and its bibliography listed in Pane's note 7 (which is misprinted on page 92 of his essay, under the heading "Capitolo quinto" instead of "Capitolo quarto"). See also Vanvitelli, *Lettere*, 351 (1756) and 914 (1761).

66. See note 57 and Giorgio Morelli, "Appunti bio-bibliografici," which lists the pictures and books in the Vanvitellis' Roman house. Vanvitelli might have considered himself something of an *illuminato*: he read Newton and Voltaire as well as Metastasio (*Lettere*, 127 [1753] and 290 [1755]). His interest in the preeminence of Rome and the Romans was sustained by his readings in G. Vasi, *Delle Magnificenze di Roma antica e moderna* (1753) and A. M. Bandini, *De Obelisco Caesaris Augusti e Campi Martii ruderibus nuper eruto commentarius . . .* (Rome, 1750). See also chapter 2, note 76.

67. Vanvitelli, *Lettere*, 744 (1760) and 746 (1760). We learn from the second of these letters that he also possessed prints of the Escorial. In letter 284 (1754) he tells of going to the Marchese Galiani's to consult about the Vitruvius edition. This would be *L'Architettura di M. Vitruvio Pollione colla traduzione italiana e comento del Marchese Berardo Galiani, Accademico ercolanense, e architetto di merito dell' Accademia di San Luca. Dedicata alla maestà di Carlo re delle Due Sicilie . . .* (Naples, 1758), the first really good translation of Vitruvius into Italian.

68. The story of Vanvitelli's desire to go to Spain is told throughout the *Lettere*. Letter 623 (1759) alludes to rumors that he is to be asked to go; in 630 (1759) he is not all that anxious to do so—after all, Caserta is far from complete, and he would have to sacrifice his salary as architect of St. Peter's; yet he does not wish to do what Fuga has done and imply to the king that he does *not* want to go (659 [1759]). In any event the king says Vanvitelli must finish the palace at Caserta first (667 [1759]). But the queen adds that as soon as that palace is far enough along the architect must build a new staircase in the royal palace at Madrid, just like the one at Caserta. In letter 692 (1759), Vanvitelli is studying Spanish. He also hears (700 [1759]) that the Royal Palace at Madrid is a poor thing and that its staircase is merely a temporary wooden one. However, letter 716 (1760) begins a series of letters lamenting the fact that Carlo, now that he has arrived in Spain, is ignoring him. How else explain that the measurements for the new staircase have not been sent? There are rumors of a planned new palace in Madrid (736, [1760]), and the Museo di San Martino, in Naples, possesses a drawing (20897) by Vanvitelli of a staircase for the old palace. The present staircase in the Royal Palace at Madrid was designed by Vanvitelli's student Francesco Sabatini, who worked on other royal palaces in Spain and arrived at Aranjuez on May 4, 1760 (letter 749). Sabatini was also commissioned to erect an extension to Buen Retiro (754, [1760]). Finally it appears that Sabatini will also build the new stairs for the Madrid palace (784, [1760]). These indeed copy the stair at Caserta (844, [1761]). In August 1761 hope revives that Vanvitelli may go to Spain nonetheless (888): the Prince of Jaci, Neapolitan ambassador to Madrid, says that Carlo III wants him there. When the architect meanwhile entertains Anton Raphael Mengs at Caserta, the latter agrees that the building is so far along that it can only be finished as Vanvitelli wishes—that is, whether he remains in Naples or not. In later letters Vanvitelli speaks of other, unspecified designs for Carlo's Spanish projects (1206 [1765]).

But it also becomes clear that despite the neglect of him by the regency council and Ferdinando IV, he will remain in Naples. Meanwhile for the Foro Carolino see Eduardo Nappi, "Verità e leggenda nella storia dell'arte napoletana. I. Il Foro Carolino," *Annali di storia economica e sociale*, 8 (1967):189 ff. Nicolo Carletti, *Topografia universale della città di Napoli* (Naples, 1776), pp. 254 ff., criticizes the distribution of triglyphs and metopes in the present buildings' entablature, which are then combined with Ionic dentils. We also learn that the sculptor Pietro Solari, who worked on garden sculpture at Caserta, made a full-scale model of the equestrian statue of Carlo di Borbone. This was based on a prototype discovered at Herculaneum—probably the bronze statue of Balbus now in the Museo Nazionale—and was set in place in the Foro Carolino, after which it was destroyed. Nappi meanwhile shows that the Foro Carolino with its equestrian project and fourteen roof statues symbolizing Carlo's virtues was one of the major eighteenth-century sculptural *cantieri* of Naples, along with the Cappella Sansevero, the Annunziata, and Caserta itself. See also Sasso, *Monumenti*, vol. 1, pp. 433 ff. Also Vanvitelli, *Lettere* 478 (1757), 480 (1757), 606 (1759), 866 (1761), 974 (1762), and 1161 (1764); Arnaldo Venditti, *Architettura neoclassica a Napoli*, (Naples, 1961), p. 156 ff.; for the Largo del Palazzo see Vanvitelli, *Lettere*, 184 (1753) and 188 (1725); Giulio Briganti, *Gaspar van Wittel e l'origine della veduta settecentesca* (Rome, 1966), p. 248; for other works see Venditti, "Opera," pp. 100 ff., 132 ff.

69. Vanvitelli, *Lettere*, 1414 (1768) and 843 (1761). (Lettera, 19-2).

70. Other urban projects are listed in the records of the Archivio di Stato, Napoli, under *Trattati leggi e decreti di Carlo III* (Naples, 1734-1759), pp. 97-198. See also Venditti, "Opera napoletana," pp. 131 ff.

71. Venditti, "Opera," p. 148; G. B. D'Addosio, *Origine, vicende storiche e progressi della real S. Casa dell'Annunziata di Napoli* (Naples, 1883), which shows that Carlo and then Ferdinando were interested directly in the design and execution of the work. This was a good thing, for there was much rancor about Vanvitelli's role and about the quality of the design. In 1769 Vanvitelli resigned as architect and was replaced by Gioffredo (p. 206). Subsequently supervision went back to Vanvitelli—in 1771. After Luigi Vanvitelli's death in December 1772 his son Carlo took over. See also Vanvitelli, *Lettere*, 715 (1760) and 1079 (1763), which show that for the dome of his Neapolitan church Vanvitelli wished to use that of San Carlo ai Catinari, Rome, by Rosato Rosati, 1620, as model. See also letter 1082 (1763).

72. Vanvitelli, *Lettere*, 1161 (1764). For the Palazzo Teora designs see letters 1380 (1767) and 1392 (1767).

73. Ibid., letters 86 (1752) and 184 (1753), which make clear that even at this early point he was working intensively on Neapolitan projects.

74. Quoted in Chierici, *Caserta*, pp. 21-22 ff.

75. Vanvitelli, *Lettere*, 1384 (1767), hears that the emperor is planning to come to Naples incognito to find out if in fact Ferdinando is as gross in manner as he is made out to be. Meanwhile the emperor's daughter Maria Giuseppina died in Rome in 1767. She, who had been Ferdinando's intended, was then supplanted by her sister Maria Carolina.

76. Vanvitelli, *Lettere*, 1335 (1767).

5 The River-Road

1. Vanvitelli, *Lettere*, 1180 (1765). According to letter 108 (1753), Vanvitelli also sent a copy of a book entitled *La Via Appia*, whose author he does not give, to Leonardi, presumably to help the latter with his contributions to the *Dichiarazione*.

2. The first is the Giardino Inglese to the east of the fountain of Diana. This has a swan lake, a Gothic chapel, a ruined temple, and a botanical garden, among other things. Though planned in 1768 definitive work did not begin until 1782 in the reign of Ferdinando IV. The gardenist was one John Andrew Graefer. The other appendix is the Bosco Vecchio to the west of the parterre, together with the *castelluccia*, or play castle, erected for the princes in 1769, rebuilt in 1819 as a summerhouse. The Peschiera Grande was built in 1762–1769, also after Carlo's departure for Spain, for Ferdinando's naumachias. See Christoph Thoenes, *Neapel*, p. 604 ff.; Touring Club Italiano, *Napoli e dintorni* (Milan, 1976), pp. 590 ff., and *Campania* (Milan, 1981) pp. 239 ff.

3. The distance from the south front of the palace to the beginning of the first cascade is just under 9500 U.S. feet, or c. 11,260 Neapolitan palmi. According to dimensions given by Vanvitelli, *Lettere*, 191 (1754) Caserta's garden is deeper than the garden at Versailles by 183 palmi or c. 154 U.S. feet.

4. For the gardens see the bibliography.

5. Vanvitelli, *Dichiarazione*, p. ii, also below, note 16.

6. Ibid. See also Velleius Paterculus, *Historia*, vol. 2, p. 25; Silvius Italicus, vol. 8, p. 115 ff.; A. De Franciscis. "Templum Dianae Tifatinae," *Archivio storico di Terra di Lavoro*, 1 (1956):301 ff.; Jörg Garms, "Die Briefe des Luigi Vanvitelli am seinen Brüder Urbano in Rom: Kunsthistorisches Material," *Römische historische Mitteilungen*, 13 (1971):278, shows that Vanvitelli read Mazzocchi. D'Onofri, *Elogio*, p. cxlv, says the name of the place comes from "casa irta," or *erta*—a steep or sloping citadel. According to Vico Capua was once the capital of the whole Mediterranean area (*Diritto*, p. 396).

7. See note 1; also G. De Lillo, *Le Acque del condotto carolino per la città e borgate di Caserta* (Caserta, 1896); R. De Stefano, "Luigi Vanvitelli ingegnere," pp. 171 ff.; Venditti, "Opera"; D'Onofri, *Elogio*, pp. clv–clvi.

8. Vanvitelli, *Dichiarazione*, p. ii, pl. xiii.

9. See note 3; also Vanvitelli, *Lettere*, 181 (1753) and 1249 (1766). In the latter, Ferdinando Galiani, royal secretary to the Neapolitan ambassador to Paris, great friend of Tanucci's, and a *philosophe*, is quoted as follows in praise of the waters of Caserta: "These waters run constantly through the fountains, and are clear, limpid, and copious. Those at Versailles are green, they stink, they are turbid, and run only a few hours at a time." The Prince of Francavilla, Michele Imperiale, claimed that the waterworks at Caserta were finer not only than those at Versailles but at Marly as well—that there was nothing in France as good (letter 572 [1758]). Meanwhile Vanvitelli, hearing these things with satisfaction, is awaiting a sketch by his assistant Carlo Murena of the park at the Villa Lante, Bagnaia (letter 203 [1754]). Vanvitelli (letter 76 [1752]) also says the king belittled his brother's new palace-building at San Ildefonso, adding that the queen (letter 782 [1762]) thought Caserta's gardens, especially, would be superior. He writes also that the fountains at the Corsini Villa, based on those at Chantilly, are bad and little (letter 966 [1762]). Vanvitelli himself visited villas at Frascati, Castello, and Albano (letter 1155 [1764]).

10. Fagiolo dell'Arco, *Caserta*, pp. 57 ff.; Yves Bottineau, *L'Art de cour dans l'Espagne de Philippe V, 1700–1746* (Bordeaux, 1962), pp. 259 ff., 520 ff.; Luigi Vanvitelli Jr., *Vita*, p. 187. For Juvarra see chapter 4, note 62.

11. See his *La Théorie et la practique du jardinage* (Paris, 1709), pl. 1. Venditti, "Opera," says that Vanvitelli knew Versailles through prints, meanwhile adding that the powerful horizon-

tal planes at Caserta may have been influenced by the landscapes painted by Vanvitelli's father.

12. A major figure in the creation of what Vanvitelli called the "allusive poetic fables"—the fountain sculptures—was the Abbate Porzio Leonardi (Vanvitelli, *Lettere*, 97 [1752]). As his and Vanvitelli's ideas for the fountains developed, plans for publishing the original garden scheme were left unchanged as a way of documenting the first thoughts (Venditi, "Opera," p. 107).

13. Not to mention Pontano's *De hortis hesperidum* (c. 1500), which takes up a theme that goes all through the period of interest, for example in Metastasio's opera of that title and the similarly titled opera by Giuseppe Passari, with music by J. C. Bach, seen by Vanvitelli in 1765 (*Lettere* [1175]). Vico says (*Diritto*, p. 401), that "all peoples founded in religion and virtue have some Hercules as their author," that is, as the transporter of their Hesperidean garden; and that the excellent, pious, prudent, and strong are so because they dominate land cleansed by waters that are perhaps symbolized by the "Hydra" that Hercules tames (ibid., p. 13).

14. Vanvitelli, *Lettere*, 203 (1754). In the previous year (letter 167) Fogliani's wife had spoken to the architect about a trip to Versailles to see the fountains, but a few months later (182) Carlo decreed that there was to be no such trip, saying to Vanvitelli: "I am happy with what you are doing for me, and you have no need to see the work of others."

15. Venditti, "Opera," vol. 2, notes 29 and 62; Di Stefano, "Vanvitelli ingegnere," pp. 171 ff.; Vanvitelli, *Lettere*, 85 (1752), 89 (1752), 158 (1753), 962 (1762), 1043 (1763), 1048 (1763), 1073 (1763), 1066 (1763), and 1180 (1765). Vanvitelli's report on the aqueduct deserves to be reconstructed. It would have been as important as the *Dichiarazione*. And it was far more controversial. Some of the discussion centered on the Neapolitan citizen groups who objected that the aqueduct would in fact diminish the city's water supply. Vanvitelli and his backers denied this. The result was an official report by Vanvitelli, edited by Tanucci (who was also, curiously, the person to whom the report was addressed) of which a manuscript, apparently incomplete, is now in the Biblioteca Nazionale, Naples (Sez. manoscritti XV-A-9, busta 2, c. 65). Vanvitelli spent much time and effort on his report. And not only Tanucci but Leonardi helped. Allegorical sculpture was envisioned as part of the scheme. See, for the latter, letters 81 (1752) and 60 (1752), in which Leonardi is given material on the Neapolitan festival machines. Letter 265 (1754) records Leonardi's work on the aqueduct book, as do 268 (1754) and 700 (1759). In this last Leonardi is asked to ponder a supplement with a text and four engraved plates showing the proposed structure, which is now to run from Ponte in Airola, in the north, down through Valle di Durazzano. The engravings would give elevations of the bridges and tunnels. Subsequently, in 718 (1760), the architect records Tanucci's desire to send the aqueduct report to Carlo in Spain; 718 (1760) and 720 (1760) reveal that Leonardi was the author. A version corrected by Tanucci is returned for comment to Leonardi (754 [1760]). But two years later the architect complains that even after the great system has been put in operation there is still silence on the subject of the report's being printed (964 [1762]). And it never was.

16. See Nicolini, *Reggia*, pp. 113 ff., which records many statues that were paid for and are no longer there, and V. Maderna, F. Petrelli, M. Siniscalco, and N. Spinosa, *Le Arti figurative a Napoli nel settecento: Documenti e ricerche* (Naples, 1979), which does the same, and prints documents for some of the present sculptures (pp. 155 ff., 199 ff.). Vanvitelli probably designed the fountains personally. He always maintained his role as a figure artist. In the *Lettere*, 875 (1761) he describes his figure compositions for the tapestries in Ferdinando's chamber in the Palazzo Reale,

made on the occasion of his marriage to Maria Carolina. And his name appears as "pictor et architectus" on the aqueduct inscriptions (letter 92 [1752]). See also Gino Chierici, "Luigi Vanvitelli pittore," in *Bollettino d'arte*, 30 (1937):513 ff.; Nicola Spinosa, "Luigi Vanvitelli e i pittori attivi a Napoli nella seconda metà del settecento: Lettere e documenti inediti," *Storia dell'arte*, 4 (1972): 193 ff.; Roberto Pane, "Luigi Vanvitelli, l'uomo e l'artista," *Napoli nobilissima*, 3rd ser., 12 (1973): 3 ff.; Franco Strazzullo, "Pittori e scultori del '700 a Napoli nelle relazioni di Luigi Vanvitelli," *Atti dell'Accademia Pontaniana*, 23 (1974):204 ff. and 24 (1974):1 ff. Fagiolo dell'Arco, *Caserta*, p. 60, thinks Vanvitelli made all the designs for the Caserta fountains in the 1760s.

17. Vanvitelli, *Vita*, pp. 196 ff. The inscriptions on the Ponte della Valle, which date from 1754, make it clear that the Acqua Carolina was a recension of the Acqua Julia and that Carlo di Borbone built this mighty bridge as a kind of surrogate for the abandoned arch. See also *Lettere*, 1107 (1763). Though abandoned, the scheme does indicate that in Vanvitelli's mind (1) the whole sequence of the river-road could be linked to the king and (2) that he was thinking of tying together the beginning of the river-road and the palace facade two miles away. This second concept, though without the royal statue, seems to have stayed in Vanvitelli's mind as we shall see. The other abandoned ideas for sculpture are also revealing. Among them were Venus as queen of love in her chariot (letter 18 [1751]); a fountain of nymphs; Andromeda and her marine monster; Arethusa (see the discussion of the Ceres fountain below); the birth of Venus; Egeria turned into a stream—to a total of nineteen (Venditti, "Opera," pp. 127 ff.). And according to Venditti, ibid., p. 2, no. 266, between 1754 and 1759 there arrived at Caserta, from Carrara, no less than forty mythological statues, including termini, sent by an artist named Giovanni del Medico. See also Caroselli, *Caserta*, p. 60. Vanvitelli himself collected antique fragments for the Caserta workshops from Mondragone, Pozzuoli, Nettuno, and other places—mostly columns, capitals, and the like, but also some figure sculpture. This is recorded in the Biblioteca Nazionale manuscript mentioned in note 15. The architect also sent for volumes of engravings of classical statues in the Capitolino, Odescalchi, and Pisano collections (*Lettere*, 192 [1754]). The ubiquitous Paolo Rolli, who engraved so many of the plates for Vanvitelli's, Baiardi's, and Mazzocchi's books (Garms, "Briefe," *Mitteilungen*, p. 204), is mentioned in a letter of 1751 in which Vanvitelli sends a sketch to Urbano so that Rolli can develop further "fables" to be set up in the garden. Indeed Vanvitelli was prolific with fountain ideas. In the *Lettere* he says he is thinking of making more such sketches, smaller than the designs in the *Dichiarazione* (letter 80 [1752]), and in 84 (1752) there is a plan for twenty-four of these. In letter 192 (1754) he records the need for a sculptor to start to work but first wants him to study the Caracci Gallery in the Farnese Palace (n.b., the latter being now the property of Carlo). In letter 196 (1754) Vanvitelli tells Urbano that the sculptors now at Caserta are not good enough for major work, though he supports and befriends Tommaso Solari, who did do important things for Vanvitelli there (letter 347, [1756]). In letter 499 (1757) Del Medico's termini arrive and are found unsatisfactory. Mazzocchi, *Aeneas tabulas*, pp. 149 ff., prints quite a disquisition on this kind of statue, a pedestalled bust of Terminus, Roman god of boundaries. They were invented, he says, to express the idea of "every type of god" though they often depicted famous men. Whatever Vanvitelli's disapproval of Del Medico's termini in 1757, we find that forty of them had been ordered by 1764 (1138). Some of them, no doubt, are what presently line the planted hemicycle just north of the palace (fig. 5.6). But Vanvitelli was more interested

in fountains than in termini. In 1765 and thereafter he seems to have been designing fountains for one or more of Carlo's estates in Spain (1176 [1765] and 1178 [1765]). From 1181 (1765) we learn that the designs are bound into a volume and that a certain Abbate Clementi has written four sets of Latin verses for them—verses Vanvitelli finds full of youthful fire—while Tanucci has praised the designs. Unhappily, at Murcia, on their way to the king, the wagon carrying the book was mired in mud and the drawings partly ruined. Vanvitelli's son Pietro, who was accompanying the designs, will try to restore them (1196 [1765]). In letter 1200 (1765) Paolo Pini presents them to the king and Vanvitelli plans to send two further designs. The latter, if not the whole group, seem to have been for San Ildefonso (1289 [1766]). Finally, another set of sculptures designed by Vanvitelli were four statues, *Humility*, *Prayer*, *Innocence*, and *Perseverence* for the Minims of San Luigi di Palazzo, Naples (1326 [1767]). This church no longer exists; I do not know where the sculptures are. Much research remains to be done on Vanvitelli as a figure artist and especially on the Spanish fountains, for a number of important eighteenth-century sculpture groups decorate Carlo's gardens in Spain.

18. Vanvitelli, Jr., *Vita*, fig. 178. In the *Lettere*, Vanvitelli records that he gave the king models of the conduits planned for the river system in the garden (letter 165 [1753]). Giancarlo Alisio, *Urbanistica napoletana del settecento* (Bari, 1979), fig. 41, publishes this, without comment, as an alternative plan for the garden and town of Caserta.

19. Bottineau, *L'Art de cour*, fig. xviii.

20. Just to make everything more complicated Vanvitelli, *Lettere*, 147 (1753) makes it clear that in this year a "new" garden plan was presented to the sovereigns. This was probably the scheme recorded in the *Dichiarazione* of 1756, which therefore does not actually represent the first project.

21. According to Fagiolo Dell'Arco, *Caserta*, p. 60, when in 1768 the aqueduct was completed it turned out that the water issued from the top of the hill rather than the bottom as planned. Yet already in 1763 Vanvitelli says the water was intended to issue from the top (*Lettere*, 1106).

22. Strazzullo, "Primi anni," p. 462, a letter of December 1751; *Lettere*, 62 (1752), 64 (1752), 164 (1753), and 355 (1756). This last includes a sketch of how the statues at Tivoli could actually be transported to Caserta if a low enough price could be agreed on.

23. For the Villa d'Este see Carl Lamb, *Die Villa D'Este in Tivoli* (Munich, 1966), with earlier bibliography; also D. R. Coffin. *The Villa in the Life of Renaissance Rome* (Princeton, N.J., 1979), pp. 311 ff., 361 ff. Another possible source is the less famous Villa Palagonia, Bagheria, near Palermo, with its river-road like Caserta's. But the river-road perhaps has a more obvious prototype in Sicily in Vittorio Amedeo II's scheme (unrealized but certainly not unknown) for the gardens of the royal palace at Messina. This consists essentially of one long axial boulevard—perhaps only a road and not a river—extending from a palace whose plan is much like that of the Palazzo Reale, Madrid, and which was drawn out by Juvarra in 1714 [Messina, University, Instituto di Disegno]. *Mostra di Filippo Juvarra architetto e scenografo* (Messina, 1966), fig. 42.

24. Lamb, *Villa d'Este*, pls. 146 ff.

25. Venditti, "Opera," p. 106, who mentions, as well, the water-chains at Caprarola and Frascati. For the Villa Lante, Bagnaia, see Coffin, pp. 358 ff., who describes an original series of six fountains tracing the history of man from the Golden Age—fountains of the Golden Age itself, of the Deluge, of the Tiber and Arno, and of Pomona and Flora, in a single direct axis, designed by Carlo Maderno

and others. Cardinal Gianfrancesco Gambara, one of the builders of Bagnaia, it should be noted, was a connection of the Farnese family's.

26. See Judith Colton, *Le Parnasse françois, Titon du Tillet and the Origins of the Monument to Genius* (New Haven, Conn., 1979), pp. 148 ff. For the garden sculptures at Caserta see Luigi Izzo, *La Scultura decorativa nel parco reale di Caserta* (Naples, 1970); Fagiolo dell'Arco, *Caserta*, p. 92, n. 3; Flavia Petrelli, "La Fontana di Diana e Atteone a Caserta," *Antologia di belle arti*, 2 (1978):53 ff.; N. Spinosa, ed., *Arti figurative*, pp. 155 ff., 199 ff. For contemporary Diana-iconography connected with this region see H. Dessau, *Inscriptiones latinae selectae*, 3257–3266, and Francesco Daniele, *Monete*, pp. 69 ff., which illustrates figures from coins of Diana and wild boar or stags.

27. Fagiolo Dell'Arco, *Caserta*, pp. 61 ff.

28. *Scienza nuova*, paragraph 528. See also *Diritto*, pp. 145, where Vico says the first of all religions was that of fountains, again giving the story of Diana and Actaeon as an instance. Diana herself, meanwhile, is a symbol of women's sudden death (ibid., p. 748). She and Actaeon lead to water- and fire-rites in marriage, for anciently brides were captured "by water and fire" (ibid., p. 421).

29. Vanvitelli had planned a different Venus fountain. See note 17.

30. *Scienza nuova*, paragraph 529.

31. Ibid.

32. Izzo, *Scultura decorativa*, p. 16. According to Niccolo Carletti, *Topografia universale della città di Napoli* (Naples, 1776), p. 162, there were in ancient times twin temples to Ceres and Persephone on the site presently filled by San Gregorio Armeno.

33. Ibid. Izzo notes that there is disagreement between Chierici and De Filippis (F. De Filippis, *Il Palazzo reale di Caserta e i Borbone* [Naples, 1968]), as to whether the rivers are the Anapo and the Simeto (Chierici) or the Oreto and the Simeto (De Filippis). On the other hand Domenico Bartolini, *Viaggio da Napoli alle forche Caudine ed a Benevento e di ritorno a Caserta e a Monte Cassino* (Naples, 1827) claims, with justice, that one of the rivers must be the Arethusa, in reference to Ovid's story. See note 17 for the proposed Fountain of Arethusa.

34. *Scienza nuova*, paragraphs 541, 546.

35. Ibid., paragraph 547. Vico also makes Diana the symbol of continence, Venus that of honest life, and Ceres that of lawgiving (*Diritto*, p. 498). Daniele, *Monete*, p. 39, illustrates Ceres in ancient coins of the region as a sceptered woman, as in the Caserta statue.

36. *Scienza nuova*, paragraph 597.

37. Vico, *Diritto*, p. 495, stresses that Ceres' laws are those of agriculture, of raising abundance, or life, up from Earth and the Underworld. Indeed Aeneas, descending to her lower kingdom with his golden bough, was reenacting those laws (*Diritto*, vol. 2, p. 500).

38. See note 33.

39. Quoted in Paturelli, pp. 93 ff.

40. *Scienza nuova*, paragraph 307.

41. Ibid., paragraph 721.

42. Ibid., paragraphs 770–73.

43. Bartolini, *Viaggio*, passim; Chierici, *Reggia*, p. 81; Izzo, *Scultura*, p. 12. Every trace of the uncompleted main figures seems to have vanished. Venditti, "Opera," p. 128, quoting Fagiolo dell'Arco, has already noted the correspondence between the Dolphin, the Ceres, and the Aeolus Fountains as fountains of water, earth, and air. But the suggestions I make seem more complete. For the Neptune fountain see *Dichiarazione*, p. II, pl. xiii. Coffin notes, furthermore, in *The Villa in the Life of Renaissance Rome*, p. 320, that from 1572 a dismembered Neptune fountain existed at the Villa d'Este, Tivoli in the lower garden. For the Caserta group see Chierici, p. 81, and Izzo, p. 12.

44. *Scienza nuova*, paragraphs 549, 650.

45. Caroselli, *Reggia*, p. 50.

6 Palace Geometry

1. See Giovanni Aliberti, "Economia e società da Carlo III ai Napoleonidi (1734–1806)," *Storia di Napoli*, vol. 8, pp. 77 ff., for the growth of the bureaucratic machine in Carlo's reign; also Moscati, *I Borboni d'Italia* (Naples, 1920), p. 55.

2. See Giuseppe De Nitto, "I Disegni di Mario Gioffredo per la reggia di Caserta presso la Biblioteca Nazionale di Napoli," *Napoli nobilissima*, ser. 3, 14 (1975):183 ff. (reprinted Naples, 1981). The drawings are catalogued as "Vedute di un palazzo reale" under "Carte geografiche," Sala 6, Misc. C, 164/7; Ba. 26 (76[1–4]). See also Renato de Fusco, "Architettura," in *Storia di Napoli*, vol. 8, p. 382, and Arnaldo Venditti, "L'Opera napoletana di Luigi Vanvitelli," in Roberto di Stefano, ed., *Luigi Vanvitelli* (Naples, 1979), p. 102. Another set of these plans, once the property of Giovanni Paturelli, son of the Carlo Paturelli who worked with Vanvitelli at Caserta and who was *capomaestro* from 1767, is now in a private collection in Caserta. See Anon., "Un Progetto grandioso di un palazzo reale del Vanvitelli [sic]," *Bollettino mensile dell'Ufficio del lavoro della città di Caserta* (May/June 1922):16 ff. and (July/Aug. 1922):4 ff., and bibliography in De Nitto, "I Disegni."

3. Gioffredo, *Dell'Architettura*, p. 8.

4. Venditti, "Opera," p. 102.

5. Juan Bautista Villalpando, *In Ezechielem explanationes, etc.*, (Rome, 1596–1604). For the temple see vol. 2, pars secundum, disc. 1, isagog., cap. 7, p. 18; also René Taylor, "El Padre Villalpando (1552–1608) y sus ideas estèticas," *Academia, Anales y Boletìn de la real Academia de San Fernando* (1952):9 ff. Also René Taylor, "Architecture and Magic: Considerations on the *Idea* of the Escorial," in D. Fraser, H. Hibbard, and M. Lewine, eds., *Essays in the History of Architecture Presented to Rudolf Wittkower* (New York, 1967), pp. 81 ff.; and Wolfgang Herrmann, "Unknown Designs for the 'Temple of Jerusalem' by Claude Perrault," ibid., pp. 143 ff. A more complete picture of the phenomenon is given in Helen Rosenau, *Vision of the Temple: the Image of the Temple of Jerusalem in Judaism and Christianity* (London, 1979).

6. See chapter 4, notes 12, 13.

7. See De Fusco, "Architettura," p. 382.

8. This has to do with the fact that in real life, as opposed to the imagined realm of descriptive geometry, planes must have a certain thickness. That thickness almost always destroys the outer correspondences if the inner ones fit, or vice versa. See March and Steadman, *Geometry of Environment*, p. 209.

9. Gaspard Monge's *Géometrie descriptive* [1795] (Paris, 1811), seems to be the first truly mathematical book on the subject and develops these ideas much further than would have been possible in the 1750s. But Monge's sections on measurements, projection, and the mapping of volumes are all outgrowths of this geometrical tradition. As to the later destiny of Gioffredo's basic scheme—square pavilions linking long colonnaded or walled wings into square courts—see Carditello, the villa erected by Francesco Collecini, Vanvitelli's pupil, in 1787 (G. C. Alisio, *Siti reali dei Borboni*, p. 48 and his fig. 28).

10. See Gino Chierici, "Note vanvitelliane," *Atti del VIII convegno nazionale di storia dell'architettura* (Rome, 1956), p. 153.

11. Vanvitelli, *Lettere*, 22 (1751) and 525 (1758).

12. Bottineau, *L'Art de cour*, pp. 117 ff.

13. The manuscript is in the Biblioteca Nazionale, Naples, BNN ms. autografi XV-A-9. The text is published by Fichera, *Vanvitelli*, pp. 181 ff.

14. The courtyards were the cause of much discussion. In the *Lettere* Vanvitelli brags to Monsignore Clementi that each of the four at Caserta is larger than the single one in the Palazzo Reale, Madrid (letter 200 [1754]).

(The courts at Caserta are 200 by 300 palmi; that at Madrid 163 Neapolitan palmi square.) In letter 425 (1757) Vanvitelli denies the rumor, circulated he thinks by Fuga, that he had borrowed the courtyard designs at Caserta from Stupinigi. And indeed there is no resemblance between the two, though as noted the crossing at Caserta is like one of Juvarra's preliminary ideas for Stupinigi (figs. 4.16, 6.13). Vanvitelli's original notion had been to make each courtyard different, so that the building would seem to be composed of four different palaces, an aspect of Vanvitelli's conception of Caserta as a four-part family home (see chapters 7 and 8). The queen liked the idea but the king did not (letter 58 [1752]).

15. Carlo's liking for architectural geometry matched his liking for the geometry of military formations. Not only did the army mark out the plan of the future palace at Caserta at the foundation-stone ceremony, but the king staged similar ceremonies in Spain, including one with horses forming squares and circles and then moving around on a large drill field "with respective order, symmetry, and all to the sound of musical instruments" at the palace at Aranjuez (D'Onofri, *Elogio*, p. clx).

16. Fichera, *Vanvitelli*, p. 182.

17. For the *baciamano* see Moscati, *Borboni*, p. 55.

18. See Fagiolo dell'Arco, *Reggia*, p. 24, and Venditti, "Opera," pp. 103 ff., for general discussions of Caserta's prototypes; also Rudolf Wittkower, *Art and Architecture in Italy, 1600–1750* (Harmondsworth, England [1958], 3rd rev. ed. 1973), pp. 395–97, H. Rose, "Nicodemus Tessin der Jüngere und der Neubau des Schlosses von Stockholm," in *Festschrift Heinrich Wölfflin* (Munich, 1924), pp. 245 ff., and E. Battisti, "J. Juvarra a San Ildefonso," *Commentari* (1958), pp. 273 ff.

19. For vertical bays as vectors see March and Steadman, *Geometry of Environment*, pp. 87 ff.

20. Tanucci was worried that riffraff might have access to the courtyards at Caserta (as they did at the Palazzo Reale) but Vanvitelli felt he could design access facilities that would prevent this (*Lettere*, 526 [1758]).

21. Vico in fact claims that the Sacred Council of Naples is a vestige of the early family parliaments headed by family kings, for the head of the Sacred Council is called "Sacred Royal Majesty," though he is not necessarily the king. The members of the council are "soldiers" or "knights" (*milites*), a vestige of the time when only noblemen were allowed to be soldiers, on the grounds that only such men could trace their ancestries sufficiently to claim membership in original heroic families. The Sacred Royal Council of Naples is absolute: its decisions admit of no appeal, and only the Council itself can change its decisions (*Scienza nuova*, paragraph 1082). For the structure of the Neapolitan government the best guide is Iole Mazzoleni, *Archivio di Stato di Napoli. Archivio Borbone: Inventario sommario* (Rome, 1961), vol. 1, preface.

22. Moscati, *Borboni*, p. 55.

23. Even D'Onofri, *Elogio*, p. clvii, mentions this defect. Nonetheless, as Roberto Pane notes (*Architettura dell'età barocca*, pp. 249 ff.), the design is remarkable from a geometric viewpoint; for example, the pilasters on the exterior line up with the interior walls, as is not the case at Capodimonte. Meanwhile the fact that the rooms for petition and decree are particularly geometric matches Vico's notion (*Diritto*, pp. 386–387) that both in Greek and "Italic" the sounds of the voice are signified by geometric forms—acute and oblique angles, straight and divided lines, semicircles, and the like. And the shapes used reflect the sounds themselves, says Vico, or their speech functions: *I* is a thin straight line, *O* the most copious of sounds. *A* has maximum stability since it stands at the beginning of the alphabet. That children can learn the immutable principles of geometry proves that such things, which also include virtue and knowledge, are not forgotten with the demise

of the individual memory but remain as "irrefragable proofs" in the collective memory of mankind (ibid., p. 387).

24. It was Carlo who insisted that these cellars, or at least that their engraved cross-sections, be included in the *Dichiarazione* (Vanvitelli, *Lettere* 438 [1757]).

25. See chapter 4.

26. D'Onofri, *Elogio*, p. cxlvi, says it was Carlo's particular architectural responsibility to design, with compass in hand, the layout and the central crossing. Note that a comparable feature is conspicuously absent both at Capodimonte and at the Palazzo Reale. D'Onofri says Carlo also designed the towers and dome. The attributions are affirmed by Celano (*Notizie del bello* 5:787) and for that matter by Vanvitelli (*Lettere*, 132 [1753]). The king's desire for absolute symmetry and absolute correctness of angles gave rise to gossip (denied by Vanvitelli) that the palace had been built 40 palmi out of square (letter 244 [1754]). On the contrary, in accordance with the king's express wish, the axis did not deviate even two degrees (letter 38 [1751]).

27. *Diritto*, pp. 386–87.

28. Ibid.

29. Quoted by Vanvitelli, *Lettere*, 58 (1752).

7 Public Poetry

1. G. L. Hersey, "Alfonso II, Benedetto e Giuliano da Maiano e la Porta Reale," *Napoli nobilissima*, ser. 3., 4 (1964):77 ff.

2. See chapter 4, note 29.

3. G. L. Hersey, *The Aragonese Arch at Naples, 1443–1475* (New Haven, Conn., 1973), pp. 53 ff.

4. Vanvitelli, *Lettere* 717 (1760).

5. For other sources see ibid., letter 717 (1760), and letter 943 (1762), in which the architect asks his brother Urbano to send him a drawing of a statue pedestal in the Villa Doria Pamphili for use at Caserta, while in letter 911 (1761) he asks for a drawing of one of the columns from the facade of Sant'Andrea della Valle. In 372 (1756) he talks of using columns from the Serapeum at Pozzuoli for the courtyard portals at Caserta, remarks that again emphasize the classico-cinquecento nature of Vanvitelli's inspiration.

6. *Dichiarazione*, p. xiii. For other allegorical figure schemes by Vanvitelli see the *Lettere*, (875 [1761]). These are for tapestries for the king's bedroom in the Palazzo Reale in Naples: Felicity, Fecundity, Justice, Peace, Pleasingness (*Piacevolezza*), Benignity, Religion, Heroic Virtue, Magnificence, and Liberality. For the standard iconography of Justice, see Vincenzo Cartari, *Le Immagini degli dei degli antichi* (Venice, 1625), p. 345, and for Magnificence Cesare Ripa, *Della novissima iconologia . . .* (Padua, 1625), p. 405, which also prescribes that the goddess hold an architectural plan; see also Justice (ibid., pp. 278, 280), Clemency (p. 102) and Peace (p. 493). They all differ from Vanvitelli's formulas. On the other hand, for the 1622 catafalque for Paul V, Bernini designed virtues including Verity, Magnificence, Clemency, and Justice that may well have inspired Vanvitelli. See M. Fagiolo dell'Arco, *L'Effimero barocco: Strutture della festa nella Roma del '600* (Rome, 1977), vol. 1, pp. 49 ff.

7. *Dichiarazione*, p. xiii.

8. Ibid.

9. Vico, *Scienza nuova*, paragraph 25. In the *Diritto*, p. 433, Vico stresses that statues and simple words (*signa*) were needed by early heroic men because of their paucity of language.

10. Vico, *Diritto*, vol. 2, pp. 506–507.

11. Vanvitelli, *Lettere*, 476 (1756).

12. *Dichiarazione*, pls. ii, viii. In a typical *sproposito* Anthony Blunt, while failing to mention the planned Hercules Fountain in the lower vestibule, does say that the gardens' "principal feature is the mile-long layout of

water, beginning at the top with a cascade, over which presides a figure of Hercules resting. . . . Half-way down this narrow band is enlarged into an English Garden" (*Neapolitan Baroque and Rococo Architecture*, p. 174). There is no figure of Hercules at the cascade, and the English Garden is entered just below the Venus Fountain, at the beginning of the sequence. Blunt is confusing Caserta's English Garden with its Parco Reale, and its Hercules with the nineteenth-century one at Vaux-le-Vicomte, which does indeed survey the axis of the gardens from their most distant point.

13. See chapter 4, note 16.

14. Marcello De Venuti, *Descrizione delle prime scoperte dell'antica città d'Ercolano* (Rome, 1748), pp. 1 ff., 16. De Venuti, like Vico, assumes that Hercules was a real person who later became mythic, and shows how the artistic traditions of the Hercules myths may be read as legacies of this reality. De Venuti is a key figure in this whole matter. He was in charge of the excavations at Herculaneum for a time, as well as writing about Bourbon iconography. De Venuti also discusses Hercules' trip to Sicily to recover one of the oxen of Geryon and talks of an ancient medal showing Hercules crowned by Victory (pp. 16–18), an analogue to Vanvitelli's conception for the vestibule statue, which was to have been crowned by Glory. In line with the new emphasis on Hercules, Tanucci was thinking of transferring the antiquities of Herculaneum from Portici to Caserta (*Lettere*, 1415 [1768]). In 816 (1760) we learn that Cardinal Alessandro Albani had wished to present the court at Caserta with an antique statue of Hercules, a work received from Mario Guarnacci. Vanvitelli has a low estimate of it. For more on Herculean imagery at Caserta see Garms, "Briefe," p. 205. Nor should we forget Zurbarán's series, *Los Trabajos de Hercules*, at Philip V's Buen Retiro, whose garden once boasted the Pietro Tacca equestrian statue of Philip IV now in the Plaza de Oriente, Madrid.

15. See chapter 4.

16. Mazzocchi, *Aeneas tabulas*, pp. 85, 92, 116, 118.

17. Francesco Daniele, *Monete antiche di Capua* (Naples, 1802), pp. 88 ff.

18. For other Renaissance Hesperidean gardens and their myths see Hans Henrik Brummer, *The Statue Court in the Vatican Belvedere* (Stockholm, 1970), pp. 235–38, and Coffin, *Villa in the Life of Rome*, p. 329, where the Villa d'Este is described as such a garden.

19. In a similar mood Vanvitelli called Carlo's enemy, Frederick II of Prussia, "the Hydra"; *Lettere*, 788 (1760).

20. *Diritto*, pp. 459–60.

21. Ibid., pp. 690–91.

22. Ibid., pp. 744, 355.

23. Ibid., pp. 13, 648–49.

24. Ibid., pp. 16, 477.

25. Ibid., p. 405.

26. Ibid., p. 433.

27. *Odyssey* XI 600.

28. *Diritto*, pp. 159–60.

29. Ibid., p. 459. Let us also remember that Vico had traced Maria Amalia's "Scythian" descent back to Hercules (*Breve ragguaglio*, [Naples, 1738], s.v.).

30. D'Onofri, *Elogio*, p. clx.

31. *Civiltà del '700 a Napoli* (1979), 1, no. 148. See also Natalis Comes' poem *De venatione* in his *Mythologiae, sive explicationis fabularum libri decem* (Geneva, 1641), pp. 1084 ff.

32. Vanvitelli, *Lettere*, 622 (1759) and 626 (1759). In the full-scale model, the water jets were painted. However, when the king came over to examine them more closely, an upper jet turned into real water. Carlo was delighted (627 [1759]).

33. Ennemond Petitot, the Vanvitelli of Carlo's brother's realm at Parma designed a Hercules for the park at Colorno: it was yet another version of the Farnese type. See [Regione Emilia Romagna. Commune di Colorno], *La Reggia de Colorno nel '700* (1979), no. 23. As to "Hercules' town," Vanvitelli had many connections with the publications on Herculaneum. He sent a copy of the Accademia Ercolanense's *Antichità* to his brother Urbano (letter 127 [1753]), having read the first four volumes; indeed he had even been asked by Tanucci to write on the newly discovered paintings (506 [1757]), and he was commissioned by the king to design twenty-four initials, vignettes, and friezes for the first volume (391, [1756]). He was also concerned with Baiardi's *Prodromo* (431 [1757]), which as noted had appeared earlier, in 1752, as a companion to the *Dichiarazione*. In letter 445 (1757) Vanvitelli records his intention of sending three volumes of the *Prodromo* to Porzio Leonardi.

34. *Dichiarazione*, p. xvi. See also Ripa, *Iconologia*, pp. 280.

35. For the vestibule and stair sculptures see *Civiltà del '700*, 1:32–40.

36. Vico, *Diritto*, p. 635; *Scienza nuova*, paragraph 558.

37. *Dichiarazione*, pp. xvii–xix. For earlier images of Veritas see Fritz Saxl, "Veritas Filia Temporis," in *Essays Presented to Ernst Cassirer*, edited by R. Klibansky and H. J. Paton (Oxford, 1936), pp. 197 ff., and especially Matthias Winner, "Bernini's 'Verità'" in *Munuscula discipulorum. Kunsthistorische Studien Hans Kauffmann zum 70. Gebürtstag 1966* (Berlin, 1968), pp. 393 ff.

38. See Citti Siracusano, "La Decorazione pittorica della reggia di Caserta," in *Le Arti figurative a Napoli nel settecento*, pp. 301 ff.; also Nicola Spinosa, "Un Gioco per i sovrani," *Strenna napoletana* (1974), pp. 53 ff., which deals with the wooden model of the *scala regia*; also Siracusano, "Pittura," p. 546 (and for the painting program at Caserta as a whole), ibid., pp. 516 ff.; Caroselli, *Reggia*, p. 38. The notion that divine mythologies ought to be painted on a ceiling, as opposed to other parts of a room, receives Vico's implicit support when (*Diritto*, p. 748) he defines "poetic characters" as having originated in metaphor, "and metaphor, by the strength of similitude, carefully and seriously transforms images, and what, to our ancestors, were inherited fables, through the mediation of our [Vichian] principles; so that, for example, the strength that the gods were thought to have first possessed on earth, afterward was the strength they had in heaven." As to Hercules' standing at the foot of this whole complex, he appears in the *Diritto*, p. 491, as the "sustainer of Olympus" and hence as one of those who accomplished, or at least who continues, this "transfer." Finally, according to Carletti, *Topografia universale della città di Napoli*, p. 148, the sun (Apollo) was worshipped by the ancient Neapolitans "under the image of Hercules," and in the latter's temple. Before his return to Naples in 1766 Corrado Giaquinto had painted a vault fresco, *The Birth of the Sun with Apollo and Allegorical Figures* (now destroyed) in the Royal Palace, Madrid.

39. Vanvitelli, *Lettere*, 266 (1754), 399 (1756), 404 (1756), and then passim 640 through 1396 (1759–1767).

40. For Justice, Pity, and similar goddesses see Ripa, *Iconologia*, pp. 278–280, 426 ff. respectively. For Astraea see Vico, *Diritto*, p. 750, and *Scienza nuova*, paragraph 30.

41. Vico, *Diritto*, pp. 146–47.

42. Ibid., pp. 494–95.

43. Ibid., pp. 494, 652–53.

44. Ibid., pp. 441, 730.

45. For Clio and Thalia, see Ripa, *Iconologie*, pp. 364, 369. For the names, attributes, and varying identities of the muses, especially unconventional ones, see Comes, *Mythologiae*, pp. 500 ff.

46. Vico, *Diritto*, pp. 203, 480.

47. Ibid., pp. 478, 496, 519.

48. Ibid., p. 496.

49. Ibid.

50. Vanvitelli, *Lettere*, 12 (1751), 65 (1752), 66 (1752), and 67 (1752). In February 1753 Carlo, conversing with the Piedmontese minister and showing him some small marble colonnettes as the trophies of one of his dominions, also showed off thirty-two huge monoliths destined for the vestibule. The set was not yet complete, he said, because columns of Giallo da Verona were still lacking; but happily such columns had now been found, buried, in his dominions (see Schipa, *Borboni*, pp. 317–18). See also Raffaello Causa, "Appunti per una storia di neoclassicismo a Napoli," *Strenna napoletana* (1974): 61 ff.

51. Saint-Non, *Voyage pittoresque*, vol. 2, pp. 261 ff. *Dichiarazione*, p. xvi; also Strazzullo, "Autografi," and Vanvitelli, *Lettere*, 1 (1751), 79 (1752).

52. For Renaissance precedents for this attitude, see Sebastiano Serlio, *Tutte le opere d'architettura* (Venice, 1619), fols. 2r, 6. For foreign reactions see Aniello Gentile, *Caserta nei ricordi dei viaggiatori stranieri* (Naples, 1980), pp. 23 ff.

53. See Hersey, *Pythagorean Palaces*, pp. 88 ff. Mazzocchi, *Aeneas tabulas*, pp. 149 ff., has an essay on herms and termini, the origins of their forms and the reasons why they were often dedicated to great men.

54. Vanvitelli, *Dichiarazione*, p. iii; Garms, "Briefe," passim; Strazzullo, "Primi anni," Caroselli, *Reggia*, pp. 23 ff.

55. Vanvitelli, *Lettere*, 46 (1751). The inscription is by Porzio Leonardi.

56. Vico, *Scienza nuova*, paragraph 81.

57. Caroselli, *Reggia*, pp. 34 ff. During the most intense periods of activity about 3000 persons were at work on the building and gardens. In 1753–1763 there were 1655 male workers, including 300 *capomaestri*, 200 female workers—some employed on construction—405 Christian and Turkish slaves, 166 convicts, 438 guards, 14 administrators, 9 superintendents, and 18 court servants listed. Total: 2905. Even more were employed in 1769–1773, but in 1774–1799, after Luigi Vanvitelli's death and under the supervision of his son Carlo, only 892 people were at work on the project.

8 The Family Romance

1. Strazzullo, "Autografi," pp. 198 ff.; M. Asso, "La Cappella Palatina," *Archivio storico di Terra di Lavoro*, 10 (1973):15 ff.

2. *Lettere*, 839 (1761). There had been a plan afoot to send Vanvitelli to Versailles—but to see the fountains, not the chapel (letters 167 and 182 [1753]).

3. Ibid., 74 (1752), 76 (1752), 496 (1757), 498 (1757), and 507 (1758). Vanvitelli wants the column bases designed after those in two Roman chapels: the Gavotti, in San Nicolo da Tolentino, and that of San Luigi Gonzaga in Sant' Ignazio.

4. See ibid., 390 (1756), 510 (1757), 502 (1757), and 646 (1759); Caroselli, *Reggia*, p. 38; A. M. Clark, "Sebastiano Conca and the Roman Rococo," *Apollo*, (1967), pp. 327 ff.; also Giovanni Tescione, "Il Laboratorio delle pietre dure di Napoli e l'altare della palatina della reggia di Caserta," *Studi in onore di Riccardo Filangieri*, 3 (Naples, 1959):187 ff.; Valentina Maderna, "Il Tabernacolo della cappella di Caserta," *Antologia di belle arti*, 5 (1978):62 ff. For Bonito see G. Cosenza, "Giuseppe Bonito," *Napoli nobilissima*, ser. 2, 11 (1902):81 ff., 103 ff, 122 ff, and 154 ff, and 12 (1903):12 ff.

5. For the Halls of Representation and the apartments see Spinosa, *Le arti figurative*, pp.

269 ff., 301 ff., 385 ff.; also Thoenes, *Neapel*, pp. 600 ff.; Touring Club Italiano, *Napoli e dintorni*, pp. 608 ff., and Fichera, *Vanvitelli*, pp. 100 ff.; also Chierici *Caserta*, pp. 30 ff. Vanvitelli, *Lettere*, 572 (1758), speaks of putting off the designing of the furniture and similar objects, though there are preliminary drawings by him and his son Carlo (and others of the *équipe*) in the archives at Caserta that record various decorative schemes for the main rooms.

6. See C. Garzya, *Interni neoclassici a Napoli* (Naples, 1978), which gives a complete and scholarly survey of the subject not only in Naples but at Caserta as well.

7. Antonio Marotta, *La Reggia e le fontane di Caserta* (Caserta, n.d.), p. 14.

8. For Mondo see Nicola Spinosa, "Domenico Mondo e il rococo napoletano," *Napoli nobilissima*, ser. 3, 6 (1967):204 ff.; M. Volpi, "Domenico Mondo pittore 'letterato,'" *Paragone: Arte* (1959), no. 119, pp. 51 ff. An oil sketch for the final fresco is discussed in *The Golden Age of Naples* (Detroit, 1981), no. 32.

9. For the iconography see Ripa, *Iconologia*, p. 61 (Authority), p. 388 (Loyalty); p. 493 (Peace); p. 524 (Preeminence); p. 468 (Obedience); p. 253 (Puissance); and p. 268, 270 (Generosity).

10. For the statue of Alessandro Farnese see Filippo de' Rossi, *Descrizione di Roma moderna formata nuovamente con le autorità del Cardinale Baronio . . .* [1697] (Rome, 1708), vol. 2, p. 275 and [Ecole française de Rome], *Le Palais farnèse* (Rome, 1980). Simone Moschino, to whom De' Rossi attributes the statue, was born in Orvieto c. 1560 and died in Parma in 1610. From 1578 he was in the service of the Dukes of Parma, including Alessandro III. See also Herbert Keutner, "Über die Entstehung und die Formen des Standbildes im Cinquecento," *Münchner Jahrbuch der bildenden Kunst*, 7 (1956):138 ff., esp. 164 ff. A program similar to that of the room in which this statue stands was designed by Juvarra in 1735–36 at San Ildefonso. The moving spirit seems to have been Carlo di Borbone's mother, Elisabetta Farnese. Various painters, some of them Neapolitan, were to depict events in the life of Alexander, each of which symbolized one of his royal virtues. See Eugenio Battisti, "Juvarra a San Ildefonso," *Commentari*, no. 9 (1958):277 ff.

11. See, for a similar connection between the Farnese and Alexander's wedding, the Fresco in the Farnesina, Rome, by Sodoma (1511–12); also S. J. Freedberg, *Painting of the High Renaissance in Rome and Florence* (Cambridge, Mass., 1961), pp. 140–41. The fresco had of course been commissioned by the Chigi.

The villa did not become a Farnese possession until 1580. In 1730 it became the property of the future Carlo di Borbone. Vittorio Gleijes in his *Guida storica, artistica, monumentale, turistica, della città di Napoli e dintorni* (Naples, 1979), p. 490, lists the objects installed in the Hall of Alexander the Great during Murat's reign and removed when the Bourbons were restored.

12. Vico, *Scienza nuova*, paragraph 46.

13. Ibid., paragraph 1023.

14. For the model artists' village at San Leucio, see De Fusco, "Architettura," p. 402, with earlier bibliography, especially Renato De Fusco and F. Sbaudi, "Un Centro comunitario del settecento in Campania," *Comunità*, no. 86 (1961), pp. 56 ff.

15. For Dominici see C. Siracusano, "Antonio Dominici, pittore alla corte dei Borbone di Napoli," *Quaderni dell'istoria dell'arte medioevale e moderna*, no. 3 (Messina, 1979):33 ff.

16. Marotta, *La Reggia*, p. 14.

17. Caroselli, *Reggia*, p. 57; Nicolini, *Reggia*, p. 142.

18. M. P. Maresca and V. Vaccaro, "Massoneria ed ermetismo nella Napoli del '700," *Psicon*, 4 (1975):101 ff. See also Tommaso Pedio, *Massoni e giacobini nel regno di Napoli* (Matera, 1976), pp. 48 ff., 75 ff. Maria Carolina was a member of the lodge called Saint-Jean

du Secret et de la parfaite Amitié, founded in 1774. Gennaro Vico, Giambattista's son, was also a mason. Giovanni Gravier's great compilation of Neapolitan histories, *Raccolta di tutti i più rinomati scrittori dell'istoria générale del Regno di Napoli*, published in Naples in 1769 and frequently cited in the foregoing pages, was dedicated to Maria Carolina as a well-known patroness of the arts and sciences. It contains a particularly rich selection of earlier mythographers.

19. For the *lituus* see Vico, *Scienza nuova*, frontispiece and paragraph 9. The use of the *lituus* is the first sign that barbarian man began to learn of divine things. For Füger see A. Stix, *H. F. Füger* (Vienna-Leipzig, 1925).

20. Vico, *Scienza nuova*, paragraphs 569, 604.

21. Marotta, *La Reggia*, p. 14.

22. Vico, *Diritto*, p. 580.

23. Ibid., p. 546.

24. Ibid., pp. 496, 497.

25. *Scienza nuova*, paragraph 499.

26. Ibid., paragraph 776.

27. *Diritto*, p. 14.

28. Cartari, *Imagini*, pp. 402, 404.

29. *Diritto*, p. 496.

30. Two paintings by Nicolas Poussin that are relevant here are *Midas at the Source of the Pactolus*, Musée Fesch, Ajaccio (Corsica), and *Midas Washing at the Source of the Pactolus*, Metropolitan Museum, New York.

31. Vico, *Scienza nuova*, paragraph 667; *Diritto*, pp. 694, 695.

32. See David Irwin, *English Neoclassical Art* (London, 1966), fig. 14; also Dora Wiebenson, "Subjects from Homer's Iliad in Neoclassical Art," *Art Bulletin*, 46 (1964):23 ff. Gavin Hamilton's painting in turn was clearly influenced by a composition engraved by Pietro Testa, reproduced by Wiebenson on p. 29. On the other hand Calliano's Hector is probably drawn from Thorvaldsen's relief, *The Wrath of Achilles at the Departure of Briseis*, 1805, now in the Thorvaldsen Museum, Copenhagen.

33. Vico, *Diritto*, p. 750; *Scienza nuova*, paragraphs 713, 1042.

34. Vico does not mention Ripa or Cartari; but his frequent recourse to the ideas of Natalis Comes and Voss, whom he does mention quite frequently, suggests that iconographical books were an important part of his source material. Indeed his explication of the frontispiece of the *Scienza nuova* is an example of emblem analysis very much in the Ripa/Comes tradition.

35. Vico, *Scienza nuova*, paragraph 733.

36. Ripa, *Iconologie*, p. 387.

37. Sigmund Freud, *The Sexual Enlightenment of Children* (New York [1963], 1968), pp. 41 ff.

9 Epilogue: Neptune's Triumph

1. Vanvitelli, *Lettere*, 72 (1752), 453 (1757), and 709 (1760); Caroselli, *Reggia*, p. 57. The theater was begun in the 1750s but abandoned, then begun again in 1768.

2. There are forty-two boxes in all. The fifth row was reserved for the royal regiment of Liparotti, alternating with the Royal Ferdinando Battalion, the fourth for employees of the royal household. Among the better boxes no. 7 went to royal counsellors, no. 8 to captains general, no. 3 to the minister from Spain, no. 4 to the Minister from France (L. Nicolini, *La Reggia di Caserta*, p. 142).

3. Vico, *Diritto*, p. 459. The scene of Apollo and Python had been included in a Medici festival held in 1589. One of the intermezzi to a production of the comedy *La Pellegrina* by Bastiano de' Rossi depicted Python as a great dragon, slain by Apollo in his role as god of universal harmony. The intermezzo is thought of as one of the most "operatic" of these early works. Here, as in the ceiling of the theater at Caserta, Apollo overcomes his enemy in an enactment of the triumph of harmony over disharmony, in a theatrical setting conceived as a model of the universe. Arthur Blumenthal, *Theater Art of the Medici* [exhibition catalogue], Dartmouth College, Hanover, N.H., 1980, pp. 11 ff., with bibliography.

4. Vico, *Diritto*, p. 748.

5. Ibid., pp. 459, 514.

6. Ibid., pp. 742–46.

7. Ibid., 480, 519.

8. Caroselli, *Reggia*, p. 57; Nicolini, *Reggia*, p. 142.

9. Nicolini, pp. 150 ff.; Vanvitelli, *Lettere*, 1117 (1764) recalls that in that year, on the king's birthday, January 20, the opera was also performed, with music by Tommaso Traetta, and with magnificent sets, at the Teatro San Carlo in Naples.

10. Pietro Metastasio, *Opere*, edited by Mario Fubini (Milan, 1968 ff.), vol. 1, pp. 1 ff. *Didone Abbandonata* was provided with musical scores by Sarro, as mentioned, and by Domenico Scarlatti (Rome, 1724), Tommaso Albinoni (Venice, 1725), Leonardo Vinci (Rome, 1726), and dozens of others. At the time of the Caserta production treatments by Michele Mortellari and Giuseppe Schuster were current in Naples.

11. *Aeneid* I 132 ff.

12. See chapter 2, note 32.

13. Vico, *Diritto*, p. 713.

14. Ibid.

15. Ibid., p. 500.

16. Ibid., pp. 713, 720. Vico, *De mente heroica* (Naples, 1732), p. 14.

17. For the planned capital, only small parts of which were built and which was to spread southward from the palace, see E. Martucci, *La Città reale: Caserta e i suoi fasti* (Caserta, 1928); Venditti, "Opera," p. 105; for the strict relation between the planned capital and the garden layout at Caserta, see De Fusco, "Architettura," p. 398. The urbanist aspects of Vanvitelli's planned town are discussed by Giancarlo Alisio, *Urbanistica napoletana del settecento* (Bari, 1979), pp. 26 ff. The *Dichiarazione* displays a rather considerable geometric town in front of the palace with a public theater, domed churches, and uniform blocks of housing and office space. From this it is clear that the capital was to contain a considerable part of the bureaucracy—though precisely what part is not certain. The town, especially that part of it around the oval palace forecourt, was a continuation of the geometries and spatial and ornamental hierarchies of the garden and palace proper. However, only two quadrants of the planned six were ever built. The scheme, with its oval piazza and goosefoot of avenues, is clearly derived from the Place d'Armes at Versailles. Around this oval were to be stables and barracks for cavalry and infantry as well as housing for sections of royal and government staffs. In figure 5.8, *E* marks the winter riding school, while an open-air cavalry exercise yard stands behind.

Bibliography

Except for the catalogue section, which is arranged chronologically, the bibliography is alphabetical. Items dealing with Carlo di Borbone are marked with an asterisk (★), those dealing with Vanvitelli or Caserta with a dagger (†), and those with Vico with a section sign (§).

Anonymous and Collective Works (Alphabetically Arranged)

Autori vari. *Le Antichità di Ercolano esposte* [Reale accademia ercolanense]. Naples, 1757–1792.

†Autori vari. *Le Arti figurative a Napoli nel settecento: Documenti e ricerche.* Naples, 1979.

Autori vari. *Fonti documentari per la storia degli scavi di Pompeii Ercolano Stabia.* Naples, 1979.

Autori vari. *Settecento napoletano.* Naples, 1962.

★*Breve ragguaglio della rinomata fiera che sotto la direzione di Don Ferdinando Sanfelice Cavaliere Napoletano si celebrò nel mese di luglio dell'anno 1738 in occasione del real maritaggio del nostro Re Don Carlo Borbone. Dedicato agli eccellentissimi eletti della fedelissima città di Napoli.* Naples, 1738.

†*Caserta—la Versailles d'Italia.* Milan, n.d.

★*Descrizione delle feste celebrate dalla fedelissima città di Napoli per lo glorioso ritorno dalla impresa di Sicilia della Sacra Maestà di Carlo di Borbone Re di Napoli, Sicilia, Gerusalemme, ecc.* Naples, 1735.

★*Funerali per Carlo III re delle Spagne e per l'infante di Napoli Don Gennaro Borbone.* Palermo, 1789.

★*Inscrizioni pei funerali celebrati alla gloriosa memoria di Carlo III re delle Spagne da Cavalieri dell'insigne ordine di San Gennaro.* Naples, 1789.

★*Narrazione delle solenne reali feste fatte celebrare in Napoli da sua Maestà il re delle Due Sicilie Carlo infante di Spagna Duca di Parma, Piacenza, ecc., per la nascita del suo primogenito Filippo Real Principe delle Due Sicilie.* Naples, 1749.

★*Officium in regis Caroli Borboni et Amaliae Saxonicae nuptiis . . . di G. B. Vico, G. Martorelli, A. Mazzocchi, etc.* Naples, 1738.

†"Un Progetto grandioso di palazzo reale del Vanvitelli," *Bollettino mensile dell'Ufficio del Lavoro della città di Caserta.* (March/June 1922), 16 ff.; (July/August 1922), 4 ff.

★ *Relazione della solennità celebrata al 23 maggio 1734 nella real chiesa di San Lorenzo Maggiore per la felice ingresso di sua maestà che Dio guardi Don Carlo di Borbone.* Naples, 1734.

★*Vita serenissimorum Parmae, Placentiae ducum . . . primis studiis Caroli Borboni . . . ,* Naples, 1735.

Bibliography

Exhibition Catalogues (Chronologically Arranged)

Catalogo della mostra bibliografica della stamperia reale di Napoli Pompeiiana. Naples, 1950.

Il Paesaggio napoletana nella pittura straniera. Palazzo Reale di Napoli, 1962.

Painting in Italy in the Eighteenth Century, Rococo to Romanticism. The Art Institute of Chicago et al., 1970.

†*Catalogo dei documenti e dei modelli. Mostra vanvitelliana.* Edited by D. De Marco and G. Fiengo. Naples, 1973.

†*Mostra vanvitelliana. Catalogo dei documenti e dei modelli.* Naples, Palazzo Reale, 1973–74.

†*Catalogo della mostra di incisioni di opere vanvitelliane.* Edited by Mario Rotili. Naples, 1977.

Mostra: Da Palazzo degli studi a museo archeologico. Naples, 1977.

Pompeii AD 79. Edited by J. Ward-Perkins and A. Claridge. Boston, 1978.

Pompeii as Source and Inspiration: Reflections in Eighteenth and Nineteenth-Century Art. Ann Arbor, University of Michigan, 1977.

★*Civiltà del '700 a Napoli, 1734–1799.* Florence, 1979.

[Regione Emilia Romagna. Commune di Colorno.] *La Reggia di Colorno nel '700.* 1979.

[Comune di Ancona.] *Il Lazzaretto di Luigi Vanvitelli.* Ancona, 1980.

Gaspar van Wittel (1652/3–1736). Disegni dalle collezioni napoletane. Edited by Walther Vitzthum. Gaeta, 1980.

Pittura sacra a Napoli nel '700, edited by Nicola Spinosa. Naples, Palazzo Reale, 1980–1981.

[Regione Toscana Giunta Regionale.] *Il Giardino storico italiano. Problemi di indagine fonti letterarie e storiche* [1978]. Florence, 1981.

★*The Golden Age of Naples: Art and Civilization under the Bourbons, 1734–1805.* Detroit Institute of Arts, 1981; Art Institute of Chicago, 1981–82.

Works by Individual Authors

★Achaintre, Nicolas-Louis. *Histoire généalogique et chronologique de la maison royale de Bourbon*. . . . Paris, 1825–26.

★Acton, Harold. *The Bourbons of Naples (1734–1825)*. London, 1956; Italian ed., Milan, 1962.

★Ajello, Raffaele. "Carlo di Borbone." *Dizionario biografico degli italiani.*

———. *Il Problema della riforma giudiziaria e legislativa nel regno di Napoli durante la prima metà del secolo XVIII.* Naples, 1961.

★———. "La Vita politica napoletana sotto Carlo di Borbone." *Storia di Napoli*, vol. 7. Naples, 1972, pp. 716 ff.

★Aliberti, Giovanni. "Economia e società da Carlo III ai Napoleonidi (1734–1806)." *Storia di Napoli*, vol. 8. Naples, 1971, pp. 75 ff.

Alisio, Giancarlo. "L'Ambiente di Piazza Dante in antichi rilievi inediti." *Napoli nobilissima*, ser. 3, 4 (1965):185 ff.

★———. *Siti reali dei Borboni: Aspetti dell'architettura napoletana del settecento.* Naples, 1976.

†———. "Sviluppo urbano e struttura della città." *Storia di Napoli*, vol. 8. Naples, 1971, pp. 313 ff.

†———. *Urbanistica napoletana del settecento.* Bari, 1979.

†Ansaldi, Giulio. "Luigi Vanvitelli e il neoclassico." *Atti del VIII convegno nazionale di storia dell'architettura* [1953]. Rome, 1956.

†Asso, M. "La Cappella palatina." *La Provincia di Terra di Lavoro,* 10 (1973):15 ff.

Astori, F. A. *De Vita Mari Gioffredi architecti commentariolum.* Naples, 1785.

Baiardi, Ottavio. *Prodromo delle antichità d'Ercolano . . .* Naples, 1752.

Ballerini, G. *Descrizione delle statue esistenti nella villa reale di Napoli.* Naples, 1842.

Bartolini, Domenico. *Viaggio da Napoli alle Forche Caudine ed a Benevento e di ritorno a Caserta ed a Monte-Casino del Signor D. D. B.* Naples, 1827.

Battisti, Eugenio. "J. Juvarra a San Ildefonso." *Commentari: arte* (1958):273 ff.

†———. "Lione Pascoli, Luigi Vanvitelli, e l'urbanistica italiana del settecento." *Atti del VIII convegno nazionale di storia dell'architettura* [1953]. Rome, 1956, pp. 51 ff.

★Beccattini, Francesco. *Storia del regno di Carlo III di Borbone. . . .* Venice, 1790.

Beloch, Julius. *Campanien.* Berlin, 1879.

Bérard, Jean. *La Colonisation grècque de l'Italie méridionale et de la Sicile.* Paris, 1950.

§Berlin, Isaiah. *Vico and Herder: Two Studies in the History of Ideas.* New York, 1977.

§Bidney, D. "Vico's New Science of Myth." *Giambattista Vico: An International Symposium.* Baltimore, 1969, pp. 259 ff.

Blessich, A. "La Carta topografica di Napoli di Giovanni Carafa Duca di Noja." *Napoli nobilissima,* ser. 1, 4 (1895):183 ff.

†Blunt, Anthony. *Neapolitan Baroque and Rococo Architecture.* London, 1975.

★Bologna, Ferdinando. "Solimena al palazzo reale di Napoli per le nozze di Carlo di Borbone." *Prospettiva,* 16 (1979):53 ff.

Borelli, G. *Sanmartino.* Naples, 1966.

†Bottari, Giovanni Gaetano. *Dialoghi sopra le tre arti del disegno* [1754]. Florence, 1770.

Bottineau, Yves. *L'Art de cour dans l'Espagne de Philippe V, 1700–1746.* Bordeaux, 1962.

———. "Felipe V y el Buen Retiro." *Archivo español de arte,* 31 (1958):117 ff.

Bouvier, René, and André Laffargue. *Vita napoletana nel XVIII secolo.* Naples, 1960.

Boyer, F. *Le Monde des arts en Italie et la France de la Révolution et de l'Empire.* Turin, 1969.

Briganti, Giulio. *I Vedutisti.* Rome, 1968.

———. *Gaspar van Wittel e l'origine della veduta settecentesca.* Rome, 1966.

Campolongo, Emmanuele. *La Mergellina: Opera pescatoria.* Naples, 1761.

———. *Il Proteo: Componimento . . . per le nozze di Ferdinando IV.* Naples, 1768.

Capasso, Bartolommeo. *Sull'antico Sito di Napoli e Palepoli.* Naples, 1889.

†Capasso, Gaetano. *Ricordo di Vanvitelli.* Naples, 1974.

Carafa, Giovanni. *Lettera di Giovanni Carafa duca di Noja contenente alcune considerazioni sull'utilità e gloria, che si trarrebbe da una esatta carta topografica della città di Napoli, e del suo contado.* Naples, 1770.

Caramuel Lobkowitz, Juan. *De la Architectura civil.* Vigevano, 1678.

★Carignani, Giuseppe. *Il Tempo di Carlo III, re delle Due Sicilie.* Naples, 1865.

[Carlini, Antonio Niccolò.] *De vita Mari Gioffredi neapolitani architecti commentariolum.* n.p., n.d.

†Caroselli, M. R. *La Reggia di Caserta: lavoro, costo, effetti della costruzione.* Milan, 1968.

†Carreras, Pietro. *Studi su Luigi Vanvitelli.* Florence, 1977.

Cartari, Vincenzo. *Le Immagini degli dei degli antichi.* Venice, 1625.

★Cattaneo, C. *Orazione funebre per la morte di Carlo III.* Naples, 1788.

Bibliography

Causa Picone, Maria. "Volaire." *Antologia di belle arti*, 5 (1978):24 ff.

———. *La Cappella Sansevero*. Naples, 1959.

Causa, Raffaello. *Pitloo*. Naples, 1956.

Caylus, Anne-Claude-Philippe de Tubières de Grimouard de Pestels de Lévis, comte de. *Correspondance du comte de Caylus avec le père Paciaudi*. Paris, 1877.

Celano, Carlo. *Notizie del bello, dell'antico e del curioso della città di Napoli* [edited and updated by G. B. Chiarini]. Naples, 1856–1860.

Cestari, G. *Descrizione della topografia ed antichi edifici della città di Napoli*. Naples, 1782.

Chevallier, E. "Les Peintures découvertes à Herculaneum, Pompei et Stabie vues par les voyageurs du XVIII siècle." *Gazette des beaux-arts*, 90 (1977):177 ff.

Chierici, Gino. "L'Albergo dei poveri a Napoli." *Bollettino d'arte*, 25 (1932):439 ff.

†———. "I Disegni della raccolta vanvitelliana nella reggia di Caserta." *Rassegna di architettura* (1936):168 ff.

†———. "Luigi Vanvitelli pittore." *Bollettino d'arte*, 30 (1937):513 ff.

†———. "Note vanvitelliane." *Atti del VIII convegno nazionale di storia dell'architettura* [1953]. Rome, 1956, pp. 145 ff.

†———. *La Reggia di Caserta*. Rome, 1930.

Ciechanowiecki, Andrew S. "Sculpture in Naples." *The Golden Age of Naples* (exhibit catalogue), vol. 2, pp. 286 ff.

Cioffi, Irene. "Corrado Giaquinto's *Rest on the Flight into Egypt*." *Bulletin of the Detroit Institute of Arts*, 58 (1980):5 ff.

Comes, Natalis. *Mythologiae, sive explicationis fabularum libri decem*. Geneva, 1641.

Comoli Mandracci, Vera. "Le 'Delizie farnesiane' di Colorno." *Arte lombarda*, 10 (1965): 107 ff., and 11 (1966):57 ff.

Conte, C. *Gli Stabilimenti di beneficenza a Napoli* Naples, 1884.

§Corsaro, A. "Vico and Mathematics." *Giambattista Vico: An International Symposium*. Baltimore, 1969, pp. 425 ff.

Cortese, Nicola. "Nella Napoli colta della seconda metà del settecento," in *Cultura e politica a Napoli del XV al XVIII secoli*. Naples, 1965.

Corti, E. C. *The Destruction and Resurrection of Pompeii and Herculaneum*. London, 1976.

Cosenza, G. "Giuseppe Bonito." *Napoli nobilissima*, 11 (1902):81 ff., 103 ff., 122 ff., 154 ff.; ibid., 12 (1903):12 ff.

§Croce, Benedetto (and Fausto Nicolini). *Bibliografia vichiana*. Naples, 1947.

§———. "Estetici italiani della seconda metà del settecento," in *Problemi di estetica*. 4th ed. Bari, 1949, pp. 383 ff.

——— ("Don Fastidio"). "Il Museo sotto i Borboni." *Napoli nobilissima*, 1st ser., 15 (1906):30 ff.

★———. "Sentenze e giudizi di Bernardo Tanucci," in *Uomini e cose della vecchia Italia*. Bari, 1956, pp. 15 ff.

———. "Shaftesbury in Italia," in *Uomini e cose della vecchia Italia*. Bari, 1956, pp. 272 ff.

———. *Storia del regno di Napoli*. Bari, 1958.

D'Addosio, G. B. *Origine, vicende storiche e progressi della real santa casa dell'Annunziata di Napoli*. Naples, 1883.

★D'Aquino, Andrea Lettieri. *L'Eroismo del magnanimo, generoso, ed invitissimo re di Napoli Carlo di Borbone ragionato, e palesato con orazione panegirica*. Naples, 1740.

Daniele, Francesco. *Monete antiche di Capua*. Naples, 1802.

De Dominici, B. *Vite dei pittori, scultori ed architetti napoletani*. Naples, 1742; with O. Giannone, *Aggiunte alle "vite dei pittori,"* etc. edited by O. Morisani. Naples, 1941.

De Eisner Eisenhof, A. *Le Porcellane di Capodimonte*. Naples, 1925.

De Filippis, Felice. *Le Antiche residenze reali di Napoli*. Naples, 1971.

†———. *Caserta e la sua reggia.* Naples, 1954.

———. "I Modelli degli arazzi per la règgia di Caserta." *Commentari,* 18 (1967):67 ff.

†———. *Il Palazzo reale di Caserta e i Borboni di Napoli.* Naples, 1968.

———. *Pittori tedeschi a Napoli nel settecento.* Naples, 1943.

———. *La Reggia di Napoli.* Naples, 1942.

De Franciscis, A. "L'Esperienza napoletana del Winckelmann." *Croniche pompeiane,* 1 (1975):7 ff.

De Fusco, Renato. "L'Architettura nella seconda metà del settecento." *Storia di Napoli,* vol. 8. Naples, 1971, p. 369 ff.

———. "Un Centro comunitario del settecento in Campania." *Comunità,* 86 (1961):56 ff.

†———. *Luigi Vanvitelli.* Naples, 1973.

†———. "Vanvitelli e la critica del settecento." *Napoli nobilissima,* ser. 3, 6 (1967):14 ff.

†De Lillo, G. *Le Acque del condotto carolino per la città e bargate di Caserta.* Caserta, 1896.

Del Pezzo, N. "Siti reali: Capodimonte." *Napoli nobilissima,* ser. 1, 6 (1902):65 ff., 170 ff., 188 ff.

———. "Siti reali: i campi flegrei e gli astroni." *Napoli nobilissima,* ser. 1, 1 (1892):119 ff., 149 ff., 170 ff.

§De Mauro, T., "G. B. Vico dalla retorica allo storicismo." *La Cultura,* 6 (1968):167 ff.

De Nitto, Giuseppe. "I Disegni di Mario Gioffredo per la reggia di Caserta presso la Biblioteca Nazionale di Napoli." *Napoli nobilissima,* ser. 3, 14 (1975):183 ff.

★De Rosa, Giuseppe. *Istoria d'Europa che incomincia da'negoziati della pace di Risnich del 1697 sino a' due trattati di Belgrado del 1739 conchiusi fra l'emperadore, la Moscovia a la Porta.* Naples, 1740.

§De Ruggiero. *Il Pensiero meridionale nei secoli XVIII e XIX.* Bari, 1922.

De Seta, Cesare. *Architettura, ambiente e società a Napoli nel '700.* Turin, 1981.

†———. "Disegni di Luigi Vanvitelli architetto e scenografo," in Roberto di Stefano, ed., *Luigi Vanvitelli.* Naples, 1973, pp. 275 ff.

†———. "Luigi Vanvitelli, l'antico e il neoclassico." *Prospettiva,* 15 (1978):40 ff.

———. *Napoli nel settecento.* Naples, 1977.

———. *Storia della città di Napoli dalle origini al settecento.* Bari, 1973.

★Desormeaux, Joseph-Louis-Ripault. *Histoire de la maison de Bourbon.* Paris, 1772–1788.

De Venuti, Marcello. *Descrizione delle prime scoperte dell'antica città di Ercolano.* Rome, 1748.

★Di Donato, Giuseppe. *Orazione funebre di Carlo III il grande, re di Spagna, etc.* Naples, 1789.

Di Giacomo, Salvatore. "L'Albergo dei Poveri," in *Napoli d'oggi.* Naples, 1900.

———. "Le Reggie di Napoli, Capodimonte e Caserta," in *Palazzi e ville che non sono più del re.* Milan, 1921.

†Di Stefano, Renato, ed. *Luigi Vanvitelli.* Naples, 1973.

†———. "Luigi Vanvitelli, ingegnere e restauratore," in *Luigi Vanvitelli.* Naples, 1973, pp. 171 ff.

★Donatone, Guido. *La Real fabbrica di maioliche di Carlo di Borbone a Caserta.* Caserta, 1973.

★D'Onofri, Pietro. *Elogio contemporaneo per la gloriosa memoria di Carlo III.* Naples [1789?].

§Donzelli, Maria. *Contributo alla bibliografia vichiana (1948–1970).* Naples, 1973.

Doria, Gino. *Il 'Largo del Palazzo' a Napoli e Gaspare degli occhiali.* Milan, 1964.

———, Ferdinando Bologna, and G. Pannain. *Settecento napoletano.* Portici, 1962.

———, and Oreste Ferrari. *Vedute napoletane dalla raccolta Lemmermann.* Naples, 1957.

★Dumas, Alexandre. *I Borboni di Napoli.* Naples, 1865.

★Dussieux, Louis-Etienne. *Généalogie de la maison de Bourbon, de 1256 à 1871,* 2d ed. Paris, 1872.

Enggass, Robert. *Early Eighteenth-Century Sculpture in Rome: An Illustrated Catalogue Raisonné.* University Park, Pa., 1976.

Fagiolo dell'Arco, Marcello, and S. Carandino. *L'Effimero barocco: Strutture della festa nella Roma del '600.* Rome, 1977.

†———. *Funzioni simboli valori della reggia di Caserta.* Rome, 1963.

†———. "Luigi Vanvitelli." *Dizionario enciclopedico di architettura e urbanistica.* Rome, 1969.

Faraglia, N. F. "Il Largo del palazzo." *Napoli nobilissima,* ser. 1, 2 (1892): Fascicules 9, 10.

———. "La Real pinacoteca di Napoli nel 1802." *Napoli nobilissima,* ser. 1, 4, (1895): 109 ff.

Félibien, André. *Entretiens sur les vies et sur les ouvrages des plus excellens peintres anciens et modernes; avec la vie des architectes.* Paris, 1725.

Ferdinando IV di Borbone, re delle Due Sicilie. *Origine della popolazione di San Leucio e i suoi progressi fino al giorno di oggi correspondenti al buon governo di essa di Ferdinando IV.* See under Tescione, T.

Fernandez Murga, F. "Roque Joachín de Alcubierre, descubridor de Herculano, Pompeya y Stabia." *Arquivo español de arqueología,* 35 (1962):3 ff.

Ferrari, Oreste. "La Manifattura di Capodimonte." *Arte figurativa,* no. 3 (1960):24 ff.

†Fichera, Francesco. *Luigi Vanvitelli.* Rome, 1937.

†Fiengo, G. *Gioffredo e Vanvitelli nei palazzi dei Casacalenda.* Naples, 1976.

Filangieri, Gaetano. *Documenti per la storia, le arti e le industrie delle provincie napoletane.* Naples, 1883–1891.

Fittipaldi, T. "Il Monumento del canoncio Alessio Simmaco Mazzocchi nella basilica di Santa Restituta in Napoli." *Campania sacra,* no. 5 (1974):142 ff.

———. "Sculture inedite di D. A. Vaccaro, Bottigliero, Pagano, e Sammartino." *Napoli nobilissima,* ser. 3, 19 (1979):133 ff.

★Flumeri, Giuseppe. *In Funere Caroli III Magni Hispaniarum Regis,* etc. Naples, 1794.

Fontana, Domenico. *Dichiarazione del nuovo real palazzo cominciato nella piazza di San Luiggi.* Naples, 1604.

Galanti, Gennaro Maria. *Descrizione dello stato antico ed attuale del contado di Molise, con un saggio storico sulla costituzione del regno.* Naples, 1781.

———. *Nuova descrizione storica e geografica delle Sicilie.* Naples, 1786.

§———. *Saggio sopra i primi abitatori dell'Italia.* 2d ed. Naples, 1783.

†Galasso, Elio. *Vanvitelli a Benevento.* Benevento, 1959.

Galiani, Ferdinando. *Dialogues sur le commerce des blèds* [1769], edited by Fausto Nicolini. Milan/Naples, 1959.

Gambardella, A. *Note su Ferdinando Sanfelice architetto.* Naples, 1970.

†Garms, Jörg. "Beiträgen zu Vanvitellis Leben, Werk und Milieu." *Römische historische Mitteilungen,* 16 (1974):107 ff.

†———. "Die Briefe des Luigi Vanvitelli am seinen Brüder Urbano in Rom: Kunsthistorisches Material." *Römische historische Mitteilungen,* 13 (1971):277 ff.

†———. *Disegni di Luigi Vanvitelli nelle collezioni pubbliche di Napoli e di Caserta.* Naples, 1973.

†———. "Notizie intorno al corpus de' disegni vanvitelliani (addenda e corrigenda al catalogo della mostra, Napoli 1973)." *Napoli nobilissima,* ser. 3., 17 (1974):45 ff.

†———. "Vanvitelli und Spanien. Ein Projekt für die Ehrenstiege des Madrider Königspalastes." *Storia dell'arte,* 11 (1971):173 ff.

Garzya, C. *Interni neoclassici a Napoli*. Naples, 1978.

Gentile, Aniello. *Caserta nei ricordi dei viaggiatori stranieri*. Naples, 1980.

Giannantonio, P. *L'Arcadica napoletana*. Naples, 1962.

Giannone, Pietro. *Istoria civile di Napoli*. Palmyra, 1752.

Gioffredo, Mario. *Dell'architettura di Mario Gioffredo architetto napoletano. Parte prima nella quale si tratta degli ordini dell'architettura de' greci, e degli italiani*. Naples, 1768.

§Giovanni, A. Bianca. *Il Concetto di poesia in Giambattista Vico*. Messina/Florence, 1967.

Giustiniani, L. *Dizionario geografico-ragionato del regno di Napoli*. Naples, 1803.

Glaser, J. *Schloss Schönbrunn*. Schönbrunn/Vienna, 1962.

★Gleijes, Vittorio. *Carlo di Borbone re di Napoli*. Naples, 1976.

Gonzàlez-Palacios. "Il Trasporto delle statue farnesiane da Roma a Napoli." *Antologia di belle arti*, 6 (1978):74 ff.

Gori, A. F. *Notizie del memorabile scoprimento dell'antico città di Ercolano vicina a Napoli . . .* Florence, 1748.

Goudar, Ange. *Naples, ce qu'il faut faire pour rendre ce royaume florissant . . . .* Paris, 1769.

Gregori, M. "Liani: Ritrattista di eccezione," *Paragone*, no. 309 (1975):103 ff.

Griseri, A. "Francesco De Mura tra le corti di Napoli, Madrid, e Torino." *Paragone* [arte], 13 (1962):22 ff.

Guarini, Guarino. *Architettura civile* [1737]. Edited by Bianca Tavassi La Greca. Milan, 1968.

Guarino, G. *Vita ed opera di Alessio Simmaco Mazzocchi*. Caserta, 1908.

§Guarnacci, Mario. *Origini italiche o siano memorie istorico-etrusche sopra l'antichissimo regno d'Italia, e sopra i di lei primi abitatori*. Lucca, 1767.

Guerrieri, G. "Alessio Simmaco Mazzocchi e le accademie ercolanensi et etrusca." *Archivio storico per la provincia di Terra di Lavoro*, 4 (1975):283 ff.

Guimbaud, Louis. *Saint-Non et Fragonard*. Paris, 1928.

Gwynn, John. *London and Westminster Improved*. London, 1776.

Hamilton, William. *A Collection of Engravings from Ancient Vases Mostly of Pure Greek Workmanship Discovered in Sepulchres in the Kingdom of the Two Sicilies*. Naples, 1791–1795.

Hersey, George. *Alfonso II and the Artistic Renewal of Naples, 1485–1495*. New Haven, Conn., 1969.

———. "Alfonso II, Benedetto e Giuliano da Maiano e la Porta Reale." *Napoli nobilissima*, ser. 3, 4 (1964):77 ff.

———. *The Aragonese Arch at Naples, 1443–1475*. New Haven, Conn., 1973.

———. *Pythagorean Palaces: Magic and Architecture in the Italian Renaissance*. Ithaca, N.Y., 1976.

§Ignarra, Niccolo. *Alexii Symmachi Mazochii vita*. Naples, 1772.

Izzo, Luigi. *La Scultura decorativa nel parco reale di Caserta*. Naples, 1970.

Keohane, Nannerl O. *Philosophy and the State in France: The Renaissance and the Enlightenment*. Princeton, N.J., 1980.

Kronig, W. "Der königliche Jagd-Pavillon in Fusaro-See bei Neapel und Filipp Hackerts Jahreszeiten-Bilder." *Wallraf-Richartz Jahrbuch*, 29 (1967):219 ff.

———. "Il Padiglione borbonico a Fusaro e le 'Quattro Stagioni' di F. Hackert." *Napoli nobilissima*, ser. 3, 7 (1968):3 ff.

†Latronico, N. *Vanvitelli e le sue opere*. Caserta, 1879.

LeGuillou, Jean-Claude. "Aperçu sur un projet insolite (1668) pour le château de Versailles." *Gazette des Beaux-Arts*, ser. 5, 95 (1980):49 ff.

Lepore, Ettore. "La Vita politica e sociale" [of Greco-Roman Naples]. *Storia di Napoli*, vol. 1. Naples, 1976, pp. 141 ff.

Leppmann, W. *Pompeii in Fact and Fiction*. London, 1968.

Liberatore, R. *Viaggio pittorico nel regno delle Due Sicilie*. Naples, n.d.

Liverani, G. "Porcellane di scavo da Capodimonte." *Faenza*, 5/6 (1959):120 ff.

Lorenzetti, C. *L'Accademia de' belle arti di Napoli*. Florence, 1952.

Lotz, Wolfgang. "La Sosta di Goethe a Caserta." *Archivio storico di Terra di Lavoro*, 3 (1960–1964).

Madelin, Louis. "Comment le roi soleil dirigeait ses ministres." *Historia* (March, 1953), 293 ff.

Maderna, Valentina. "Il Tabernacolo della cappella di Caserta." *Antologia di belle arti*, 5 (1978):62 ff.

Maffei, Scipione. *Tre Lettere del signor marchese Scipione Maffei*. Verona, 1748.

Maiuri, Amedeo. *Saggi di vari antichità*. Venice, 1954.

Mancini, Franco. "Il 'Trucco' urbano." *Civiltà del '700 a Napoli*, vol. 2, pp. 301 ff.

———. "Feste apparati e spettacoli teatrali." *Storia di Napoli*, vol. 8. Naples, 1971, pp. 651 ff.

———. *Feste ed apparati civili e religiosi in Napoli del viceregno alla capitale*. Naples, 1968.

———. *Scenografia napoletana dell'età barocca*. Naples, 1964.

Mandalari, Mario. *La Reggia di Caserta e la sua recente trasformazione*. Caserta, 1888.

★Manzi, Pietro. *Carlo di Borbone e Luigi Vanvitelli antesegnanti delle moderne caserme*. Naples, 1969.

———. "L'Urbanizzazione del paesaggio agrario nel Mezzogiorno attraverso la cartografia." in *Atti del XXII congresso geografico italiano*. Salerno, 1975, pp. 167 ff.

Maresca, P., and V. Vaccaro. "Massoneria ed ermetismo nella Napoli del '700," *Psicon*, 4 (1975):101 ff.

†Marotta, Antonio. *La Reggia e le fontane di Caserta*. Caserta, n.d.

†Martorelli, L. *Vita ed opera di Luigi Vanvitelli*. Caserta, 1923.

†Martucci, E. *La Città reale: Caserta e i suoi fasti*. Caserta, 1928.

†Mattiae, G. "Il Disegno a due ordini per la facciata di San Giovanni in Laterano," in *Atti del VIII convegno nazionale di storia dell'architettura* [1953]. Rome, 1956, pp. 83 ff.

§Mazochi, Alexii Symmachi. *Commentariorum in regii Herculanensis musei aeneas tabulas heracleenses*. Naples, 1754.

Mazzoleni, Iole. *Archivio di Stato di Napoli. Archivio borbone. Inventario sommario*. Rome, 1961.

†Melani, A. "Il Palazzo e il parco di Caserta." *Arte italiana decorativa e industriale* (1906): pp. 42 ff., 51 ff., 58 ff.

Mele, E. "Viaggiatori stranieri a Napoli, II. D. L. Fernandez de Moratini." *Napoli nobilissima*, ser. 1, 15 (1906):27 ff.

Metastasio, Pietro. *Opere*. Edited by Mario Fubini. Milan, 1968.

———. *Opere*. Edited by Fausto Nicolini. Bari, 1912.

Milizia, Francesco. *Memorie degli architetti*. Bassano, 1785.

†Minieri-Riccio, Camillo. "Autografo di Luigi Vanvitelli." *Archivio storico delle province napoletane*, 5 (1880):196 ff.

———. *Cenno storico delle accademie fiorite nella città di Napoli*. Naples, 1879.

Miola, A. "La Facciata della reggia di Napoli." *Napoli nobilissima*, ser. 1, 1 (1892):14 ff.

Molajoli, Bruno. *Notizie di Capodimonte.* Naples, 1957.

§Momigliano, Arnaldo. "Vico's 'Scienza Nuova.'" *History and Theory*, 5 (1966):3 ff.

†Mongiello, Giovanni. *La Reggia di Caserta.* Caserta, 1954.

†Morelli, G. "Appunti bio-bibliografici su Gaspar e Luigi Vanvitelli." *Archivio della società romana di storia patria*, ser. 3, 23 (1969):128 ff.

Mormone, Raffaello. "Architettura a Napoli 1650–1734." *Storia di Napoli*, vol. 6. Naples, 1970, pp. 1087 ff.

———. "La Scultura (1734–1800)." *Storia di Napoli*, vol. 8. Naples, 1971, pp. 549 ff.

★Moscati, Ruggiero. *I Borboni d'Italia.* Naples, 1970.

★Muzio, Michele Luigi. *Diario del viaggio fatto dalla maestà di Carlo III re delle Spagne . . . da Barcellona a Milano ed a Francfort . . .* Naples, 1712.

Napoli Signorelli, Pietro. "Gli Artisti napoletani della seconda metà del sec. XVIII." *Napoli nobilissima*, ser. 2, 1 (1921):10 ff.

★———. *De' Funerali in morte del cattolico monarca Carlo III.* Naples, 1789.

———. *Vicende della coltura nelle Due Sicilie.* Naples, 1785 ff.

Nappi, Eduardo. "La Famiglia, il palazzo e la cappella dei principi di Sansevero." *Revue internationale d'histoire de la banque*, 11 (1975):1 ff.

†———. "Verità e leggenda nella storia dell'arte napoletana. I. Il Foro Carolino." *Annali di storia economica e sociale*, 8 (1967):189 ff.

★Nardi, Carlo. *De' Titoli del re delle Due Sicilie colle spiegazioni del D. Carlo Nardi al re.* Naples, 1747.

§Nicolini, Fausto. *La Giovinezza di Giambattista Vico (1668–1700).* 2d ed. Bari, 1932.

———. *Della Società nazionale di scienze lettere e arti e di talune accademie napoletane che la precedono.* Edited by F. Tessitore. Naples, 1974.

†Nicolini, L. *La Reggia di Caserta (1750–1775). Ricerche storiche.* Bari, 1911.

Oncken, Alste-Horn. *Ausflug in elysische Gefilde. Das europäische Campanienbild des 16. und 17. Jahrhunderts und die Aufzeichnungen J. F. A. von Uffenbachs.* Göttingen, 1978.

Pacelli, V. "Contributo a Francesco Celebrano pittore." *Studi di storia dell'arte in onore di Valerio Mariano.* Naples, 1971, pp. 259 ff.

Pacichelli, G. B. *Ill Regno di Napoli in prospettiva.* Naples, 1703.

Palermo, S. *Notizie del bello, dell'antico, e del curioso che contengono le reali ville di Portici, Resina, lo Scaramento di Pompejano, Capodimonte, Cardito, Caserta e San Leucio.* Naples, 1792.

Pane, Giulio. "Ferdinando Fuga e l'Albergo dei Poveri." *Napoli nobilissima*, ser. 3, 5 (1966):72 ff.

Pane, Roberto. *Architettura dell'età barocca in Napoli.* Naples, 1939.

———. *Architettura del rinascimento in Napoli.* Naples, 1937.

†———. "L'Attività di Luigi Vanvitelli fuori del regno delle Due Sicilie." *Luigi Vanvitelli*, pp. 43 ff.

———. *Ferdinando Fuga.* Naples, 1956.

†———. *Luigi Vanvitelli secondo centenario MCMLXXIII. Opere e particolari inediti in 32 foto di Roberto Pane.* Naples, 1973.

†———. "Luigi Vanvitelli, l'uomo e l'artista." *Napoli nobilissima*, ser. 3, 13 (1973):3 ff.

†———. "Vanvitelli e la grafica." *Congresso internazionale di studi. Vanvitelli e il '700 europeo.* Naples, 1978.

★Parochi Palmieri, F. *In laudem Caroli III, Siciliarum inde Hispaniarum et novis orbis catholici regis.* Naples, 1819.

Bibliography

Parrino, D. A. *Teatro eroico e politico dei governi dei vicerè del regno di Napoli.* Naples, 1875.

†Paturelli, Ferdinando. *Caserta e San Leucio.* New ed., edited by Gaetano Capasso. Naples, 1972.

§Peci, Enzo. *Ingens Sylva. Saggio sulla filosofia di G. B. Vico.* Verona, 1966.

Pellegrino, Camillo. *Apparato alle antichità di Capua o vero discorsi della Campania felice, ecc.* Naples, 1771.

Petrelli, Flavia. "La Fontana di Diana e Atteone a Caserta." *Antologia di belle arti,* 2 (1978):53 ff.

Petrie, Charles. *King Charles III of Spain. An Enlightened Despot.* London, 1971.

§Piovani, P. "Piranesi e Vico." *Giornale critica della filosofia italiana,* 48 (1969):318 ff.

Piranesi, Giovanni Battista. *Delle Magnificenze ed architetture de' romani.* Rome, 1761.

Possenti, E. "Restauro di sei arazzi di fabbrica napoletana della reggia di Capodimonte." *Bollettino d'arte,* 29 (1935):141 ff.

Praz, Mario. "Le Antichità di Ercolano." *Civiltà del '700 a Napoli* (1979), 1:35 ff.

Prota Giurleo, U. "I Bibiena a Napoli." *Partenope,* 3 (1960):175 ff.

Pugliese Carratelli, Giovanni. "Il Mondo Mediterraneo e le origini di Napoli." *Storia di Napoli,* vol. 1, Naples, 1975.

★Quattromani, Gabriele. *Della vita e delle opere di Carlo Borbone re delle Due Sicilie. Saggio.* Naples, 1976, pp. 99 ff.

†Quintavalle, A. O. "Luigi Vanvitelli e il suo barochismo." *Marzocco* (June 1928).

Ripa, Cesare. *Della novissima Iconologia. . . .* Padua, 1625.

†Robotti, Ciro. "L'Opera di Gioffredo e di Vanvitelli per il giardino di Villa Campolieto." *Storia dell'arte,* 35 (1979):49 ff.

Robson, E. "La Guerra dei sette anni." *Storia del mondo moderno,* 7 (1968):620 ff.

Rocco, Benedetto. *Elogio del Cavalier Gioffredo disteso da B. R.* Naples, 1785.

§Romano, Damiano. *Difesa istorica delle leggi greche venute in Roma contro alla moderna opinione del Sign. D. Gio. Battista Vico.* Naples, 1736.

Romano, E. *La Porcellana di Capodimonte.* Naples, 1959.

Rosci, Mario. "Filippo Juvarra e il 'nuovo' gusto classico alla metà del settecento," *Atti del VIII convegno nazionale di storia dell'architettura* [1953]. Rome, 1956.

Rose, H. "Nicodemus Tessin der Jüngere und der Neubau des Schlosses von Stockholm." *Festschrift Heinrich Wölfflin.* Munich, 1924, pp. 245 ff.

†Rotili, Mario. "Il Progetto vanvitelliano per la fontana di Trevi." *Samnium,* 27 (1954):54 ff.

§Rousseau, François. *Le Règne de Charles III d'Espagne (1759–1788).* Paris, 1907.

Ruffo, Vincenzo. *Saggio ragionato sull'origine ed essenza dell'architettura civile.* Naples, 1789.

———. *Rinnovazione de' progetti relativi all'abbellimento e alla pulizia della città di Napoli.* Naples, n.d.

†Rufini, E. "L'Importanza di un epistolario inedito di Luigi Vanvitelli." *Studi in memoria di Gino Chierici.* Rome, 1965, pp. 281 ff.

†Rufini, T. *Regesto delle lettere di Luigi Vanvitelli.* Rome, 1962.

Ruggiero, M. *Storia degli scavi di Ercolano.* Naples, 1885.

Russo, G. "La Città di Napoli dalle origini al 1860," in Mario Napoli, ed., *Contributi allo studio della città,* Naples, 1960.

———. *Napoli come città.* Naples, 1966.

Rykwert, Joseph. *The First Moderns: The Architects of the Eighteenth Century.* Cambridge, Mass., 1980.

Saint-Non, J. C. Richard, Abbé de. *Description historique et critique de l'Italie*. Dijon, 1766.

———. *Voyage pittoresque ou description des royaumes de Naples de la Sicile*. Paris, 1781–1786.

Sarnelli, Pompeo. *Nuova Guida de' forastieri curiosi di vedere, e di riconoscere le cose più memorabile di Pozzuoli, Baja, Cuma, Misena [sic], Gaeta*. Naples, 1782.

Scherillo, Antonio. "Suolo e sottosuolo di Napoli. *Storia di Napoli*, vol. 1. Naples, 1975, p. 1 ff.

†Schiavo, Armando. "Luigi Vanvitelli e la Cappella Sanpajo." *Archivio della società romana di storia patria*, ser. 3, 26 (1972):43 ff.

†———. "Il Progetto di Luigi Vanvitelli per Caserta e la sua reggia." *Bollettino del centro di studi per la storia dell'architettura*, Rome (1953):45 ff.

†———. "Progetto di Mario Gioffredo per la reggia di Caserta." *Palladio*, ser. 2 (1950):160 ff.

†———. "Reminiscenze e lieviti nei prospetti della reggia di Caserta." *Archivio storico di Terra di Lavoro* (1959):223 ff.

†———. "Santa Maria degli Angeli alle Terme." *Bollettino del centra studi di storia dell'architettura*, 8 (1954):15 ff.

†Schipa, Michelangelo. "Per l'Addobbo, l'ingradimento e le decorazioni della reggia di Napoli alla venuta di Carlo di Borbone." *Napoli nobilissima*, ser. 1, 11 (1902):109 ff.

★———. "Reali delizie borboniche." *Napoli nobilissima*, ser. 2, 3 (1923):171 ff.

★———. *Il Regno di Napoli al tempo di Carlo di Borbone*. Naples, 1904; reprinted Naples, 1923.

Schräder, Hermann. *Die Sirenen nach ihrer Bedeutung und kunstlerischen Darstellung im Alterthum*. Berlin, 1868.

Selvaggi, B. "La Città di Napoli attraverso le sue piante topografiche: Napoli borbonica." *Ingegneri*, 6 (1963):33 ff.

§Serai, Francesco. "Commentariolum de rebus Alexii Mazochii," in Mazzocchi, *Opuscula*, vol. 1, Naples, 1771, pp. vi ff.

Seznec, Jean. "Herculaneum and Pompeii in French Literature of the Eighteenth Century." *Archaeology*, 11 (1949):150 ff.

Sigismondo, G. *Descrizione della città di Napoli e suoi borgini*. Naples, 1788–1789.

Siracusano, C. "Antonio Dominici, pittore siciliano alla corte del Borbone di Napoli." Messina, University: *Quaderni dell'istoria dell'arte medioevale e moderna*, 3 (1979):33 ff.

Sirri, Raffaele. "La Cultura a Napoli nel settecento." *Storia di Napoli*, vol. 8. Naples, 1971, pp. 165 ff.

Smith, R. *Schiarimenti archaeologici ad alcune statue antiche nel real giardino di Caserta*. Caserta, 1869.

†Smith, R. C. "Some Drawings by the Architect Luigi Vanvitelli," *Art Quarterly*, 11 (1939):331 ff.

§Solari, Gioele. "Vico e Pagano. Per la storia della tradizione vichiana a Napoli nel secolo XVIII," in G. Solari and Luigi Firpo, eds., *Studi su Francesco Mario Pagano*. Turin, 1963, pp. 165 ff.

†Spaziano, Giovanni. *Il Palazzo reale di Caserta*. 3rd ed. Capua, 1973.

Spinosa, Nicola. "Domenico Mondo e il barocco napoletano." *Napoli nobilissima*, ser. 3, 7 (1967), pp. 191 ff.

———. "Francesco Liani, pittore emiliano al servizio della corte di Napoli." *Paragone: Arte*, no. 309 (1975):38 ff.

†———. "Un Giocattolo per i sovrani." *Strenna napoletana* (1974):53 ff.

†———. "Luigi Vanvitelli e i pittori attivi a Napoli nella seconda metà del settecento. Lettere e documenti inediti." *Storia dell'arte*, 14 (1972):193 ff.

———. "La Pittura napoletana da Carlo a Ferdinando IV di Borbone." *Storia di Napoli*, vol. 8. Naples, 1971, pp. 453 ff.

†Strazzullo, Franco. *Autografi vanvitelliani della biblioteca nazionale di Napoli*. Naples, 1973.

†———. "Autografi vanvitelliani inediti sulla cappella reale." *Arte cristiana*, 39 (1952):198 ff.

†———. *Edilizia e urbanistica a Napoli del '500 al '700*. Naples, 1968.

†———. "Lettere a Luigi Vanvitelli." *Arte cristiana*, 61 (1973):287 ff.

†———. "Nuovi documenti su Luigi Vanvitelli." *Fuidoro* (1955):266 ff.

†———. "Pittori e scultori del '700 a Napoli nelle relazioni di Luigi Vanvitelli." *Atti dell'accademia pontaniana*, 24 (1974):1 ff.

†———. "I Primi anni di Luigi Vanvitelli a Caserta." *Archivio storico di Terra di Lavoro*, 3 (1960–1964):437 ff.

———. *Tradizioni sacre popolari e scultura del '700 a Napoli. Da un manoscritto di P. Napoli Signorelli*. Naples, 1968.

★Tanucci, Bernardo. *Bernardo Tanucci ed il suo più importante carteggio*. Florence, 1942.

★———. *Lettere di Bernardo Tanucci a Carlo III di Borbone (1759–1776)*. Edited by Rosa Mincuzzi. Rome, 1969.

———. *Lettere al Galiani*. Edited by Fausto Nicolini. Bari, 1914.

Taylor, René. "Architecture and Magic: Considerations on the *Idea* of the Escorial," in Douglas Fraser, Howard Hibbard, and Milton S. Lewine, eds., *Essays in the History of Architecture Presented to Rudolf Wittkower*. New York, 1967, pp. 81 ff.

———. "Hermetism and Mystical Architecture in the Society of Jesus," in Rudolf Wittkower and Irma B. Jaffe, eds., *Baroque Art: The Jesuit Contribution*. New York, 1972, pp. 63 ff.

Tescione, Giovanni. *L'Arte della seta a Napoli e la colonia di San Leucio*. Naples, 1932.

———. "Il Laboratorio delle pietre dure di Napoli e l'altare della palatina della reggia di Caserta." *Studi in onore di Riccardo Filangieri*. Naples, 1959, vol. 3, pp. 187 ff.

Tescione, T. *San Leucio e l'arte della seta nel mezzogiorno d'Italia*. Naples, 1961.

Thoenes, Christoph, with Thuri Lorenz. *Neapel und Umgebung*. Stuttgart, 1971.

Vallecchi, F. "La Fabbrica di Capodimonte." *Antichità viva*, 1 (1962):29 ff.

Valsecchi, F. "L'Eredità del passato," in M. Fubini, ed., *La Cultura illuministica in Italia*. Turin, 1957.

†Vanvitelli, Luigi. *Dichiarazione dei disegni del real palazzo di Caserta*. Naples, 1756.

†———. *Lettere della biblioteca palatina di Caserta*, edited by Franco Strazzullo. Galatina, 1976–77.

†———. "Relazione sull'acquedotto di Caserta." Biblioteca nazionale di Napoli, sezione manoscritti XV-A-9, busta 2, c. 65.

†Vanvitelli, Luigi the Younger. *Vita di Luigi Vanvitelli*. Edited by Mario Rotili. Naples, 1975.

Vasi, G. *Delle Magnificenze di Roma antica e moderna*. Rome, 1753.

Venditti, Arnaldo. *Architettura neoclassica a Napoli*. Naples, 1961.

†———. "L'Opera napoletana di Luigi Vanvitelli," in R. Di Stefano, ed., *Luigi Vanvitelli*. Naples, 1972, pp. 99 ff.

★Venturi, Franco. "Un Bilancio della politica economica di Carlo di Borbone. L'Economia del commercio di Napoli di G. B. Maria Tanucci." *Rivista storica italiana*, 4 (1969): 882 ff.

———. "Napoli capitale nel pensiero dei riformatori illuministi." *Storia di Napoli*, vol. 8. Naples, 1971, pp. 3 ff.

———. *Settecento riformatore. Da Muratori a Beccaria*. Turin, 1969.

§Vico, Giambattista. *Autobiografia*. Edited and continued by the Marchese di Villarosa. Naples, 1818.

§———. *The Autobiography*. Edited and translated by Max Harold Fisch and Goddard Bergin. Ithaca, 1944.

§———. *Il Diritto universale [De universi iuris uno principio et fine uno]*. Edited by Fausto Nicolini. Bari, 1936. Translated as *The New Science of Giambattista Vico* by T. G. Bergin and M. H. Fisch. Ithaca, 1948.

§———. *La Scienza nuova seconda*. Edited by Fausto Nicolini. Bari, 1953.

§———. *Opere*. Edited by Fausto Nicolini. Milan, 1953.

§———. *Opere giuridiche*. Edited by Nicola Baddaloni. Florence, 1974.

§———. *Scritti storici*. Edited by Fausto Nicolini. Bari, 1939.

§———. *Versi d'occasione e scritti di scuola*. Edited by Fausto Nicolini. Bari, 1941.

§Villa, Giovanni. *La Filosofia del mito secondo G. B. Vico*. Milan, 1949.

Villani, P. *Mezzogiorno tra riforme e rivoluzione*. Bari, 1962.

Vinciguerra, M., "Le Reggenza borbonica nella minorità di Ferdinando IV." *Archivio storico per le province napoletane*, 1 (1915):576 ff.; 2 (1916):100 ff.; 3 (1917):184 ff.

Vitruvius Pollio. *L'Architettura di M. Vitruvio Pollio colla traduzione italiana e comento del Marchese Berardo Galiani, accademico ercolanense, etc*. Naples, 1758.

Volpe, F. "La Carestia del 1764 nel Cilento nella cronaca di un contemporaneo." Salerno, University: *Quaderni contemporanei*, 4 (1971): 180 ff.

Volpi, M. "Domenico Mondo pittore 'letterato.'" *Paragone*, 10 (1959):51 ff.

Voss, Gerard. *De Theologia Gentili*. Amsterdam, 1641.

Wildenstein, Georges. "L'Abbé de Saint-Non artiste et mécène." *Gazette des Beaux-Arts*, 44 (1959):225 ff.

Winckelmann, J. J. *Gedanken über die Nachahmung der griechischen Werke in der Malerei und Bildhauerkunst*. Dresden, 1755.

———. *Geschichte der Kunst des Altertums*. Dresden, 1764–1767.

———. *Nachrichten von den neuesten Herculanischen Entdeckungen*. Dresden, 1764.

———. *Sendschreiben von der herculanischen Entdeckungen*. Dresden, 1762.

———. *Versuch einer Allegorie, besonders für die Kunst*. Edited by Albert Dressel. Leipzig, 1866.

†Wittkower, Rudolf. *Art and Architecture in Italy, 1600–1750*. Harmondsworth, England, 1958; 2d ed., 1965.

Zeri, Federico. "Un Appunto su Vernet a Napoli." *Antologia di belle arti*, 5 (1978):59 ff.

†Zevi, Bruno. "Luigi Vanvitelli e la reggia di Caserta: Versailles tra i contadini del sud." *L'Espresso*, April 1, 1973.

List of Illustrations

Plate 1
Luigi Vanvitelli. The Royal Palace of Caserta, 1752 on, garden facade. Photo Ente Provinciale per il Turismo

1.1
Giuseppe Piermarini. Facade of Palazzo Belgioioso, Milan, 1777. Photo Alinari

1.2
Luigi Rusca. Barracks for Belosersky Regiment, St. Petersburg. From Rusca, *Receuil des dessins de différents bâtiments*

1.3
Sir Aston Webb. New facade, Buckingham Palace. From *The Architectural Review*, 1912

1.4
Etienne-Louis Boullée. Design for a vaulted hall. London, RIBA

1.5
Luigi Vanvitelli. Caserta, lower floor vestibule. Photo Alinari

1.6
J. N. L. Durand. Plan and elevations of a large hall. From Durand, *Précis de Leçons d'Architecture*, 1801–1805

1.7
Boullée. Project for new envelope for Versailles, c. 1785. Paris, Bibliothèque Nationale

2.1
Pietro Fabris. Ventotene, Capo dell'Arco. From Hamilton, *Campi Phlegraei* (1779)

2.2
Pietro Fabris. The island of Ventotene. From Saint-Non, *Voyage pittoresque* (1781)

2.3
Map of the environs of Naples. From Saint-Non

2.4
The grotto of Pozzuoli: plan, section, view. From P. A. Paoli, *Antichità di Pozzuoli* (1768)

2.5
Michelangelo Naccherino and Tommaso Montani. Fontana Santa Lucia, Naples, 1606. Photo Alinari

2.6
Fontana Santa Lucia, relief of Hercules, Amphitrite, and Neptune.

2.7
Fontana Santa Lucia, relief of Neptune, Triton, and Amphitrite

2.8
Fontana Santa Lucia, siren console

2.9
Fontana Santa Lucia, arms of Alfonso Pimentel

3.1
Filarete. Labyrinth. From Filarete, *Trattato* (1460s)

3.2
Filarete. Reservoir

3.3
After Francesco di Giorgio. Republican palace. From the *Trattati* (1480s)

3.4
After Francesco di Giorgio. Prince's palace

3.5
Francesco di Giorgio. Palace on the Campidoglio, Rome. From the *Trattati*

3.6
Giuliano da Sangallo. Projected Tribunali Palace for Naples, c. 1488. Florence, Uffizi

Illustrations

3.7
Bramante. Projected Tribunali Palace for Rome, c. 1506. Florence, Uffizi

3.8
After Bramante. Tribunali Palace for Rome, mapped onto a regular grid of 11.5-palmo squares

3.9
Sketch plan of the Escorial. After Kubler, *Building the Escorial*

3.10
Juan Caramuel Lobkowitz. Plan of the Temple of Diana at Ephesus. From his *Architectura Civil* (1678)

3.11
Leibniz's system of binary arithmetic. After Leibniz, *Opera* (1768)

3.12
After Vincenzo Scamozzi. A reconstruction of Pliny's villa at Laurentum, plan. From his *Idea dell' Architettura* (1619)

3.13
Pierre Lescot. Plan for remodeling the Louvre and the Tuileries, 1598. Paris, Bibliothèque Nationale

3.14
Israël Silvestre. Plan of Versailles in 1667. Paris, Bibliothèque Nationale

3.15
Versailles. Sketch plan of present building. Courtesy Yale Slide and Photograph Collection

3.16
Versailles. King's private apartments, begun in 1677. After Pierre Verlet, *Versailles*

3.17
Versailles, dauphin's apartments. After Verlet

3.18
Louis Le Vau. Project for a geometrical envelope for Versailles, 1668. Stockholm, National-museum

3.19
Domenico Fontana (with later niches by Vanvitelli). Palazzo Reale, Naples, 1600–1602. Photo Alinari

3.20
Palazzo Reale, Courtyard

3.21
Engraved plan of the Palazzo Reale, Naples, before 1837. Naples, Biblioteca Nazionale

3.22
Antonio Canevari and Giovanni Antonio Medrano. Palazzo di Capodimonte, Naples, 1738–1838. Photo Alinari

3.23
Capodimonte from the side. Photo Alinari

3.24
Capodimonte, courtyard. Photo Mimmo Jodice

3.25
Capodimonte, plan of ground floor. Caserta, Reggia

3.26
Capodimonte, plan of main floor. Caserta, Reggia

3.27
Capodimonte, main-floor plan mapped onto a grid

4.1
The Kingdom of the Two Sicilies. From Saint-Non

4.2
Francesco Solimena. *Carlo di Borbone at the Battle of Gaeta*. Caserta, Reggia

4.3
Francesco Liani. Portrait of Queen Maria Amalia, c. 1755. Naples, Capodimonte

4.4
Ferdinando Fuga. Albergo dei Poveri, Naples. From Sasso, *Monumenti*

4.5
Vanvitelli. Alternative project for the Foro Carolino. From Sasso

4.6
G. B. Natali. Porcelain cabinet from the royal villa at Portici, 1757–1759. Naples, Capodimonte.

4.7
Carlo di Borbone as Aeneas welcomed by Parthenope and the river Sebeto. From *Descrizione delle Feste* (1735)

4.8
Vanvitelli. Vignette from the *Dichiarazione*.

4.9
Vincenzo Rè. Castel Nuovo decorations. From Rè, *Narrazione* (1749)

4.10
Rè. Guglia for fireworks in the Largo del Castello. From the *Narrazione*

4.11
Rè. Cuccagna in the Largo del Palazzo. From the *Narrazione*

4.12
Rè. Frontispiece from the *Narrazione*

4.13
Mario Gioffredo. Church of the Spirito Santo, Naples, 1774 on Nave and vault. Photo Mimmo Jodice

4.14
Church of the Spirito Santo, dome. Photo Mimmo Jodice

4.15
Giacinto Diano (?). Portrait of Luigi Vanvitelli. Caserta, Reggia

4.16
Filippo Juvarra. Early scheme for Stupinigi Palace, c. 1729. Turin, Museo Civico

4.17
Alessandro Galilei. Church of San Giovanni in Laterano, facade, 1735. Photo Alinari

4.18
Nicola Salvi. Trevi Fountain, Rome, 1732–1751; 1762. Photo Alinari

4.19
Vanvitelli. Church of the Annunziata, Naples, 1760–1782. Nave vault. Photo Mimmo Jodice

4.20
Vanvitelli, Church of the Annunziata, dome. Photo Mimmo Iodice

4.21
Anton Raphael Mengs. Portrait of Ferdinando IV at nine, 1759–1760. Madrid, Prado

5.1
Philipp Hackert. *The Palace of Caserta from the Convent of the Capuchins*, 1782. Naples, San Martino

5.2
Caserta, principal facade. Photo Ente Provinciale per il Turismo

5.3
Caserta, gardens. Photo Jacelli

5.4
Caserta, view of the planned gardens of 1756 from the south. From the *Dichiarazione*

5.5
Caserta, view of the planned gardens of 1756 from the north. From the *Dichiarazione*

5.6
Caserta, air view of the royal palace and gardens. Photo Ente Provinciale per il Turismo

5.7
Detail of fig. 5.4.

5.8
Caserta, planned gardens of 1756. From Vanvitelli, *Dichiarazione*

5.9
Robert de Cotte. Proposed garden at Buen Retiro, 1714–1715. Paris, Bibliothèque Nationale

5.10
A. J. Dézallier d'Argenville. "Disposition générale d'un magnifique jardin tout de niveau," from his *La Théorie et la practique du jardinage* (1709)

5.11
Caserta, details of the palace plan and of the 1756 garden, analyzed as examples of cyclical and dihedral symmetry. *A*, garden of Pomona; *B*, boscage with outdoor salon; *C*, central crossing of palace at ground-floor level; *D*, southern entrance to palace; *E*, "theatrical prospect with chambers" in the garden; *F*, the four corners of the palace at the level of the *piano reale*, or second floor, showing how room configurations approximate a complete 360-degree clockwise cycle. Examples *A–E* all display dihedral or mirror symmetry. Example *F* shows a four-part cycle symmetry.

5.12
Vanvitelli. Sketch for proposed garden at Caserta, c. 1760 (?). Caserta, Museo Vanvitelliano

5.13
Caserta, map of the gardens, palace, and palace square. From Thoenes, *Neapel und Umgebung*

5.14
G. B. Piranesi. Waterfall at the Villa D'Este, etching, 1761. From Lamb, *Die Villa D'Este*

5.15
Villa Lante, Bagnaia, upper garden

5.16
Caserta, Cascade and Fountain of Diana, mainly executed by Paolo Persico, with Angelo Brunelli and Pietro Solari, 1785–1789. Photo Alinari. (See also pls. 2, 3.)

5.17
Fountain of Diana, Diana. Photo Jacelli

5.18
Fountain of Diana, Actaeon. Photo Alinari

5.19
Fountain of Diana, detail of Diana's group. Photo Mimmo Jodice

5.20
Fountain of Diana, detail of more distant nymphs. Photo Mimmo Jodice

5.21
Fountain of Diana, Actaeon's dogs. Photo Mimmo Jodice

5.22
Fountain of Diana, balustrade figure. Photo Mimmo Jodice

5.23–5.25
Fountain of Diana, balustrade figures. Photo Mimmo Jodice

Illustrations

5.26
Caserta, Fountain of Venus and Adonis from rear. Photo Mimmo Jodice

5.27
Fountain of Venus and Adonis, mainly by Gaetano Salomone, late 1770s and early 1780s. Photo Alinari

5.28
Fountain of Venus and Adonis, detail of Venus and Adonis. Photo Mimmo Jodice

5.29
Fountain of Venus and Adonis, two putti and dog. Photo Mimmo Jodice

5.30
Fountain of Venus and Adonis, putto's face. Photo Mimmo Jodice

5.31
Fountain of Venus and Adonis, boar

5.32
Caserta, Fountain of Ceres, mainly by Gaetano Salomone, 1783. Photo Ente Provinciale per il Turismo

5.33
Fountain of Ceres, river god

5.34
Fountain of Ceres, river god. Photo Ente Provinciale per il Turismo

5.35
Boar's head in parapet (Paolo Persico or Pietro Solari, 1782)

5.36
Fountain of Ceres, triton-satyr

5.37
Caserta, Fountain of Juno and Aeolus, by Salomone Persico, Andrea Violani, and Angelo Brunelli, 1779–1785. Photo Alinari

5.38
Fountain of Juno and Aeolus, relief by A. Brunelli of Peleus and Thetis. Photo Soprintendenza per i Beni Culturali

5.39
Fountain of Juno and Aeolus, gallery behind cascade. Photo Ente Provinciale per il Turismo

5.40
Fountain of Juno and Aeolus, the Winds. Photo Ente Provinciale per il Turismo

5.41
Fountain of Juno and Aeolus, chained slave-pair on the parapet. Photo Ente Provinciale per il Turismo

5.42
Vanvitelli. Sketch of balustrade figure. Caserta, Reggia

5.43
Caserta, Dolphin Fountain. Photo Alinari

5.44
Dolphin Fountain, detail of hell beast. Photo Ente Provinciale per il Turismo

6.1
Mario Gioffredo. Project for the royal palace and town of Caserta, perspective, c. 1755. Naples, Biblioteca Nazionale

6.2
Gioffredo. Early site plan for Caserta. Naples, Biblioteca Nazionale

6.3
Gioffredo. Site plan for Caserta. Naples, Biblioteca Nazionale

6.4
Gioffredo. Plan of second and third floors of the palace of Caserta. Naples, Biblioteca Nazionale

6.5
Gioffredo. Plan of upper floors of the palace of Caserta. Naples, Biblioteca Nazionale

6.6
Juan Bautista Villalpando, reconstruction of Solomon's temple. From Villalpando, *In Ezechielem explanationes* (1596–1604)

6.7
A plaid graph generated by the coordinates or edges of the plan in figure 6.3

6.8
The upper left-hand corner of Gioffredo's ground-floor plan

6.9
Redrawn detail from fig. 6.8 showing the outer row of pavilions and ranges and the interpenetrations, within them, of *a*-modules and *b*-modules

6.10
Plan of Capodimonte redrawn as a nine-court palace

6.11
Buen Retiro at the beginning of the eighteenth century. Paris, Bibliothèque Nationale

6.12
Vanvitelli. Early plan for the royal palace at Caserta. Caserta, Règgia

6.13
Vanvitelli. Plan of the ground floor of the palace at Caserta, 1756. From the *Dichiarazione*

6.14
Vanvitelli. Plan of the main floor, or *piano reale*, of the palace at Caserta

6.15
Vanvitelli. Plan of upper floor of the palace at Caserta

6.16
Transformation of four of Gioffredo's courts (fig. 6.3) from squares (*A*) to overlapped squares (*B*) to Vanvitelli's proportions of 4:3 (*C*)

6.17
Caserta, Vanvitelli's plan mapped onto a 14-palmo grid. The ranges are 96 palmi wide; the porticoes are 88 wide and project 30; the lateral ranges are 206 palmi long; the front and rear ranges 306.

6.18
Vanvitelli. Garden facade of the palace at Caserta, 1756, from the *Dichiarazione*

6.19
Vanvitelli. Town facade of the palace at Caserta, 1756. From the *Dichiarazione*

6.20
Robert de Cotte. Garden facade of first project for Buen Retiro, 1712–1714. Paris, Bibliothèque Nationale

6.21
Robert de Cotte. Buen Retiro, court facade. Paris, Bibliothèque Nationale

6.22
Figure 6.19 with drum and towers removed

6.23
Robert de Cotte. Section of an alternative project for Buen Retiro. Paris, Bibliothèque Nationale

6.24
Vanvitelli. Section through the palace at Caserta, showing the stair hall in horizontal section. From the *Dichiarazione*

6.25
Vanvitelli. Study for Caserta facade. Caserta, Reggia

6.26
Vanvitelli. Drawing for longer facade of typical court, with temple front for the palace. Caserta, Reggia

6.27
Caserta, narrower court facade of the palace. Photo Ente Provinciale per il Turismo

6.28
Caserta, section along main axis of the palace. From the *Dichiarazione*

6.29
Caserta, circulation system of the palace. From the *Dichiarazione*

6.30
Caserta, palace courtyards seen from central octagon. Photo Ente Provinciale per il Turismo

7.1
Caserta, detail of northern facade. From the *Dichiarazione*

7.2
Caserta, southern facade, corner pavilion. Photo Ente Provinciale per il Turismo

7.3
Caserta, courtyard, window in *piano reale*

7.4
Caserta, window in upper story

7.5
Caserta, southern portal, detail of Colossi. From the *Dichiarazione*

7.6
Michelangelo and assistants. Tomb of Julius II, finished 1547, Rome, San Pietro in Vincoli. Photo Alinari

7.7
Claude Perrault. Design for the east front of the Louvre, detail. Paris, Bibliothèque Nationale

7.8
Caserta, lower vestibule. Photo Mimmo Jodice. (See also pl. 7.)

7.9
Andrea Violani. Adaptation of the Farnese Hercules, 1770–1773, Caserta, lower vestibule. Photo Ente Provinciale per il Turismo

7.10
Hercules and the Nemean lion, after an antique original, from Mazzocchi, *Aeneas Tabulas* (1754)

7.11
Francesco Celebrano. *Ferdinando IV and His Court at a Boar Hunt*, 1770s. Naples, Museo San Martino. (See also pl. 4.)

7.12
Violani. Adaptation of Medici Venus, 1768–1773. Caserta, lower vestibule. Photo Mimmo Jodice

7.13
Violani. Copy of Roman Germanicus, 1762–63. Caserta, lower vestibule. Photo Mimmo Jodice

7.14
Tommaso Solari (after Pierre Legros the Younger). Apollo, 1761. Caserta, lower vestibule. Photo Mimmo Jodice

7.15
Solari. Antinous (after Campidoglio type), 1759. Caserta, lower vestibule. Photo Mimmo Jodice

7.16
Caserta, stair hall from entrance to crown prince's quarters. Photo Mimmo Jodice. (See also pl. 5.)

7.17
Caserta, lion by Paolo Persico. Photo Ente Provinciale per il Turismo

7.18
Gaetano Salomone. *Truth*, 1776. Caserta, stair hall. Photo Soprintendenza per i Beni Culturali

7.19
Solari. *Royal Majesty*, 1776–77. Caserta, stair hall. Photo Soprintendenza per i Beni Culturali

7.20
Violani. *Merit*, 1776. Caserta, stair hall. Photo Soprintendenza per i Beni Culturali

7.21
Stair hall, view from above. Photo Mimmo Jodice

7.22
Girolamo Starace. *Apollo's Kingdom*, 1768–69. Caserta, stair hall. Photo Mimmo Jodice. (See also pl. 6.)

7.23
Apollo's Kingdom, central panel. Photo Mimmo Jodice

7.24
Apollo's Kingdom, central figures. Photo Mimmo Jodice

7.25
Apollo's Kingdom, lower figures. Photo Mimmo Jodice

7.26
Apollo's Kingdom, right-hand figures. Photo Mimmo Jodice

7.27
Caserta, royal palace, lower vestibule. Photo Ente Provinciale per il Turismo

7.28
Caserta, upper vestibule. Photo Ente Provinciale per il Turismo

7.29
Caserta, upper vestibule. Photo Ente Provinciale per il Turismo

7.30
Caserta, upper vestibule, vault. Photo Mimmo Jodice

7.31
Columns, pilasters, termini, and atlantes. From Guarino Guarini, *Architettura Civile* (1737)

7.32
Pasquale Mattei. *Manovre al Campo di Marte*. Caserta, Reggia

8.1
Caserta, chapel of the royal palace, 1768. Photo Alinari

8.2
Caserta, chancel of the palace chapel. Photo Ente Provinciale per il Turismo

8.3
Caserta, chapel, entry beneath royal loge. Photo Ente Provinciale per il Turismo

8.4
Caserta, chapel, winged head in door. Gaetano Salomone, 1777. Photo Ente Provinciale per il Turismo

8.5
Vanvitelli. Planned Halls of the Ambassadors, of Alessandro Farnese, and of Alexander the Great at the royal palace at Caserta. From the *Dichiarazione*

8.6
Caserta, Reggia, Hall of the Ambassadors, late 1780s. Photo Alinari

8.7
Tommaso Bucciano. Bust of Bourbon queen in the Hall of the Ambassadors. Photo Mimmo Jodice

8.8
Domenico Mondo. *Bourbon Arms Sustained by Virtues*, 1787, in the Hall of the Ambassadors. Photo Soprintendenza per i Beni Culturali per la Campania. (See also pl. 8.)

8.9
Luigi and Carlo Vanvitelli. Hall of Alessandro Farnese at Caserta, late 1780s. Photo Ente Provinciale per il Turismo

8.10
Tommaso Bucciano. *The Flight of Hannibal from Capua*, 1787. Caserta, Hall of Alessandro Farnese. Photo Ente Provinciale per il Turismo

8.11
Simone Moschino, after a design by Gaspare Celio. *Alessandro Farnese, Vanquisher of Heresy and Liberator of the Province of Escaut, Crowned by Victory*, late sixteenth century. Caserta, Hall of Alessandro Farnese. Photo Mimmo Jodice

8.12
Camillo Guerra. *Carlo di Borbone at the Battle of Velletri*. Caserta, Hall of Alexander the Great. Photo Mimmo Jodice

8.13
Gennaro Maldarelli. *The Abdication of Carlo di Borbone in Favor of Ferdinando IV*, 1849. Photo Soprintendenza per i Beni Culturali

8.14
Tito Angelini. *The Family of Darius Seeking Mercy from Alexander*. Caserta, Hall of Alexander the Great. Photo Ente Provinciale per il Turismo

8.15
Mariano Rossi. *The Marriage of Alexander and Roxana*, 1787. Caserta, Hall of Alexander the Great. Photo Ente Provinciale per il Turismo. (See also pls. 9, 10.)

8.16
Antonio Domenici. Spring Chamber of the Old Apartments, late 1770s. Caserta, Reggia. Photo Jacelli

8.17
Spring Chamber, Caserta. Photo Soprintendenza per i Beni Culturali

8.18
Antonio Dominici. Autumn Chamber of the Old Apartments, late 1770s. Caserta, Reggia. Photo Ente Provinciale per il Turismo. (See also pl. 11.)

8.19
Studio of Ferdinando IV. Caserta, Reggia. Photo Ente Provinciale per il Turismo

8.20
Antonio Dominici. *Apollo and Minerva*, 1782–83, for Maria Carolina's *salottino*. Caserta, Reggia. Photo Mimmo Jodice

8.21
Maria Carolina's bath, 1782–83, Caserta, Reggia. Photo Mimmo Jodice. (See also pl. 12.)

8.22
Gennaro Fiore. Putti, Maria Carolina's bath. Caserta, Reggia. Photo Mimmo Jodice. (See also pl. 13.)

8.23
Fedele Fischetti. Ceiling, Maria Carolina's bath. Caserta, Reggia. Photo Mimmo Jodice

8.24
Anton Raphael Mengs. Portrait of Queen Maria Carolina. Madrid, Prado

8.25
Friedrich Heinrich Füger. *The Age of Gold*, 1782. Caserta, Old Apartments, library. Photo Mimmo Jodice. (See also pl. 14.)

8.26
Füger. *Envy and Wealth*. Photo Mimmo Jodice

8.27
Füger. *The School of Athens*. Photo Mimmo Jodice. (See also pl. 15.)

8.28
Füger. *The Rebirth of the Arts*. Photo Mimmo Jodice. (See also pl. 16.)

8.29
Detail of fig. 8.26, Envy

8.30
Detail of fig. 8.26, Wealth treading on lyre

8.31
Detail of fig. 8.27, self-portrait of Füger as Raphael (on far right)

8.32
Detail of fig. 8.27, the unveiling of Venus

8.33
Mourning Venus. From Vincenzo Cartari, *Imagini degli dei*, 1625

8.34
Detail of fig. 8.28, goddess

8.35
Detail of fig. 8.28, putto

8.36
Antonio de Simone and others. Hall of Mars, 1807 on. Caserta. Photo Alinari

8.37
Antonio Calliano. *The Death of Hector and the Triumph of Achilles*, 1815. Caserta, Hall of Mars. Photo Ente Provinciale per il Turismo. (See also pl. 17.)

8.38
Antonio de Simone and others. Hall of Astraea, c. 1815. Caserta. Photo Jacelli. (See also pl. 18.)

8.39
Giacomo Berger. *The Triumph of Justice with Astraea between Verity and Innocence*, 1815. Photo Ente Provinciale per il Turismo

8.40
Gaetano Genovese and others. Throne room at Caserta, 1839–1845. Photo Ente Provinciale per il Turismo. (See also pl. 19.)

8.41
The throne at Caserta. Photo Ente Provinciale per il Turismo

8.42
Gennaro Maldarelli. *Laying the Cornerstone of the Reggia*, 1844. Caserta, throne room. Photo Ente Provinciale per il Turismo. (See also pl. 20.)

9.1
Theater of the royal palace at Caserta, 1768–1772. Photo Jacelli

9.2
The royal box at Caserta's theater. Photo Ente Provinciale per il Turismo

9.3
Vanvitelli. Design for an opera setting. Caserta, Reggia. Photo Soprintendenza per i Beni Culturali

Index

Absolute palace, the, 45 ff.
Absolutism, in Naples, 50 ff.
Abundance, figure of, 230
Acheron, 24
Achilles, 238, 241, 246
Actaeon, 110, 117, 125, 132, 137, 190, 252; dogs of, 119
Acton, Harold, 66
Acton, Lord, 68
Adonis, 106, 108, 127, 131
Aeneas, 3, 21, 24, 25, 68, 72, 133, 136, 138, 182, 241, 252, 253, 255; and Carlo di Borbone, 76; and Golden Bough, 200, 238
Aeneid, The, 252
Aeolus, 110, 138, 181, 252; Fountain of, 207
Aetna, 130, 131
Africa, 255
Africus, 136
Agrigento, harbor of, 181
Alba, house of, 136
Alcmeno (character in *Partenope*), 28
Alexander and Bucephalus, 218
Alexander the Great, 11, 246; and Africa, 222; and Darius, 218; and Vico, 222
Alexandria, 222
Alfonso I, il Magnanimo (King of Naples), 175
Alfonso of Calabria, 15
Alitersus, 73
Alpheus, 132
Altar of the Miserable, 234, 241
Amor, 106, 108
Amphion, 201, 207, 255; statue of, 249
Amphitrite, 19, 21
Anceus, 73
Anchises, 24, 252
Ancona, Arco Clementino, 90; Cappella San Siriaco, 90; Gesù, 90
Angelini, Tito, 246; *Episodes in the Life of Alexander*, 218

Antinous, 187
Apollo, 12, 21, 24, 52, 64, 187, 228, 230, 248, 252; as Conditor Legu, 201; husband of Parthenope, 73; lyre of, 233; Starace fresco of, 196–202
Apulia, 202, 205
Aquari (denizens of Naples), 80
Aqueduct, 23
Aranjuez, 4, 65, 104
Architectura obliqua, 41
Architectura recta, 41, 45, 149
Architectural Review, The, 6
Arco, Fagiolo dell', Maurizio, 3
Arethusa (river), 131, 132, 230
Argonauts, the, 21
Ariadne, 228
Aristotle, 234
Army and navy secretariats, at Caserta, 168
Arnaud, Tommaso, 246
Arno (river), 111
Assyrians, 86
Astarita, 82
Astipalea, 73
Astraea, 81, 194, 196, 200, 228, 237, 241, 243, 245, 246; house of, 243
Astronomy, 235
Atalanta, 104, 108
Athena, 137, 138
Athens, 29, 233; Altar of the Miserable at, 234
Atlantes, 202, 205
Augean Stables, 25
Augustus, 24, 178
Augustus III (King of Poland), 65
Avernus, 12, 23, 131, 136

Babylon, 96
Babylonia, 221
Bacchus, 104, 108, 228
Baciamano, 97, 155 169, 185, 207

Index

Bagnaia, Villa Lante, 111, 113, 141
Baia, 12, 27; Temple of Diana at, 86
Baiardi, Ottavio, 22; *Prodromo della Antichità*, 26, 27
Barletta, harbor at, 181
Beauty, figure of, 81
Belliazzi, Raffaelle, 56
Berger, Giacomo, *Triumph of Justice*, 241, 245
Bergstrom & Witmer, 9
Bernini, Gianlorenzo, 41; colonnade of St. Peter's, 109; Vatican Verità, 196
Bianchi, Pietro, 245
Bibiena, family, 173
Blenheim Palace, 6
Blore, Edward, 4
Boccaccio, *De Genealogia Deorum*, 2
Bodin, Jean, 32, 50
Bonaparte, Giuseppe, 238, 246
Bonito, Giuseppe, 222; *Immaculate Conception*, 207, 211, 248
Borbone, Carlo di, 4, 9, 11, 21, 22, 25, 26, 29, 31, 96, 98, 104, 246, 255; abandons Capodimonte, 60; *Abdication*, by Maldarelli, 218; and Alessandro Farnese, 215; as artist, 71; birthday of, 205; career of, 64–82; as Carlo III of Spain, 25; and column shafts, 202; and de Cotte, 153; departure for Spain, 93; education, 65; and Farnese collection, 182; favors Vanvitelli, 87; and festivals, 72–82; and Gioffredo, 82, 83; in Camillo Guerra, 218; and his palaces, 53; as hunter, 185; and Magna Graecia, 182; military acts, 65 ff.; patronage of, 96; policy in Naples, 65; rebuilds Naples, 68–71; Renaissance predecessors of, 36; and Sicily, 73; as ruler of the New Sphere, 76; in Spain, 40, 109; statue by Belliazzi, 56; and Tivoli, 110
Borbone, Ferdinando II di, 218, 246
Borbone, Ferdinando IV di (earlier name of Ferdinando I), 23, 71, 222, 238, 241, 249, 253, 255; marriage of, 95; neglects Caserta, 93

Borbone, Filippo di, 81, 113; and Parma and Piacenza, 65
Borbone, Filippo di (son of Carlo), 77, 194
Borbone, house of, 211
Borbone, Luigi di, 65
Boreas, 228
Borromini, Francesco, 41, 211
Bottari, Giovanni, 90
Boullée, Etienne-Louis, 6, 148; project for Versailles, 9
Bourbon, dynasty, 68, 241. *See also* Borbone
Bramante, Donato, Tribunali Palace in Rome by, 38–40
Briano, Collina di, 98, 109, 110, 113
Brunelleschi, Filippo, 33
Brunelli, Angelo, 113, 137, 228
Bucciano, Tommaso, 212; *The Flight of Hannibal*, 215
Bucephalus, 218
Buckingham, Duke of, 4
Buen Retiro, 56, 65, 104, 153, 156, 165, 171; gardens of, 109
Buonaparte, Giuseppe, 71

Cadmus, 118
Caduceus, symbolism of, 237
California, 253
Calliano, Antonio, 241; *Death of Hector*, 238, 243
Calliope, 28
Calumny, figure of, 243
Cammas, Guillaume, 3
Campania, 12, 26, 82, 98, 108, 182
Campbell, Colen, 3
Canevari, Antonio, 60, 82
Capodimonte, porcelain works at, 68
Capri, 12, 74
Capua, 98
Caramuel Lobkowitz, Juan, 41, 42, 44, 90, 149, 163

Carasale, Angelo, 60
Carletti, Niccolo, 86; treatise on architecture, 63
Carlini, Niccolo, 82, 83, 85; on Gioffredo, 87; treatise on architecture, 85
Carracci, Annibale, 68
Cartari, Vincenzo, 2, 235
Carthage, 133, 222, 252, 253, 255
Caryatids, 205
Casalanza, Treaty of, 239
Caserta Nuova, 98, 109, 175
Caserta (Royal Palace), 22, 25; aedicules, 177; Aeolus fountain, 111, 133, 207; antechambers, 170; bedroom, 170; and Capodimonte, 60; Ceres fountain, 127–133; chapel, 208–220; coffeehouse, 104, 109; cubic modules in, 177; definitive design, 156–173; Dolphin Cascade, 138; Dolphin Fountain, 182; dome, 205; facades, 175; and family romance, 82; functions in, 165–171; Fountain of Diana and Actaeon, 113–122; Fountain of Juno and Aeolus, 133; Fountain of Venus and Adonis, 122–127; gardens, equestrian statue, 109; gardens, geometrical structure, 107; gardens, iconography, 108; gardens, Neptune Fountain, 110; gardens, orchard, 106; gardens as rooms, 106 ff.; geometry in, 142, 174; Gioffredo scheme for, 154, 156; Gioffredo scheme for, distributions, 151; Gioffredo scheme for, geometry, 68, 149; Hall of Alessandro Farnese, 218, 228, 246; Hall of Alexander the Great, 182, 218, 241, 246; Hall of Ambassadors, 212–215, 238; Hall of Astraea, 246; Hall of Baciamano, 238; Hall of Bodyguards, 170, 212; Hall of Halberdiers, 212; Hall of Mars, 238, 241, 246; Hall of the Untitled, 175, 212, 218, 238; Halls of Representation, 212, 221, 238; Headquarters for General Patton, 9; Herculean iconography in, 186; Museo Vanvitelliano, 246, 253; Neptune Fountain, 252; New Apartments, 238–241; Old Apartments, 222–228, 249; Old Apartments,

Autumn Chamber, 228; Old Apartments, bath, 228; Old Apartments, bath salottino, 228; Old Apartments, library, 229–238; Old Apartments, Spring Chamber, 222; Old Apartments, Winter Chamber, 228; Palazzo Reale, 2, 3, 4, 53, 253; Piano Reale, 177; planned museum, 170; planned observatory, 153, 170; planned seminary, 170; poetry in, 174; Porta Reale, 181; prefigured by Sangallo, 36–38; roof statues, 177; royal family accommodations, 171; Superintendent of Fabric, 207; symmetry in, 163; theater, 248–255; Throne Room, 245; window system, 177; workmen for, 207; written scheme for by Vanvitelli, 154; Zampilliero, 127
Cassel, 104
Castle Howard, 3, 6
Cebes' Tablet, 2
Celebrano, Francesco, 68, 185, 246; *Ferdinando at Hunt*, 218
Celio, Gaspare, 215
Central tribunals, 168
Ceres, 2, 21, 104, 110, 131, 137, 138, 141, 181, 182, 194, 212, 228, 238; and Venus, 132
Chalgrin, Jean-François, 85
Chambers, Sir William, 3
Chantilly, 104
Charles IX of France, 45
Charlotte (Queen of England), 4
Charon, 23
Chiaia, 27
Circe, 30
Cities, problem of their size, 30 ff.
Claude Lorrain, 28
Cleanto (character in *Partenope*), 28, 72
Clemency, 184; lion of, 194; statue of, 178, 181, 234
Clio, 201
Cocceius, 22
Cochin, Charles-Nicolas, Comte de Caylus, 27
Coffeehouse at Caserta, 104, 109

Collina di Briano. *See* Briano
Colorno, palace at, 65, 71
Columbus, Christopher, 255
Comes, Natalis, *Mythologiae*, 2
Commonwealths, Herculean, 180
Compasses, symbolism of, 181
Conca, Sebastiano, 68
Conrad of Querfurt, 15
Corinthian order, 205
Correggio (Antonio Allegri), 68
Corsica, 53
Cronaca di Partenope, 29, 30
Cuccagna, 72, 77
Cumae, 23, 27, 28, 29, 82, 136, 255
Cunego, Domenico, 241
Cupid, 126, 127, 131
Cyane, 131, 132
Cybele, 178, 237, 238
Cythera, 125, 253

Daedalus, 255
Da Gama, Vasco, 255
Daniele, Francesco, 27
Darius, 218
David, Jacques-Louis, 238
De Cotte, Robert, 171; and Buen Retiro, 109, 153, 156; chapel at Versailles by, 208
Deiopea, 136
De Simone, Antonio, 238
De Sormeaux, J. L. R., *La Maison de Bourbon*, 53
De Venuti, Niccolo Marcello, 182
Dézallier d'Argenville, Antoine-Joseph, 104
Diana, 12, 106, 110, 117, 118, 125, 126, 137, 141, 182, 194, 212, 249, 252; circus of, 104; grove of, 104; nymphs of, 118–119
Dichiarazione. *See* Vanvitelli
Dido, 252, 253; and Aeneas, 255; palace of, 253
Diomedes, 182

Dis, 15, 23, 24, 136, 238
Dolphins, 141
Dominici, Antonio, 228
Dryden, John, 15
Ducerceau, Jacques, 41
Durand, Jean-Nicolas-Louis, 6, 148

Echo, 106, 108
Egyptian influence, 29
Eletti of Naples, 71
Elpinice (character in *Partenope*), 28
Eminence of Rank, 212
Endymion, 106, 108
Envy, figure of, 233, 237
Epaminondas, 236
Ephesus, Temple of Diana at, 41 ff., 163
Ercole, 133, 182
Erymanthian boar, 185
Eryx (King of Sicily), 73
Escorial, the, 4, 40, 41, 56, 65, 156
Etruscan civilization. *See* Italic civilization
Euboia, 27, 29
Eundos, 73
Eurus, 136
Euterpe, 201

Fabius, Quintus, 200
Faith, figure of, 81
Fame, figure of, 81
Families, barbarian, 178
Family romance, 11, 246 ff.
Famine of 1764, 25 ff., 72
Fanzago, Cosimo, 82, 83
Farnese, Alessandro, 11, 182, 215, 221, 237, 247; statue of, 215–218
Farnese, Elisabetta (Queen of Spain), 65, 218
Farnese, family, 65, 182, 221
Farnese collection, 68, 71, 146; and the Bourbons, 236

Fasces, symbolism of, 181, 241
Félibien, Jean-François, 43
Ferdinando I of Aragon (King of Naples), 40; Tribunali Palace of, 36, 38
Fichera, Francesco, 3
Filandro (character in *Partenope*), 28
Filarete (Antonio Averlino), 33
Filomarino, Giovanni Battista, 22
Fiore, Gennaro, 228
Fischetti, Fedele, 68, 228
Flora, 104, 108
Florence, Pitti Palace, 65, 71
Fogliani d'Aragona, Giovanni, 83
Fontana, Carlo, 90
Fontana, Domenico, 53, 83, 89; plan of Palazzo Reale, 56
Fortitude, figure of, 212, 238, 243; lion of, 194
Fourier, Francois-Charles-Marie, 9
Fragonard, Jean-Honoré, 110
Francis I (King of France), 40, 48
Franz I (Roman Emperor and Grand Duke of Tuscany), 229
Freemasons, 229
Freud, Sigmund, 194; and "family romance," 246–247
Füger, Heinrich Friedrich, 229, 230, 235, 236, 238; *Age of Gold*, 230, 237, 238, 247; *Envy and Wealth*, 230, 236; *Rebirth of the Arts*, 230; *School of Athens*, 230, 236, 238
Fuga, Ferdinando, 25, 60, 82, 87, 90, 93
Fusaro, 12

Gaetani, family, 182
Galanti, G. M., 30, 43; and in-migration, 36
Galiani, Bernardo, 181; and Vanvitelli, 93; Vitruvius edition, 85
Galiani, Celestino, 22
Galiani, Ferdinando, 21
Galilei, Alessandro, 88, 90

Gargaphia, 118
Gennaro, San, 73
Genovese, Antonio, 21, 22, 181
Genovese, Gaetano, 246
Gentile, Aniello, 4
Gentleness, figure of, 243
Geometric planning, 32 ff.
George II (King of England), 4
Germanicus, 187
Germany, 9
Geryon, 182
Giannone, Pietro di, 21
Gioffredo, Mario, 11, 25, 32, 33, 64, 68, 89, 90, 171; career of, 82–87; Caserta project, 142–153, 207; Caserta project, functions of 41, 71, 142–146; Naples, Santo Spirito, 93, 208; treatise on architecture, 85; and Vanvitelli, 88
Giordano, Tommaso, 60
Girardon, François, 110
Giunte for Caserta, 168
Glory, statue of, 185, 187
Glycon, 186
Goethe, Johann von, 15
Golden Age, the 131
Golden Bough, 249
Goths, 87
Goudar, Ange, 30
Graces, the, 81, 228, 230
Greece, and Alexander, 222
Greed, figure of, 237
Gros, Baron Antoine-Jean, 238
Guarini, Guarino, 41
Guerra, Camillo, *Battle of Velletri*, 218
Gynn, John, *London and Westminster Improved*, 4

Hackert, Jakob Philipp, 71, 228
Hadrian, 178
Halle, 230

Hamilton, Gavin, 187; *Achilles and Hector*, 241
Hamilton, Sir William 187
Hapsburg, house of, 65
Hardouin-Mansart, Jules, 48
Hebrews, 86
Hector, 11, 239, 241, 246
Heemsteede (near Utrecht), 104
Helen of Troy, 137, 138, 200
Henry III (King of France), 48
Hera, 137
Herculaneum, 26, 86, 136, 237
Hercules, 3, 12, 19, 21, 22, 25, 26, 29, 52, 64, 68, 104, 108, 184, 187, 190, 212, 234, 241, 245, 247, 255; as Atlas, 202; at Caserta, 181, 182; the Founder, 194; Fountain of, 218; as Glory of Hera, 185; lustrations of, 215; and Nemean lion, 201; in Rossi fresco, 221
Heresy, 218
Herrera, Juan de, 40
Hesiod, 130
Hesperia, 26, 73, 182
Hesperides, 108, 182, 255; Gardens of the, 21, 26, 200, 237
Hippocrene, 104, 201; River, 237
Hobbes, Thomas, 50
Homer, 20, 30, 236, 237
Horace, Ode to Augustus, 73
Hunting, as royal sport, 185
Hydra, Lernian, 73, 184, 187, 212, 235, 249
Hymen, 235
Hypostyle, 147

Iberia, 104
Ignarra, Niccolò, 27
Iliad, scene from, 238, 239
Ilium. *See* Troy
Immortality, figure of, 236
Indolence, figure of, 243
Innocence, figure of, 243

Index

Ischia, 12
Istro (River), 76
Italic civilization, 24, 29
Ius naturalis, 60

Japan, 9
Jerusalem, temple at, 153
Joli, Antonio, 246
Jove. *See* Jupiter
Julius II, 40; begins Tribunali Palace, 38–40
Juno, 110, 136, 138, 241; fountain (*see* Aeolus Fountain)
Jupiter, 52, 131, 137, 228, 241
Justice, 200, 212; figure of, 178, 181, 243; geometric, 52; mathematical, 241
Juvarra, Filippo, 89, 90, 149

Kaufmann, Emile, 6
Khorsabad, 153
Koch, Joseph Anton, 238
Kokorinov, A. F., 3
Kremlin, 9

La Gamba, Crescenzo, *Apollo and Python*, 249
Ladon, 249
Lampedusa, Giuseppe, *The Leopard*, 228
Latium, 136
Laughter, figure of, 81
Laurentum, Pliny's villa at, 43 ff.
Le Vau, Louis, 45
Leah (statue on Julius tomb), 177
Leibniz, Gottfried Wilhelm, 21, 32, 50; zero/one arithmetic of, 43
Lemercier, Jacques, 45
Leningrad, Academy of Art, 3
Leo, house of, 243
Leonardi, Porzio, 23
Leonardo da Vinci, 149
Lescot, Pierre, 45, 46

Lethe, 23, 110
Lex, 2; aequatrix, 51–52, 194; rectrix, 51–52, 194
Liani, Francesco, 66
Liberality, 201
Licomedes, 73
Ligorio, Pirro, 110
Lilibeo, 130
Lituus, 130, 230; symbolism of, 243
Locke, John, 21
Loire Valley, 40
London, Buckingham Palace, 4, 6; Crystal Palace, 9; Hyde Park, 4; Somerset House, 3
Longhena, Baldassare, 3
Loreto, Holy House, campanile, 90
Louis XIII (King of France), 46, 71
Louis XIV (King of France), 9, 45, 65, 178
Louis XV (King of France), 26, 65
Louis XVI (King of France), 222
Louvre, Grande Galerie, 71
Loyalty, 212
Lucrino, 12
Lucullus, 22
Lyre, meaning of, 201, 249

Macerata, 90
Madrid, 22, 66; court at, 96; Palazzo Reale, 89; Prado, 4; Royal Palace, 65
Magellan, Ferdinand, 255
Magna Graecia, 43, 66, 82, 132, 138, 215, 221; as Tuscan kingdom, 77
Magnanimity, figure of, 243
Magnificence, statue of, 178, 181
Magri, Gaetano, 187, 196
Magri, Giuseppe, 196, 228
Maiuri, Amedeo, 26
Majesty, statue of, 190, 194, 200, 205
Maldarelli, Gennaro, *Laying the Cornerstone of Caserta*, 218; *Abdication of Carlo di Borbone*, 218
Marches, the, 90

Marcus Aurelius, 185, 236
Mare Siculum, 133
Maria Amalia (Queen of the Two Sicilies), 66, 73, 76, 104
Maria Anna of Hapsburg, 65
Maria Carolina of Hapsburg-Lorraine (Queen of the Two Sicilies), 95, 228, 229, 253, 255
Maria Theresa (Empress of Austria), 65, 229
Marie Antoinette (Queen of France), 229
Marly, 104
Marotta, Antonio, 212
Mars, 118, 228, 239, 243
Martini, Francesco di Giorgio, 33, 36
Martorelli, Jacopo Orazio, 27
Masucci, Domenico, 238, 245
Mattei, Pasquale, *Manovre al Campo di Marte*, 207
Mazzocchi, Alessio, 22, 26, 27, 66, 86, 98, 171; inscription on aqueduct, 133
Meander, 73
Medes, 86
Medici, house of the, 65
Medici, Cosimo de', 236, 246
Medicis, Cathérine de, 45
Medrano, Carlo, 83, 90, 151
Memphis, 76, 96
Menelaus, 182
Mengs, Anton Raphael, 96, 229
Mercury, 196, 200, 201, 228, 241; discovers lyre, 201; and Merx, 200
Merit, statue of, 190–194, 205
Metae, 141
Metastasio, Pietro, 3, 22, 29, 89, 221, 229; *Didone Abbandonata*, 11, 173, 249–255; *Partenope*, 27, 28, 72
Michelangelo Buonarroti, 202; and Palazzo Farnese, 177
Midas, 230, 233, 238
Milan, Belgioioso Palace, 4
Minerva, 200, 201, 228, 233, 236

Miseno, 136; Cape, 12, 24, 27
Misenus, 25, 77; companion of Aeneas, 24
Modesty, figure of, 243
Molise, regiments from, 207
Monarchism, 52 ff.
Mondo, Domenico, 68, 249; Bourbon Arms, 212
Montalto, Cardinal, 111
Montani, Tommaso, 15
Monte Sant' Angelo, Apulia, 202
Montevergine, 27
Morosini, Nicola, 187
Moschino, Simone, 215
Murat, Gioacchino, 238, 246
Muses, the, 201

Naccherino, Michelangelo, 15
Naples, 2, 66, 98; Albergo dei Poveri, 25, 90, 234; Annunziata, 93; Bacino Angioino, 53; Bay of, 241; Biblioteca Nazionale, 146, 151; Borgo Loreto, 93; Capodimonte, 82, 146, 147; Capodimonte, Medrano scheme, 146; Castel Capuano, 53; Castel dell'Oro, 53; Castel Nuovo, 27, 53, 73, 77; Castel Nuovo, and festivals, 72; cavalry barracks, Ponte della Maddaloni, 93; Fontana Santa Lucia, 15–20, 21, 22, 72, 246; Foro Carolino (Piazza Dante), 65, 68, 71–72, 93, 175; Gesù e Maria, 53; harbor, 181; Kingdom of, 9; kings of portrayed, 246; Largo del Castello, 77; Largo del Palazzo (Piazza Plebescito), 68, 77; meeting of 1845 Congress of Sciences, 246; Miradois, 56; Neptune Fountain, 53; Oratorio della Scala Santa, 95; Palazzo Bovio, 95; Palazzo Calabritto, 93; Palazzo di Capodimonte, 72; Palazzo Casacalenda, 83, 95; Palazzo degli Studi, 71; Palazzo donn'Anna, 60; Palazzo Filomarino, 22; Palazzo Fondi, 95; Palazzo Reale, 27, 53–56, 60, 68, 71, 77, 82, 83, 89, 146; Palazzo Teora, 95; Piazza di Nilo, Alma Mater, 30; Poggioreale, 71, 146; Porta Reale, 175; San Ferdinando, 53; San Francesco di Paola, 53; Santa Caterina da Siena, 83; Spirito Santo, 83–85, 90; SS Marcellino e Festo, 95; SS Trinità, 95; Teatro San Carlo, 77; Temple of Dioscuri, 86; Tribunali, 45; University of, 21, 146; Via Posillipo, 60; Viceroy's Palace, 27; Villa Comunale, 15
Narcissus, 106, 108
Nash, John, 4
Neapolis, 255. *See also* Naples
Nemean lion, 182, 190, 201
Neptune, 19, 21, 73, 132, 136, 141, 252; Enthroned in Triumph, 253; Fountain, 104, 106, 113
Neroni, Lorenzo Maria, 207
Netherlands, The, 215
New York (city), 15
Nile (river), 230
Notus, 136
Nymphenburg, 104

Obedience, 212
Olympus, 202, 228
Optimates, 74
Orcus, 200
Orpheus, 21, 126, 127, 255; statue of, 249; teacher of Midas, 230
Orythia, 228
Ourabouros, 81
Ovid, 118, 122, 126

Pachino, 130
Pactolus, 237; River, 230
Paestum, 83, 86, 237
Paisiello, 249
Palace, the absolute, 32, 45 ff.
Palinuro, 24, 136
Palinurus (companion of Aeneas), 24, 25
Palladio, Andrea, 41
Pallas, 81, 104
Palmyra, 96
Paris, Judgment of, 137–138
Paris, Louvre, 93; Cour Carrée, 45; St. Philippe-du-Roule, 85; Tuileries, 45, 93
Parma, 53, 71, 215
Partenope (Metastasio), 72
Parthenope, 15, 28, 29, 30, 31, 32, 72, 77, 82, 194, 201, 211, 238, 255; genealogy of, 73; as Queen of Naples, 81; in Biagio Troisi, 74
Pastoral poetry, 201
Patton, General George S., 9
Peace, statue of, 178, 181, 212
Pegasus, 230
Peleus, 137, 138
Peloro, 130
Perrault, Claude, East Front of Louvre, 177, 178
Persephone, 131, 136, 228
Persepolis, 86, 153
Perseus, 104, 108
Persia, 221
Persians, 86
Persico, Paolo, 68, 113, 119, 190
Perugia, 90
Pesaro, 90
Phidias, 236
Philip II (King of Spain), 40, 215
Philip V (King of Spain), 65
Phlegraean Fields, 12, 22, 23, 185; nymphaea, 15
Phoenicians, 255
Piacenza, 53
Piermarini, Giuseppe, 4
Pini, Marco, 96
Piranesi, Giovanni Battista, 110, 111
Piscina Mirabilis, 22, 23
Pity, 196, 200; figure of, 237, 241
Pius IX, 66
Plaid Graph, 147
Plato, 233, 234
Plebs, 200, 201, 230

Pliny, 41, 43
Plough, symbolism of, 28
Poland, 76, 104
Pomona, 106
Pompeii, 26
Pontano, Giovanni Gioviano, 15
Ponte della Valle, 133
Portici, 26; collection at, 146; figure of, 77; Villa Reale, 60, 65, 71, 82
Poseidon, 137
Posillipo, Monte de, 22
Pozzuoli, 22, 73, 136; Aeneas's city, 205; grotto at, 22; Serapeum, 202
Procida, 12, 27, 29
Proserpine, 182
Prudence, figure of, 238
Psyche, 106, 108
Pudicity, 196, 200; figure of, 241
Pufendorf, Samuel, 21, 50
Puissance, 212
Puteolum. *See* Pozzuoli
Pythagoras, school of, 182
Pythagorean commonwealth, 66, 182
Pythagorean justice, 52
Pythagorean mathematics, 233
Pythagoreanism, 32; in geometry, 43
Python, 249

Queens of Naples, in Hall of Ambassadors, 212
Queirolo, Francesco, 68

Rachel, statue on Julius tomb, 177
Raphael, 68; *School of Athens*, 234, 235
Rè, Vincenzo, 72, 77, 81, 82, 113, 181, 194, 211
Real Accademia Erculanense, 26
Regency Council, 93
Republican palaces, 36
Resina, Villa Campolieto, 83, 95
Rinaldi, Antonio, 4

Ripa, Cesare, 2, 196, 212, 241
Rivoli, palace of, 89
Robert, Hubert, 71, 110
Roman Empire, 86
Rome, 24, 31, 73, 96, 184, 186, 255; Arch of Marcus Aurelius, 36; Basilica of Constantine, column from, 215; Baths of Diocletian, 93; Chapel of the King of Portugal, 93; Convent of Sant'Agostino, 93; Palazzo Farnese, 6, 177; Palazzo Farnese, Sala Grande, 215; "Palazzo Maggiore," 36; Palazzo Odescalchi, 93; San Giacomo degli Spagnuoli, 83; Santa Cecilia, Cappella delle Reliquie, 228; Santa Maria degli Angeli, 93, 202; St. John Lateran, 211; St. Peter's, 109, 202; Temple of Jupiter, 36; Tribunali Palace, 38–40, 41, 45; Vatican, 196; Vatican, *School of Athens*, 234
Romorantin, France, 40
Romulus, 184
Rossi, Giovanni Battista, 222
Rossi, Mariano, 222, 249; *Marriage of Alexander*, 219
Roxana, marriage of, 221
Royal palaces, in Francesco di Georgio, 36
Rusca, Luigi, 4
Rykwert, Joseph, 6

Sacred Royal Council, 168
St. Cloud, 104
St. Lawrence, 40
St. Petersburg, Belosersky barracks, 4
Saint-Simon, Duc de, 6
Salomone, Gaetano, 68, 122, 127, 137, 190, 211, 228
Salvi, Niccolò, 90
Samia, 73
Samos, 73
Sanchez de Lana, Isidoro, 75
Sanfelice, Ferdinando, 72, 82
Sangallo, Giuliano da, 36; Tribunali Palace in Naples, 45

San Ildefonso, 4, 71
San Leucio, 222
Sannazaro, Jacopo, 25, 75
Sannicandro, Prince of, 25, 64
Santestebán de Puerto, Count, 65
Savoy, Carlo Emanuele, King of, 66
Saxony, 76, 104
Scamozzi, Vincenzo, 41, 43, 45; and Pliny, 44
Schiavo, Armando, 3
Schönbrunn, 4, 104
Scipio Africanus, 76
Scythians, 86
Sebeto (river), 15, 28, 72, 77, 81, 104
Serlio, Sebastiano, 41
Serra, Fray Junipero, 253
Sicily, 66, 130, 131, 138, 202, 253
Sirens, the, 30
Siti Reali, 31
Slaves, in Aeolus Fountain, 138
Socrates, 233, 236
Solari, Pietro, 113
Solari, Tommaso, 187, 190
Solimena, Francesco, 82
South America, 53
Spain, 26, 53, 64
Sparta, 29
Splendor, figure of, 81
Spring, 201
Stabiae, 26
Starace Franchis, Girolamo, 106, 215, 221, 236, 241, 249
Stupinigi, 89
Styx (river), 131, 238
Sublime, the, 96

Tagliacozzi Canale, 72
Tanucci, Bernardo, 25, 26, 64, 72, 218, 229
Tartarus (river), 132, 230

Index

Termini, 205
Tetrastyle, 149
Thalia, 201
Thebes, 118, 201
Theseus, 234
Thetis, 137
"Thickness problem," 149
Thrace, 126
Tifata, Monte, 104
Tifatine Mountains, 98
Tiller, symbolism of, 181
Tischbein, Johann Heinrich Wilhelm, 228, 238
Titian (Tiziano Vecelli), 68
Tivoli, Villa d'Este, 110
Toledo, Juan Bautista de, 40
Torregaveta, 12
Toulouse, Capitole, 3
Trajan, 180
Trinacria, 138. *See also* Sicily
Troisi, Biagio, 76; poem to Carlo, 74
Troy, 184, 222, 239, 241
Truth, statue of, 194, 205; statue of, by Bernini, 196
Turin, Duomo, 89; Palazzo Madama, 89
Tuscan Sea, 133
Two Sicilies, Kingdom of the, 53, 65, 133, 138, 221
Tyche, 180, 237, 238
Typhon, 130, 131, 132, 253
Tyre, 222, 255
Tyrrhenian Sea, 28

Ulysses, 29, 182, 184
United States of America, 9

Vaccaro, Domenico Antonio, 72, 82
Vanbrugh, Sir John, 3
Van Wittel, Gaspar, 88
Vanvitelli, Carlo, 238
Vanvitelli, Luigi, 2, 4, 11, 22, 23, 25, 29, 31, 43, 68, 82, 90; alterations to Palazzo Reale, 56; career of, 87–97; and Carlo di Borbone, 88; and Caserta chapel, 208; and Caserta gardens, 104; Caserta plan (1756), 137; church in Naples, 208; and columns, 202; complaints to Carlo, 97; death of, 109; and design for Hall of Alessandro Farnese, 228; *Dichiarazione*, 3, 83, 98, 106, 108, 109, 113, 156, 165, 174, 178, 182, 186, 196, 205, 211, 212, 215; early sketch for Caserta Nuova, 109; and French gardens, 108–109; functional analysis of Caserta, 155; and Hercules statue, 186 inscription in stair hall, 245; *Lettere*, 64, 104, 202; and Michelangelo, 93, 177; and myth, 113; and Neapolitan architecture, 95; and Neptune Fountain, 252; and Neroni, 207; and Old Apartments, 222; in Rome, 38–40; and Santa Maria degli Angeli, 202; sketches for slaves, 138; stair-hall iconography, 190; stair-hall program, 194; and Tanucci, 229; vignette in *Dichiarazione*, 76; written Caserta scheme, 154
Vanvitelli, Luigi, the Younger, 88
Vaux-le-Vicomte, 104
Venice, San Giorgio Maggiore, 3
Venus, 2, 106, 118, 127, 131, 136, 137, 138, 141, 182, 187, 194, 200, 212, 228, 235, 252, 253
Verlet, Pierre, 48
Versailles, 4, 6, 9, 32, 45, 108, 110; chapel at, 208; Cour de Marbre, 48; Cour des Cerfs, 48; gardens of, 104; irregular plan of, 46–50; of Louis XII, 71; Louis XIII, 46, 71; Louis XIV, 45; Salon de la Pendule, 48
Vertumnus, 106
Vespucci, Amerigo, 255
Vesuvius, 23, 77, 82, 98, 228
Via Appia, 98, 109
Via Tescione, 133
Vicaria Civile, Naples, 168
Vicaria Criminale, Naples, 168
Vico, Giambattista, 2, 3, 11, 22, 25, 26, 27, 29, 97, 181, 229; and Achilles, 239; and Aeneas, 136; and Alexander, 221, 222; and architectonic justice, 86; and Astraea, 81, 200, 241; and Bourbon policy, 53; and derivation of *ara*, 234; and Diana, 113, 119; *Diritto universale*, 131, 181, 255; and early myth, 32; and Füger, 230; followers of, 86; and Gioffredo, 82; and Hercules, 73; and monarchism, 50 ff.; and Neptune, 75; and number poetry, 60; and oneness of monarchy, 133; poetic institutions and, 234; Pythagorean justice, 50–52; and *relegendo*, 178, 180; and Romanness, 88; *Scienza nuova*, 131, 241, 243; sonnet to Carlo, 76; sonnet to Ferdinando Sanfelice, 76; speech to Carlo, 74
Victoria, Queen, 4
Victory, and Alessandro Farnese, 215; figure of, 81
Villalpando, Juan Bautista, 146, 151
Villareale, Valerio, 238; *Minerva between Legislation and Reason*, 245
Violani, Andrea, 137, 182, 186, 190, 211
Virgil, 12, 15, 22, 25; *Aeneid*, 26, 72–73, 133, 252; *Eclogues* and *Georgics*, 108
Vistula (river), 104
Vitruvius, 42, 83, 86, 148, 205; Galiani edition, 85
Vitruvius Britannicus, 3
Vittone, Bernardo, 41
Von Kaunitz, Ernst, 95
Voss, Gerard, 2
Vulcan, 137, 252, 253

Washington, D.C., Pentagon, 9; White House, 9
Watteau, Antoine, 125
Wealth, figure of, 236
Webb, Sir Aston, 6
Willamowitz-Müllendorf, 27
Winckelmann, Johann, 27, 86
Wittkower, Rudolf, 3

Zephyr, 104, 108
Zeus, 137. *See also* Jupiter